DATE DUE

NOV 1 8 2003			
DEC 0 2 2003			
JUN 0 4 2004			
			Demco

Enlarging NATO

Enlarging NATO

The National Debates

EDITED BY
Gale A. Mattox
Arthur R. Rachwald

LYNNE
RIENNER
PUBLISHERS

BOULDER
LONDON

To Robert, Inga, and Elizabeth,
who will live in a world with an undivided Europe

Published in the United States of America in 2001 by
Lynne Rienner Publishers, Inc.
1800 30th Street, Boulder, Colorado 80301
www.rienner.com

and in the United Kingdom by
Lynne Rienner Publishers, Inc.
3 Henrietta Street, Covent Garden, London WC2E 8LU

Library of Congress Cataloging-in-Publication Data
Enlarging NATO : the national debates / edited by Gale A. Mattox and Arthur R. Rachwald.
     p.   cm.
   Includes bibliographical references and index.
   ISBN 1-55587-908-X (alk. paper)
   1. North Atlantic Treaty Organization—Membership.   I. Mattox, Gale A.   II. Rachwald,
Arthur R.

UA646.3.E53   2001
355'.031091821—dc21

                                                                          2001019005

British Cataloguing in Publication Data
A Cataloguing in Publication record for this book
is available from the British Library.

Printed and bound in the United States of America

       The paper used in this publication meets the requirements
 (∞)   of the American National Standard for Permanence of
       Paper for Printed Library Materials Z39.48-1984.

 5   4   3   2   1

CONTENTS

PREFACE

Transformations as dramatic as the disintegration of the Soviet Union and its communist empire, the collapse of the Warsaw Treaty Organization (WTO), and the enlargement of the North Atlantic Treaty Organization (NATO) to include three Central European countries have profoundly redefined the international political system. The Cold War division of Europe came to an end, together with the totalitarian political order and economic centralization that prevailed among the Central and Eastern nations for over forty years. Communism has been replaced by democracy, free market economics, and a sweeping realignment toward the West. At the earliest possible opportunity, the entire region sought stability, prosperity, democracy, and security in alliance with the nations and international institutions of Western Europe and the United States. Ultimately, the aspiration of the many nations in this region has been membership in NATO and the European Union.

This volume, a product of these changes, was first conceptualized in the summer of 1998, when we joined the faculty of the International Summer School in Krynica, Poland. For several years the school had been organized by the Batory Foundation in Poland, with funding provided by the Soros and Ford Foundations. The program's objective was to bring together more than one hundred promising young scholars and government officials from countries and republics of the former Soviet bloc for a four-week intensive study of Western political theories, democratic institutions, and political developments. While the students were learning about the Western approach to government and society, we had the opportunity to gain a better understanding of the complexities of the region's social and economic transformations, including a comprehensive understanding of the democratic debates over the enlargement of NATO. Thus, the temptation to organize systematically the various aspects and arguments of this truly international debate became irresistible.

The idea of NATO enlargement has had broad political ramifications not only for existing members and new members of the alliance, but also for those states not offered membership in the first round, as well as Russia and Ukraine, who in all likelihood will not become NATO members in the foreseeable future. Unquestionably, the issue of enlargement has been particularly controversial and emotional for the nations of Central and Eastern Europe and Russia. The debate has focused on such issues as the need for the alliance after the end of the Cold War, the nature of Russia's democratic transition and the international intentions of the new Russian state, and the desirability of extending the alliance beyond its traditional Atlantic-Mediterranean theaters of operation. As for the Central and Eastern European states, the debates have focused primarily on the wisdom of placing regional security in the hands of distant powers to the West. Such reservations about the West's sincerity are a by-product of historical decisions such as Munich, the Stalin-Hitler Pact, and Yalta. These memories continue to play a defining role in the political calculations of the Poles, Czechs, Hungarians, and others. Just as difficult to overcome, however, has been the post–World War II image of Europe confined to the Atlantic region and autonomous from its Central and Eastern regions. This Iron Curtain "in reverse" was particularly pronounced during the enlargement debates in the United States. This book seeks to convey a better understanding of all the perceptions and misconceptions, hopes and fears, calculations and miscalculations that prevailed during the first round of NATO's enlargement to the East.

We would like especially to express gratitude to all our contributors, who provided their expertise in the following chapters, and who responded patiently to our queries and suggestions. We also appreciate assistance provided by Ensign Christopher K. Barker (U.S. Navy), who spent endless hours on various editorial aspects of this publication; Sarah Wahba, Kathleen Young, and Eric Schmitt, who checked reference data and undertook numerous administrative tasks; Angela M. Wheeler, who provided the invaluable experience necessary to translate several diverse word processing languages into one coherent version; and Susan Sheahan, who painstakingly took on the index. We also appreciate the support and research opportunities provided by the U.S. Naval Academy. Finally, we would like to extend heartfelt thanks to our spouses for their encouragement, patience, support, and understanding during our involvement with this project.

—*Gale A. Mattox and Arthur R. Rachwald*

ACRONYMS

AFSOUTH	Allied Forces South
ARRC	Allied Command Europe Rapid Reaction Corps
AWS	Electoral Action-Solidarity
BALTBAT	Baltic Battalion
CAP	Common Agricultural Policy (European Union)
CBO	Congressional Budget Office
CDU-CSU	Christian Democrat Union–Christian Socialist Union
CEE	Central and Eastern Europe
CFE	Conventional Forces in Europe
CFSP	Common Foreign and Security Policy (European Union)
CIS	Commonwealth of Independent States
CJTF	Combined Joint Task Force (NATO)
COMECON	Council for Mutual Economic Assistance
CSCE	Conference on Security and Cooperation in Europe
CSSD	Social Democrats of the Czech Republic
DM	deutsche mark
DoD	Department of Defense (U.S.)
EAPC/NACC	European Atlantic Partnership Council (formerly North Atlantic Cooperation Council)
EFTA	European Free Trade Area
EMU	European monetary union
ESDI	European Security and Defense Initiative
ESDP	European Security and Defense Policy
EU/EC	European Union (formerly European Community)
FDP	Free Democratic Party (Germany)
FLA	future large aircraft
G-7	Group of Seven Industrial States
GDP	General Defense Plan (Estonia)
GDP	gross domestic product
GDR	German Democratic Republic (East Germany)

IFOR	Implementation Forces (Bosnia)
IMF	International Monetary Fund
KDU-CSL	Christian and Democratic Union–Czechoslovak People's Party
KPN	Confederation of Independent Poland
KSCM	Czechoslovak Communist Party
MAP	Membership Action Plan
MFA	Ministry of Foreign Affairs
MOD	Ministry of Defense (United Kingdom)
NAA	North Atlantic Assembly
NAC	North Atlantic Council
NACC/EAPC	North Atlantic Cooperation Council (now European Atlantic Partnership Council)
NATO	North Atlantic Treaty Organization
NCO	noncommissioned officer
NGO	nongovernmental organization
NIS	Newly Independent States (formerly USSR)
NSF	National Salvation Front
ODA	Civic Democratic Alliance (Czechoslovakia)
ODS	Civic Democratic Party (Czechoslovakia)
OSCE/CSCE	Organization for Security and Cooperation in Europe (formerly Conference on Security and Cooperation in Europe)
PARP	Planning and Review Process (NATO)
PCI	Partito Comunista Italiano
PDS	Party of Democratic Socialists (Germany)
PDSR	Party of Social Democracy in Romania
PESC	La politique etrangére de sècuritè commune
PfP	Partnership for Peace
PSL	Polish Peasant Party
RC	Rifondazione Comunista Party
RCSS	Governmental Center for Strategic Studies
ROP	Movement for the Rebirth of Poland
RRF	rapid reaction force
SACEUR	Supreme Allied Commander Europe
SEA	Euro-Atlantic Association
SFOR	Stabilization Forces (Bosnia)
SLD	Democratic Left Alliance
SNOG	Senate NATO Observer Group
SOFA	Status of Forces Agreement
SPD	Socialist Party of Germany (Social Democrats)
SPR	governmental strategic programs

SPR-RSC	Association for the Republic–Republican Party of Czechoslovakia
START	Strategic Arms Reduction Talks
UN	United Nations
US	Freedom Union (Czech Republic)
USSR	Union of Soviet Socialist Republics
UW	Union of Liberty
WEU	Western European Union
WMD	weapons of mass destruction
WTO	Warsaw Treaty Organization
WTO	World Trade Organization

1

Introduction: European Security and the Enlargement of NATO

GALE A. MATTOX AND ARTHUR R. RACHWALD

The end of the Cold War raised fundamental questions for the United States and Europe over the design of a future European security system that would both maintain peace and stability and enhance the democratic evolution of the countries of the former Warsaw Pact. The breakdown of the Soviet empire produced a chain of relatively weak nations in the center of Europe. The potential remained high that this vacuum of power could re-ignite the traditional rivalries or prompt other threats to stability, including dominance in the region of the German-Russian rivalry or growth of militant nationalism and ethnic conflicts, which would undermine yet-tenuous democratic governments. Following several years of intensive deliberations within the newly emerging democracies among NATO members and within and between NATO and the former Warsaw Pact states, NATO invited Poland, the Czech Republic, and Hungary to join the Atlantic Alliance. At the same time, the alliance recognized the need to define its relations with the East by signing bilateral partnership agreements with Russia and Ukraine and by broadening the agenda for the North Atlantic Cooperation Council (NACC, renamed the Euro-Atlantic Partnership Council, EAPC) so that security in Europe would include as well states not invited to join the NATO alliance as formal members.

This entirely new security concept for Europe required a radical revision of the traditional thinking that the only and now obsolete purpose of NATO was to protect its members from Soviet threat. In essence, support for NATO enlargement symbolized not only an acceptance of new members but also an endorsement of a new conceptual foundation for the alliance. In its fiftieth anniversary summit in Washington during the spring of 1999, NATO adopted its New Strategic Concept, which coupled an ambitious agenda for reforming and redefining the alliance in many of its core functions with an attempt to reassure the remaining European states that had not been extended an invitation to join as full NATO members. These other members were offered the Membership Action Plan laying out the requirements for future membership and, to be clear in its intent to be inclusive, even listing a potential nine states that might fulfill those requirements and explicitly stating its desire to maintain an "open door" in the future. In particular, the alliance agreed that support for democracy and market economies, as articulated in the NATO charter, and the absence of ongoing conflicts are the most effective long-term guarantee for the peaceful resolution of disputes on the European continent.

An often overlooked aspect of the discussion over the appropriate approach to European security in the post–Cold War era are the deliberations in the NATO member states after 1989 and 1991 over the role of NATO and the breadth of its commitment to states outside the existing membership of sixteen. The member states asked whether enlargement would threaten or enhance the security that had attracted them to NATO at the time of their membership. In addition, discussions in some nonmember states led officials to conclude that an alliance that once represented the enemy now appeared to be the future guarantor of security. These deliberations are interesting for their insights into the expectations of both the states that gained membership and those that were unsuccessful. Finally, the future success of the alliance will obviously be influenced as well by those states that posed a historical threat, but which NATO now hopes will accept the need for close cooperation to avoid any future misunderstandings with the potential to destabilize the continent.

The primary purpose of this volume is to analyze and compare the domestic deliberations over enlargement in selected countries in order to facilitate a better understanding of the political motives leading to each country's decision either to support or oppose the idea of European security anchored in a larger NATO. To this end, we asked a group of distinguished international security scholars with expertise in transatlantic and European affairs to address the deliberations in twelve selected European states. Collectively these twelve contributions offer a more comprehensive analytical picture of the domestic NATO enlargement debate than has been offered to date, thereby broadening the understanding of various views and attitudes toward one of the most important security decisions of our time.

Specifically, the contributors address the domestic political deliberations over NATO enlargement in four categories of countries directly or indirectly involved in this process: first, the current members of the alliance asked to assume additional security obligations and to overhaul the old, threat-based, strategic doctrine of NATO (i.e., the United States, Great Britain, France, Germany, and Italy); second, the three Central European states invited to join the alliance in the first round of enlargement and the states that played a central role in defining the debate and pressuring the current alliance to enlarge (i.e., Poland, the Czech Republic, and Hungary); third, two disappointed states not included in the first group of invitees but hopeful that in the not so distant future NATO's door will open to additional qualified candidates (i.e., Romania and Estonia); fourth, Russia and Ukraine, who, while not excluded from future membership, are less likely to be included in any enlargement in the near future, if at all, but are likely to play a prominent role in determining the stability of the continent and even the success or failure of NATO to assure security into the twenty-first century. Both Russia and Ukraine have concluded bilateral strategic partnership agreements with NATO, the Founding Act and the Ukraine-NATO Charter, respectively, which provide for ongoing, regular consultations on issues of mutual concern and interest. It is important to note, however, that Russia orchestrated a powerful international campaign against enlargement, while Ukraine adopted a cautiously positive attitude reflecting the country's ambiguous position between NATO and Russia, between former "West and East."

THE HISTORICAL LEGACY

The main geostrategic characteristic of Central and Eastern Europe (CEE) has been an inherent weakness in determining its own destiny and yet a central position attractive to other larger and more powerful nations. The modern history of these countries has its origins in the Congress of Vienna (1815), when the eastern part of Europe was carved up among feudal states, such as Prussia and Austria, and European empires, as in the case of Russia and Turkey. It is not surprising, therefore, that until the outbreak of World War I, national self-determination was a central aspiration for these nations.

World War I was beneficial for a number of states and its end result—the simultaneous defeat of Germany, Russia, the Austro-Hungarian Empire, and the Ottoman Turkish empire—marked a return to the earlier political map of Europe for several nations, including Poland, the federation of Czechs and Slovaks (Czechoslovakia), and Hungary. At the same time, however, following the Treaty of Versailles (1919), the United States abandoned the European continent together with its rejection of Wilsonian idealism. This left behind an enormous vacuum of power in Europe, which was promptly exploited by the Nazis in Germany and the Communists in Russia.

The Western policy of appeasement in Munich (1938) and the signing of the Nazi-Soviet Pact (August 1939) marked a return to the spheres-of-influence policy in Europe. Exactly twenty years after World War I Europe was again at war, which started in Central Europe with the 1939 Nazi-Soviet invasion of Poland. While the Western powers after World War II attempted to avoid the punitive decisions taken after World War I and at Versailles, their hope for a similar approach by the Soviet Union in the countries over which it exercised influence as a result of the agreements made at Yalta, Potsdam, and in the last stages of the hard-fought war did not materialize. If the failures of the foreign ministers' conferences to agree on a peace treaty and attempts at joint governance in Germany and elsewhere were not sufficient evidence of the end of any cooperation between the wartime allies, then the 1948–1949 Berlin crisis made clear the futility of partnership with the Soviet Union in rebuilding a democratic continent.

Instead of peace, Western Europe and the United States plunged into a Cold War with the Soviet Union. As conceived in 1945 at Yalta, the division of Europe along the Elba River had placed the countries of Central and Eastern Europe under the influence of Moscow and the sociopolitical system of Marxism-Leninism for forty-five years. At a time when democratic political systems and a free market economy had produced an unprecedented stability and prosperity (a so-called economic miracle) in the West, CEE populations had experienced forced collectivization, state-dominated industrialization, and the imposition of communist political systems. The impact on the societies and the political and economic—not to mention social and cultural—structures was immense. In order to perpetuate its domination of the region, Moscow had relied on two basic pillars. In domestic politics, a single communist party controlled the political system and was expected to follow policies originated in Moscow. In foreign and security policy, Moscow used the instrument of the 1955 Warsaw Treaty Organization (WTO, or Warsaw Pact) to guarantee that in international affairs all member nations spoke and acted in unison.

While the 1970s ignited the hope for a change in domestic and international realities, particularly for the Central Europeans during the period of *ostpolitik* highlighted by the 1975 Helsinki Agreement, the superpowers remained at nuclear standoff until the mid-1980s when the Cold War began its historic thaw. In domestic terms, the thaw meant the end of single-party rule and, in foreign and security terms, it meant the disintegration of the Warsaw Pact. Central and Eastern European domestic and international realities were altered fundamentally. Almost half a century after the end of World War II, these nations became independent. With independence, however, came domestic and international vulnerability.

As the Berlin Wall fell in November 1989, the fall of other Central and Eastern European governments was not far behind—Poland had begun down the road to change in 1980 as had Hungary, in a different way but also in the 1980s. Soon, the Czechs experienced a "velvet" revolution in 1989, and other governments followed suit, the bloodiest in Romania. The disintegration of the former Soviet bloc was complete with the Russian events of 1991 and the end of the Warsaw Pact dissolution the same year. As the Russians pulled back troops from the former Warsaw Pact and, even more significantly, from the Baltic states, those governments began to revisit the issue of immediate and long-term security. Despite Russian reforms and pronouncements, there continued to be a nervousness about the security of the former Warsaw Pact states. Though their attempts to join the European Community and NATO at first appeared hopeful, both the former Warsaw Pact states and the current NATO members became more cautious about the implications of hasty enlargement. Nonetheless, other approaches emerged to assure steady progress toward reform as well as continental stability.

A EUROPEAN OR TRANSATLANTIC FRAMEWORK?

With the Cold War finally over, the former satellites of Moscow wasted no time. Almost overnight, the region began a period of economic transformation—some countries more quickly than others, but all in some manner. Public attention focused on the tremendous economic expectations of the population. With this in mind, CEE governments naturally turned first to the European Union (EU), which held out the promise of the same robust markets and economic assistance it had accorded Spain and Portugal at the time of their entries into the union. Initial discussions raised the hope that the CEE would be integrated swiftly into the EU and that economic progress could be achieved for CEE citizens who had suffered the collectivizations and state-dominated economies that had plagued the region since World War II. Consumer demand was rising, and EU entry was expected to expedite the process of economic reform and raise the standard of living for the formerly communist bloc states.

Although sympathetic in principle and initially forthcoming with European treaties according trade and other benefits, EU member states became increasingly more skeptical of rapid integration of these countries (from an economic perspective the Council for Mutual Economic Assistance, or COMECON, countries) as industries in the EU lost market shares to the less expensive textile and other manufacturers in the East, where labor was cheap and eager to lure business. It was not hard for the EU to justify moving slowly on enlargement to the East—it had pledged dual commitment to both deepen and broaden the EU. Under the Maastricht Treaty, the EU embarked on a range of reforms to "deepen" integration in all three of its major pillars, including a European Monetary Union. In addition, negotiations with Finland, Austria, and Sweden to "broaden" EU membership were progressing rapidly and would mean, in contrast to the earlier Spanish entry and the potential CEE and any other "Eastern" membership, a net financial gain for the union.

Despite the attraction of the EU, it became clear to the CEE states that if they were to be included in the broader community of Western nations, it would have to be through another means—NATO proved a logical approach.

The difficulties of quick entrance into the EU were also becoming clear to other countries eager to stabilize the region, particularly Germany and the United States. As the EU option receded, the natural alternative to assure permanent incorporation of the formerly communist nations into a community of Western values was through a security institution. There was a brief period in which a number of policymakers, most predominantly German foreign minister Hans-Dietrich Genscher, flirted with encouraging the Conference on Security and Cooperation in Europe (CSCE; since 1994, OSCE) to put greater emphasis on European security. But the Gulf War had drawn on the assets of NATO states even though it was not a NATO mission. The resulting need for funds together with the obvious disadvantages of decisionmaking in an organization of fifty-three or fifty-four members such as the CSCE convinced the United States and Europe that NATO's success in the post–World War II era and the impressive cooperation and policymaking processes honed in NATO would provide the best structure for stability and security in the center of Europe. While the conflict in the Gulf followed by the crises in the former Yugoslavia convinced NATO members that the alliance remained the most viable institution to assure European security, there was no consensus on enlarging the alliance before 1994.

To the contrary, NATO undertook several major efforts, short of membership, to bring non-NATO states into the alliance structure, including the North Atlantic Cooperation Council in 1992, which provided a forum for discussion of issues of mutual interest as did the Western European Union (WEU), which extended early associate membership. Regional efforts, such as in the Baltic region, to encourage cooperation and lower tensions were also initiated, accelerated, and encouraged as well by states outside the region, such as the United States. Probably the most substantial effort was the January 1994 establishment of the Partnership for Peace (PfP) program with the objective of close cooperation between NATO and non-NATO members to reduce any perceptions of threat and achieve greater cooperation in securing the stability of the European continent. PfP membership was opened to all European states and, despite initial hesitation and delay in joining, even Russia eventually became a partner, albeit without enthusiasm.

For the populations who felt they had risked, or potentially risked, their lives and possessions to participate in the revolutions of 1989 and assertions of independence in 1991, associate and affiliate memberships were not sufficient. If the reform processes failed, what assurances would they have that the status quo of the past forty-five years would not return with all the consequences? Further, what implications might a reversal of democratic processes in Russia have for the former Warsaw Pact states?

WEIGHING THE ALTERNATIVES FOR SECURITY IN EUROPE

There were several hypothetical international security options open for these states. First, they could apply for full membership in the WEU in the hope that the three major European powers, France, Germany, and the United Kingdom, would collectively assure the security of the CEE and for even the Newly Independent States (NIS). The apparent weakness of this scenario is that the Western European states are themselves unable to provide for their own security without U.S. nuclear and conventional guarantees, especially against a Russian-dominated Commonwealth of Independent States (CIS). Relying on the WEU alone would be as unwise, perhaps even as catastrophic, as reliance on French and British security guarantees had been in 1939.

The second security option in the post–Cold War environment could have been bilateral relations with a united Germany, particularly for the CEE. Since Germany was the country most directly threatened by a potential instability in the East, including economic chaos, excessive nationalism, demographic pressures, and organized crime, perhaps Germany would have an interest in bilateral economic, political, and military arrangements with each individual Eastern neighbor even at the price of weakening its ties with the West. Several nations of the region, notably Hungary, Romania, Slovakia, Bulgaria, and Croatia, had had historic, friendly, and beneficial relations with Germany, while Poland and the Czech Republic might contemplate closer ties to Germany as an alternative to a relationship with Russia. Even without the backdrop of Germany's history and the potentially negative implications of the newly united Germany overpowering its European and U.S. partners, since 1949 Germany has been successful in anchoring itself in economic (in the EU) and security (in NATO) terms to multilateral institutions. To alter this successful formula, through which Germany had experienced unprecedented growth and economic prosperity as well as political and military stability, would be foolhardy.

The "French option" enjoyed a considerable degree of popularity in Poland, the Czech Republic, and Romania immediately after their revolutions. This option was inspired by a combination of two factors: continuing fear of Germany and a belief that the Treaty of Versailles security bridge linking France with Poland and other Central European states could be sufficiently strong to assure stability on the continent. In the early 1990s, this security alternative received considerable attention in Poland, primarily for sentimental reasons. It was quickly recognized as unrealistic from several perspectives. Under President François Mitterrand, France was much more concerned with Russia than with its traditional allies in Central Europe. In addition, an exclusive French–Central European security understanding would place countries of the region in an uncomfortably and unnaturally anti-U.S. and anti-German position. And, finally, neither the economic nor military power of France was considered sufficient to counterbalance the proximity of Russia, particularly a nationalistic Russia.

A fourth security alternative focused on the military potential of the Visegrad Four—Poland, Hungary, the Czech Republic, and Slovakia (Czechoslovakia until January 1993). Those four countries discussed as well the inclusion of Ukraine, especially because Ukraine had been a nuclear power for several years since achieving its independence. The historical source of this idea was the Polish-Lithuanian Commonwealth, which for four centuries had contained the combined pressure of Germany, Russia, Austria, Sweden, and Turkey, until the partitions of Poland at the end of the eighteenth century dissolved the union. This thought of recasting Central and Eastern Europe into the third nuclear power center on the continent enjoyed some support in Poland where 25 percent of voters favored a pronuclear candidate during the 1991 presidential elections and were attracted to an alliance with a nuclear power between the former two blocs. There was support as well from Ukrainians who saw an opportunity to use the Visegrad agreement as an opening to the West. But in reality no serious politician appears to have given this option serious consideration. Although for the smaller nations, but also for Poland, a Visegrad Group would have provided a degree of security, the option was more likely viewed by most as potential leverage to admittance into NATO and the EU. Such factors as the relative economic weakness of the countries involved, the lack of unity among them, and, above all, their desire to join the West rather than to perpetuate the notion of Eastern Europe quickly put an end to serious consideration of a Visegrad Group as a substitute for NATO and other options.

The fifth option of a possible return to the Russian geostrategic orbit was also on the political table. It was never a popular idea, but a potential resurgence of Russian power, particularly if Russia appeared to be firmly committed to democratic and free market reform, made it a potentially attractive option. However, the Russian ideas of "near abroad" and "far abroad" and the inclination to foment conflicts among former republics to justify "peacekeeping" operations as in Chechnya were feared instead as a manifestation of Moscow's imperial ambitions (sometimes labeled the "Monrovsky Doctrine") and a signal that the Russians might regress into a less than democratic state. In this case, it might be prudent to make accommodations with the Russians ahead of time, because a negotiated *modus vivendi* would be more advantageous than one unilaterally imposed by the Russians in the future. The "common European house" idea advanced by the last Soviet leader Mikhail Gorbachev became suspect as a design to convert Central and Eastern Europe into a semidemilitarized zone and one that might preserve Moscow's ultimate authority over the region. In this option, relations between the Russian Federation and the former Warsaw Pact states would resemble relations between Finland and the USSR during the Cold War. While Finland was allowed to practice democracy and adopt a free market economic model, it operated within understood constraints. Meanwhile, its foreign policy was strictly circumscribed by Moscow.

Although this form of accommodation with the superpower in the East might have been highly popular in previous decades, in the 1990s it had very few serious advocates. It was feared that continuing dependency on Russia for security in the region would threaten the fruits of the 1989 revolution. For most Central and Eastern Europeans, the essence of this revolution was to return the region to Western civilization. At the same time, the war in Chechnya evoked memories of the post–World War II Russian brutalities in Poland, Hungary, East Germany, and Czechoslovakia. Furthermore, Vladimir Zhirinovsky's ultranationalistic political platform and his success in elections to the Russian parliament in December 1993 helped to establish a strong consensus that there was no alternative to the Euro-Atlantic option. NATO, in the opinion of the Central European states, would shield them from possible internal and external threats.

THE DECISION TO JOIN NATO

Thus, Central and Eastern Europeans came to the conclusion that there was no alternative to a NATO security system on the continent. All available historical alternatives had dangerous flaws that could in a short period of time propel European nations into another debilitating conflict. Almost half a century after World War II, Western Europe had prospered with U.S. security guarantees provided by the transatlantic partnership. For the former members of the Warsaw Pact under the shadow of Moscow, a membership in NATO appeared as an ideal solution for a number of reasons.

First, the smaller nations of Europe were understandably reluctant to enter bilateral security agreements with a stronger neighbor; unequal partnerships are seldom advantageous to the weaker side. NATO, on the other hand, is a multilateral security organization that includes a superpower, several powerful states, and many smaller nations. The dilemma of approaching Germany, France, the UK, or Russia to provide security was unattractive in comparison. In a multilateral security organization founded on a one state–one vote principle, the rights of smaller members are protected, and there is also considerable room for an individual state to exert some influence within the framework of the larger organization.

Second, membership in NATO enhanced the prospect of security ties with the United States, the only remaining superpower. In the post–Cold War circumstances, the United States and Europe, both West and East, would be linked together. Within the framework of NATO, the alliance could pursue friendly relations with Moscow without isolating Russia as during the Cold War. Further, Russia could eventually become an equal partner in the alliance, removing the temptation to reassert its historical imperial hegemony in any part of Europe. The area of stability and prosperity in Europe would encourage Russia to adopt the same values as other states in Europe, including democracy, free market economies, and peaceful relations with neighbors.

Third, in addition to potential external threats, local and internal conflicts over issues such as border disputes, the status of ethnic minorities, domestic power struggles, and the rising influence of ultranationalistic groups have proliferated and confronted the states of Central and Eastern Europe as well. In the West, NATO is credited with assuring a democratic path of development and the prevention of numerous conflicts, especially between Greece and Turkey, as well as the necessary structure for reconciliation between former enemies as in the historic French-German reconciliation. A CEE enlargement of NATO was expected to facilitate historic German-Polish and German-Czech reconciliations, not to mention the settlement of other outstanding disputes among countries of the region. In this way, countries invited to join NATO would not only receive security guarantees from the West, but they would also contribute to peace and order on the continent.

ATLANTIC ALLIANCE MEMBERS DECIDE ON ENLARGEMENT

Despite the efforts in the EU and NATO to include the CEE, Russia, and the NIS in some manner in their institutions but without formal membership, Germany, the United States, and other "Western" countries had become convinced that only through formal membership in one of the two communities would the road to democratic regimes and real economic reform for those states be effective. In summer of 1994 President Clinton visited Central Europe and committed the United States to the goal of membership in NATO for qualified countries. In December 1994 NATO officially adopted the objective of enlarged NATO membership and nine months later presented enlargement guidelines to interested states. Generally, the guidelines for acceptance into NATO included democratic processes, market economies, civilian control of the military, and an absence of outstanding border disputes. Each interested country was expected to work out an individual program to achieve these goals with NATO. The alliance deemed three states to have met the criteria and offered them membership in July 1997 at the Madrid summit meeting—Poland, the Czech Republic (Slovakia, at that time, did not meet the requirements), and Hungary. While other states were named as the most likely future candidates in the subsequent Madrid document, specifically Slovenia and Romania at the insistence of Germany and France, respectively, the first offer was limited to the named three. After ratification by member states of the necessary NATO treaty change, formal entry occurred on 12 March 1999.

This is not to overlook debate and dissension within the alliance (cases of which are detailed by each of the volume authors), but also at times vitriolic opposition by Russia. The Russians had only reluctantly negotiated a PfP program; they felt that as a nuclear power and still a significant force in Europe, Russia should be accorded a special status. An alliance of "sixteen plus one" was suggested; in May 1997 before the Madrid summit, the NATO-Russia Founding Act was signed with a provision for the Permanent Joint Council to discuss issues of interest to both NATO and Russia. Russia trumpeted the unprecedented influence it could have in NATO while the United States reiterated to critics that Russia could not in this way exercise a veto over NATO matters. The act was a compromise, and its operation, particularly during crises such as Kosovo, has been uneven. Although the Russian vehemence over enlargement was substantial and costly to East-West relations, since enlargement the Russian focus has been on dissuading NATO from adding additional members, particularly the Baltics, which provide Russia's western access via the Baltic Sea to Europe. Coupled with the clashes over Kosovo and then Chechnya, further enlargement would be a red flag to the Russians.

As the largest European nation in size next to Russia with a population the size of France, Ukraine was also granted a special (but necessarily different) status, and it signed the NATO-Ukraine Charter also with provisions for regular meetings and consultative mechanisms. While it has expressed a desire to join NATO, its continuing economic disarray and myriad other problems have meant that formal EU and NATO membership is clearly not a near-term possibility. Instead Ukraine has tried through its relations with both the West—where it obviously sees a greater chance for assistance—and the East—to which its Russian-speaking minority continues to be closely tied—to maintain good working relations and keep its options open.

THE DOMESTIC DEBATES

The weighing of security options by the newly democratic states and the new conceptual framework for European security and subsequent reforms by

NATO were accompanied by discussions within each involved country over their own appropriate role as well as the impact on national security. With the domestic context as an analytical focus on the NATO debate, the contributors to this volume examine several important facets of the international efforts to reshape the security map of Europe. In some respects, all authors aim to address the following: (1) How did the country's historical legacy and geographic location influence its attitude toward security and how is the security of the state perceived in the post–Cold War era? What are the perceived threats? (2) What were the factors that led to the country's decision to support, seek, or reject enlargement? What rationale was given for opposing the decision (either in favor or against membership)? (3) How did the country's constitutional framework and the interaction of other international and domestic issues influence the ratification of the NATO Accession Act? Or, in the case of the nonmembers, what was the reaction to the enlargement and expansion of NATO? (4) What was the reaction to the criteria for membership, that is, democratic processes, free market reforms, civilian control of the military, and settlement of border and other disputes? (5) What were the main arguments presented in favor and against the enlargement, and how extensive was public involvement in the ratification process? (6) Which segment of the country's political spectrum, including political parties and interest groups, supported and which opposed the enlargement? (7) As applicable, what was the nature of the parliamentary debate over enlargement? (8) Finally, what might be expected in terms of future enlargements? The following chapters address these issues and add an important dimension to the understanding of the individual and collective decisions with respect to membership in NATO.

PART 1

Accepting New Allies?

2

The United States: Stability Through Engagement and Enlargement

GALE A. MATTOX

The U.S. decision to support NATO enlargement was largely bipartisan and, as with most foreign policy initiatives, not a priority issue for the public. In contrast to public interest, executive and legislative policymakers viewed the enlargement of NATO as a major national security decision with substantial implications for fundamental U.S. interests and relationships. As a result, enlargement prompted interagency debate up to the time of a presidential decision in mid-1994 and a robust congressional discussion at the time of the required Senate ratification for treaty revision in 1998. A major factor in both was the political imperative to encourage emerging democracies by drawing them into the Atlantic community versus the military considerations over additional U.S. commitments at a time when the military was undergoing substantial post–Cold War reduction and restructuring.

But while there was no broad public debate, enlargement caught the attention of two interested communities. On the one hand, it drew support from the Eastern European, especially Polish, ethnic communities, and, on the other, it evoked opposition by scholars concerned with the impact of enlargement on the pace and progress of the nascent Russian democracy. This concern over Russia's direction in the case of NATO enlargement loomed large in the discussion both inside the government in the interagency realm and outside the government within the community of Russian scholars and experts.

15

NEW SECURITY CHALLENGES

The security dilemmas of the 1990s posed entirely new challenges for the United States. With the fall of the Berlin Wall in 1989, the United States began the slow process of reevaluating and responding to the consequent changes both on the European continent and globally. After the disintegration of the Soviet Union in 1991, the United States became the world's single super-power, and the potential for an East-West nuclear war receded almost overnight. The U.S. and many foreign publics breathed a collective sigh of relief.

The euphoria was also evident in Europe, and predictions of the outbreak of ethnic tensions were hotly debated and rejected.[1] While other countries expected the United States to assume additional responsibilities as the remaining superpower, the U.S. public perception of threat diminished. Americans waited for the "peace dividend," which they expected to accompany the demise of the Soviet Union and disappearance of Cold War threats. The Gulf War ironically confirmed both of these expectations—the United States reacted quickly with a large force in conjunction with over twenty allies to move Iraq out of Kuwait.

In fact, after moving U.S. forces from Europe (poised for over forty years to confront the Soviet Union at the Fulda Gap) to the Persian Gulf during the war, the Bush administration brought most of them back to the United States and began to downsize the U.S. military significantly.[2] With the advent of hostilities in the Balkans shortly thereafter, President Bush assumed, and was reassured by the Europeans, that Europe would address conflicts on the continent. By 1992, the U.S. force level in Europe hovered around 100,000, after having reached heights around 325,000 at the end of the Cold War.

The even larger question was whether NATO, as an organization established to counter the Soviet Union, would remain the cornerstone of Western security. After a brief flirtation with the idea of replacing NATO with the Conference for Security and Cooperation in Europe (CSCE/later OSCE), NATO members turned instead to adapting NATO to the demands of the post–Cold War.[3]

At the same time, Europeans began to address as well the implications of the end of the Cold War for the European Union (EU), which was then introducing the provisions of the Single European Act (SEA), scheduled to be in place by 1992. Although there was an initial enthusiastic discussion of widening the EU to include the newly emerged democracies of Central and Eastern Europe, the focus turned to completion of the process to deepen integration through the Maastricht Treaty, particularly threatened after the Danish vote, and the admittance of Finland, Austria, and Sweden. Rather than move the process forward on broadening membership, the Europe Association Agreements negotiated with the new democracies actually served to slow the process of any EU enlargement.[4]

By 1993–1994 it had become clear that there would be no quick entry to the EU for the newly emerging democracies. The United States, with the encouragement of Germany, began to consider seriously NATO membership as the vehicle to consolidate and encourage the political and economic transition already under way in Europe. Enlargement would, once and for all, tie the Central Europeans who had suffered greatly during the Cold War to the NATO community of democratic values, not to mention free markets.

RESPONDING TO NEW CHALLENGES

As the U.S. force commitment decreased in Europe, there was close attention as well to adapting NATO alliance strategy to reflect the changes in threat. The London summit and then the Rome summit both addressed the need for the alliance to rethink its strategy in the post–Cold War era.

The first major issue in this rethinking was the future of NATO. Within the academic community as well as within broader policy circles, the need for NATO given the dramatic changes to the East-West relationship came under consideration. But while there was discussion of alternatives to the alliance, the U.S. consensus to continue to pursue security for the European continent through NATO was strikingly strong. The reasons for this support were diverse and ranged from those determined to maintain a presence in the event of a Soviet reemergence to those convinced of the success of NATO during the Cold War and impressed by the institutional culture that had permitted peaceful resolution of any number of challenges to those who wanted change and felt it would be most successful by building on the current structure.[5]

But while there emerged consensus to maintain the Atlantic alliance, there was no agreement on the best approach to assure that the newly emerging democracies in Central Europe and the former Soviet Union would remain committed to reform. Although enlargement to the East came under discussion initially, there were objections based on nervousness over the potentially high cost of bringing those countries up to standards, concerns over the future direction of the new democracies, and convictions that membership in the European Union should precede NATO membership.

In 1991 the State Department circulated and then submitted a proposal to NATO that resulted in the establishment of a North Atlantic Cooperation Council (NACC) at the Rome summit in November as part of the new "strategic concept." The rationale (which was also supported by Germany) was to provide a forum within the alliance for the new democracies and NATO members to address common problems. But within the first year, the inadequacy of the NACC and the unwillingness of the EU to take the lead in enlargement was clear. When the Clinton administration entered office, attention focused on the options for a more satisfactory inclusion of selected Central and Eastern European countries in the Atlantic security community.

THE U.S. ENLARGEMENT DEBATE: AN OVERVIEW

Elected under the motto of "It's the economy, stupid," the new Clinton officials did not anticipate major change in European security. But the demands of the mounting Balkan conflict made clear that the process of restructuring European security had not yet successfully addressed the range of potential challenges to European stability. The enlargement of NATO became one of the major policy initiatives for the administration in this respect. From 1993, the new administration found itself quickly embroiled internally in a discussion of the benefits and costs of enlargement to which it responded in fall of 1993 with a proposal for a Partnership for Peace (PfP). NATO formally established PfP in January 1994 to include all the states of the former Warsaw Pact and the newly independent former republics of the Soviet Union (initially, with the exception of Tajikistan) in a program for common exercises and military coordination.[6]

But almost before NATO even started its PfP program, President Clinton announced in speeches given in January and July 1994, in Prague and Warsaw respectively, a commitment to NATO membership for eligible Central European aspirants. The United States then turned to defining how enlargement would occur in the NATO alliance, which states would be offered membership, and when NATO would enlarge.[7] Beginning in early 1994, Republicans in Congress also began to discuss the need for enlargement. The Senate offered its first expression of interest in late January, and the House followed in April.[8] As the Atlantic alliance coalesced around a policy of enlargement in 1995–1996, the decision encountered increasingly more opposition from both states outside the alliance and their own expert communities, particularly the intellectual community of Russian experts and scholars. This opposition became more vocal with the Madrid decision in July 1997 and played a significant role in the next year's Senate ratification debate.

With the 1999 admission of three new members, NATO's first involvement in conflict since its establishment in 1949 consumed the alliance. Both in NATO generally and in the United States, the discussion of further enlargement took a backseat to Kosovo. But it is highly probable that the new Bush administration will address and encourage future enlargement. Both Republican and Democratic presidential candidates declared themselves committed to further enlargement during the 2000 campaign, but there were no explicit decisions on which countries or deadlines beyond the 2002 target date for beginning the process, which had been laid out in the 1999 summit documents to be elaborated in NATO at a later date.

THE GOVERNMENT DEBATES ENLARGEMENT, 1993–1994

While President Bill Clinton clearly entered office in 1993 with a domestic focus, the events in Somalia only eight months later impressed on the administration and president the need to clarify a new role for the United States in the post–Cold War era. It was not surprising that the U.S. *National Security Strategy* document issued in 1994 prompted heated debate, fundamentally between the State and Defense Departments, requiring the National Security Council to mediate.[9] Its title *Engagement and Enlargement* reflected a commitment, despite Somalia, to assume a leadership role globally with respect to U.S. interests and to support efforts to achieve free market reforms and democratic governance by bringing emerging democracies into the community of Western values.

For most Europeanists within the State Department, NATO enlargement was a logical step in this effort, although enlargement had its detractors as well; for the Defense Department, the prospect of extending the NATO nuclear and conventional defense guarantee to a group of nascent democracies was sobering, and there was veiled, at times even vehement, opposition from the military. The initiative also had only reluctant support in the Office of the Secretary of Defense. With the military downsizing under way, DoD was struggling to maintain coherence in its force structures and deployments; any additional commitment with the extension of the U.S. nuclear guarantee to other countries was viewed skeptically, to say the least.

The public is said to be the final word in a democracy, but it is not often clear what they want to say in foreign policy. On the one hand, there is data against extending U.S. commitments, particularly after the Somalia debacle. And with respect to the prospective NATO invitees, a Chicago Council on Foreign Relations poll found 50 percent opposed to U.S. troops defending Poland against a Russian invasion. At the same time, however, 61 percent expressed support for increased U.S. commitment to NATO.[10]

A compromise for which Deputy Assistant Secretary of Defense Joe Kruzel took responsibility was the announcement in January 1994 at the Brussels NATO summit of the PfP program.[11] While the states for whom NATO membership was clearly a long-shot were enthusiastic about PfP as a manner in which to be at the table, albeit without a vote, other states who desired membership looked suspiciously at PfP as a shield for the West to avoid real commitment.[12]

Support for PfP in NATO was quick; the European Union had already recognized the substantial responsibility and dangers of enlarging the EU to include the newly emerging democracies. Furthermore, the Europeans were in the midst of their own reduction in forces and not inclined to expend the possible budgets an EU enlargement might require. PfP offered an attractive option to be inclusive while at the same time not overburdening the alliance when members were unsuccessfully confronting the mounting crisis in the Balkans. By extending the opportunity to the former Warsaw Pact states through PfP to undertake joint exercises, NATO could assure that the pact would not be reconstituted as its former members grew close to the West, that the forces for reform in those countries would be encouraged, and that cooperative operations would reinforce the mutual objective of European stability.

Each country turned then to negotiating the extent and outlines of its PfP agreement with NATO. Within several months, the Atlantic alliance announced its first joint PfP exercises. By any measure, the program was a success, despite the typical delays in launching some of the exercises, not uncommon for the large NATO bureaucracy with a cast of sixteen members and a need for consensus.

President Clinton's trip to Eastern Europe moved the United States on this debate. In January 1994 in Prague and again even more forcefully in July in Warsaw, Clinton announced that it was no longer a question of whether; rather, it was a question of when, how, and which countries were now ready to assume the responsibilities of NATO membership. The remarks in Warsaw committed the United States more forcefully to enlargement than Clinton had in Prague, but still without a timeline. There is substantial speculation about Clinton's motives. Some attribute his announcement to the ethnic communities' pressure in the year before a midterm election, others to an attempt to preempt the Republican adoption of NATO enlargement as official party policy. Certainly neither of these potential motivations discouraged the Clinton decision. But it is also difficult to attribute the decision strictly to political motives—the ethnic constituency is modest, and the broad public appeal of any foreign policy issue short of war is questionable at best. Much more in character was the explanation he gave, which Deputy Secretary of State Strobe Talbott reiterated, that it was time to recognize the hardships these countries endured on the "other side of the East-West divide," and bring qualified states into the NATO alliance as soon as possible.[13]

The presidential decision obviously quieted a substantial degree of the interagency opposition, but it also required strict admonishments from the newly appointed Assistant Secretary of State Richard Holbrooke to DoD officials, some at surprisingly high levels, to stem the vocal opposition in fall of 1994. The importance of Richard Holbrooke as a champion for the NATO enlargement cause was not inconsequential in the final U.S. support and eventual December 1994 NATO summit adoption of this new direction for the alliance.[14] Also important was the support of Deputy Secretary Talbott, who also worked to reconcile NATO and Russian policy within the government.

THE INTRA-ALLIANCE DEBATE, 1995–1996

After the NATO summit agreement, the alliance began the process of drafting guidelines for the eventual membership process. The period 1995–1997 marked the consolidation and design of a process whereby three new members joined NATO in 1999. There were three major issues addressed in this period by the United States and NATO: (1) intra-alliance consensus-building from the December 1994 summit decision to the 1995 agreement on the Enlargement Study; (2) negotiations with potential members; and (3) initiatives undertaken to mollify opposition to enlargement, particularly by Russia.

On the first issue, following the 1994 decision to pursue the objective of enlargement, the alliance partners entered a phase of negotiation on admission requirements for new members. The process was vintage NATO—slow and frustrating but ultimately successful. NATO released an incredibly crafted consensus document in September 1995 outlining the basic requirements of enlargement—democratic governance, free market reform, and civilian control of the military as well as resolution of outstanding border disputes. (See Appendix F.)

While intra-alliance cooperative efforts leading up to the Enlargement Study completed in September 1995 and agreed on at the summit produced allied consensus on the requirements for new members, that consensus became fragile in the weeks prior to the July 1997 Madrid summit and was nearly overturned in Madrid.[15] At the summit France, Germany, and Italy attempted to reverse what the United States had considered a done deal by proposing Romania (France) and Slovenia (Germany and Italy) respectively for inclusion in the first phase of new membership.[16] Driven by the conviction both that more than three new members could undermine the necessary U.S. congressional support for the treaty revision and that these two countries would stretch U.S. and NATO resources beyond their capabilities to bring new members up to NATO standards, the United States expended its influence to convince allies of the folly of more than three members in the first phase. In return, the United States agreed to a clause in the Madrid communiqué committing NATO to future enlargements and taking the unusual step of mentioning Romania and Slovenia explicitly as examples for future membership.

With respect to the second issue of negotiation and agreement with potential members, the Enlargement Study offered all interested countries an individual briefing of the necessary steps to potential membership. NATO assigned several teams to conduct these briefings to discuss the general and specific expectations. While the process proved to be a learning experience in many aspects, it also sparked a number of necessary reforms, for instance the shift to civilian control of the military in Poland.

To respond particularly to the domestic skeptics who feared that the United States would be confronted with the need to resolve standing disputes soon after enlargement, the alliance also stipulated that all border challenges and disputes be resolved before NATO membership. This led, for instance, to a constructive Hungarian-Romanian agreement on contentious border issues. In sum, while not a perfect process, the attempt to hold potential members to generally specified guidelines proved useful in meeting the oft-stated U.S. objective that new members needed to be "not just consumers (of security), but also producers."

The third and most challenging issue in this period was mollifying the opposition to enlargement, or "NATO expansion," as the opponents even now continue to call it.[17] There was both a slowly gathering domestic opposition and an opposition outside the alliance. The domestic opposition will be addressed below. The major external opposition came predominantly from Russia. Despite an unexpected interest in Russian membership in NATO expressed by President Yeltsin at one point, there was general condemnation of what Russia viewed as the continuation as well as expansion of the NATO threat. Repeated U.S. and NATO assurances that enlargement would provide enhanced stability on the continent and not create dividing lines did not seem to quiet Russian fears.

On the bilateral level, the United States pursued two initiatives to reassure the Russians that the NATO decision to extend its membership did not indicate any attempt to create new divisions: one, in arms control and, two, in support of Russian membership in a number of organizations dealing with trade. The first offered discussions on Strategic Arms Reduction Talks (START) III (while waiting for START II ratification), and the second offered to support Russian efforts to gain membership in the Organization for Economic Cooperation and Development (OECD), the World Trade Organization (WTO), and in some form the Group of Seven (G-7).

On a third initiative, the United States crafted a response, adopted by NATO, of three "no's" to assure the Russians: NATO had "no intention, no plan, and no reason to deploy nuclear weapons on the territory of new members, nor any need to change any aspect of NATO's nuclear posture or nuclear policy—and [did] not foresee any future need to do so."[18] Building on this approach laid out by former Secretary of State Warren Christopher in December 1996 at a NATO foreign ministers meeting in Brussels, Secretary of State Madeleine Albright continued to underscore it in a number of public addresses, adding often "We do not contemplate permanently stationing substantial combat forces."[19] To assure those

worried about defense of NATO territory, the three no's did not extend to conflict situations, so there would be no Russian veto when national interests were
threatened, but no new Berlin Walls would be erected.

U.S. policymakers recognized the thin line this policy forced them to
walk in terms of their commitment to potential full member states, but the
need to be forthcoming to the Russian state, which had undergone a tremendous transformation since the days of the Cold War, was clear.[20] But it was
also clear that Russia could not be seen to dictate the terms of enlargement. In
blunt Kissinger style, the former secretary of state voiced his own misgivings:

> I will hold my nose and support enlargement even though . . . dangerous.
> . . . Whoever heard of a military alliance begging with a weakened adver-
> sary? NATO should not be turned into an instrument to conciliate Russia or
> Russia will undermine it.[21]

Despite these efforts, the Russian opposition grew more shrill as the July
1997 Madrid summit neared. The European allies were also increasingly
nervous about the impact of enlargement on Russia. Proposals for an appropriate response ranged from support for the Russian concept of an alliance of
sixteen-plus-one to an agreement for a forum for closer consultation and coordination. The result of the subsequent discussion of various options was the
May 1997 NATO-Russian Founding Act establishing a Permanent Joint
Council (PJC) in Brussels for discussions, but not a veto, of alliance issues.[22]

The NATO-Ukrainian Charter on a Distinctive Partnership followed the
Russia-NATO Founding Act also with the purpose of allaying concerns of
exclusion from NATO. For the Ukrainians, the charter (agreed before the
Founding Act, but in deference to the Russians not signed until afterward) had
the additional benefit of underscoring Ukrainian independence from Russia
while not causing the alarm that membership in NATO would have sparked.[23]

THE DOMESTIC DEBATE, 1997–1999

NATO enlargement did not loom prominently in public debate after the
Madrid summit. In fact, the decision did not register to any extent with the
broad U.S. public. The discussion remained a largely elite debate but one that
drew more attention beginning in late spring 1997. To assure Senate passage
of the required NATO treaty revision, the administration had Jeremy Rosner
set up office in March 1997 at the State Department to oversee the campaign
for enlargement. Over the next year he worked to broaden support, not only
from ethnic communities but also from other groups. Critical backing came
from Republicans, who had run in 1994 on the Contract with America and

supported the NATO Enlargement Facilitation Act of 1996, which passed the Senate 81 to 16. A two-thirds Senate majority is a high hurdle, and in order to avoid a close call similar to the experience with the Chemical Weapons Convention when it came to voting on a change to the NATO treaty, all stops were taken out to swing support.[24]

The impact of the decision about to be made in Madrid prompted in particular the community of Russian scholars, but also other concerned elites, to mobilize against enlargement in the weeks before the summit. Whether an earlier agreement on the Founding Act would have assured greater Russian acquiescence and therefore a lower level of concern is unknown. The primary concern of U.S. Russian experts was the deleterious impact enlargement could have on U.S.-Russian relations. They feared that it might cause Russia to move away from reform and back into some of the practices of the previous regimes. In a last-minute attempt to reverse the decision, a letter from members of Congress and one from members of Congress together with academics were forwarded to the president to protest the anticipated Madrid decision. As a movement against enlargement, these letters constituted the proverbial "too little, too late."

After the July 1997 decision in NATO, U.S. scholarly opposition increased and became more vocal. Michael Mandelbaum voiced one of the most outspoken opinions, warning of the dire consequences to the U.S.-Russian relationship. Susan Eisenhower added her concerns about the potential for Russia to turn away from reforms.[25] Other prominent opponents included George F. Kennan and Senator Sam Nunn, recently retired from Congress, as well as a number of editorialists such as Thomas Friedman.[26]

For the remainder of 1997 and until the final vote, the administration focused on assuring bipartisan support for enlargement and a positive Senate vote. Republican Senate majority leader Trent Lott established the Senate NATO Observer Group (SNOG), which supported enlargement. Finally, administration officials testified frequently over the year in Congress: Secretaries Madeleine Albright (State) and William Cohen (DoD), among others such as Chairman of the Joint Chiefs of Staff General Henry Shelton, appeared in October 1997 before House committees and again before the Senate Foreign Relations Committee with jurisdiction. The House and Senate testimony attempted to reassure particularly on the issue of cost, and the final spring 1998 Senate hearings found a very receptive Senate chair, Jesse Helms. Without his support, the consent of the Senate would have been far more difficult.[27]

Perhaps the more skeptical congressional opposition came from the House of Representatives, which does not have a vote in treaty ratification but held hearings in fall 1997 before the final Senate hearings in spring 1998. The major concern in the House deliberations was the extension of U.S. military commitments, but the potential cost of enlargement also worried members. The range of estimates was striking, from U.S.$13 billion over fourteen years by the Congressional Budget Office (CBO) to U.S.$5–6 billion over fifteen years from RAND to U.S.$1.5–2 billion over twelve years by the Department of Defense. The CBO and RAND studies assumed four new members, including Slovakia, while the DoD assumed only three, but was officially classified.[28] The bottom line was that the cost could only be calculated imperfectly.

When Senator Helms called a vote in March 1998, the committee vote was an overwhelming 16 to 2 with four conditions and a number of declarations assuring that the costs would not grow and NATO would continue to safeguard U.S. interests. There were also statements on Russia. The opposition came from the extremes. On the left Senator Paul Wellstone voted against the resolution on the grounds that NATO was a relic of the Cold War and should be disbanded or undergo radical change. On the right, Senator John Ashcroft argued that the alliance was becoming diluted with too many members and missions. But with only two negative votes, the treaty moved to the full Senate.

On the Senate floor, seventeen senators offered a threatening resolution calling for a delay in the U.S. ratification of the treaty. Senator Patrick Moynihan also attempted a delay until after EU enlargement. The administration countered his resolution by arguing that the United States had control over neither the timing nor the nature of EU enlargement. Late in the game, Senator John Warner argued unsuccessfully for a mandated pause in enlargement after the first three new members. The leading Democratic member of the Senate Foreign Relations Committee, Senator Joseph Biden, took the lead in responding to the various attempts to derail enlargement, particularly on a pause and on dilution of mission. In the end, the 30 April 1998 U.S. Senate vote (80 to 19) clearly supported the treaty revision without crippling amendments and with a comfortable margin over the required 67 (two-thirds) votes.

INTEREST GROUPS/OTHER INFLUENCES

During the U.S. debate, charges were leveled at two interest groups for undue influence in the U.S. decision to seek NATO enlargement—the Eastern European ethnic communities and the defense industry. In the former case, there is no question that particularly the Polish-American community actively petitioned officials both in the government and in the Republican Party for NATO enlargement. The Polish-American Congress became very involved in such lobbying. Its president, Edward J. Moskal, wrote President Clinton in October 1995 concerned that "Time is not on our side," and that the answer to Who? and When? might be "No one and never."[29] The cause also attracted influential support from personalities such as former National Security Advisor Zbigniew Brzezinski. The smaller Czech- and Hungarian-American communities, meanwhile, were not as organized or effective and their impact was less substantial.

In the case of influence by the defense industry, the connection is much more tenuous and subtle. That companies were attempting to sell their arms and platforms to the emerging democracies is not in doubt, but the charges, particularly by enlargement opponents, that enlargement was driven by the defense industry desire to sell new members weapons is difficult to confirm. In fact, the financial ability of these countries to purchase arms in substantial numbers is questionable. At best U.S. industry might have hoped for some immediate purchases but could only expect profits in the long term. While there appears to be a correlation between congressional support for enlargement and districts that contain defense industries, it is also true that those districts traditionally have Republican or prodefense Democratic majorities and typically vote in favor of a whole range of defense issues.

In addition to these two groups, the U.S. Committee to Expand NATO combined the efforts of a number of disparate interests in order to lobby the administration as well as Congress. Finally, other affected groups such as labor, veterans, and Eastern European diplomats tried to influence the decision. The fact that lobbying against enlargement was so modest and so late may explain its obviously slight impact. In addition to the Russia experts mentioned earlier, John Lewis Gaddis faulted NATO enlargement for lack of strategic vision and commented that he could recall "no other moment in my own experience as a practicing historian at which there was less support, within the community of historians, for an announced policy position."[30]

BEYOND THE 1999 ENLARGEMENT

At the time of the 12 March 1999 admittance of the three new member states to NATO, the United States reiterated its commitment to an open process of enlargement. Just over a week later, NATO became involved in an air war in Kosovo. This first conflict for NATO since its inception in 1949 obviously turned attention to the Balkans. Even the long-awaited NATO fiftieth anniversary celebrations in Washington were muted and focused on the conflict. If there had been hopes by aspirant states of a signal from the alliance about the next phase of enlargement, those hopes were not realized.

But this did not mean that the issue was ignored. Rather, the alliance agreed to a Membership Action Plan (MAP), which explicitly stated the intention of NATO to expand and listed the potential states.[31] There was also a clearer definition of the requirements for membership, albeit not exact standards. While there was U.S. support for the MAP and for a clear signal to the disappointed states "in-waiting," the Kosovo crisis might be seen as almost fortuitous in its impact—the United States could signal support for further enlargement, which had wide domestic support, but delay immediate decisions due to the burdens of the Balkan war. Furthermore, the decision to name Macedonia and Albania, even if at the end of the list, demonstrated U.S. support and showed appreciation for the efforts of those countries in the warring region.

The anticipated date for the next consideration of enlargement at the end of 2002 also permitted Poland, Hungary, and the Czech Republic time to demonstrate their intention to reform and restructure the military to conform to NATO standards. After 1999, the Clinton administration has repeated a number of times its commitment to an "open process" of enlargement. The support for NATO enlargement cuts across party lines as well. Vice President Al Gore underscored his position in favor of enlargement during his campaign for president in early fall 2000, and Governor George W. Bush issued an equally strong, if not stronger, endorsement for enlargement in the week before the election. Clearly both viewed this issue to be of concern to at least a portion of the voters, considering it sufficiently important to warrant an explicit policy. As President Bush refashions U.S. foreign and defense policy, the U.S. position regarding enlargement will become clearer.

An interesting policymaker to watch will be National Security Advisor Condoleezza Rice. She opposed the first NATO enlargement before the 1996 Russian elections but then supported NATO efforts when the decision could no longer be detrimental to Russia.[32] Critical factors affecting this issue will include Russian attitudes, particularly with respect to the Baltic states. There is no question that any discussion of NATO membership for states on the Russian border will draw heavy criticism. The state of U.S.-Russian relations may aggravate or mollify the impact of the Russian opposition.

An interesting factor that has received surprisingly little attention is the European Union process of enlargement. While many U.S. policymakers in the immediate post–Cold War era had unsuccessfully pushed for EU enlargement as a logical precedent to NATO enlargement, that EU enlargement may now fully occur before the next opening of NATO and could prompt an entirely different set of circumstances. Most strikingly Estonia has been named for the first EU wave. Another new element, the launch of a European Security and Defense Policy (ESDP) with a 60,000-person army will make use of a range of NATO assets. In other words, Estonia, through its EU membership, could become a de facto NATO member if it chooses to join the ESDP as many expect. The other two Baltic states are expected to join the EU as well, and could exercise the same defense option.[33]

For the United States, the Baltic states will probably pose the largest dilemma for future enlargement. There was already substantial support during the first enlargement for their admission, but it was successfully argued that their reform process was not as far along as the other candidates and that there should be more assistance as PfP partners for greater military standardization before the alliance considered their membership. Even more convincing was the sense that although the Russians would oppose the admission of former Warsaw Pact allies Poland, Hungary, and the Czech Republic, they would, in the end, come to terms with it. In contrast, the admission of their former republics, which surround the Russian exclave Kaliningrad, would be more threatening. The opposition could be such that the already slow democratic reform process in Russia would be severely threatened or even overturned.

However, the issue of membership for the Baltic states will emerge again during the discussion of the second if not subsequent enlargements. Chairman of the Senate Foreign Relations Committee Jesse Helms announced his support of their admission to NATO at the beginning of the new session of Congress in 2001. Although this will not necessarily lead to an official U.S. position—indeed, the opponents from the first wave in the scholarly and expert communities that follow Russia will argue vehemently against such a position—it will assure its consideration.

The case of Romania and Slovenia may prove more difficult than envisioned in July 1997 when the two were included in the summit communiqué. Since that time, Romanian reform has fallen substantially behind that of other Central European countries. Slovenia also remains hopeful, and may again in the next wave find a strong supporter in the Italians and Germans. There may also be an ideological rationale for its admittance as a model to the Balkan region. But the Austrian announcement that it would not seek NATO membership might argue against admitting Slovenia with its long border on Austria. Additionally, its modest defense establishment has been criticized as falling short of a reasonable contribution to NATO. During the 1997 Madrid summit discussions, Slovenia also attracted support from selected senators (for example, Republican Senator William Roth, who even sent President Clinton a supportive letter). Unclear is whether their support, based primarily on the potentially stabilizing impact of Slovenia on the Balkan region, will persist into the next round.

Conversely, the early discussion of enlargement had assumed Slovakia would join in the first wave, but it fell so far behind in its privatization and other efforts that it was taken out of consideration and not even discussed to any extent in Madrid.[34] The United States made no secret of its disdain for President Vladimir Meciar and his programs. Since his defeat for re-election, however, the United States has felt a commitment to respond to renewed reform efforts.

Discussion of membership in the alliance for all these states and others such as Bulgaria will almost unavoidably unleash a debate between those concerned with stretching the military responsibilities of the United States and those who place high value on the political signal it sends to the emerging democracies.

CONCLUSION

NATO enlargement was hotly debated behind closed doors within the government and particularly between the State and Defense Departments until summer 1994, when President Clinton made it clear he would support enlargement.[35] For President Clinton, NATO enlargement reflected the objectives of engagement and enlargement articulated in *National Security Strategy,* approved in 1994 as the road map for the new administration. Open debate within the government abated after 1994, although it was clear that muted opposition continued from primarily two groups: those concerned that extending membership to three new countries would stretch U.S. defense capabilities dangerously in Europe and those worried that NATO enlargement would unnecessarily challenge or even destabilize an emerging, but uncertain, Russia. Active debate moved outside the government following the presidential decision and focused on these two issues.

In contrast, there was no significant debate of enlargement in the U.S. Congress until the final stages of the hearing process. This had several causes. Except for very specific communities with large Polish-American, and to a much lesser extent Czech- and Hungarian-American, populations, the issue had virtually no visibility for the public until the very last stages of congressional debate. Even then, the issue had only a limited audience. In addition, the Republicans had adopted the objective of enlargement before the 1994 election in their Contract with America. They had joined with the Democrats in a 94 to 3 Senate vote in January 1994 after the president's remarks in Prague. This was followed by several other resolutions over the next few years that drew little debate beyond whether the Baltic states should be included. The Republicans during this period were supportive of enlargement, and the issue was more one of whether they or the president could be more forthcoming on enlargement. The fact that both President Clinton and the Republicans were in agreement on enlargement essentially removed the issue from partisan debate.

In the 1996 presidential election, Republican candidate Robert Dole and incumbent Clinton differed only in timing: The Republicans pushed for an accelerated timetable while Clinton cautioned that the NATO process needed to be deliberate. This fundamental bipartisanship carried over into the congressional debate of the treaty revisions in 1998, with only two Senate Foreign Relations Committee votes (one each on left and right) registered against enlargement (16 to 2) and a more than comfortable two-thirds majority vote (80 to 19) on the Senate floor in favor of treaty revisions to enlarge the alliance. Despite the fact that Congress considered the issue seriously only during the final year of a five-year process, Senator Lott cited forty hours of Senate debate, fifty senatorial statements, and twenty defeated amendments, leaving no question of Senate advice and consent.

It was in these final stages that the most vigorous public debate took place, primarily initiated by those who feared repercussions from Russia. Russia had indeed expressed its displeasure over enlargement, and although its opposition had been shrill at points, it was resigned at others. Initially reticent with an opinion, Russia voiced inconsistent views throughout the process. It spoke adamantly against enlargement when it perceived that it would actually occur, but then backed off to the point of suggesting Russian membership, moderating its commentary in light of the NATO-Russia Founding Act. Yet in the final stages, Russia again weighed in loudly when the U.S. scholarly community mobilized. This latter effort of course proved unsuccessful, and the Russians appear to have been surprisingly quick to resign themselves to the new NATO membership.

Future enlargement will depend on a number of factors, but support from both presidential candidates during the 2000 campaign indicates that the Bush administration will remain open to further enlargement when the discussion begins and that the issue should find bipartisan support. Indeed, Secretary of State Colin Powell anticipated the interest in further enlargement in his confirmation hearings. With the philosophical issue of the appropriateness of opening NATO resolved, current members will likely concentrate on the political, economic, and military progress made by prospective members as well as the state of U.S.-Russian relations. To an even greater extent than in the first round, the next enlargement will likely attract much expert input and succeed only with strong bipartisan support.

NOTES

The views expressed in this chapter are solely those of the author and do not represent the views of the U.S. government or any oranization or other agency with which the author is affiliated.

1. John Mearsheimer's dire predictions of ethnic tensions and eventually conflict were the topic of hot debate and angry denunciation in 1991 when published. His panel at the annual conference of the American Political Science Association (APSA) attracted over 200 scholars and only one of the many questions and responses during

the discussion session supported his theses. (Note: he also predicted in the same article the emergence of Germany as a nuclear power and suggested the inevitable demise of the EU in the Q&A. On these points, history has not borne him out.)

2. By the end of his term, President Bush had reduced forces from over 325,000 in Europe before 1989 to officially 100,000, headed for 75,000. Three hundred and twenty-five thousand equals approximately 800,000 total Americans including dependents and civilian personnel—a very substantial presence, by any count.

3. For a chronology of the period 1949–1994 on European security, see Catherine McArdle Kelleher, "The Future of European Security: An Interim Assessment," *Brookings Occasional Papers* (Washington, D.C., 1995). See especially pp. 160–173 for a European Security Chronology.

4. There have been a number of explanations for the seeming change of heart by the EU on enlargement, including the impact on the employment market of the flood of low-cost workers from the East into the European Union after the revolutions of 1989 as well as the attraction of low-cost labor and associated costs in the East for investors who otherwise might have invested in the EU. The EU official explanations for not enlarging have ranged from the need first to introduce the Single Market and the Maastricht program (that is, in "Eurojargon," deepen the EU community rather then widen it) and consolidate the enlargement then under way with Austria, Sweden, and Finland. Note that this wave of enlargement was to countries who became net contributors to the EU coffers. Later in 1997 the EU argued that it should first deal with the introduction of the European Monetary Union (EMU) before enlargement to the East. See Ian Davidson, "In the Fast Lane," *Financial Times*, 19 February 1997: 12.

5. German Foreign Minister Genscher floated the idea of a greatly strengthened CSCE informally, but the idea of creating a secure Europe through an organization grown to fifty-four nations, with the disintegration of the Soviet Union and Eastern bloc, confronted members with an impossible task.

6. North Atlantic Treaty Organization, *Partnership for Peace: Invitation* (Brussels, 10–11 January 1994). See Appendix D for excerpts.

7. President Clinton's first speech mentioning enlargement was in January 1994 in Prague with a more forceful articulation in July 1994 in Warsaw. Vice President Gore used similar language in his European speeches of September 1994. None of these did more than indicate a U.S. commitment to enlargement—there was no mention of when or how or even which states.

8. Republican support came primarily from members of Congress with heavily Central European constituencies—in April 1994 from Representatives Gilman and Hyde and in summer 1994 from Senator Lugar who called PfP "a policy for postponement." James M. Goldgeier, *Not Whether but When: The U.S. Decision to Enlarge NATO* (Washington, D.C.: Brookings Institution Press, 1999), 80. The book provides a detailed discussion of the NATO decision.

9. White House, *A National Security Strategy of Engagement and Enlargement* (Washington, D.C., July 1994).

10. Jeremy D. Rosner, "NATO Enlargement's America Hurdle," *Foreign Affairs* 75, no. 4 (July/August 1996): 12. There are equally uneven polls from the University of Maryland School of Public Affairs polling program.

11. Others claimed ownership, including the Germans, but Kruzel clearly played a major role in its design and later in its implementation.

12. Not only did those states receive a seat at the table through PfP to the point of an active joint exercise program, they moved into NATO headquarters in Brussels in

the rooms previously occupied by the security services whose primary responsibility during the Cold War had been, ironically, to assure headquarters security from precisely those states.

13. See Strobe Talbott, "Why NATO Should Grow," *The New York Review of Books*, 10 August 1995. Talbott wrote the article to counter the beginning of opposition to enlargement, particularly that of Senator Sam Nunn who had given a very critical speech in Norfolk, Virginia, on "The Future of NATO in an Uncertain World," 22 June 1995. Even earlier Secretary Christopher testified on the president's conviction to enlarge in testimony on 30 June 1994 before the Senate Foreign Relations Committee.

14. Richard Holbrooke, "America, a European Power," *Foreign Affairs* 14, no. 2 (April 1995): 38–53.

15. North Atlantic Treaty Organization. *Study on NATO Enlargement* (Brussels, September 1995). (See Appendix F.)

16. The French support for Romania is presumed to have two sources: first, historic French ties to Romania, which have meant, among other things, that the second language of Romania is French and, second, a French desire to counter what is considered an emerging bloc of allies for the Germans with the membership of Poland, the Czech Republic, and Hungary.

17. When the issue of expanding NATO membership was first raised, the term *expansion* was used. However, the U.S. administration shifted to *enlargement* to avoid a term used with reference to the ambitions of the Soviet Union during the Cold War.

18. See Section 4, para. 2, of the *Founding Act on Mutual Relations, Cooperation and Security Between NATO and the Russian Federation* for more complete wording (Appendix G).

19. Statement by the Honorable Madeleine Albright, secretary of state, before the Senate Foreign Relations Committee, 7 October 1997, in Lawrence Chalmer and Jonathan Pierce, *NATO 1997: Year of Change* (Washington, D.C.: NDU Press, 1997).

20. Talbott also attempted to calm the fears of the Russians that NATO enlargement was directed toward them. See Strobe Talbott, "Russia Has Nothing to Fear," *New York Times*, 18 February 1997: A25.

21. Goldgeier, *Not Whether but When,* 113.

22. Among others, former Secretary of State Henry Kissinger has been critical of the Founding Act and the Permanent Joint Council. While acknowledging the possible need to reach out to Russia at the time of enlargement, he has suggested that such efforts not be attempted within the alliance where the Russians might eventually in fact have a veto.

23. See Appendix G for the Founding Act on Mutual Relations, Cooperation and Security Between NATO and the Russian Federation and Appendix H for the Charter on a Distinctive Partnership Between the North Atlantic Treaty Organization and Ukraine (excerpts).

24. The effort was substantial and included also what became known as the SNOG, the Senate NATO Observer Group, favorable to the policy.

25. One of many critical articles and books on this subject is Michael Mandelbaum, *Dawn of Peace in Europe* (New York: Twentieth Century Fund, 1996).

26. George F. Kennan, "A Fateful Error," *New York Times*, 5 February 1997: A23.

27. After the Madrid summit, Senator Helms had been much more skeptical, but he became convinced that neither enlargement cost nor Russia would weaken NATO. See Goldgeier, *Not Whether but When,* 127.

28. A detailed summary of all three studies is included in Todd Sandler and Keith Hartley, *The Political Economy of NATO: Past, Present, and into the 21st Century* (Cambridge: Cambridge University Press, 1999), 83. Note that the RAND and DoD

studies assume a low threat; the CBO study assumes a resurgent Russia. The U.S. share of the costs for DoD is 16.7 percent; CBO, 11.9 percent; and RAND, 13 percent. See also Ronald Asmus, Richard Kugler, and F. Stephen Larrabee, "What Will NATO Enlargement Cost?" *Survival* (Autumn 1996): 5–26. For an alternative analysis of these studies, see Amos Perlmutter and Ted Galen Carpenter, "NATO's Expensive Trip East: The Folly of Enlargement," *Foreign Affairs* 77, no. 1 (1998): 2–6.

29. For discussion of the ethnic communities, see Goldgeier, *Not Whether but When,* 100.

30. John Lewis Gaddis, "History, Grand Strategy, and NATO Enlargement," *Survival* (Spring 1998): 15.

31. The order in which the states were listed was hotly debated and closely watched: Romania, Slovenia, Estonia, Latvia, Lithuania, Bulgaria, Slovakia, Yugoslav Republic of Macedonia, and Albania. Washington Summit Communiqué, "An Alliance for the 21st Century" (Washington, D.C., 24 April 1999).

32. Condoleezza Rice, "Now, NATO Should Grow," *New York Times*, 8 July 1996: A13.

33. Under the new policy, all three Baltic republics could actually become members simultaneously if they were all to achieve the acceptable standards.

34. It is interesting that all the early U.S. studies of NATO enlargement included Slovakia, but as Meciar refused to undertake true reform, the United States withdrew its support for the country as did other NATO members. With the subsequent change in government and significant reform effort, the United States would find it hard to deny membership and, in fact, might prove one of its strongest supporters. For instance, see Congressional Budget Office, "The Costs of Expanding the NATO Alliance," *CBO Papers* (Washington, D.C., March 1996).

35. In fact, James Goldgeier argues that without the 1994 presidential decision that NATO enlargement was the right thing to do, the limited support in the bureaucracy could not have moved the policy alone. Only National Security Adviser Lake and UN Ambassador Albright were strongly in favor, together with a small group of dedicated government officials. See Goldgeier, *Not Whether but When,* 153.

3

Germany: Consensus Politics and Changing Security Paradigms

DANIEL J. WHITENECK

In no other NATO country was the issue of enlargement raised earlier and discussed with more attention than the newly united German republic. The revolution that unified West and East Germany in 1989 and 1990 was still being digested when the momentous events that led to the collapse of the Soviet Union in 1991 took place. In 1992 the Maastricht Treaty marked the beginning of another sea change in European politics, the transformation of the European Union. This was followed by economic and political instability in Russia and many countries of Eastern Europe as they struggled with the initial effects of radical reform measures. The threat of political instability creating new security threats was given concrete form at this time by the savage war in the Balkans. The fear that such fighting could break out in other states subject to political and ethnic instability was at the forefront for NATO leaders and the foreign policy establishments of the European states.

It is hardly surprising that this environment produced a rethinking of German national security policy. That rethinking would find its expression in significant German efforts to extend the institutions of the West into Central and Eastern Europe in an attempt to create a more stable continent with Germany at its center and no longer on the front line of a security divide. This would be a radical departure from the foreign and security policy that had dominated Germany from 1955 to 1989. It would bring into debate Germany's role in Europe, and indeed in all the political and security organizations concerned with Europe. The manner in which the debate took place within Germany demonstrated that the shift in national security strategies had been accomplished by consensus politics. The discussions managed to balance the unique national interests of Germany with its important relationships to NATO, the European Union, Russia, and the states of Eastern and Central Europe.

CHANGING GERMAN SECURITY INTERESTS

Germany's historical legacy was to be *the* frontline state in NATO's forty-year standoff with the Soviet Union. It was impossible for West Germany to be anything else, just as it was impossible for East Germany to be anything but a garrison state for thousands of Russian troops. With more than a million soldiers and several thousand nuclear missiles stationed on their soil for the entire Cold War, the political and economic costs of European security were enormous for Germans on both sides of the divide.

The events of 1989, and the unification of Germany within NATO, meant that the new German state would have to throw away its security policies and quickly move to help create a new security paradigm in the center of Europe. In the midst of the chaos of the period from 1989 to 1991, it was the constancy of Germany's position within NATO that provided the grounding for a new security policy to be launched.

First, the threat of a unified Germany emerging as a "great power" in the center of the continent was constrained by historic changes in the consciousness of German leaders and public opinion on Germany's role in Europe and the continued leadership of NATO by the United States.[1] This was evidenced by the actions of the Kohl government as it reaffirmed its commitment to act within multilateral institutions like NATO and the Western European Union (WEU). It moved to strengthen multinational units with France, it stressed the continuity of the long-standing policy not to pursue weapons of mass destruction, and it immediately called for reductions in military forces below those called for in the Conventional Forces in Europe (CFE) negotiations. German public opinion and elite opinion strongly supported these policies. In 1991 Germans favored the continued role of NATO as the "best guarantor" of European security by a 57 percent to 28 percent margin. They also supported the continued presence of foreign troops by a 55 percent to 28 percent margin. Elite opinions were even more in favor of maintaining NATO's role in Europe and Germany's position within NATO under U.S. leadership.[2]

Second, Germany in the years from 1989 to 1991 was totally preoccupied with the internal politics and economics of unification. The process that so many had waited for and never thought would happen so suddenly had a tremendous impact on the German economy and its budget, electoral politics at the local and national levels, and social policy. Germany was spending up to DM 150 billion (150 billion deutsche mark; U.S.$100 billion dollars) per year on integrating the East. This huge financial transfer attempted to deal with a situation wherein the territories of the former German Democratic Republic (GDR) had a gross domestic product (GDP) that was 7 percent of the West, a 33 percent unemployment rate, and labor productivity 70 percent below that of the West. All of these combined to produce internal migration on the order of one million people moving from East to West.[3]

Third, Germany expressed repeatedly its concerns that future security questions in Central and Eastern Europe not contribute to insecurity and instability for Russia and the former states of the Soviet Union and the Warsaw Pact. Germany provided early economic assistance to the Soviet Union (subsequently Russia) on a scale much larger than any other state with a commitment of DM 70 billion over a five-year period in 1990. In comparison, the rest of the European Union (EU) provided DM 24.6 billion combined, the United States DM 8.4 billion, and Japan DM 4.1 billion. The bill for providing for the 380,000 Soviet troops while they were in Germany and after they returned home reached DM 12 billion (about U.S.$8 billion).[4] Diplomatically, Chancellor Helmut Kohl and Secretary Mikhail Gorbachev signed the Treaty on Good Neighborliness, Partnership, and Cooperation in November of 1990. Kohl and Foreign Minister Hans-Dietrich Genscher were also muted in their criticism of Gorbachev's crackdown on Lithuania in 1991. Chancellor Kohl went to NATO's Rome summit in 1991 and argued for further arms reductions and increased confidence-building measures between NATO and Russia.[5]

As for Eastern Europe, Kohl and Genscher called for early EU enlargement into the region. They recognized that the conflict raging in the Balkans was founded on some of the same conditions that could be found in Eastern Europe. The prospect of EU membership could help the region transition to market economics, help stabilize fledgling democracies, and quell the reasons for ethnic hostilities. Kohl and French President François Mitterrand had dominated the 1989 EU summit on these issues by creating the European Development Bank to promote development in Eastern Europe and bring the EU and the European Free Trade Area (EFTA) countries into a closer relationship. Germany and Russia shared an interest in regional stability. Neither could impose order on the region for their own particular reasons. Russia feared the rise of an anti-Russian coalition in the region and Germany feared an economic and political reaction from ethnic conflict and refugee flows. EU expansion into the region was less traumatic for the Russians than NATO expansion because of the U.S. factor.[6]

These factors together meant that the old focus of German security, the forward defense of its territory from a massive attack by Warsaw Pact troops, could be radically altered. The Russian threat was buried by German unification and the collapse of the Soviet Union. Germany was securely anchored in

Western institutions, NATO, and the EU, and it was committed to a policy of continuity within them. Germany's security policy would now be shaped by the processes of NATO enlargement and the changing nature of NATO's security role in Europe.

GERMANY, NATO, AND THE NEW EUROPE, 1993–1994

Germany faced new security policy choices as unification began to fade and NATO and the EU struggled to create a new European order. Germany's policy options were framed by NATO's new strategic concepts, by the impact of the Balkan debacle, and by the emergence of German power within the EU. Within these broad parameters, Germany's elites, and to some extent the public, dealt with the new security issues. German focus would have to shift from territorial defense to active security provision outside of NATO's member states, that is, to shift from a specific and well-known threat to a general and unknown threat to "stability in Europe." To deal with these issues, German defense and foreign policy officials would make enlargement of NATO an answer at the heart of the debate.

The atmosphere in Germany in 1993 was heavily influenced by the unrest to the East and South. Russian elections seemed to portend a looming chaos as the economy collapsed. In that supercharged climate, nationalist politicians were finding fertile ground in the loss of power and prestige suffered by Russia as its political and economic conditions slowly disintegrated. Closer to home, Czechoslovakia split in two. The economic reforms in Poland, the Czech Republic, Hungary, and Slovakia were not proceeding as fast or as well as expected. The Baltic states were clamoring for membership in Western institutions as insurance against a reassertion of Russian power. In the Balkans, the EU, the Organization for Security and Cooperation in Europe (OSCE), and the UN had all failed to stop the bloody war. It led to 400,000 refugees in Germany alone, lost economic opportunities throughout the region, and paralysis of the EU politically as peace plan after peace plan was scuttled by the differing foreign policy agendas of EU members.

At this time German elite and public opinion were closely aligned. Ninety-two percent of elites believed NATO was essential to European security and 70 percent of the general public agreed. The public also supported strong alliance ties for Germany within NATO. When asked to identify a security threat in the post–Cold War world, they identified the threat of Balkan-style conflict spreading to the territory of the former Soviet Union. At the same time, 88 percent of the broader public favored improving ties with the United States and 92 percent favored improved cooperation with France to handle European problems.

The fear of a spreading Balkan-type conflict was reflected when 80 percent of the public opposed further immigration increases. On the larger questions of new security roles for Germany, the role of the armed forces, and future European security, the German public was undecided and did not express a clear preference for either a pacifist or activist security policy.[7]

Among the political parties, there was broad support for changes in fundamental security policies to address the new concerns. The governing CDU-CSU (Christian Democrat Union–Christian Socialist Union) and FDP (Free Democrats) coalition as well as influential security policy experts in the SPD (Social Democrats) all supported the continuation of German security policy within the NATO framework, the creation of the EU's CFSP (Common Foreign and Security Policy), and the extension of significant aid to Eastern Europe. The parties disagreed, however, on the use of military force outside of German and NATO territory. The CDU-CSU backed its use under NATO auspices. The FDP leaned toward the CDU-CSU position. The SPD supported the use of force only under UN auspices. At their 1993 party conference, the Green/Alliance 90 coalition voted by a 90 to 10 margin to oppose the use of military force of any kind, even in a situation like Bosnia.[8]

Germany's security policy choices at this time were therefore open to some degree of change, particularly after the constitutional court ruling in 1994 that made its participation in NATO actions at least legally permissible. With the exception of the Green/Alliance 90 opposition, there was public and elite support for a strong role for Germany within existing institutions.

The options for Germany to pursue a more independent security policy, as a leader of a Central European bloc of states or as part of a special Berlin-Moscow relationship and condominium in Eastern Europe, were foreclosed with no support from the elites or the public. The two options remaining for Germany were to help create a "core Europe" by deepening the relationship among the Western European states at the heart of the EU or to help create a "broader Europe" by expanding the Western institutions.[9] The debate over the future of German security policy would be based on these options as the government and the political class struggled to create a consensus broad enough to bring along the public.

The Balkan war proved that the OSCE and the UN were unable to provide adequate European security. It also proved that the main threat to the future security of NATO's European members would stem from common problems along the periphery of the alliance. What was needed was a NATO response to the changed security environment. NATO was needed as an insurance policy, not only for its members who faced that periphery on the new "frontline," but also by the newly emerging democracies if they were to avoid the fate of the Balkans.[10]

ENLARGEMENT: "EXPORTING STABILITY"

It was Manfred Wörner, NATO's secretary general, who would put the alliance's enlargement on the agenda in a 10 September 1993 speech. Volker Rühe, German minister of defense, seized on the idea as a solution to many of the security problems after the Cold War. Rühe set the tone of the debate for the next five years. The enlargement debate, in Germany at least, centered on the issues of strategic policy and choices, far more than budgetary concerns or changes in force levels, or burden sharing.[11]

Enlargement served a number of strategic objectives, including taking Germany off the frontline of NATO, pushing the defense perimeter of the alliance eastward, and preventing a security vacuum from developing in Central Europe. The withdrawal of Russian power could not be filled with a unilateral German presence or with a weak coalition of former members of the Warsaw Pact. The OSCE and the UN could not provide a security framework for the region. Furthermore, the EU did not possess the structures or the presence of the United States to deal with security issues. Stability for the new democratic governments would result instead from the enlargement of NATO. It would reinforce confidence in the region and create the climate for EU economic action as a prelude to EU expansion. Last, but not least, enlargement served German national interests. NATO, not Germany alone, would foot the bill for security. The United States would continue its preeminent role in NATO, but Germany would be the dominant power in Central Europe.

On 21 October 1993, Volker Rühe called for NATO membership for the Visegrad countries (Poland, Hungary, the Czech Republic, and Slovakia). He supported the plan to create Partnership for Peace (PfP) as a stepping stone to NATO membership.[12] In November, Foreign Minister Klaus Kinkel of the FDP took a different position and supported opening up the Western European Union to the East. He assured the Russians that this was not a back door to NATO.[13]

There was, therefore, from the beginning of the enlargement discussions, a division that would shape the enlargement debate until the 1997 Madrid summit. On the one side, Rühe argued for rapid expansion of NATO to stabilize the region around Germany. On the other side, Kinkel argued for a phased relationship with neighboring states by enlarging first the EU in order to avoid creating political instability for the most important Eastern neighbor, Russia. At this early stage, Chancellor Kohl supported a process leading to NATO membership (not just WEU membership) for the Visegrad countries. In an early 1994 Bundestag speech, he supported PfP and eventual NATO enlargement. Kohl did, however, rein in Rühe on the speed of NATO expanded membership. He expressed concerns about the relationship with Russia, which he had worked to maintain through the trials of the post-Soviet period.[14]

The enlargement debate within the government and within the elite circles of party politics and security policy experts reflected the differences between the foreign and defense ministries. Rühe had proposed a German military force of 370,000 troops, with an eventual target of 340,000, as a result of the changed strategic situation before enlargement became an issue. These numbers compared with almost 700,000 troops in East and West Germany before 1989.[15] Kinkel lined up against Rühe by promoting an EU enlargement that would precede NATO enlargement to help Eastern Europe without alienating Russia.[16]

By early 1994, Chancellor Kohl made a number of statements on enlargement in summits with Boris Yeltsin, at meetings of the EU, the OSCE, and the G-7 (Group of Seven Industrial States), and in the North Atlantic Council (NAC).

During the 1994 elections, Kohl came down squarely in favor of expanding the alliance. He argued that "keeping the U.S. in Europe was an irreplaceable basis for keeping Europe on a stable footing."[17] Kohl left no doubt when he said, "The European transatlantic community is not a closed group. It depends on its effort and its sharing its free democratic ideas with all who want it."[18]

The debate now moved outside the government to include other political figures in Germany. On the opposition benches, the SPD was split as it grappled with the legacy of supporting a special relationship with Russia as the key to maintaining security in Central and Eastern Europe. SPD parliamentary chair Hans-Ulrich Klose supported expansion, but only on a very slow timetable. Rudolph Sharping, named defense minister in 1998, had reservations about enlargement. He voiced concern about Russia's legitimate security interests and encouraging antidemocratic and anti-Western Russian forces.[19] Karsten Voigt, soon to be president of the North Atlantic Assembly and a leading SPD spokesman on security policy, supported NATO enlargement, as well as that of the EU. This put him close to the position of Foreign Minister Kinkel and squarely within the mainstream of German domestic opinion. At this time, Germans supported the membership of Visegrad states by more than two to one, and thought that security issues were still important enough to stay within the NATO alliance by a majority of 69 percent.[20]

The only political opposition came from the Greens/Alliance 90 and the Party of Democratic Socialists (PDS), formerly the East German Communist Party. Their 1994 platforms called for the disbanding of NATO, the end of compulsory military service, unilateral German disarmament, and reliance on collective security mechanisms within the UN and the OSCE. This policy was opposed by leading Green parliamentarian Joschka Fischer as keeping the Greens from being part of a governing coalition in the future. But on this point Fischer was defeated by the dominant Green perspective expressed by Ludger Volmer.[21]

By December 1994 and into 1995, the debate in Germany subsided. At the 1994 OSCE summit, the Russians objected to NATO expansion, but Kohl put the alliance ahead of the German-Russian relationship. Kohl met with Yeltsin in early 1995 and reiterated his understanding of Russian fears toward NATO expansion, but assured him there would be no extension of NATO into the territory of the former Soviet Union or to the borders of Russia proper. NATO approved a study of enlargement at the Brussels NATO summit in December 1994, and the process moved from the political realm to the bureaucratic realm. It would remain there until the Madrid summit of 1997 and the subsequent parliamentary debates over ratification.

The 1994 enlargement debate in Germany was connected to another debate over national security policy, NATO, and collective European security. The rationale for enlarging NATO and stabilizing Central and Eastern Europe also opened the door to the deployment of troops for a variety of missions that might be proscribed by the German constitution depending on its interpretation by the Constitutional Court. This debate was very important to the enlargement issue because it was argued by some that enlargement increased the chances for small-scale NATO contingencies on the periphery of Europe.

The enlargement debate took a back seat in the summer of 1994 to the debate over whether or not German troops could take part in missions outside of Germany. The issue was resolved by the Constitutional Court when it announced on 12 July 1994 that German troops could participate in UN, NATO, or WEU missions as part of multinational coalitions. This was a key objective in the foreign policy goals of foreign ministers Genscher and Kinkel, as well as Defense Minister Ruhe and Chancellor Kohl.[22] Within ten days the Bundestag approved German participation in NATO naval operations in the Adriatic in support of the Balkan arms embargo, an important step in Germany's new security policy. It signaled a broad consensus across the political classes for a new role for Germany within the alliance.[23] Germany had been a lead actor on enlargement, it had taken a diplomatic initiative in recognizing Slovenia, it was taking a leading role in relations with Russia, and it was participating in NATO peacekeeping actions in the Balkans, as well as UN actions in Somalia and Cambodia.

By the spring of 1995, the initial phases of the NATO enlargement debate had been resolved in Germany. The real debate was over the speed of the process, with Defense Minister Rühe arguing for rapid expansion (under five years) and Foreign Minister Kinkel arguing for a slower pace more in line with the EU's plans for expansion (between ten and fifteen years). Chancellor Kohl had come down closer to the Rühe position than Kinkel's. He had promised Poland admission by 2000, and was publicly committed to the other Visigrad states.

ENLARGEMENT: LEADING TO MADRID

The debate in Germany throughout 1996 and into 1997 took place among the political leaders and policy elites. It concentrated not on the costs but on Germany's new security environment, policy options, and relationships with states to the East and the West.

There was a great deal of latitude for this debate because German public opinion was not influential in any one direction at this time. In 1996 75 percent of the public was in favor of improved relations with Poland and 77 percent supported better relations with Russia.[24] These opinions are hard to reconcile because at the time improved relations with Poland meant bringing Poland into the West yet improved relations with Russia meant keeping Poland out of Western institutions. In late 1996 32 percent of Germans did not have an opinion on extending NATO membership to the Visegrad states. The same poll found that the rest were widely split in their opinions. There were 14 percent who wanted membership extended at once, 31 percent within five to ten years, and 13 percent after ten years. Ten percent, however, wanted to deny membership to Poland, Hungary, and the Czech Republic forever.[25] Public opinion was shaped by a constant message from the government and from leading opposition security specialists that NATO enlargement would prevent a repeat of Balkans-like conflicts and bring security to Germany's borders.[26]

The costs of NATO enlargement were seen in Germany not in absolute terms but in relative terms. Opinion leaders were able to demonstrate that the German share of the NATO costs of expansion would be significantly less than the costs of creating political and economic stability in the region unilaterally. The German budget would be used not to pay for the renationalization and modernization of all forces of the new members but for those forces deemed necessary to the alliance.[27] This meant that the process of enlargement and integration would take place over a generation, just as it had with West Germany and Spain. The costs would also be lessened by the collapse of Russia and the subsequent breathing space this afforded. Integration and modernization of the new members would be able to proceed without the urgency that attended similar processes in the Cold War, enhanced even further with a NATO-Russia understanding. The relationship with Russia had become a top priority of the government and was at the heart of its estimates on lowering the costs of enlargement.[28] The Kohl government found support throughout the governing coalition and from prominent SPD and Green politicians when Chancellor Kohl took a leadership role in trying to shape an agreement between NATO and Russia.

During this period NATO was conducting its enlargement study and Germany was expanding its role in the WEU, in NATO's Rapid Reaction Force, and in NATO's Bosnia operations. At the same time Kohl, Kinkel, and Rühe engaged in intensive discussions with their Russian counterparts in an attempt to secure an understanding on enlargement and consultative procedures for future security issues.

Chancellor Kohl met with Russian President Yeltsin four times in fourteen months and committed Germany to a position that it "was not our intention to bring NATO's political and military machinery up to Russia's borders." Kohl was trying to wrap expansion, new strategic concepts, and relations with Russia all into one package deal that Yeltsin would be able to accept.[29]

Kohl was supported by active involvement from Foreign Minister Kinkel and Defense Minister Rühe. They worked on Germany's relationships with the prospective new members and assured Yeltsin that Germany was even more firmly rooted in Western institutions that would act as constraints on unilateral action that might be perceived as threatening by Russia.

Kinkel went to Warsaw on 13 June 1995 and pledged that Germany was "Poland's advocate." This was later supported by Kohl's pledge of "no second-class membership" for any of the new members. In addition to Poland, there was a signing of the German-Czech Declaration of Reconciliation. This paved the way for Czech membership in NATO, already strongly supported by the personal appeals of President Václav Havel. Lastly, Kinkel had strong public backing for Hungary's membership in the NATO alliance. Grateful for the role Hungary played in the unification process in 1989, President Roman Herzog made a personal trip to Hungary where he supported NATO membership.

Kinkel also made sure that there would be no replay of past German-Russian deals. He promised, "We will not go over the heads of countries . . . and decide with Russia what kind of membership they are to have." Kinkel also stressed to Foreign Minister Yevgeniy Primakov that Russia would benefit from NATO expansion because it would limit ethnic tensions and internal instabilities in countries on Russia's borders.[30]

Defense Minister Rühe downplayed the German influence on the enlargement process, preferring instead to underscore the sovereign right of states to choose their alliance memberships. In 1996 he was able to announce that Germany would be a part of a new NATO Combined Joint Task Force Naval Headquarters in the Baltics through the Partnership for Peace program. In early 1997, he announced an agreement with France and Poland on defense cooperation. He oversaw the changes in Germany's geostrategic doctrine, moving the country away from a static homeland defense to a smaller force fully integrated into NATO's rapid reaction forces for peacekeeping and crisis management missions. This change in security doctrine was accomplished at the same time that Germany was decreasing other military forces and budgets. Rühe was able to show the Russians a German military cut in half between 1994 and 1997, from 670,000 troops to 340,000 troops. He was also able to point to a defense budget of 1.7 percent of GDP.[31] It was not only good for securing Russian acquiescence to expansion, but the decreased expenditures also made it easier to sell expansion to members of the opposition and the public.

Throughout 1996 and 1997 support for NATO enlargement became the dominant position in the SPD and even managed to gain a foothold among the Greens. The SPD defeat in the 1994 Bundestag, and hence chancellor, elections led to a reevaluation of both domestic and international policies. The SPD chancellor, Helmut Schmidt, had been a strong anchor of NATO from the middle of the 1970s until Kohl's rise to the chancellor position in 1982. The SPD member who carried on that tradition in the 1990s was Karsten Voigt. As spokesman on security issues for the SPD in the Bundestag and in 1995 as the chairman of the North Atlantic Assembly, Voigt was able to move the SPD toward a consensus position on NATO enlargement.

Voigt was supported by Gerhard Schröder, who would become the chancellor in 1998, and Rudolph Scharping, who would become defense minister in the Schröder government. These SPD leaders were also interested in moving the party closer to the center on domestic politics, as Bill Clinton and Tony Blair had done over the previous years in the United States and Britain. Opposition to Voigt was posed by Oskar Lafontaine, party leader and keeper of the flame for the left wing of the party throughout the 1980s and 1990s, who argued that the SPD should oppose NATO expansion and German participation in NATO peacekeeping in Bosnia.[32]

Voigt countered in 1995 when, as chair of the North Atlantic Assembly, he supported expansion to Eastern Europe without forward-based troops or the deployment of nuclear weapons. This "soft expansion" would pose less threat to Russia and yet still extend the NATO security umbrella. The idea was opposed vigorously by the Eastern Europeans and the Kohl government ("no second-class members," many said), but it demonstrated a willingness by the pragmatists in the SPD to support NATO enlargement.

By the spring of 1997, Voigt had accepted enlargement and was bringing the SPD with him. In a speech to the Party Congress in Frankfurt, Voigt told his fellow party members that the time had come to avoid the party difficulties of the past and recognize that the enlargement of NATO was a step "to undoing the splitting of Europe and a step to the stabilizing of peace on our continent."[33]

Voigt and Scharping represented a current of opinion that could be found across parties in Germany. Among the political elites in ministries and structures of the dominant parties, the pragmatists ruled. Those who saw the need for a wider Europe, including an expanding EU and NATO, recognized that Germany had succeeded because it was embedded in multilateral institutions.

Since the end of the Cold War, Germany had been able to cut the armed forces in half, and at the same time it had made those forces more useful to new missions by extending their multilateral involvement in the WEU and NATO organizations. Germany created closer ties to France within the EU while simultaneously expanding its power within the organization. And Germany had forged closer ties with Washington within NATO by coming to agreements on the issues of enlargement, PfP, and the structure of the North Atlantic Cooperation Council (NACC).[34]

Opposition to NATO enlargement on the eve of Madrid was left to the PDS and the party activists of the Greens. Green members of the Bundestag were split. Pragmatists, led by Joschka Fischer, were interested in making the Greens an acceptable member of a future governing coalition with the SPD. They recognized that to do this, they were going to have to make compromises with long-held party positions on foreign and defense policies. NATO enlargement was clearly coming, and to be on the wrong side of the consensus would give the Greens no room for bargaining on other important issues.

Fischer was defeated at the 1996 summer party conference, as the Greens voted to oppose enlargement. Fischer pointed out that the platform vote was not binding on Bundestag members. This laid a marker for politicians in the SPD, letting them know that there were members of the Greens who were willing to enter into a coalition government after the 1998 elections.[35]

THE FORMALITIES OF THE ENLARGEMENT DEBATE: FROM MADRID TO BUNDESTAG VOTE

NATO's decision to invite Poland, Hungary, and the Czech Republic to become new members came in May of 1997. Even though the vote in the Bundestag to ratify this decision was not held until the spring of 1998, there was no doubt as to its outcome long before then. Within the government, intense debate had already taken place between the foreign and defense ministers. The chancellor had been personally involved in the important negotiations for German relations with Russia, the United States, and the new members. The level of debate within the opposition left the pragmatists dominant in the SPD. All of this created a strong German consensus for enlargement before the 1997 Madrid summit vote took place.

German leaders had been the first to raise the issue of enlargement. Germany was the leading provider of aid to Eastern Europe and Russia. And it had been the first state to argue for the dual expansion of both NATO and the EU, holding up its own successes (stabilization, growth, and integration) as a role model of the benefits of enlargement. German security policy had much to gain from broadening NATO membership, moving from a policy of territorial defense to full partnership in NATO's new missions and creating a zone of stability around itself as insurance against future Bosnias. Expansion would fill the power vacuum in the region left by the departing Russians and guard against their possible return. It would also prevent Germany from pursuing a unilateralist foreign policy in the region that would be politically and economically costly. Furthermore, it would prevent the states of Central and Eastern Europe from renationalizing their security policies or scrambling to create weak coalitions to protect against German or Russian dominance. These important ramifications for German foreign policy supported the foreign policy establishment as it headed into the formal Bundestag ratification debate on enlargement.

In December of 1997 the Cabinet formally approved the enlargement of NATO and moved the measure to the Bundestag. Defense Minister Volker Rühe anticipated 95 percent of the Bundestag would support ratification. Foreign Minister Kinkel, at the ministerial meeting of NATO in Brussels, noted that the door had not been closed to future members, and that ratification of this round would encourage potential future members to meet the NATO standards for membership all the more quickly. The government was supported by the editorial policies of Germany's major newspapers in December. These included *Süddeutsche Zeitung, Der Tagesspiegel, Frankfurter Allgemeine Zeitung, Die Welt,* and *Märkische Oderzeitung.*

Chancellor Kohl addressed the Munich Wehrkunde Conference on Security Policy in February 1998. He saw the scheduled March vote on NATO enlargement as the first step in completing construction of a common European house through a community of democratic nations that hold common fundamental values.

As the vote on enlargement approached, it became clear that the SPD had come far in its foreign policy position. It was facing an election in the fall of 1998 in which it was heavily favored to recapture the chancellor's office for the first time in sixteen years. It had a national candidate, Gerhard Schröder, who succeeded in winning middle-class and business votes to the SPD. Moreover, it had a foreign policy elite who were moving beyond the old battles and adapting to the realities of life after the Cold War.

Right after the Madrid summit the SPD had effectively isolated Lafontaine, as Voigt, Schröder, Scharping, and Günter Verheugen all came out in favor of NATO expansion, the NATO-Russia Founding Act, and NATO's new strategic concepts.[36] As the vote neared, Voigt summed up the compelling arguments for enlarging NATO. In so doing, he echoed the words that had been voiced for years by Kinkel from the Foreign Ministry. Voigt said that German foreign policy priorities were deepening European integration, extending transatlantic ties, stabilizing Eastern and Central Europe, and solving the problems in the Balkans. He stated that the extension of the EU and

NATO would avoid renationalizing the security policies of European states and that Russian opposition to expansion was based on obsolete interests in spheres of influence. Voigt also concluded that Europe needed an array of different institutions, including NATO, the EU, and the OSCE, in order to further integrate and handle the complexity of the problems facing the periphery of the continent.[37]

That this position was now overwhelming among German elites was demonstrated by polls that showed 76 percent of elites favoring enlargement, compared to 60 percent of the general public.[38] Only the activists among the Greens and the PDS (former communists in the East) remained in the opposition.

The leading foreign policy spokesman for the Greens, Joschka Fischer, was on board as the decision reached the Bundestag. After rejecting his arguments in favor of NATO enlargement at their pre-election party conference in March, half of the Greens in the Bundestag sided with Fischer when the time came for the vote.

By the time the Bundestag voted on ratification, all of the reservations had been cleared away. The economic costs had been directed into the NATO budget, where the lion's share would be eaten up by the United States and the Germans would be able to point to the shared costs absorbed by other rich NATO members like France, Britain, and Italy. The concerns over Russia had been finessed with the NATO-Russia Founding Act and the creation of the Permanent Joint Council mechanism for NATO-Russia consultations and confidence building. The fears of expanding German commitments to solve ethnic problems in Central and Eastern Europe were resolved by treaties among members states and between members and PfP states who wished to join in the future. Such treaties had been a condition of invitations for membership extended early in the process by NATO. The success of the implementation and stabilization forces (IFOR and SFOR) in Bosnia defused the opposition to NATO in general. There were no casualties among peacekeepers and there was no resumption of the fighting. German foreign policy elites could point with pride to Germany's role both on the land in the Balkans and on the seas of the Adriatic as the multilateral institutions on which they had staked their reputations held together to implement the Balkan peacekeeping plan.

The vote in the Bundestag on 26 March 1998 was overwhelming. Out of 672 members, 555 voted in favor of enlargement. This included the membership of the CDU-CSU and FDP governing coalition, the SPD, and half of the Green members. A mere 37 members opposed the proposition, with only the PDS voting as a group against enlargement.

For the first time since its establishment in 1871 Germany would have no conflicts with any of its neighbors. Those neighbors would be stable, democratic partners in both security and economic institutions. Germany would not have a unilateral policy toward the East and Russia. And the strategic, moral, and political interests of Germany would be served by existing European structures. These were accomplishments worthy of a consensus among the leaders of Germany and among the people who had elected them.

THE NEXT STAGE OF ENLARGEMENT: CAN THE CONSENSUS BE REPEATED?

As NATO now looks beyond the first round of enlargement and prepares for the next decade, what will the German role be? Germany stood poised between the United States and France on the issue of expanding NATO to four or five countries at Madrid. Germany made it clear that there was support for expanding the alliance to include Slovenia and Romania in the first round in 1997. This position was in line with the desires expressed by France and Italy, but the Kohl government also understood that the strengthening of transatlantic ties and the maintenance of U.S. leadership in NATO required it to be open to compromise on the issue.

Parliamentary resolutions leading up to Madrid in 1997 placed all the major parties on the record supporting the membership efforts of Poland, Hungary, and the Czech Republic, plus Slovenia and Romania. The first three states were easy to understand and have been fully explained above. Slovenia, however, proved a special case. Heavily Catholic Slovenia received support from the Catholics in Bavaria (that is, the CSU). Kohl's CDU had been the first to recognize Slovenian independence in 1991. This act was deemed by some security analysts to have sparked the break-up of Yugoslavia, and the CDU was anxious to demonstrate that its diplomacy was not a mistake. The SPD also supported Slovenian membership, as a way to bring stability to the region without further extension of military power. Romanian membership, meanwhile, was key to French interests and was supported by the interests of Franco-German solidarity heading into the summit.

In the face of opposition from the United States, Kohl adopted a mediating position at Madrid that successfully satisfied the United States as well as German domestic political opinion. However, the summit concluded with invitations to Poland, Hungary, and the Czech Republic only, leaving the door open for future expansion. Germany and the United States were able to agree that a second expansion round would be limited, but that both countries remained committed to such an expansion.[39]

A second expansion round could certainly be limited to Slovenia and Romania, mentioned in the Madrid communiqué explicitly, or to Bulgaria (now undertaking reform more successfully than Romania), given the importance of the Balkans in NATO's future. For the foreseeable future, the missions in Bosnia and Kosovo will keep NATO engaged there for years. Membership for Slovenia and Romania, especially, would serve political and strategic interests.

All of these options would be acceptable to Germany. They would further integrate potential EU members and help stabilize NATO's Southern flank. They would also keep NATO enlargement from moving closer, ideologically, to the strategic interests of Russia. The Kohl government and the Schröder government have exhibited the same concerns for creating a stable relationship with Russia throughout Eastern Europe. But in the aftermath of Kosovo, pushing NATO enlargement to the door of the former Soviet Union would test the fragile understanding reached at Madrid.[40]

During talks on the second round of enlargement in 1997 and 1998, the Kohl government ended up split on the issue of including the Baltics. A degree of stability had been established in the region without extending NATO membership. Through the PfP and economic cooperation agreements with the EU, the Baltic states, Sweden, Finland, Germany, and Denmark had created cooperative naval strategies, peacekeeping forces, and economic enterprise zones. All of this had been accomplished without Russian interference or opposition. The extension of NATO, according to opponents, would be a decisive move away from policies designed to engage the Baltic region with the West without disturbing relations with Russia. While Volker Rühe has been skeptical of Baltic membership in NATO, Klaus Kinkel and the FDP had long championed the cause of the Baltics.

The Schröder government has since been able to avoid this split. It clearly places a priority on the German-Russian relationship, and it recognizes that there is nothing to be gained by pursuing an enlargement strategy that has no chance of support in the United States. The Social Democrats can point to the Bundestag vote at the time of the first enlargement, when the Bundestag voted to accept the three applicants then pending and then voted to support "future membership" for the Baltics without any specifics.[41] The German support for the Baltics in the next NATO round will be tempered by concern over the impact on Russia, including the complications over the future of the enclave of Kaliningrad.

Germany has come a long way since 1989. Although it contributed security through the stability it brought to Central Europe, it spent the first forty-five years of its membership taking advantage of the security offered by NATO. It also served as the arena for the Cold War standoff between East and West. The issue of enlarging NATO forced Germany to debate its role in Europe and accept its new position as a security provider. As the leader of the enlargement debate on the European side of the Atlantic, Germany accepted new responsibilities and new missions within NATO and the EU. It exercised those responsibilities with a broad consensus among its political leaders that insured both continuity and progress with the change of government in 1998. Now, as NATO looks toward another round of enlargement in the first decade of the twenty-first century, the role of Germany and its relations with Russia and the states of Central and Eastern Europe will again take center stage. The issue will be the same one that Volker Ruhe expressed in 1993. Once again, Germans will be asked to export stability and serve as the political, economic, and security anchor for new members of the democratic community of states.

NOTES

I would like to thank the American Institute for Contemporary German Studies and the Friedrich Ebert Stiftung for use of their facilities in the preparation of this chapter.

1. Bregor Schollgen, "Putting Germany's Post-Unification Foreign Policy to the Test," *NATO Review* 41, no. 2 (April 1993): 15–22; Jonathan Bach, *Between Sovereignty and Integration: German Foreign Policy and National Identity After 1989* (New York: St. Martin's Press, 1999); Philip Zelikow and Condoleezza Rice, *Germany Unified and Europe Transformed* (Cambridge: Harvard University Press, 1995).

2. Thomas Berger, *Cultures of Antimilitarism: National Security in Germany and Japan* (Baltimore: Johns Hopkins Press, 1998); Wolfgang Schlor, "German Security Policy," *Adelphi Paper*, no. 277 (International Institute for Strategic Studies, June 1993); Keith B. Payne and Michael Ruhle, "The Future of the Alliance: Emerging German Views," *Strategic Review* (Winter 1991): 37–45.

3. Robert Gerald Livingston, "United Germany: Bigger and Better," *Foreign Policy*, no. 87 (Summer 1992): 157–174.

4. Angela Stent, "The One Germany," *Foreign Policy*, no. 81 (Winter 1990–1991): 53–70; W. R. Smyser, "USSR-Germany: A Link Restored," *Foreign Policy*, no. 84 (Fall 1991): 125–141; Joyce Marie Mushaben, *From Post-War to Post-Wall Generations* (Boulder: Westview Press, 1998).

5. Manfred Wörner, "NATO Transformed: The Significance of the Rome Summit," *NATO Review* 39, no. 6 (December 1991): 3–8; Michael Legge, "The Making of NATO's New Strategy," *NATO Review* 39, no. 6 (December 1991): 9–14.

6. Leigh Bruce, "Europe's Locomotive," *Foreign Policy*, no. 78 (Spring 1990): 68–90; Jiri Dienstbier, "Central Europe's Security," *Foreign Policy*, no. 83 (Summer 1991): 119–127; Daniel N. Nelson, "Europe's Unstable East," *Foreign Policy*, no. 82 (Spring 1991): 137–158.

7. Erika V.C. Bruce, "NATO's Public Opinion Seminar Indicates Continuing, but Not Unshakeable Support," *NATO Review* 40, no. 2 (April 1992): 1–8; Erika V.C. Bruce, "The Image of the Alliance: Public Opinion Seminar Gauges Support," *NATO Review* 41, no. 6 (December 1993): 6–11; RAND Corporation, *Germany's Geopolitical Maturation: Public Opinion and Security Policy* (Santa Monica, Calif.: RAND Corporation, 1994); Elizabeth Hann Hastings and Phillip K. Hastings, *Index to International Public Opinion* (London: Greenwood Press, 1994–1995); "Meinungsseite," *Frankfurter Allgemeine Zeitung*, 2 July 1993; "Meinungsseite," *Die Zeit*, 30 July 1993.

8. Wolfgang Schlor, "German Security Policy," *Adelphi Paper*, no. 277 (International Institute for Strategic Studies, June 1993).

9. Richard Woyke, "NATO Faces New Challenges," *Aussenpolitik* 44, no. 2 (1993): 120–126. The IISS speech by Wörner may be found online at http://www.nato.int/docu/speech/1993.

10. Richard Woyke, "NATO Faces New Challenges," *Aussenpolitik* 44, no. 2 (1993): 120–126. The IISS speech by Wörner may be found online at http://www.nato.int/docu/speech/1993.

11. *Süddeutsche Zeitung* (22 October 1993).

12. "Rühe Views European Unification, U.S. Role," *Bonn Bulletin* (October 1993): 981–984.

13. "Kinkel Discusses Coalition Problems, FDP Course," *Der Spiegel* (22 November 1993): 41–44.

14. Lothar Ruehl, "European Security and NATO's Eastward Expansion," *Aussenpolitik* 45, no. 2: 115–122; Ronald Asmus, Richard L. Kugler, and F. Stephen Larrabee, "NATO Enlargement: A Framework for Analysis" and Michael E. Brown, "The Flawed Logic of NATO Enlargement," in *NATO's Transformation: The Changing Shape of the Atlantic Alliance,* ed. by Philip H. Gordon (London: Rowman and Littlefield, 1997).

15. Ibid.

16. *Süddeutsche Zeitung* (14 May 1994).

17. W. R. Smyser, "Germany's New Vision," *Foreign Policy,* no. 97 (Winter 1994/1995): 140–157; Karl-Heinz Kamp, "The Folly of Rapid NATO Expansion," *Foreign Policy,* no. 98 (Spring 1995): 116–131.

18. "President Clinton in Europe: Naples Economic Summit, Visits to Baltic States, Poland, Germany," *Foreign Policy Bulletin* (September/October 1994): 68.

19. Richard R. Moeller, "The Ambivalence of the SPD and the End of Its Ostpolitik," *German Politics* 5, no. 1 (April 1996): 121–136; Karsten Voigt, "Eastward Enlargement of NATO," 1995.

20. Elizabeth Hann Hastings and Phillip K. Hastings, *Index to International Public Opinion* (London: Greenwood Press, 1994–1995).

21. Mary Hampton, "Poland, Germany, and NATO Enlargement Policy," *German Comments* 49 (January 1998): 85–94.

22. Klaus Kinkel, "Peacekeeping Missions: Germany Can Now Play Its Part," *NATO Review* 42, no. 5 (October 1994): 3–7.

23. Karl Kaiser, "40 Years of German Membership in NATO," *NATO Review* 43, no. 4 (July 1995): 3–8.

24. Elizabeth Hann Hastings and Phillip K. Hastings, *Index to International Public Opinion 1996–1997* (London: Greenwood Press, 1997), 165.

25. Ibid.

26. "Optimismus Über NATO-Ost-Erweiterung," *Frankfurter Allgemeine Zeitung* (13 June 1996).

27. North Atlantic Treaty Organization, *Enlargement Study* (Brussels: NATO Press, 1995).

28. Wolfgang Pfeiler, "NATO in the East," *German Comments* 42 (April 1996): 38–42; Gernot Erler, "NATO zwischen Einbindung und Ausgrenzung," *Blätter für Deutsche und Internationale Politik* (August 1997): 927–936.

29. "Kohl: Bei Ost Erweiterung der NATO Müssen Russlands Sicherheits interessen Beachtet Werden," *Frankfurter Allgemeine Zeitung* (5 February 1996).

30. Joerg Kastl, "European Security Without Russia." *Aussenpolitik* 48, no. 1 (1997): 31–38; Heinrich Vogel, "Opening NATO: A Cooperative Solution for an Ill-Defined Problem," *Aussenpolitik* 48, no. 1 (1997): 22–31; Mary Hampton, "Poland, Germany, and NATO Enlargement Policy," *German Comments* 49 (January 1998):

85–94; Piotr Dutkiewicz and Slawomic Lodzinski, "The Grey Zone: Poland's Security Policy Since 1989," in *NATO Looks East*, ed. by Piotr Dutkiewicz and Robert Jackson (London: Praeger Publishing, 1998).

31. Werner Link, "Integration and Balance," *German Comments* 41 (January 1996): 17–23; Peter Schmidt, "German Security Policy in the Framework of the EU, WEU, and NATO," *Aussenpolitik* 47, no. 3 (1996): 211–222; Michael O'Hanlon, "Transforming NATO: The Role of European Forces," *Survival* 39, no. 3 (Autumn 1997): 5–15; Karl Kaiser, "Reforming NATO," *Foreign Policy*, no. 103 (Summer 1996): 128–143.

32. "Voigt für Schnelle NATO-OST-Erweiterung," *Frankfurter Allgemeine Zeitung*, 10 May 1996: 2; "Für oder Gegen die Ost-Erweiterung der NATO?" *Frankfurter Allgemeine Zeitung*, 8 March 1997: 16; Josef Janning, "A German Europe—A European Germany? On the Debate over Germany's Foreign Policy," *International Affairs* 72, no. 1 (1996): 33–41.

33. Karsten Voigt, "Rede auf dem Parteitag des UB Frankfurt" (speech given at the Party Congress, Frankfurt, 19 April 1997).

34. Gunther Hellmann, "The Sirens of Power and German Foreign Policy: Who Is Listening?" *German Politics* 6, no. 2 (August 1997): 29–57.

35. "Grüne Schliessen NATO-Erweiterung nicht aus," *Frankfurter Allgemeine Zeitung*, 12 June 1996: 1; "Bislang Sagten die Bündnisgrünen nein zur NATO," *Die Taz*, 9 April 1997: 3.

36. "SPD Plant Antrag zur NATO Erweitung," *Frankfurter Allgemeine Zeitung*, 7 June 1997: 3; "SPD Stimmt mit Regierung überein in allen Wesentlichen Fragen der Aussen-und Sicherheitspolitik," *Süddeutsche Zeitung*, 19 June 1997: 2.

37. Karsten Voigt, "German Foreign Policy Beyond the East-West Conflict" (19 April 1997).

38. "NATO Enlargement: The National Debates over Ratification," *NATO Academic Forum* (October 1997).

39. Karl-Heinz Kamp, "NATO Entrapped: Debating the Next Enlargement Round," *Survival* 40, no. 3 (Autumn 1998): 170–186.

40. "Voigt: eine Unideologische Aussenpolitik," *Frankfurter Allgemeine Zeitung*, 14 January 1999: 12.

41. Yaroslav Bilinsky, *Endgame in NATO's Enlargement: The Baltic States and the Ukraine* (London: Praeger Publishing, 1999).

4

France: NATO's "Renovation" and Enlargement

PAUL GALLIS

France developed its policy for NATO enlargement in the context of a broader proposed redesign for European security policy. Intellectually, the general outline of French objectives was logical and defensible. For French leaders, enlargement entailed potential security risks because the alliance would be expanding its territory and because expansion would come in the face of Russian opposition. The debate over enlargement also coincided with the debate over reform of the European Union's (EU's) institutions and direction, including the EU's own enlargement and its fitful struggle to develop greater political cohesion and its Common Foreign and Security Policy (CFSP). For these reasons, France demanded that NATO's "renovation" occur before the entry of new members. Paris wanted NATO to clarify its mission, and put in place an institutional restructuring that would reflect that mission, and it wanted Europeans to build a consensus in the EU over a security and defense identity. Once the sixteen members had reached consensus on the alliance's future course, in France's view, NATO might then more comfortably accept new members. In France, these discussions took place untroubled by public debate over enlargement of the alliance, as French popular interest in the issue was desultory at best.

Several developments arose to defeat French policy. Competing priorities led to contradictions that Paris never sorted out, particularly in relations with Germany and Russia. Internal political developments deflected President Jacques Chirac from his initial course, and weakened his hand. France could not find a willing ally, either for its desired course in European security policy or, more narrowly, for its avenue to enlargement. Economic strictures undercut the argument that French officials were making in Brussels for a stronger voice in NATO policymaking. Finally, France was playing the wrong game at the wrong time. At a moment when it was seeking tradeoffs with the United States, the nature of its military restructuring put into doubt the weight of its offer on the table, and the crisis in Bosnia undermined its call for European leadership in continental security affairs.

PREEMINENCE OF THE EUROPEAN UNION

French leaders have sought to maintain what they believe to be their country's traditional, central role in European affairs. The creation of policies to build European unity and the development of independent French foreign policy initiatives have been cornerstones of this role since the late 1940s. France was a progenitor of the European Coal and Steel Community, the forerunner of the European Union, that forged a place for Germany in continental political life after the war. Additionally, Paris has used military power to sustain influence in geographically distant locations. The Suez crisis of 1956, combat operations in Africa and the Middle East, and an independent nuclear force have underscored the French intention to shape developments deemed important to security.

After his election to the presidency, Jacques Chirac tried to enhance for France its position as a leader in the European Union. His prime minister, Alain Juppé, called for an "inner circle," defined as "a small number of states around France and Germany," willing to move forward to European monetary union (EMU) in 1999 and to develop the CFSP backed by a military force able to project enough power to handle crises threatening the union's interests.[1] Developing an eventual CFSP for the EU, in the view of Juppé's foreign minister, Hervé de Charette, "far from weakening France's influence and authority in the world . . . will increase their impact and audience."[2]

These ambitious objectives sometimes became entangled in a rhetorical fusillade aimed at the United States, a tendency that led to suspicion in both the Clinton administration and Congress about France's ultimate goals. President Chirac wished to see the European Union become "an active and powerful center, the equal of the United States," in the twenty-first century. In his view, the EU should become "one of the great centers of decision-making and action in the world,"[3] with France playing a "catalytic role" in forging such leadership.[4] De Charette added that "we don't want a world dominated by a sole power [the United States], but rather one organized around the principles of multipolarity." France's first priority is the European Union, which "is, for its members, a formidable amplifier of power."[5] Privately, French officials (joined by officials from several other EU member countries) decried what they viewed as an effort by some U.S. officials to establish a "competition" between NATO and the European Union. They had sharp criticism for U.S.

officials who openly denigrated EU economic growth and potential or EU efforts to resolve security issues on the continent. Particularly galling was that these U.S. officials represented a government that for many years had urged greater European integration as a means to bring stability to the continent, a key U.S. interest.[6] They interpreted the disparaging comments about the European Union by U.S. officials as an effort to raise NATO's estimation and, with it, the U.S. role on the continent.

In 1994 and 1995, France struggled unsuccessfully to find an ally in its effort to make the European Union a stronger international player in political and defense policy. For many years, France and Germany had worked together as the engine that pushed the European Community, and then the European Union, toward greater economic and political integration. But the effort to forge a joint French-German plan for a CFSP for the EU ran afoul of what many German officials saw as a tendency toward unilateralism in Paris. In the German view, Paris spoke of a common European policy toward the Middle East peace process but then supported only its own proposals. French officials spoke of joint defense efforts with Bonn but then announced a nuclear policy that included weapons if, fired to the east, would fall on German territory. And under Chirac, France, after a lengthy moratorium, undertook nuclear tests at a moment when Russia was in sharp decline and environmentalists held a strong position in the EU political spectrum. Such decisions did not inspire confidence in Bonn. When France proposed that the union appoint a "Monsieur PESC" (la politique etrangére de sècuritè commune) who would ensure that decisions on defense and foreign policy be taken in the European Council and not the European Commission, German officials suspected that Chirac and Juppé were intent on a dominant French role in shaping EU external policy.[7] The Germans remained comfortable with U.S. leadership of NATO, and with Washington's strategic nuclear deterrent for the long run, in the event of a Russian revival. While Germany wished to see a strengthened EU foreign and security policy, it did not want such a policy at the expense of a strong U.S. position on the continent.

France's inability to gain Germany as an ally in the effort to build CFSP was a key factor in the decision to move closer to NATO. In December 1995, de Charette announced that France wished to see a distinct European identity, both politically and militarily, within the alliance. Together with Germany, France saw the Western European Union (WEU) as the European pillar within NATO. The WEU would "borrow" NATO assets to accomplish missions in which the United States did not wish its combat forces to participate. The French defense minister would, after many years' absence, return "on a regular basis" to allied discussions in Brussels. And a French representative would take his place on NATO's Military Committee. But French officials made clear that a full return to NATO military structures in the form of rejoining the integrated command was contingent on the alliance undertaking a process of "reform" and "adaptation."[8] Working out the details of this process would prove to be a lengthy, tortuous task, one in which the debate over NATO enlargement would become entangled.

BUILDING EUROPEAN STABILITY:
ENLARGEMENT AND COMBINED JOINT TASK FORCES

In 1994, the Clinton administration began to make concerted efforts to form a consensus in the alliance to admit new members. For the administration, it was important to seize the opportunity to build stability in Central Europe, and enlargement would be presented as a step toward that goal. Relations with President Boris Yeltsin's government were good; President Bill Clinton believed that he could persuade Russia to accept an expanded alliance in the name of general European stability. Clinton was also clearly aware that EU expansion would require an extended period of time. NATO's requirements for membership did not involve the bureaucratic hurdles and lengthy negotiation over laws and regulations that the EU exacted from candidate states. Alliance expansion seemed therefore the more rapid course to bring willing and able states into the Western fold.[9] The Clinton administration also began to propose new alliance structures that would fulfill the goal of the 1991 NATO Strategic Concept to build lighter, more mobile forces for NATO's "new missions," such as crisis management and peacekeeping.

The French government had a more cautious, structured approach in responding to the changing post–Cold War world. In addition to believing that a civil institution, such as the European Union, rather than a military institution, such as NATO, should play the key role in shaping the continent's future, France sought more dramatic changes in NATO than did the Clinton administration. These changes centered on a greater European role in decisionmaking and in greater political authority over military affairs.

French officials used the word "renovation" to capture their view of a NATO able to operate in the post–Cold War world. France continued to desire a key U.S. role in the alliance's core function of collective defense in the event of a revived Russian threat. But the French government concentrated on changes it thought necessary to construct a more flexible alliance, one better able to respond to crises outside the NATO treaty area, and a stronger European hand in the military command structure. In the background, often unspoken publicly, was a concern that the Americans would depart Europe and leave the Europeans with a security architecture not of their own making.[10] As already noted, French officials continued to search for a way to invest a greater EU role in defense issues within a redesign of the alliance.

Enthusiasm for NATO enlargement in the French political establishment was lacking. Early discussion of expansion of the alliance was evident in the United States and in Europe in 1991 and 1992. In France, the political elite viewed enlargement as "a means to impede the construction of an autonomous defense pillar and to increase U.S. influence over East European countries."[11] The public was disengaged from the debate. Major dailies such as *Le Monde* and *Libération*, when they treated enlargement, usually embedded the discussion within analysis of the debate over NATO's missions and restructuring of alliance commands—a tendency that in many ways reflected the thinking of the French government. President François Mitterrand, who ceded power to Chirac in May 1995, was opposed to enlargement, and some within his own party were hostile to a NATO still geared to Cold War needs and led by the United States. Further on the left, Communist Party leaders opposed French membership in the alliance. Dominique Voynet, the Greens candidate in the 1995 presidential election, wrote that "France should disengage from military blocs that have lost their *raison d'être*."[12] President Chirac, in his first months in power, seemed to many to be opposed to enlargement. In Washington, embassy personnel of the principal candidate states complained that Chirac had sent their governments very negative signals about both NATO and EU enlargement.[13]

Chirac concentrated his efforts on "renovation" of the alliance. Parallel to the French initiatives, the Clinton administration was seeking to build a more stable Europe by adapting NATO structures for crisis response and by enlarging the alliance. At the January 1994 NATO summit, the allies approved in principle the U.S. proposal for Combined Joint Task Forces (CJTF). The United States saw CJTF as a mechanism that could develop greater sharing of out-of-area military burdens. As designed, CJTF would establish structures in which the Europeans might assume command for operations in which the United States did not wish to participate with combat forces. A European commander would lead a WEU force, "borrowing" NATO assets such as lift, command-and-control, and overhead intelligence. Most of these assets belonged to the United States. CJTF had a strong link to enlargement because the allies agreed that non-NATO countries might participate in such a task force, which might not provide a means to test only a country's military qualifications for alliance membership but its political will as well.

After considerable negotiation, NATO embraced CJTF at the Berlin Ministerial in June 1996. France accepted the CJTF concept but wished to enhance the overall European role. For example, France wanted a "buffet line" from which the Europeans could choose assets for dedication to the WEU before any crisis arose. Paris also sought command structures in a CJTF dominated by political control, in which the contribution to decisionmaking by the Supreme Allied Commander Europe (SACEUR) would be reduced. Foreign Minister de Charette spoke of the need for "a European [NATO] commander alongside

SACEUR" who would supervise the preparations for CJTF operations.[14] Many U.S. officials believed that Paris had a French officer in mind.

In contrast, the United States wished to maintain some control over its assets dedicated to NATO, and it wished to preserve important authority for SACEUR, not fully delineated in the early stages of CJTF, over the overall structure and strategy of a CJTF operation. And many senior Pentagon officials, backed by several key European counterparts, did not wish a French officer alongside SACEUR making decisions, in part because France for three decades had had no experience in the integrated command structure and in part because such a position should be gained through long-term military contributions and accomplishments, not as a "political" reward for engineering the shape of the European Security and Defense Initiative (ESDI) within the alliance.[15]

The U.S. position prevailed on key points. Instead of a "buffet line" for selection of NATO assets, only those assets appropriate for a specific mission would be made available. The allies agreed to preserve SACEUR's ultimate command over U.S. forces and assets acting in support of a CJTF, a powerful lever for influencing the form and objectives of a mission. As part of the discussion over CJTF and over reform of NATO's command structure in general, the United States agreed that the alliance should have more Europeans in senior commands, a victory for France and for other allies, such as Germany and Italy, that wished to see greater responsibilities in European hands. CJTF would also be an instrument for bringing prospective members more closely into the allied fold, so that they and the allies could have a closer look at one another. Countries not in the alliance were already participating in the peacekeeping force in Bosnia. CJTF could formalize elements of the command structure developed in Bosnia for the Stabilization Forces (SFOR).

NATO's Berlin Ministerial thus satisfied a number of important political objectives. The United States preserved its key role in decisionmaking in the alliance, and U.S. officials believed that the European Security and Defense Initiative, partly expressed through Combined Joint Task Forces, would develop within NATO, and not independently. France was perceived as having taken the lead among the Europeans in giving an element of concrete form to ESDI, even though few of its positions were adopted. On 8 June 1996, President Chirac declared that NATO's renovation was under way, and that within a year, with continued reform of the alliance, France would consider rejoining NATO's integrated command structure.

THE RESTRUCTURING OF FRENCH FORCES

The logic of the French position for a more Europeanized alliance seemed sound. But did France have the forces that could show Europeans the way to a "renovated" alliance, increasingly led by Europeans and able to undertake

NATO's new missions? At the same time that France was pressing for such renovation, its forces were losing their capability for projection.

Since the end of the Cold War, virtually all allied countries have been reducing their defense budgets, including the United States. The 1991 NATO Strategic Concept called for lighter, more mobile forces to be developed to conduct crisis management operations outside the NATO treaty area. Cuts in their defense budget ultimately undermined the French position at the bargaining table for enhanced responsibility in the alliance. At the height of the crisis over Bosnia in the summer and fall of 1995, French leaders knew that their forces were incapable of combating the Yugoslav army without U.S. assistance. French helicopters were too light and insufficiently armored to bring troops and equipment into the potential battlefield of Bosnia.[16]

At the same time, plans for further cuts were under discussion. If France wished to take a leading role in a European security and defense identity, then its ability to project power would seemingly have been paramount in planners' minds. The focal point of the discussion over CJTF from 1994 had been how to structure a force led by Europeans that would be able to fight beyond the treaty area. Key components of French defense planning, however, seemed to go in the opposite direction. Though Chirac announced a plan in February 1996 to restructure French forces into smaller units and to build a force of fifty to sixty thousand men for power projection, defense expenditures were cut sharply. Among the casualties was the Future Large Aircraft (FLA), able to transport tanks, helicopters, and other heavy equipment. FLA was also symbolically important because Germany was to serve as coproducer.[17]

France had long envisioned Paris and Bonn taking the lead in ESDI. But the French decision not to participate in the FLA meant that the project would lose its financial viability, and with it, a key part of the Franco-German defense initiative. The French decision further eroded Bonn's confidence in Paris as a reliable partner in the security field. French planners had designed a lighter, more mobile force but one that was now dependent on U.S. lift. This was a card thrown onto the table that Washington quickly grabbed and tucked away for future use.

COMMAND STRUCTURE AND A MORE "POLITICAL" NATO

By the summer of 1996, NATO's restructuring was moving forward, somewhat slowed by negotiation over a range of issues but grounded in the experience of the peacekeeping effort in Bosnia. At the height of the Cold War, there were over seventy substantial commands to manage forces in the event of large-scale military operations. After the Cold War, the allies reached a consensus that downsizing of defense forces throughout the alliance together with the shift toward new missions called for fewer commands as well as lighter, more mobile forces. In some capitals including Paris, the Balkans and the Mediterranean, due to instability in the Middle East and a concern over terrorism arising from Islamic revival movements, were key regions for which such forces might be used. CJTF, with its movable headquarters, was one indication of this effort to develop greater flexibility for addressing crises in NATO Europe's unstable environs. At the same time, negotiation and implementation of the Dayton Accord gave credibility to the allies' political weight in security matters beyond the treaty area.

The French government made its voice heard in the discussion over commands as well as in the role of political decisionmaking by civilian authorities in NATO military issues. In July 1996, Defense Minister Charles Millon reportedly asked U.S. Secretary of Defense William Perry to consider allowing a European to take the position of SACEUR. The idea was quickly dropped in the face of strong U.S. resistance, with a negative response as well from the other allies, who saw the United States as the glue holding NATO together.[18]

France then proposed that a European officer be given command of Allied Forces South (AFSOUTH), in Naples. While this proposal went through several formulations, its core element was that several countries—France, Italy, and Spain—would rotate the command. A consideration concerning enlargement was eventually thrown into the mix: Paris began to champion Romania as a candidate state for NATO membership. Did it not make sense, French officials asked, given the alliance's growing interests in the Mediterranean and the belief that future threats would come from the "South" rather than the "East," that a Mediterranean state take over AFSOUTH, and that a country in southeastern Europe be seriously considered for membership? In the French view, these two issues were closely linked.

U.S. officials reacted negatively. The commander of AFSOUTH was traditionally an American, giving orders to the Sixth Fleet, which carried U.S. nuclear weapons and watched over U.S. interests in the Middle East. Meanwhile, a second consideration hovered in the background. For years, U.S. officials had groaned at the maneuvering and political horse-trading so much a part of life in the European Union. It seemed to some U.S. officials that senior EU leaders were chosen more as payment for a political favor than for pure ability. Though NATO was not immune from such back-room dealing, many decisionmakers, above all in the United States but also in some allied countries, believed that security issues were too important to see such practices imported into NATO. Officials in some allied governments, including the U.S. government, could not understand why Paris, not in the integrated command structure, would believe that its flag officers might quickly walk into a senior command when they had not participated in key military decisions or trained their forces in the field with other allies. Chirac himself had said that French forces did not perform well when attempting to coordinate with allies in the

Gulf War. The Clinton administration told the French government that rotation of the AFSOUTH command could not in effect be a political statement, which might harm military efficiency, but rather that the commander in Naples must be selected purely on the experience and capability of the officer. In addition, some other allied governments with strong interests in the Mediterranean preferred to see a U.S. hand in charge of military affairs in such an unstable region. The AFSOUTH command lingered as an issue, but France would never garner sufficient backing for its position to prevail.

A more deeply seated issue setting France apart from the United States was the relation of political and military authority. In France, the memory of Bonapartism ran deep. In the late 1950s and early 1960s, during the Algerian War, rebellious French army officers in Algeria threatened a coup d'état against President Charles de Gaulle. A consensus for strong civilian control over the military, for these reasons, has been evident for many years. In the post–Cold War period, French officials believed that the new missions, such as peacekeeping in Bosnia, would bring NATO militaries more directly into contact with civilians; the delicacy of such missions provided yet another reason to enhance political control over the military and leave no important decisions to commanders in the field or at Mons.

In the United States, while civilian authority over the military is obviously paramount, officials tend to give commanders more leeway in making tactical decisions. As a result, France and the United States have openly clashed over the extent of political authority. In January 1993, while the United States and France were operating under a UN mandate in Iraq after the Gulf War, the U.S. military proposed and used (with President George Bush's consent) cruise missiles against targets in Baghdad. And in August 1995, during a NATO operation to curb Serb forces in Bosnia, the U.S. military again decided to use cruise missiles against a target. In both instances, France complained that the weapon represented a qualitative, and unwarranted, escalation against an adversary; the decision to use the missiles should therefore have been subjected first to political scrutiny by authorities of the allied states involved.[19] French officials, in their attempt to influence the new post–Cold War NATO and while considering a possible return to the integrated command structure, would repeatedly raise the issue, seeking more control in the North Atlantic Council over matters involving military operations.

THE ROLE OF RUSSIA

Chirac, in line with several other European allied leaders, was concerned that NATO enlargement might antagonize and isolate Russia. In early 1996, he began to urge that the Organization for Security and Cooperation in Europe

(OSCE) be "amplified" to play a central role in the continent's security affairs, an elevation of the institution that would give Moscow a greater voice. Chirac proposed that the OSCE's responsibilities be codified in a "treaty or charter on the security of Europe" and that those responsibilities cover crisis prevention and crisis management.[20] Some U.S. officials were miffed at this development. Were not difficult, extended negotiations with France and other allies over CJTF under way, they asked, with the intention of giving CJTF the mission of crisis management? And the principal candidate states for NATO did not want the OSCE, where Russia would have a veto, to play a central role in security affairs.

Above all, the Russian government seemed initially uncertain in its response to the French proposal on OSCE. In early 1996, the Russians explored U.S. reaction to an enhanced OSCE. They were told in Congress and by the Clinton administration that the OSCE's role must remain the same: monitoring elections, ensuring observance of human rights norms, and performing the general functions of a collective security organization. U.S. officials were adamant that the key military security issues must remain within NATO. Yet Russian officials still saw their country as having a major role in decisionmaking on the continent. They were used to the Cold War practice of spurning overtures by "lesser powers," and they preferred the prestigious, central role that appeared to go with making decisions with Washington over key issues. If the United States was saying "no" to an enhanced OSCE, then Moscow would prefer bilateral discussion with Washington or dealing with U.S. administrations through NATO. The Yeltsin government turned a cold shoulder to Chirac's OSCE proposal.[21]

Chirac then began to pursue the idea of a charter between NATO and Russia. In the French government's view, the charter would give Russia a seat at the table in discussions on European security ideas. U.S. Secretary of State Warren Christopher was at first wary of such an arrangement. Members of Congress were unlikely to support any initiative that gave Russia influence over NATO strategy or other important decisions. The administration initially preferred securing better relations with Russia through a step-by-step process, such as working with Moscow in implementing the Dayton Accord in Bosnia; if the Russians proved constructive, other steps might follow.

But France was persistent in an effort that was backed by other Europeans to ensure that the Yeltsin government, constantly under duress from more radical elements in the Duma, not find itself isolated and in an atmosphere where communists and nationalists might undermine reform. The German and Italian governments strongly urged the Clinton administration to accept the charter and to convince Congress of the need for such an agreement. Secretary of State Christopher began to explore an agreement that might give Russia a "voice but not a veto" in NATO councils. By September 1996 he had reached agreement in principle with France and other allies that the course was worth pursuing. In the end, this was a formula embraced by the alliance and, more warily, by the Russians and by Congress. NATO and Russia signed the document, to be called the Founding Act, on 27 May 1997, in Paris. (See Appendix G for excerpts from the Founding Act.)

The Founding Act met several French objectives. First, it showed that Paris could play a significant role in leading the allies to an important agreement with Russia. The Founding Act played a role in lowering tensions by restating, in a formal document, that the alliance had "no intention, no plan, and no reason" in the foreseeable future to station nuclear weapons or storage sites on new members' territory. The allies also pledged "in the current and foreseeable security environment" not to station "substantial combat forces" on new members' soil, but at the same time underscored the intention to increase interoperability, integration, and reinforcement capabilities between existing and new member states. The document thereby reassured nervous candidate states that their security was not being sacrificed to accommodate Russian concerns.[22] In the view of some French observers, the Founding Act meant that no important security question in Europe could be addressed without close consultation with Russia. Russia was now "an implicit member of NATO," a step that would enhance stability and move the alliance away from the Cold War era.[23] For President Chirac, this was an important element of NATO's "renovation."

The Founding Act, however, was not without irony and contradiction for French security policy. If Russia was to be an "implicit member of NATO," then it risked relegating the European Union's vision of a security and defense identity to a second-class status. And the OSCE, so recently championed by Paris, now seemed certain to play an even lesser role in security affairs.

POLITICS AND ENLARGEMENT

Throughout the alliance discussion of enlargement, France emphasized NATO's strategic purpose as the most central issue, and within it, the shape and direction of the European security and defense identity. By the summer of 1996, the outline of CJTF had become more clear, the debate over AFSOUTH was engaged, and Chirac had stated that return to the integrated command structure was under consideration as a result. With "renovation" seemingly under way, French leaders now turned, for the first time, to make clear decisions over enlargement.

Mitterrand had spoken of his desire for a long apprenticeship for the Central European states for membership in both the European Union and NATO. For political and economic reasons, French officials across the political spectrum initially had reservations about the candidacies of Poland, the Czech Republic, and Hungary. Economically, many French officials viewed Poland and the Czech Republic in particular as being in a more "liberal" camp, closer to the British or U.S. economic model than to the French model. In France, whether the left or the right was in power, the hand of the state was stronger than in virtually any other EU country. Bringing the three principal candidate states into NATO was a prelude to bringing them into the European Union. Such a step therefore had economic as well as strategic considerations. A European Union weighted with governments favoring a more liberal economic model could place pressure on France to step back from its more statist model, where government participation or influence in the banking and financial sector, in acquiescence to unions' demands and in support of the transportation industry, for example, was strongly evident. Admission of the three candidate states, in this view, would not only tip the political balance in the alliance in favor of Germany, the candidates' strong continental advocate, but also economically in the European Union in favor of Britain and other "liberal" states.

Why, then, did France move toward support for NATO enlargement? Several factors pushed Chirac to endorse the three countries' candidacies, aside from progress over alliance "renovation." Complaints were growing in Poland, the Czech Republic, and Hungary that France was the principal country barring the way to a decisive step in favor of their membership.[24] In addition, criticism in several influential French newspapers was also evident. To deny the three countries' membership in key European institutions, in the view of some journalists, was to deny the importance of their hard struggle to gain freedom and establish democratic governments. Some critics also thought that French hesitation was due to an overly eager desire not to antagonize Russia.[25]

By the fall and winter of 1996, Chirac began to visit the countries of Central Europe and announce his support for NATO enlargement. During this period, he clearly endorsed Poland, the Czech Republic, and Hungary as qualified to join the alliance. On state visits, he hailed their faith in democratic structures and their adherence to Western philosophies and norms.[26]

Chirac's overtures to and endorsement of Romania were more controversial. In February 1997 he visited Bucharest. France found several reasons to support a Romanian candidacy. Under Nicolae Ceaușescu, Romania had arguably seen the most repressive of the Central European governments. By early 1997, however, it had held relatively unblemished democratic elections. Other allies, including the United States, questioned Romania's progress, given that old-line communist *apparatchiks* were still in power, corruption was rampant, the intelligence community was wavering at best in its sentiment toward the West, and the economy was unreformed. France saw these blemishes but preferred to reward and encourage Romania for its steps forward. Had not, for example, Romania signed a treaty with Hungary that settled the key outstanding issues over treatment of its Hungarian minority? Military-to-military relations between Romania and Hungary were good. Strategically, Paris saw Romania as a potential anchor for the alliance's southeastern flank, an area troubled by instability. In an official visit to Bucharest in February 1997, before the Romanian Parliament, Chirac sought to underscore the friendship of two old Latin nations. French officials and journalists contended that French was the principal foreign language taught in Romania, and that Romanian culture was greatly influenced by France.[27] The Romanians, for their part, were eager to please their French guests. France was the first allied country to endorse Romania's candidacy. Chirac's hosts, in his presence, rebaptized one of Bucharest's most prominent squares "Place Charles de Gaulle," after removing a statue of Stalin that had been its centerpiece.

DOMESTIC POLITICS

Against the backdrop of Chirac's swing through the candidate states, an election campaign was under way. Chirac, sensing that the center-right could improve its position in the National Assembly, had called legislative elections for 1 June 1997, only a month before the NATO summit that would formally select the candidate states. During the campaign, however, domestic issues prevailed. By the spring of 1997, unemployment had grown to 12.8 percent and annual gross domestic product (GDP) growth was a weak 1.9 percent. The center-right ran on a platform of further budget tightening to ensure qualification for European monetary union. The Socialists and their leftist allies, meanwhile, ran on a platform calling for employment initiatives.

Little was said in the campaign about NATO enlargement, but Lionel Jospin, leader of the Socialist Party, had criticized Chirac's idea that France eventually should rejoin the alliance's integrated command structure. "If we didn't [see the value of reintegration] in the Warsaw Pact era," Jospin said, "why should we have it now when there is no threat?" In addition, he saw a "hegemonic tendency" in the United States, all the more reason to oppose drawing closer to NATO. In Jospin's view, France should "first define the way of European security, which would then allow the formulation in new, evolved terms of the relation with NATO. [President Chirac] has put the cart before the horse." Jospin believed that EU enlargement should precede NATO enlargement.[28] Jospin promised that if the left gained power, he would seek a "convergence" in foreign policy with Chirac, but that "there can be no *domaine réservé*" that would allow the president alone to shape the foreign and defense policy agenda.[29]

During the campaign Jospin accepted some of Chirac's views on foreign and defense policy. He shared the concerns of Chirac and Juppé about "the South," and he embraced the call for lighter, more mobile armed forces. But he largely avoided comment on the government's maneuvering on specific points of foreign policy before the election.

LEGISLATIVE ELECTIONS AND THE NATO SUMMIT

On 1 June 1997, French voters dealt a devastating blow to Jacques Chirac and the center-right government of Alain Juppé. Voters punished the sitting majority for its inattention to the economy and made Chirac's decision to call early elections a failed gamble that badly tarnished his credibility throughout Europe and among U.S. policymakers. Before the elections, the Socialists held only sixty-one of 577 seats; by the evening of 1 June they held 261. Chirac's weakened hand, coming only weeks before the NATO summit that would decide on candidate states for membership, adversely affected his broad plan for alliance renovation.

Lionel Jospin became prime minister and led a coalition of Socialists, Communists, Greens, and Jean-Pierre Chevènement's small Movement for Citizens, bringing France its third period of "cohabitation." Jospin's coalition contained elements sharply critical of NATO. Chevènement had long been uneasy with U.S. leadership of the alliance and had quit an earlier government over President Mitterrand's decision to join with the United States in the Gulf War. He opposed enlargement as yet another effort by Washington to enhance U.S. influence on the continent. Robert Hue, not in a ministerial seat but head of the Communist Party, had called for NATO's disbandment as a relic of the Cold War. And Dominique Voynet, the leader of the Greens who had called for an end to military blocs, became minister for the environment.

The Denver summit of the Group of Seven (G-7) industrial powers was an important event between the French elections and the NATO summit that affected French thinking on the alliance. At Denver, some of President Clinton's aides distributed material to other countries' representatives that celebrated the achievements of the U.S. economy. Some of the documents reportedly contained graphs and other data clearly marking how the U.S. economy was outstripping rival economies in growth and innovation. President Clinton gave a speech emphasizing the United States' economic prowess, an action widely criticized as "triumphalist" and in ill taste by the European press. A few days later, Prime Minister Jospin repeated his earlier remarks about tendencies toward "hegemony" evident in U.S. leadership, adding that such tendencies are "not necessarily identical with exercising the global responsibilities of a great power, even if it is a friend." He then indirectly echoed a common French view that the U.S. economy favors the rich and leaves the poor by the side of the road. "Europe does not have the same model as the United States," he said, "and she has always tried to preserve an equilibrium between the economic and the social."[30] Perhaps reading too much into his remarks, some U.S. officials worried privately that these views might signal a revived French effort to exclude from NATO and the European Union the "liberal" governments of Central Europe, which after all had expressed a desire to draw closer to the United States as one reason for wishing to join the alliance.

Such fears were unfounded. The several weeks before the NATO summit did, however, prove rocky. On 12 June 1997, the Clinton administration announced its support for Poland, the Czech Republic, and Hungary as the only candidate states, a move denounced in the French press as an act of "brutality" that would preempt meaningful discussion of candidacies at the summit. It was also clear that the United States would not entertain French requests that a European lead AFSOUTH. On the eve of the summit, Chirac made the important decision, perhaps due to his diminished political weight and the insistence of the new government, that French reintegration into the military command structure would be indefinitely postponed, given the failure of NATO to implement in-depth renovation.[31]

At the NATO summit in Madrid, France pressed its case yet again for Romania, and it backed Italy's call for a Slovenian candidacy. In retrospect, lingering concerns that France might delay or block enlargement if the alliance did not embrace its call for renovation were unfounded. France had led the effort to sign the Founding Act, a move consecrated at the summit by the final communiqué linking it to enlargement as a cornerstone of the continent's new security architecture; blocking enlargement in such circumstances was unthinkable. Both France and Italy, and several other countries supporting Romania or Slovenia, were primarily laying down markers for a future round of enlargement. On 8 July 1997, the allies agreed on Poland, the Czech Republic, and Hungary as the three candidate states. They further agreed to keep the door open to other prospective candidates.

Chirac took the occasion of the summit as an opportunity to make his case on related issues. He pledged that Romania would enter the alliance in 1999. He endorsed NATO's December 1996 cost estimate of U.S.$1.3 billion for enlargement and swiped at those who disagreed. There are higher estimates "bandied about behind the scenes at the U.S. Congress," he said. "I do not lend them any credence. We have adopted a very simple position: Enlargement must not cost anything in net terms. . . . In reality, NATO is a peacekeeping body, a crisis management system, and can accordingly afford much lighter resources in terms of both equipment and infrastructure."[32] These remarks were strange in that Congress had fully, and very publicly, debated a range of cost issues. Some French observers suspected a behind-the-scenes collaboration among Congress, the administration, and the U.S. defense industry to set prospective costs at a high level as a means to boost the U.S. economy and the defense industry's competitive position.[33] However, the administration's strongly voiced position on the purchase of high-technology defense equipment by the three candidates was quite distant from such analyses. Secretary of Defense William Cohen, for example, urged the candidate states to concentrate on more basic, less expensive equipment for command and control, rather than expend resources on high-performance aircraft, very much at the high end of the defense industry's armaments. And Chirac's remark that NATO was only a peacekeeping organization with a need for light equipment was especially odd, given the need for military action in 1995 against Slobodan Milosevic's forces in Bosnia. The Kosovo crisis of 1999 would further undercut such arguments.[34]

In the end, with minimal public or media attention, the amendment to the North Atlantic Treaty to admit Poland, the Czech Republic, and Hungary was agreed by the French National Assembly and the Senate on 17 June 1998.

France joined with other allies at the 1999 Washington NATO summit in stating that the door remains open to qualified candidate states. But it is clear that Paris has other more pressing priorities. French officials perceive their government's two problems of highest concern to be stability in the Balkans and EU enlargement.

CONCLUSION

In some ways, the larger picture of developments in Europe undercut the French position on modernization of the alliance and on enlargement. Most member states had some concern that a revived Russia might one day again threaten the continent. The conflict in Bosnia from 1991 on had preserved the belief that NATO must maintain a strong military capability. A unified Germany was gathering economic strength and testing the political waters on new issues, such as dispatching military forces outside the treaty area, a move welcomed in Washington and many other allied capitals. The European Union was pondering expansion, but with many preliminary obstacles in the way. Each of these factors carried with it the belief in every allied capital that the United States must remain squarely at the center of any debate over security. The position of the U.S. government, then, would generally prevail on any important issue, including enlargement and the broader question of NATO's missions and how they would be achieved.

At the same time, France's call for renovation before enlargement had considerable intellectual weight. It made sense to establish NATO's missions clearly before inviting new members, involving new risks and new territory to protect. It made sense to restructure forces and their command to accomplish those missions before inviting newcomers. And it made sense to strengthen ESDI before enlarging, especially since new NATO countries would likely one day join the European Union. To go against French logic on renovation implied a step toward making NATO a collective security rather than a collective defense institution—and an institution threatened by dilution in decisionmaking and military capability.

Real-world considerations, however, defeated the French logic. While there was sympathy for the French position in the German Foreign Ministry, Bonn knew that Washington was the key to German security and the key to the German near-term objective of admitting the three candidate states. Russia might have grasped the French offer to enhance the OSCE as a way to diminish the U.S. role in Europe, but Yeltsin hesitated and found the tried but no longer true road of high-level bilateral discussions with Washington preferable as a means to protect his country's interests. Chirac's effort to engage in horse-trading with the Clinton administration was more suited to the European Union Commission and Council than to NATO and was thus also a failure. Washington would not play, in part because it was dealing from a position of strength, in part because France's proffered trades seemed inappropriate to alliance councils.

Finally, internal developments in France threw President Chirac off course. His own decision to cut sharply his country's defense budget, including key components critical to a European security identity, left him with a hand at the table that seemed more bluff than substance, even a card or two short, no matter its solid intellectual underpinnings. Without adequate lift and command-and-control, the French request for more responsibility in allied decisionmaking on the road to a European security identity seemed unrealistic—to Washington as well as to other key allies. The ousting of the Juppé government served the final blow. It gave an embarrassing jolt to Chirac's reputation for political canniness, reduced his weight in NATO discussions, and put his country on a course to concentrate on domestic, rather than foreign, policy. By the time of the 1997 NATO summit, Chirac's plan for renovation of the alliance was behind the pace of events and without significant international support.

NOTES

1. "EU: Report Examines Countries' Views on IGC issues" (Foreign Broadcast Information Service, Report FBIS-WEU-96-052, Washington, D.C., 15 March 1996): 11.

2. French Senate, "Débat au Sénat sur la CIG: Intervention du Ministre des Affaires Etrangères M. de Charette," 14 March 1996 (Paris).

3. Jacques Chirac, "Pour un modèle Européen," *Libération,* 25 March 1996: 1.

4. Jacques Chirac, "Discours devant l'IHEDN" (Institut des Hautes Etudes de Defence Nationale, Paris, 8 June 1996).

5. "Union . . . amplificateur de puissance," *Le Monde,* December 1993: 1.

6. Richard Holbrooke was a leading target of such criticism. Many European officials expressed anger when, after the EU's inability to resolve a territorial dispute between Greece and Turkey in early 1996, Holbrooke said, "The Europeans were literally sleeping through the night. You have to wonder why Europe does not seem capable of taking decisive action in its own theater" (*Washington Post,* 8 February 1996: A17).

7. Henri de Bresson, "Les contentieux s'alourdissent entre Paris et Bonn," *Le Monde,* 4 December 1996: 2; and "L'idée française d'un 'M. Pesc' provoque la perplexité à Bonn," *Le Monde,* 21 March 21 1996: 2. (The acronym "Monsieur PESC" mirrors the English "Mr. Common Foreign and Security Policy.")

8. "France Increases Its Participation in the Transformation of the Alliance," *NATO Review* (January 1996): 16.

9. For the most sophisticated rationale by a U.S. official, see Strobe Talbott, "Why NATO Should Grow," *New York Review of Books,* August 10, 1995.

10. For an earlier expression of the concern that the United States was distancing itself from Europe, see the interesting editorial by then Prime Minister Pierre Bérégovoy, "L'Amérique, l'Europe, la France," *Le Monde,* 6 January 1993: 1.

11. Pascal Boniface, "The NATO Debate in France," in *NATO Enlargement: The National Debates over Ratification,* ed. Simon Serfaty and Stephen Cambone (Washington, D.C.: CSIS,1997).

12. Ibid., 43.

13. Author's notes, July–October 1995.

14. "Accord sur la réforme de l'OTAN," *Le Monde,* 12–13 May 1996: 3.

15. U.S. and allied officials, interviewed by the author, 1996.

16. Jacques Isnard, "La France est déjà contrainte d'agir dans un cadre interallié," *Le Monde,* 23–24 August 1995: 3.

17. Jacques Isnard, "Le budget militaire sera réduit de 100 milliards de francs en cinq ans," *Le Monde,* 24 February 1996: 6.

18. Daniel Vernet, "France-OTAN: Une bonne idée en panne," *Le Monde,* 29 June 1996: 1.

19. See, for example, the discussion in "France Attacks U.S. Cruise Strike on Baghdad," *Financial Times,* 21 January 1993: 1.

20. Alain Frachon, "La France peine à impose sa conception de sécurité en Europe," *Le Monde,* 4 December 1996: 2.

21. U.S. and Russian officials, interviewed by the author, 1996. (In 1994–1995 the Russian idea of a security council for OSCE had been immediately rejected by the United States, and this was certainly a factor in their reaction to the French proposal.)

22. NATO. *Founding Act on Mutual Relations, Cooperation and Security Between NATO and the Russian Federation* (Brussels: NATO Press Office, 27 May 1997).

23. The phrase is Daniel Vernet's. See Vernet, "Une nouvelle Alliance pour une nouvelle Europe," *Le Monde,* 25–26 May 1997: 1.

24. This criticism was unfair, in that several key countries had doubts about a rapid move toward enlargement. For a discussion of the views in each of the NATO countries, see Paul Gallis, "NATO Enlargement: The Process and Allied Views" (Congressional Research Service, Report 97-666F, Washington, D.C., 1 July 1997).

25. See, for example, the editorial "M. Chirac, l'Europe et l'Est," *Le Monde,* 19–20 January 1997: 13.

26. See, for example, the account of his trip to the Czech Republic. Claire Tréan, "Paris souhaite que la République tchèque intègre le plus rapidement possible l'OTAN et l'UE," *Le Monde,* 4 April 1997: 4.

27. Henri de Bresson, "Jacques Chirac espère voir la Roumanie intégrer l'OTAN en 1999," *Le Monde,* 23–24 February 1997: 2. The issue of language instruction was a debatable point, and an important one, given French sensitivity to cultural influence. During a visit to Bucharest in spring 1996, the author was told by Romanian officials that English and German far outdistanced French in schools due to growing U.S. and German importance in Europe and the world. Whether officials were telling foreign visitors what they thought the visitors wanted to hear could not be determined. In general, it would seem that French cultural influence in Romania has waned since World War II.

28. "M. Jospin critique la réintégration de la France dans l'OTAN," *Le Monde,* 5 February 1997: 5; and "Jospin's Foreign Policy . . . " (Foreign Broadcast Information Service, Report FBIS-WEU-97-108, Washington, D.C., 5 June 1997): 9.

29. Michel Noblecourt, "M. Jospin se place dans la perspective d'une cohabitation non-conflictuelle," *Le Monde,* 20 May 1997: 5.

30. "M. Jospin craint les tendances 'hégémoniques' des Etats-Unis," *Le Monde,* 26 June 1997: 34. For some of the sharp French criticism of the United States on other issues at the summit, see "À Denver, Américains et Européens s'opposent sur l'environnement," *Le Monde,* 24 June 1997: 2.

31. Daniel Vernet, "France-OTAN: Une bonne idée en panne," *Le Monde,* 29–30 June 1997: 1.

32. "Chirac News Conference After NATO Summit" (Foreign Broadcast Information Service, Report FBIS-WEU-97-192, Washington, D.C., 17 July 1997). The best study of the costs of enlargement remains Carl Ek, "NATO Expansion: Cost Issues" (Congressional Research Service, Report 97-668F, Washington, D.C., 2 July 1997).

33. See, for example, Thierry de Montbrial, "US Bids to Keep 'Absolute Control' over NATO" (Foreign Broadcast Information Service, Report FBIS-WEU-97-170, Washington, D.C., 19 June 1997): 2 (originally published in *Le Figaro*).

34. See, for example, Jacques Isnard, "La Force d'extraction au Kosovo sera un test pour la France," *Le Monde,* 12 December 1998: 3. The extraction force, formed under French leadership on the model of a NATO Combined Joint Task Force, was supposedly built for combat to pull out OSCE observers in Kosovo should they come in harm's way. When such a moment actually came, the French general commanding the force, to the consternation of many at NATO, said that his force was too light, and could only extract the observers in a "benign environment." Such moments undercut the French call for greater independence and leadership on the part of the Europeans, and were particularly poorly received in the U.S. Congress.

5

The United Kingdom: Making Strategic Adjustments

SIR TIMOTHY GARDEN

The United Kingdom moved relatively rapidly to adjust its defense policy to its perception of the new security needs after the end of the Cold War. The rush to change its defensive posture was accelerated by an urgent need to bring an overheated defense program back into budgetary balance. Throughout the Cold War, the UK had taken pride in being a significant player in NATO and in spending more than the European average percentage of gross domestic product (GDP) on defense. It is a nuclear power, a permanent member of the UN Security Council, and a country with a number of security obligations outside of NATO. It has also had to provide military support to the police in Northern Ireland. During the 1980s, Prime Minister Margaret Thatcher supported the NATO pledge for 3 percent per annum real growth in defense expenditures, and the UK met these targets despite a period of poor economic performance. Yet this growth rate was unsustainable, and the fall of the Berlin Wall signaled an opportunity for a strategic review in 1989. The UK government published a fundamental review of its defense policy in 1990. Combat capability was set to decline by around 30 percent over the next five years.

This 1990 review, known as "Options for Change," was in retrospect undertaken too early to be based on a firm understanding of the new security context. It was assumed that a resurgent Russia had the potential to threaten the West, and that traditional UK support for a strong NATO would be the primary requirement of British defense policy. Then–Defense Secretary Tom King wrote in April 1990,

> History shows that periods of great political upheaval are also likely to be periods of insecurity. Whilst we look forward to a new security order in Europe, we have no right to assume it. New arrangements must be worked at and constructed through patient negotiation and agreement. NATO provides the focus through which its members . . . can coordinate and pursue

arms control and other ways of managing international security. But NATO can only succeed if it can continue to demonstrate a willingness and ability to defend itself for so long as there remains a potential for military exploitation in Europe.[1]

The British planners adopted with alacrity the new NATO Strategic Concept and divided up their remaining forces into the three required degrees of readiness: rapid reaction, main defense, and augmentation forces. The formation of the multinational Allied Command Europe Rapid Reaction Corps (ARRC) was enthusiastically welcomed, and the UK sought and won the role of lead nation. In describing future roles for the British army, NATO commitments headed the list.[2] The ARRC was to be the UK's major contribution and would be available for "deployment anywhere within the Allied Command Europe area."[3] Defense of the United Kingdom and commitments beyond the NATO area completed the three major roles for British forces. This was a continuation of a policy that saw the major concern as a threat from the East; albeit one that was now weaker and less immediate. The United Kingdom, while welcoming the unification of Germany, seemed not to be thinking in terms of any changes to NATO membership.

The assumptions of the 1990 defense review were brought into sharp question by the Gulf War of 1990–1991, when the UK showed that it was prepared to put together a significant joint force for high-intensity warfare well outside the NATO area. The lessons of the war's ad hoc coalition building were also a factor in modifying strategic assumptions made during the review. The United Kingdom took the position that engagement of the United States was now even more important in the new world order. The experience of French forces in the Gulf had shown the importance of British membership of the integrated military structure of NATO in order to be able to play a major role in such deployments. The lukewarm support for Gulf operations from some allies, however, did not go unnoticed.

By 1993, the re-emergence of a major Russian threat seemed unlikely for the foreseeable future, and the UK government began to admit that the assumptions of 1991 were no longer valid.[4] Better relations with the Central European nations were seen as achievable through the North Atlantic Cooperation Council for NATO as well as the Forum of Consultation for the Western European Union. Experience in the former republic of Yugoslavia was beginning to shape policythinking on potential future security concerns.

The 1994 government's annual defense policy statement warmly endorsed the outcome of the NATO Brussels summit of January that year and used it as the first opportunity to trail the longer-term possibility of NATO enlargement:

NATO is also a focus for stability, valued not only by its members but also by the newly democratic states of central and eastern Europe. The work of the North Atlantic Co-operation Council has done much to cement relations. . . . "Partnership for Peace" will deepen the ties . . . through close co-operation on a range of military and political issues and open up the prospect of enlargement of the Alliance in the longer term.[5]

The statement focused on the threat of Balkan-type conflicts, while reminding the public that the evolution of Russia was still a cause for concern. The possible enlargement of NATO was not highlighted in the introduction by Defense Secretary Malcolm Rifkind.

The 1995 statement *Stable Forces in a Strong Britain* also makes interesting reading. The Conservative government inclined more toward a transatlantic relationship than toward closer integration with Europe. It saw advantage in promoting enlargement of the European Union, in the hope that this would delay integration (wider membership rather than deeper integration). However, it could see that a diluting of the membership of NATO might weaken the bonds that held the United States engaged. While trying to appear enthusiastic, the UK hoped to preserve the current arrangements:

We place great value on . . . a balance between partnership and membership in the development of the wider Europe we wish to see. But there is an unhelpful preoccupation with the latter, and in particular with membership of NATO and the European Union. Playing down the value of co-operation and playing up the significance of decisions on membership will risk re-creating the type of divide in Europe which we wish to avoid.[6]

By now the main thrust of defense policy was attached to wider security policy, not to mention Britain's interests in a stable world.

The last annual statement on defense policy to be produced by the Conservative government was published in May 1996, and much of it is colored by the experience in Bosnia. The post–Cold War change in rationale for defense forces was virtually complete. The opening statement declares:

The goal of our security policy is to maintain the freedom and territorial integrity of the United Kingdom and its Dependent Territories, and the ability to pursue its legitimate interests at home and abroad.[7]

Defense Secretary Michael Portillo was well known for his lack of enthusiasm for greater integration of the European Union. In his introduction to the annual statement, he welcomes the enlargement of NATO and says, "We shall argue vigorously at the European Union's Inter-Governmental Conference that European defense arrangements must be based on sustaining NATO's strength and effectiveness." NATO enlargement is given prominence for the first time, and the statement reports the outcome of the NATO study in an objective way.[8] There is no discussion of the issues or even an indication of the United Kingdom's view on the desirability of enlargement. The paper reports that ministers will assess progress at the Brussels meeting in December 1996 and consider the way forward.

The British public takes only a limited interest in defense policy except when a war is in prospect. At a time when NATO was agonizing over its future, little discussion took place within the UK apart from within the strategic studies elites. It was perhaps unfortunate that no further defense policy statement would be produced for two years. The election on 1 May 1997 meant that the outgoing Conservative government was not able to produce one. No significant debate on the issues took place in Parliament either. The House of Commons had a brief debate in February 1997 followed by an even shorter debate in the House of Lords the following month.

THE 1997 PARLIAMENTARY DEBATES

The House of Commons spared an hour and a half to debate NATO enlargement on 26 February 1997. The debate was opened by Bill Walker, a Conservative member of Parliament, who expressed reservations about enlargement and advocated keeping the current NATO membership strong and ensuring that the transatlantic bond was not weakened.[9] Members raised the question of potential costs but offered little in the way of hard evidence. The debate did not divide along political party lines; some Labor and Conservative members expressed concerns about the potential weakening of the alliance through the process of expansion, while others were broadly supportive. Tony Lloyd, who would become a Foreign Office minister in the Labor government, explained that the Labor Party strongly supported NATO and would also support, with some qualifications, enlargement. The debate was concluded, without any vote being taken, by the Conservative government Foreign Office minister Sir Nicholas Bonsor who emphasized the government's commitment to extending European security through an enlargement of NATO. In addressing the cost issues, he suggested that the lower estimates of $35 billion were nearer the mark than suggestions of $125 billion. In any event, he stated that the United Kingdom would keep a close eye on costs.[10]

Two weeks later, the House of Lords provided a forum for a discussion of all aspects of NATO enlargement. On 14 March 1997 (a Friday afternoon when low-priority business is done), Lord Kennet opened the debate by asking the government for its policy on the proposal. In a strong opening speech, he expressed great concern about the potential of enlargement causing a redivision of Europe, an alienation of Russia, and a remilitarization of Europe. He also complained about the lack of parliamentary debate before the government decided on its policy toward NATO expansion.[11] In the brief debate, the process of enlargement had more supporters than opponents. Lord Wallace, speaking as a Liberal Democrat, wished to see Slovenia and Romania included in the first wave of enlargement. Many speakers, meanwhile, regretted the lack of public debate about the important strategic issues involved, blaming the government for conducting its policy development behind closed doors. Lord Williams, the Labor Party spokesman, explained that his party supported enlargement for Poland, the Czech Republic, Hungary, and possibly Slovenia, but not for Romania in the first wave. He also highlighted the importance of working with Russia, and he supported the approach proposed by the United States. Winding up the debate for the Conservative government, Lord Chesham did little more than restate its support for the principle of enlargement. The debate lasted fewer than ninety minutes and caused no ripple of interest among the British public.[12]

NEW LABOR GOVERNMENT

The Labor Party was elected with a large majority of the seats in the House of Commons on 1 May 1997. The incoming Labor government had promised a thorough defense review on gaining power. They had also promised to complete the review within six months, but it was July 1998 before it was published. This meant that at the key time of shaping NATO enlargement policy, Britain was either preparing for an election (with its inevitable focus on domestic issues) or reexamining its whole foreign and defense policy assumptions for the new government. Even if this had not been the case, it would have been surprising if the public had become engaged in the NATO enlargement debate. Public knowledge and interest in NATO is remarkably low, which is not to say that the British electorate are antagonistic to NATO. They appear entirely content to leave things as they are inasmuch as they know how they are. Defense was not a significant issue between the parties at the time of the 1997 election, either. All three main parties supported, simply, a strong NATO with a significant contribution from Britain.

The primary NATO meeting on enlargement policy would take place in July in Madrid. Despite limited time and competing priorities for reform, the new government did address the NATO issue. Within two weeks of taking office, Robin Cook, the new foreign secretary, gave a major briefing on the priorities for British foreign policy. In this mission statement, he listed four goals of foreign policy, with security through NATO at the top:

> The first goal of foreign policy is security for nations. Our security will remain based on [NATO]. We must manage the enlargement of NATO to ensure that a wider alliance is also a stronger alliance and that the process reduces rather than increases tensions between East and West.[13]

This early statement of support for enlargement was not followed by any great public discussion. Before the Madrid summit of July 1997 George Robertson, the new defense secretary, indicated that the UK favored full membership for Poland, the Czech Republic, and Hungary and had sympathy for the Slovenian case but was less enthusiastic about Romania as part of the first wave of new members.[14] Seemingly, UK policy on enlargement would continue unchanged. The government believed that enlargement was a good thing, but that it needed to be managed carefully so as not to cause divisions within NATO and increase tensions in the rest of Europe.

The outcome of the Madrid summit in July 1997 was as expected regarding the UK. Tony Blair reported to Parliament on 9 July 1997, singling out for particular mention the position of Slovenia and Romania:

> I should say a particular word about Romania and Slovenia, whose applications were especially closely considered even though there was no consensus to invite them on this occasion. Both countries have indeed made remarkable progress. Romania's new Government deserves particular congratulation on the steps taken since they took office last November. A number of allies would have liked to see Romania and Slovenia included among those invited at Madrid. All, including ourselves, saw them as strong candidates for any future enlargement, but we felt that Poland, the Czech Republic and Hungary were the limit for current enlargement.[15]

Blair dismissed the question of additional costs as insignificant and promised that Parliament would have a full opportunity to debate the enlargement before ratification of the treaty. His announcement of the outcome of the Madrid summit was welcomed by the leaders of the two main opposition parties. However, Paddy Ashdown, the Liberal Democrat leader, expressed concern about the lack of strategy rather than ad hoc decisions:

> Does the Prime Minister accept that there is a necessary but growing divergence between the long-term strategic aims of the Americans in NATO and the Europeans in NATO? The Americans see NATO as a global institution, perhaps with implications for their policy on the Middle East, while we see it as an institution concerned with security in Europe.[16]

Despite a rebuttal by the prime minister, this theme has recurred in the subsequent discussions both inside and outside Parliament. The only critical voices over the principle of enlargement came from two left-wing Labor Party members.

Discussion in the main academic centers was more critical of the concept of enlargement. Jane Sharp, for example, analyzed the nongovernmental debate in the UK in a report by the Centre for Strategic and International Studies (CSIS):

> In general British public opinion is unconcerned about NATO enlargement, but opinions vary widely among the defense and foreign affairs cognoscenti just as they do in the United States. Among the sceptics, at one end of the spectrum are Cold Warriors who worry that enlargement will weaken alliance cohesion and undermine NATO's original task of collective defence. At the other are those on the left who worry [about giving] Russia a dangerous sense of encirclement that could strengthen xenophobic nationalists in the Duma and the military.[17]

Certainly for those of us involved in the academic debate, the anti-expansionists seem to have a significant majority. Former ambassadors, senior military officers, and distinguished professors used every opportunity to say that the West's policy was misguided. Articles and letters to the newspaper flourished. *The Times,* for instance, carried an editorial against expansion:

> The most urgent reason for Europeans to rise to the Albright challenge is that the centrepiece of her European strategy, the enlargement of NATO by 1999, is dangerously misjudged. Far from enhancing the security of the European continent, this imminent decision risks creating fresh sources of insecurity, inviting confrontation with Russia and . . . impairing the Alliance's capacity to respond to new dangers that wiser policies might avert.[18]

Yet the impact on UK policy of these statements was nil. It may be that the new Labor government, with its aversion to old national institutions, was peculiarly well placed to ignore the concerns of this body of academic and military great and good. Their criticisms were answered to some degree, however, by Defense Secretary George Robertson in two public speeches in the autumn of 1997.[19]

THE DEFENSE COMMITTEE

The UK Parliament has a number of select committees that have the authority to shadow particular departments of state and report on them to Parliament.

These committees are much weaker than their U.S. counterparts, but they do provide a useful way of probing the evolution of government policies. The members of each committee are themselves elected members of Parliament, and are drawn from all parties in a broadly representative manner. In January 1998, the Defense Committee began taking evidence about the UK policy on NATO enlargement, and it published its report in March 1998.[20]

The committee took oral evidence from the defense secretary, the minister of state at the Foreign Office, the prime minister of Hungary, and the defense minister of Poland. They also took written submissions from the embassies of Bulgaria, the Czech Republic, Estonia, Hungary, Latvia, Macedonia, Poland, Romania, Slovakia, and Slovenia. As with all select committee investigations, this one invited submissions from interested parties. But notably, no such submissions were made. The resulting report is the most coherent UK document on the issues surrounding the question of NATO enlargement. Like related discussions in Parliament, however, it received little publicity and no public debate. The report conclusions read, in sum:

(A) We certainly recognise the success of the PfP programme, which has also enabled prospective members to demonstrate their NATO-worthiness. However, we also recognise that most of the CEE states were not prepared to accept indefinitely this "associate status." . . .

(C) We conclude that the incentive to improve the structure and control of the military, to enhance democracy and to resolve border disputes and internal problems with ethnic minorities, which we have seen clearly exists within aspirant countries, would not have been as strong without the possibility of full membership of NATO.

(D) We recognise that potential improvements to the security environment could be put at risk if enlargement caused Russia to adopt a posture which could bring about a resurgence of Cold War antagonism.

(E) While we should be sensitive to Russian anxieties, we cannot accept that Russia should have a veto over Alliance decisions. . . .

(F) In deciding whether to endorse ratification of the accession protocols of the proposed new members, Parliament must weigh the potential political advantages of enlargement against any potential short-term costs in terms of military effectiveness. For our part, we are clear that the benefits of increased stability in central and eastern Europe outweigh any potential military costs. . . .

(H) We conclude, that it would be as well, in choosing to endorse the process of enlargement, to be prepared for the costs shared among the 19 members of NATO to drift up at least toward the mid-range between NATO's $1.5 billion over ten years and the U.S. DoD's [Department of Defense's] $5–6 billion over thirteen years.

(I) We conclude that the weight of informal opinion and the evidence we have heard supports the RAND Corporation and DoD in the assumption that the threat of a direct conventional war in Europe is insignificant in the near term and that should such a threat re-arise, NATO would have sufficient time to adjust its defensive posture. We accept, therefore, that the permanent forward positioning of NATO forces in the new members' territories is unnecessary. To do so when the risk does not justify it will in any case be interpreted as an action deliberately antagonistic to Russian concerns. The highest estimates are the CBO's [Congressional Budget Office's] more expensive options, at costs of up to $125 billion and can accordingly be disregarded. . . .

(L) . . . Even if the UK's estimated contribution of £110 million over ten years were to double to the equivalent of half of the purchase price of a Eurofighter every year we would still consider that enlargement offers excellent value for money.

(M) Despite equal or nearly equal claims from a few other countries, we conclude that none of the three countries invited to accede to NATO was an inappropriate choice. . . .

(O) We express the hope that the Committee on the Modernisation of the House of Commons will turn its attention to the current unsatisfactory arrangements for Parliamentary examination of international treaties and other aspects of the exercise of the royal prerogative in relation to ratification.

(P) We believe that we should approach any further enlargement after this round with caution.

(Q) We believe that consensus decisions are required where military operations may be employed, and we would not wish to see NATO operating with a "Security Council."

(R) We recommend that the House endorse the admission of the Czech Republic, Hungary and Poland to the North Atlantic Alliance.[21]

While the British parliamentary role is limited in treaty matters, its Defense Committee report gave clear support to enlargement as important to encouraging the continued development of democracy and lowering of other potential tensions in Central Europe even at a cost to NATO members. Acknowledging the need to consult with Russia, the committee also rejected a veto by Russia over NATO affairs. It backed the three candidates and counseled caution on future enlargements.

AN EMINENT GROUP OF LOBBYISTS

While there is no requirement under the British system for the government to seek parliamentary approval before ratification of a treaty, the prime minister had promised Parliament the opportunity to debate NATO enlargement before the UK ratified. In May 1998, some twenty-three senior figures, including former Defense Secretary Denis Healey and two former chiefs of defense staff, wrote to the prime minister to urge a reconsideration of the enlargement issue.[22] Tony Blair replied robustly on the decision to offer membership to the three countries and also said that the writers' concerns would be debated in Parliament. He had grown, however, much less positive on the question of a second round of enlargement. While acknowledging the need for a continuing discussion of further enlargement, he stated he could not

> say who will be invited next, or when. But neither do I believe that we should close the door to further enlargement at some point in the future. The contribution that NATO enlargement can, in the right circumstances, make to European stability and security is too important to be forsworn.[23]

By the summer of 1998, the lengthy defense review was coming to a conclusion and was published in early July.[24] In the end, the Defense Committee assumed that NATO would have three new members but remained uncommitted on the issue of future enlargement.

THE RATIFICATION OF PARLIAMENTARY DEBATES

As was described earlier, there is no requirement for the British government to consider a treaty in Parliament before ratification. Nevertheless, for major changes, it is normal practice to allow both chambers an opportunity for discussion, although the ultimate authority for ratification of the treaty rests with the administration. For key issues, an administration may decide to conduct a referendum before entering into a treaty obligation. But there was no suggestion that this was necessary on the issue of NATO enlargement. The House of Commons started its debate at 9:37 AM on Friday, 17 July 1998, and had finished by 11 AM that morning.[25]

The debate opened with Robin Cook making a strong argument about the rights as democratic European states of Poland, the Czech Republic, and Hungary to join NATO. He made it clear that this would increase the UK's commitments, but he also placed obligations on the new members and reminded members of the principle of collective defense in Article 5 of the Washington treaty making an attack on a NATO member an attack on all, the strongest guarantee of NATO member security. Furthermore, he maintained that

> the three new members of NATO will enjoy that guarantee; they will accept, too, the responsibility that it imposes on them. We will help to defend Poland, Hungary and the Czech Republic; they will help to defend us. The principle of collective defence will not be weakened by the expansion of NATO's numbers. On the contrary, the capability to deliver on that principle will be strengthened by the increase in numbers and the greater security of our present borders.[26]

Cook also described the process by which the applicant countries were narrowed down to three. He admitted that the UK would have supported

Slovenia, but that consensus among the sixteen NATO nations was necessary and it was a difficult decision which applicant countries to choose for membership:

> Critical to that judgment was the broad view that NATO enlargement should proceed at a pace that is consistent with NATO absorbing its expanded membership. We would do no service to the other countries that aspire to join NATO if we expanded so rapidly that NATO lost its effectiveness as the military guarantor of peace on our continent. As I have said, this will not be the last NATO enlargement. No one should be under any illusion about the magnitude of the current enlargement.[27]

On the subject of additional costs, Cook assessed the UK contribution to be as low as £110 million spread over ten years. In his response, John Maples, the Conservative Party defense spokesman, expressed concern about the rigor of the cost assessment. He also spent some time discussing the effect on Russia and the difficulties of extending the NATO security guarantee effectively to the enlarged area. When asked whether he supported the proposed enlargement or not, Maples expressed his support and underscored the need to integrate the three new members into the alliance before further expansion. He went on to say,

> We should be cautious about having more new members until it is clear how the situation in central and eastern Europe is developing. Almost all the countries that want to join fail at least one of the tests that I set out earlier. NATO has an enormous current agenda without further enlargement: the integration of the three new members; developing a new strategic concept; and building relationships with Russia and its former allies. Those are all significant tasks which will take much effort and time. Let us ensure that they are concluded satisfactorily before proceeding any further.[28]

The next main speaker was Bruce George, the chairman of the Defense Select Committee. He brought the conclusions of his committee's analysis to the attention of the House and strongly endorsed the proposed enlargement of NATO. He made it clear that the costs to the UK were well worth paying. The debate (such as it was) closed with only one further speaker. As a number of members noted in their interventions, it was a very cursory way for the UK Parliament to consider such a significant change to the strategic landscape in Europe. There was less than two hours of discussion and on a Friday morning, to boot, when the House of Commons is traditionally poorly attended. Despite the lack of need for a parliamentary vote, the UK was among the last of the NATO member states to ratify the treaty formally.

On the final afternoon of the parliamentary session before the long summer break of 1998, the House of Lords held their discussion of NATO enlargement. The debate was opened by Lord Gilbert, the minister for defense procurement. He reminded the House that he had opposed enlargement in 1996 as he had worried about undermining NATO through unrestrained enlargement.[29] He had also been concerned about costs. He had changed his mind, though, in part because the process after the Madrid summit had been well considered and each applicant had been examined on its merits. Lord Wallace, the Liberal Democrat spokesman, said,

> We should be developing and setting out publicly our own approach both to a domestic audience and to our allies in Europe and across the Atlantic.
>
> The Minister referred to consensus. It is never necessary to take a vote in NATO. It is an open secret that the majority of NATO members were in favour of enlargement to include five members on this occasion, of whom two were Romania and Slovenia, which would have solved the problem of Hungary as a land-locked state not having access. But the Americans said firmly and conclusively that they did not think they could get more than three through the Senate. Therefore on this occasion "consensus" meant a minority ruling the roost. NATO will not develop into a toothless security organization as the Minister suggested so long as it has an effective European pillar.[30]

Turning to the issue of further enlargement, Lord Wallace called the U.S. Senate resolution proposing a pause before further expansion a mistake. He promoted continued momentum in order to include Romania and Slovenia in the next round at a minimum. In terms of the Baltic states, the issue is more complicated. If the Baltic states are admitted to NATO, the alliance will need to discuss Baltic and European security as a whole and discuss how Sweden and Finland see their relations with NATO.[31]

The debate took as given that enlargement would happen and focused instead on the longer-term future of NATO. Not only was the question of the relationship with Russia seen as important, but a number of speakers were concerned about the potential differences between European and U.S. perspectives. Lord Kennet, who had been a critic of enlargement, charged that what Europe and the United States expect from NATO diverges and is becoming incompatible.[32]

Lord Carver, a former army chief of the Defense Staff, argued strongly against the whole enlargement process on the grounds that it redivided Europe into two potentially hostile camps. The discussion was characterized by thoughtful and well informed analysis of the issues. As is often the case with debates in the Lords, it received no publicity in the media. The final speech was made by Baroness Symons, the Foreign Office minister. She made no commitment for either time or candidates for further enlargement but said that the door remained open. Her concluding words announced the government's intention to ratify:

Following this debate the Government will deposit notifications of accept-
ance of the enlargement protocols with the United States Government in
Washington in accordance with our obligations under the Washington
Treaty. . . . I hope that the whole House will join me in welcoming the Czech
Republic, Hungary and Poland to the NATO alliance.[33]

THE CURRENT BRITISH POSITION

As we have seen, official opinion in the UK has moved from almost giving a
promise to Slovenia and Romania that they were next in line for NATO membership to much vaguer assurances of a future open door. In a major speech
on NATO in early 1999, Robin Cook made no reference to further enlargement.[34] The Ministry of Defense made it clear that the UK would not encourage further enlargement at the Washington summit in April 1999, but that the
UK government was committed to continuing the process. Several factors
would guide that future decision, including the readiness of the prospective
members and of NATO to integrate them as well as the impact on overall
European security.

Since 1999, to no one's surprise, there has been virtually no public or
parliamentary debate about further enlargement. Officials make it clear that
it has been hard work to prepare the three new members, particularly at a
time when NATO has had a heavy operational load to bear. Now that those
who had pushed for the original enlargement seem prepared to wait, the critics of the enlargement process are also content to keep quiet. The roles and
purpose of NATO, to be distilled in the new Strategic Concept, are where
staff work is most active. Meanwhile, the challenges of enlarging the European Union are becoming clearer; elite debates have focused more on the
implications in this area. In addition, there are also the challenges of the
European Monetary Union and the developing European Security and
Defense Policy.

To many non-British commentators, the lack of interest in the whole
adventure of NATO enlargement will seem surprising. Traditionally, all mainstream political opinion has been supportive of NATO. There are few votes to
be won by making NATO an issue in the country. The elites, both within government and outside, seek to manage the transition of NATO to the new
post–Cold War world. The debates, such as they are, have been about how this
can best be done. Given the lack of political dogma, the UK has seen itself in
the role of consensus broker between the U.S. view and that of the other main
European players. That it could not bring the French back into the integrated
military structure at Madrid was seen as unfortunate. For the future, the UK
can be expected to play a continuing role as a pragmatic member of NATO.

There are however signs that this may become more difficult as thinking about security on each side of the Atlantic diverges.

NOTES

1. *British Defense Policy 1990-1991,* Ministry of Defense Public Relations pamphlet (London: Ministry of Defense, April 1990).

2. *Britain's Army for the 90's,* Cm1595 (London: Her Majesty's Stationery Office [HMSO], July 1991).

3. Ibid., para. 14.

4. *Defending Our Future,* Cm2270 (London: HMSO, July 1993), para. 108.

5. *Statement on the Defense Estimates,* Cm2550 (London: HMSO, April 1994), para. 209.

6. *Stable Forces in a Strong Britain,* Cm2800 (London: HMSO, May 1995), para. 234.

7. *Statement on the Defense Estimates,* Cm3223 (London: HMSO, 1996), para. 101.

8. Ibid., 2; paras. 123–126 and table 2.

9. *Hansard Parliamentary Debates,* Commons, 290 (26 February 1997): cols. 257–260.

10. Ibid., cols. 271–272; 274–276.

11. *Hansard Parliamentary Debates,* Lords, 575 (14 March 1997): cols. 619–622.

12. Ibid., cols. 636–637; 638–642.

13. Tony Blair, Speech to Parliament, *Hansard Parliamentary Debates,* 297 (9 July 1997): col. 937.

14. *Financial Times* (4 June 1997).

15. *Hansard Parliamentary Debates,* Commons, 297 (9 July 1997): col. 937.

16. Ibid., col. 941.

17. Jane M.O. Sharp, "British Views on NATO Enlargement," in *NATO Enlargement: The National Debates over Ratification,* ed. by Simon Serfaty and Stephen Cambone (Washington, D.C.: CSIS, 1997), 23–24.

18. "A Higher Priority," *The Times,* 17 February 1997: 10.

19. George Robertson, "Building European Security and the Role of Defense Diplomacy" (speech given at the English Speaking Union, London, 4 September 1997) and "NATO, Its Partners and Defense Diplomacy" (speech given to the European Atlantic Group, 29 October 1997).

20. Parliament Defense Committee, *Third Report NATO Enlargement,* 18 March 1998 (London: HMSO).

21. Ibid., xxxi–xxxii.

22. "Defence Chiefs Warn Against Enlarging NATO," *Daily Telegraph,* 6 May 1998: 9.

23. Prime Minister Tony Blair, letter to Sir John Killick and others, 8 June 1998.

24. *The Strategic Defense Review,* Cm3999 (London: HMSO, July 1998).

25. *Hansard Parliamentary Debates,* Commons, 316 (17 July 1998).

26. Ibid., col. 684.

27. Ibid., col. 687.

28. Ibid., col. 695.

29. *Hansard Parliamentary Debates,* Lords, 317 (31 July 1998): cols. 1750–1751.

30. Ibid., col. 1764.

31. Ibid.

32. Ibid., col. 1769.

33. Ibid., col. 1809.

34. Robin Cook, Ernest Bevin Memorial Lecture (speech given in London, 22 January 1999).

6

Italy: Uneasy Ally

ROBERTO MENOTTI

Italy's ratification of the first round of NATO enlargement at the Madrid sum-mit in July 1997 attracted only limited public attention, to the relief of Prime Minister Romano Prodi's government.[1] A broad parliamentary debate on the future of NATO could have had dire consequences for the government. The Rifondazione Comunista Party (Refounded Communists, or RC), a component of the coalition Prodi government, openly opposed the continued existence of NATO and considered the enlargement of NATO to be highly undesirable.

The RC takes an extreme-left position on most foreign policy issues and hardly reflects the general mood of the Italian electorate. The RC's vote against ratification of the 1992 Maastricht Treaty on European Union, for instance, countered the eagerness of Italy's society to enhance integration.[2] The party's extreme position does demonstrate, though, the complexity of for-eign policy decisionmaking in modern Italy. Almost every foreign policy vote risks disrupting or destroying the very coalition that legitimizes the govern-ment in power. This risk is especially potent with respect to discussions of Italy's relationship with the United States in the field of security, defense, and mutual NATO commitments, which might reawaken the now-dormant con-troversy over Italy's role as the alliance's "unsinkable aircraft carrier" for out-of-area operations.

Thus, on the occasion of ratification of NATO enlargement, the center-left government of Romano Prodi had a strong interest in avoiding a "great debate" in order to ensure the continuation of its administration, regardless of the possible merits of such a debate about Italy's foreign policy.

THE COLD WAR LEGACY AND ITALY'S ROLE IN NATO

A large communist party (the Partito Comunista Italiano, or PCI) and a sig-nificant neutralist wing within the majority Christian Democratic Party made joining NATO in 1949 a controversial and divisive decision for Italy. During the early postwar years and even well into the 1970s, the position regarding Italy's role in NATO marked a fundamental difference between the parties in power and the opposition. Not until 1976 did the PCI officially change course by dropping its opposition to NATO, allowing, at last, a broad consensus within the government on the two cornerstones of Italian foreign policy—participation in NATO and participation in the European Community (now the European Union). The position on NATO was not unanimous, however. Some extreme leftists, as well as members of the right-wing party Movimento Sociale Italiano (MSI), remained uncompromisingly opposed to NATO. Consequently, making specific security commitments continued to be a controversial process.

Over time, the PCI became less concerned about questions of NATO's mandate and membership. It focused its critical review instead on Italy's specific role in NATO. It was in this vein that the 1982 debate over including Spain in NATO proved a low-key event:

- Ratification was expeditious. Only thirty-one members of Parliament took the floor during the formal debate sessions, demonstrating the minimal public interest in the issue.
- The majority (which included Christian Democrats, Socialists, and three minor centrist parties) was also supported by the right-wing opposition party MSI.
- The PCI voted against ratification, arguing that Spain's accession would dangerously alter the East-West strategic balance and heighten tension in the Mediterranean area. But the party's anti-enlargement campaign was relatively muted.

Italian consensus about NATO was reaffirmed in the aftermath of the Cold War, in part because of PCI's transformation into a social-democratic party, the Partito Democratico della Sinistra (PDS). But this consensus remained rather thin. The split between the left wing of the former PCI and the mainstream of the PDS, with the ensuing creation of the Refounded Communists in 1991, is testimony to the persistence of anti-NATO feelings and Italian fears of U.S. hegemony concerning European affairs. Many see the alliance as nothing more than a military-political vehicle of U.S. interests and policies.

The evolution of NATO remained a marginal issue in Italian politics in the years leading up to the Western intervention in Bosnia. A general understanding emerged that the nature of the alliance was undergoing a process of profound adjustment in the context of Euro-Atlantic and pan-European "interlocking institutions." Judgment on NATO was to be reserved until after this transformation was complete.

By the mid-1990s, Italians were gradually overcoming the Cold War mentality, but the contours of a new consensus on foreign policy, in general, and on NATO, in particular, were far from clear. The reduced level of controversy over NATO in the 1990s was due largely to the initial expectation, or unspoken assumption, that the "new NATO" would play a quiet role as the background security provider in a more cooperative and essentially benign European environment within the post-Soviet era. The dissolution of Yugoslavia, and the Bosnian crisis in particular, however, came as a shock that forced Italy to reassess its place in a NATO-centered security system.

THE BOSNIAN EXPERIENCE: NATO AS CRISIS MANAGER AND ITALY'S "EXCLUSION SYNDROME"

The bloody, prolonged conflict in Bosnia forced Italy into a new type of domestic debate, one that produced unusual alignments. Essentially, the debate pitted interventionists against anti-interventionists. "Wilsonian activists" (found both in left-wing and centrist parties, including *Forza Italia*) challenged old-style pacifists (both from the Catholic and the Communist tradition), who opposed any form of military intervention. Within the *realpolitik* group, advocates of active multilateralism, who supported forceful diplomacy when it was based on broad democratic coalitions, clashed with "neonationalists," who favored military interventions only when major Italian interests were at stake.

Positions on whether NATO should intervene in Bosnia (under a UN Security Council mandate) cut across all traditional political alignments and posed dilemmas for most major political leaders. The fluidity and instability of post–Cold War domestic alignments had already been demonstrated during the 1991 Gulf War, also conducted under the aegis of the United Nations. In that operation, important sectors of the Catholic parties adopted an anti-interventionist stance, under the umbrella of the Vatican's criticisms. The PCI, which was then deeply embroiled in its own painful transition to a post-Communist identity, also joined the anti-interventionist camp. Discussions about policy toward Bosnia proved to be similarly divisive.

The years from 1994 to 1996 were a formative period for the new politics of foreign policy in Italy. Both the center-right government headed by Silvio Berlusconi and the successive center-left coalitions resolved to support the UN-mandated Implementation Forces (IFOR; and later the Stabilization Forces, SFOR) operations in Bosnia. Support in Italy for multinational operations broadened, due to geopolitical interests, humanitarian considerations, international status, and a distinct "exclusion syndrome" from which Italy had been suffering. With regard to geopolitical interests, a violent conflict near the Adriatic coast in the heart of southeastern Europe, with the possible consequence of refugees moving toward adjacent areas, clearly touched Italian interests. As to the humanitarian justification for some form of intervention, the combination of massive and protracted human rights violations and the United Nations mandate for NATO action constituted a strong basis for Italian participation.

The exclusion syndrome is a more complex phenomenon. The first manifestation of this phenomenon resulted from the initial exclusion of Italy from NATO's Contact Group on the former Yugoslavia, established in 1994. This exclusion came as a surprise and was resented deeply in diplomatic circles. The perception of Italian marginalization was more insulting because Italy had expressed its willingness to allow use of its military bases and national airspace in the air campaign against Serbian targets in Bosnia, accepting the significant financial, logistical, and political costs that accompanied such a policy. But Italy was not satisfied to play the role of NATO's unsinkable aircraft carrier and logistical rearguard without participating in the de facto decisionmaking body, the Contact Group.

Foreign Minister Susanna Agnelli's September 1995 announcement that Italy would deny the use of its bases for new missions in Bosnia by the F-117 "stealth" bombers was a response—in practice, if not officially—to the continuing exclusion of Italy from the Contact Group. While reiterating its official support for a NATO-led air campaign, the Italian government stated that any new commitments regarding the F-117s would require a review of Italy's role at the negotiating table, which Italian leaders considered to be "not commensurate" with its overall contribution to the alliance. Thus, although Rome maintained relatively smooth relations with the United States, the leader of the Western coalition, Italy did exert unusually strong diplomatic pressure to encourage its inclusion in decisionmaking. Italy finally joined the Contact Group in 1996, during the implementation stage of the Dayton agreements.

Although NATO's role in Bosnia during 1995 and 1996 triggered a determined Italian effort to join the leading group at the core of the Western coalition, broader considerations also contributed to Italy's newly assertive position on Euro-Atlantic security issues. Fears of being relegated to a second-rank position in Europe were heightened by the possibility of Italy's exclusion from the European Monetary Union. Concerns about Italy's position were further compounded by the diminished utility of Italy's traditional tactic of dealing with a setback in progress in European affairs by strengthening its ties to the United States, or "playing the American card."

Regardless of its tactics within the alliance, Italy's lingering uncertainty about the future of the European Common Foreign and Security Policy (CFSP) and the European Security and Defense Initiative (ESDI) sustains the country's belief that NATO should remain the main forum for institutionalized political-military cooperation within Europe and between Europe and the United States.

Leaders in Italy continue to view NATO as the primary guarantor of Italy's relevance to strategic decisions on the evolution of European security.

The policy dilemmas in Italy generated by the Bosnian experience produced two divergent conclusions; these related to long-term strategy but ultimately affected the ratification of NATO enlargement by Italy:

- NATO should remain the cornerstone of crisis and security management in Europe, undertaking out-of-area operations, when necessary, in a peace-supporting role. However, this role should be closely tied to specific UN Security Council mandates.[3]
- In order to exercise significant influence on decisionmaking in the alliance, Italy can no longer play a passive or simply reactive role. The country must be directly involved in the management of those crises that affect its interests to the east and southeast, and its involvement must be within the context of NATO, which may mean relegating the United Nations to a secondary position.

Italy seems to have come full circle regarding the requirements of multilateralism in the security field, but officials need to reconcile the operational centrality of NATO and the legitimizing role of the United Nations in such operations. This will demand of Italy a serious commitment to NATO reform, including support for the enlargement process as part and parcel of the adaptation of the alliance to today's world.

Fears of exclusion from the formative process of a new Euro-Atlantic security arrangement (centered on NATO but adapted to post–Cold War requirements) necessarily influence Italy's position. As Foreign Minister Lamberto Dini openly stated in a letter to the House Foreign Affairs Committee in February 1997,

> Our country has so far succeeded in placing itself at the core of decision-making mechanisms on security in Europe, thus ensuring protection against its geo-strategically exposed position. . . . The memory of our initial exclusion from the Contact Group for the former Yugoslavia is still vivid, and could be interpreted as a concrete harbinger of a marginalization of Italy from those decision-making fora to which . . . she has a right to belong.[4]

Dini then specifically questioned a proposal put forth just days before by French President Jacques Chirac encouraging a summit on NATO-Russia relations to include France, Germany, Great Britain, the United States, and Russia. The foreign minister said that it entailed a serious risk "for inter-allied cohesion and solidarity and, above all, for Italy, which could be excluded, *de facto*, from a decision-making process that concerns her in a most delicate dimension, that of her defense and security."[5]

The frustration evident in such official statements must be put in the context of Italy's uneasy predicament, as a country geopolitically exposed to Balkan instability, under growing pressure from its allies to serve as a staging area for military operations along a broad southeastern front, and yet unsure of its role inside the security "elites" of the Euro-Atlantic standing coalition.

In sum, the debate on NATO enlargement in 1996 and 1997 can best be understood in light of the exclusion syndrome. This, added to Italy's initial reservations, ensured that Parliament would accept expansion but would do so unenthusiastically. This was probably the last important policy deliberation based on the underlying assumptions of a benign period in European security, with NATO's commitment to Bosnia being considered the exception rather than the rule. Kosovo would soon shatter those assumptions.

ITALIAN INTERESTS AND THE EVOLUTION OF THE ENLARGEMENT ISSUE

Italy was not the only European ally surprised by the Clinton administration's sudden acceleration of the enlargement process.[6] Italian officials welcomed the Partnership for Peace (PfP) initiative announced at the January 1994 Brussels Atlantic Council meeting, as did a vast majority of the foreign policy establishment, precisely because of its cautious approach in adapting NATO to the post–Cold War era. The Partnership for Peace program was accepted positively not as a step toward enlargement but, rather, as a way to postpone enlargement. Prime Minister Carlo Ciampi noted that enlargement at that stage would institutionalize existing tensions between the West and Russia, whereas PfP would encourage dialogue throughout this region. Other officials were more specific in their support for the decision not to grant the key "Article V" guarantee to any additional countries, stating that this approach would safeguard "Europe's overall unity" and allow Russia time to come to terms with its historical "demons"—a reference to Russian fears of encirclement and isolation.[7] The measured pace of NATO changes signaled by PfP soon gave way to a heightened momentum.

The primary reason for Italy's favorable attitude toward Partnership for Peace was the widespread desire to provide the European Union with the time, the opportunity, and a secure environment to define the scope and assess the implications of its own enlargement plans. When the pace of the European Union enlargement turned out to be slower than expected, it was believed that the pace of NATO expansion could also be adjusted in order to avoid any major differences in membership between the two organizations.[8] A series of papers produced by the Defense Ministry for internal circulation in 1995 demonstrate this belief. Defense officials argued that a link should be established between NATO's eventual enlargement and the expansion of the European Union—a link producing the highest possible degree of coherence, if not full "harmonization."

Just as importantly, the Defense Ministry strongly advocated the creation of a regional "niche" in southeastern Europe in which Italian leadership could be exercised on the issues of greatest concern for the country. The niche would be developed through a strong political and economic presence, and it would be designed primarily to hedge against the risk of a gradual enlargement of the EU, although it would also be a valuable addition to both NATO and the European Union. Italian officials singled out Albania, Slovenia, Croatia, Romania, Bulgaria, and Hungary as the states that should be included.

One tangible result of this policy was the trilateral agreement reached among Italy, Hungary, and Slovenia in October 1996 regarding the establishment of a multinational light-infantry brigade. This was seen as a potential core of broader forms of military-security integration in this region and, increasingly, in the Balkans. The agreement was also seen as a way to compensate Slovenia for the likely delay in its accession to NATO.

Italy's subregional diplomatic initiatives intensified following the acceleration of NATO's enlargement process and the slowdown of European Union enlargement. The situation also resulted in a renewed emphasis on preexisting diplomatic initiatives, such as the "Central European Initiative," originally designed during the late 1980s to counterbalance German influence in the area and to protect Italian commercial interests in Central and Eastern Europe. But the idea of subregional groups to the southeast took on a special significance once it became clear that the first round of NATO enlargement was imminent and would focus exclusively on Central Europe—with the possible, but not likely, addition of Slovenia and Romania.

Another crucial interest behind Italy's approach to the enlargement issue is the belief that NATO's security functions should be "omnidirectional" (the term adopted by the Italian Foreign Ministry), thus requiring a strong Mediterranean dimension. In this view, the alliance would be the core of a European security system capable of maintaining stability in all directions, to the south as well as to the east. The Partnership for Peace program reflected this perspective, making NATO's periphery into a relatively unitary strategic area. As such, the plan was well suited to address some of Italy's concerns, whereas a selective enlargement of NATO membership would inevitably generate divisions and a gradation of security commitments.[9]

Italy's initial insistence that the role of the Southern Flank should not be minimized in the future was primarily an attempt to slow down an enlargement that was focused on Central Europe. The approach was intended as a hedging strategy, designed by Italy to help it deal with uncertain developments. Enlargement was not the answer to the quest for increased security and stability in the broader Mediterranean region. However, once the "Central European option" on enlargement became alliance policy, and in the wake of the critical phase of the Bosnian crisis, Italian interests required a new approach. It became necessary to support credible candidates for membership from southeastern Europe, if only as an exercise in "damage control." Italy adapted its policy and effectively shifted its goal from slow enlargement to a wider and more inclusive expansion of the alliance.

Consequently, a set of interests were outlined to guide Italian foreign and security policy during the transition to the "active" stage of NATO enlargement, which coincided with a deepening of NATO's involvement in southeastern Europe.

First, the Mediterranean issue will remain high on Italy's foreign policy agenda, whatever the fate of NATO's evolution. A continued effort to emphasize the importance of NATO's old Southern Flank for Europe figures prominently among Italy's priorities and acquired a new meaning in the 1990s, given the existence of an "arc of crisis" stretching from the Balkans to the eastern Mediterranean. This is a lasting source of risk and instability for the entire European continent—as well as for traditional U.S. interests—and is the primary reason that Italy is a key actor within NATO.

Throughout the 1990s, Italian policymakers were torn between the temptation to rely even more than in the past on the "American connection"—represented by the U.S. Sixth Fleet based in Naples—and the aspiration to foster a more active role for Europe in Mediterranean affairs. The dilemma has reached its full complexity in the dispute between France and the United States over NATO's Allied Forces South (AFSOUTH) command in Naples. Italy supports in principle the idea of a shift in NATO commands to a more visible European presence; however, when forced to choose between a French commander in Naples and the current arrangement in which a U.S. commander is joined with an Italian deputy, Italy has consistently chosen the U.S. presence. French insistence that the top AFSOUTH post be assigned to rotating European commanders failed to win Italy's support primarily because of extreme Italian sensitivity to the role of the U.S. Sixth Fleet but also because of France's unilateral effort to address such a thorny issue. As Foreign Minister Dini explained in February 1997, "In view of the importance [of the Sixth Fleet] for the Mediterranean, we believe that the redefinition of commands throughout Europe should not involve AFSOUTH."[10] The unspoken part of this argument is that, due to its delicate geopolitical position, Italy will not go along with "Europeanization" schemes that do not offer specific assurances regarding what Italy gets in return for a relative loosening of the traditional U.S. ties in the Mediterranean theater.

Italy acts, on the one hand, out of a desire to strengthen the European foundation of the alliance and, on the other hand, out of a wish to find a proper balance between a more autonomous "Europe" and a substantial U.S. presence in the Mediterranean. The problem is compounded by the U.S. attitude toward "rogue states" (including Libya, Iraq, and Iran) nearby Italy. Italy must maintain a difficult balance, often dissociating itself from U.S. initiatives in the area (witness the careful position taken on the occasion of the U.S. air raids against Iraq in December 1998) while keeping a strong security and defense relationship with Washington—both in the context of NATO and at the bilateral level.

Italy's second major interest regarding NATO enlargement has been the long-awaited internal reform of the alliance, with special attention to the "Europeanization" process. The debate on enlargement inevitably raised the issue of the European role in NATO, which the allies had agreed was going to increase in response to the new security conditions. Indeed, the way in which this decision is implemented will have a major influence on the future shape of the alliance. Italy's acceptance of enlargement has been predicated on the expectation of a more equitable distribution of responsibilities between the two sides of the Atlantic. This viewpoint has not changed, and the initial reservations about enlargement remain, in part because of Italy's recognition of the complexity and ambiguity of the "Europeanization" process.

Even with the compromise that the future European Security and Defense Initiative could develop only in the context of NATO, the specific workings of the ESDI were undefined at the time of the first enlargement decision. Therefore, the alliance was set to expand eastward without any clear and formal agreement among the old members on how to achieve the planned upgrade of the European contribution to and responsibility within the alliance.

NATO's response to the Albanian crisis of early 1997 reinforced the perception of a dangerous lag in NATO's ability to adjust to new circumstances. The virtual collapse of Albania's economic system and the ensuing chaos in that country prodded an Italian-led intervention under United Nations auspices (named the Alba Operation), which was conducted by a small "coalition of the willing," including France, but without any participation by the United States or, for that matter, Britain or Germany.[11] The nature of the operation—essentially a "humanitarian-plus" intervention—together with its small size could account for the lack of any direct NATO involvement. Less acceptable to Italy was German and British opposition to any European Union or Western European Union role, at least in the early stages of the operation. This circumstance did not augur well for the future of ESDI or a Common Foreign and Security Policy of the European Union. At the same time, officials in the United States were debating the desirability of continued participation in the SFOR mission in Bosnia. The situation in southeastern Europe seemed to Italy to be one of persistent instability and uncertainty, with disagreements among NATO allies about whether to address the issue.

Important aspects of this problem are indivisible from the Mediterranean issues. Both solutions require the solving of an almost existential problem: how to reconcile the continuing relevance of the trans-Atlantic link with a renewed commitment to the European Union as the key to Europe's future. In this respect, events in the Balkans and the Mediterranean Basin in the course of 1996–1997 did nothing to raise Italy's confidence in an effective and institutionalized division of labor between the Europeans and the United States.

Italy's third major interest has been to incorporate Russia as a full participant in the evolving Euro-Atlantic security system. This system should not just be "open" in terms of future membership but also should be sufficiently flexible to incorporate Russia into a broader framework of consultation and cooperation.

In evaluating this interest Italian officials consider both the intrinsic value of a pan-European security structure and its usefulness in countering the recurring assumption of a five-power concert that would exclude Italy. Commercial considerations also play a significant role: Italian businesses have developed substantial economic stakes in Russia in recent years, and officials have a keen interest in cultivating these economic ties.

Foreign Minister Dini articulated Italy's position on the occasion of his meeting with U.S. Secretary of State Madeleine Albright in February 1997: "We believe such enlargement [of NATO], which will be decided by the NATO countries themselves, will also have to take place after we find a *modus vivendi*, an understanding of the nature of the close discussions and relations between NATO and Russia."[12] The foreign minister made a similar point a few days later in Moscow: "The enlargement of NATO is possible only with Russia's consent and not against Russia's will."[13] The explicit recognition of Moscow's role—almost to the point of granting Russia a veto power over NATO's decisions—arose from a background of other statements by NATO and U.S. officials. This may explain why the formal agreement establishing the NATO-Russia Permanent Joint Council was saluted in Rome as vindication for a distinctive Italian approach. Indeed, Italian diplomatic efforts toward Russia were so overt as to cause some friction between Italy and the Central European NATO candidates. The Polish government, in particular, complained about Italy's "Russia-first" attitude until officials in Rome offered Polish President Aleksander Kwaśniewski explicit assurances that Italy would fully support Poland's application.

Italy's fourth interest has been the likely composition of NATO after the first round of enlargement negotiations. Until the Madrid summit of July 1997, the Prodi government hoped to get at least one of its two "special candidates," namely Slovenia, included as one of the first-round invitees into NATO. Had this goal been achieved, Italy would have supported a relatively long "pause for reflection" in the enlargement process. Before the decisive Madrid summit, Defense Minister Beniamino Andreatta said that Italy "favors

a broader enlargement and a process that should not consist of a rapid suc-
cession of enlargements."[14] This statement bespeaks both a concern for the
"left-out" countries and a certain uneasiness about an unpredictable open-
ended expansion process.

Confronted with the determination of key NATO allies to proceed with
enlargement despite official Russian opposition, and with the likely rejection
of both Slovenia and Romania as new members, Rome once again adopted a
fall-back policy of damage control. This entailed insisting on the fullest possible Russian involvement in allied discussions of relevant security issues as
well as cultivating closer relations with the "left-out" countries in southeastern Europe. Indeed, Italian officials considered the specific reference to
Romania and Slovenia in the final communiqué of the Madrid summit to be a
partial diplomatic victory; consequently, they offered tempered but uncondi-
tional support for the "open-door" policy, at least as a matter of principle.

It should be noted that the seriousness of Italy's support for Slovenia's
application to NATO has been questioned by some observers, given Italy's
choice essentially to link Slovenia and Romania and propose their accession
as a package. This approach was the result of an arrangement with France, but
not only did it fail to be persuasive at the Madrid summit, it also furthered the
impression in Washington that the Europeans were engaging in parochial calculations and rather cynical deals. Given this failed strategy, perhaps the
counterproductive nature of the "five-country format" for the first round of
enlargement could have been anticipated; Slovenia by itself stood a slightly
better chance.[15] In hindsight, this seems an obvious case to make, and it lends
credibility to the thesis of a half-hearted pro-Slovenia effort in Rome.

TOWARD UNENTHUSIASTIC RATIFICATION

Italy initially regarded a slow-moving enlargement of NATO (based on Partnership for Peace as a clearinghouse) as the best option, especially when considered in connection with the enlargement of the European Union. The guiding assumption was that the most logical and effective strategy for
establishing the long-term stabilization of Central and Eastern Europe would
be the gradual enlargement of the EU, instead of a selective and controversial
extension of security guarantees through NATO.

Prior to parliamentary ratification, officials repeatedly made this argument; in fact it dominated the NATO discussions in Italy. The chairman of the
House Foreign Affairs Committee, Achille Occhetto, declared that "the pro-
motion of economic development and the integration of new democracies do
not appear to be a task for the Atlantic Organization, but rather for the European Union," a view shared by the chairman of the Senate Foreign Affairs
Committee, GianGiacomo Migone.[16] Even more explicit was the position

taken by the deputy chairman of the Senate Committee, Saverio Porcari, of the right-wing Alleanza Nazionale, who argued in favor of an expansion of the European Union's borders prior to any NATO enlargement.[17]

These high-level statements notwithstanding, significant components of the foreign policy establishment, especially within the ranks of the professional bureaucracy, usually have been hostile to the idea of rapid enlargement of the EU. This already ambiguous situation was only worsened by the first round of NATO enlargement. The decisions on NATO expansion almost forced Italy to choose between a "non–European Union enlargement"—which would give NATO absolute primacy and further reduce the stabilizing potential of the EU—and a negotiation open to a broad group of aspirants. Germany reportedly advocated the latter course based on the "harmonization" thesis and called for the admission of only three countries (Poland, Hungary, and the Czech Republic) to both NATO and the EU. This approach, though, would have created a near-permanent club of "left outs," which had been precisely the main Italian objection to the strategy of NATO enlargement since at least 1993.

The other major objection to fast-track NATO enlargement had to do with Russian reactions. Here the Prodi government resolved to walk a fine line by arguing, in the words of Undersecretary of State for Foreign Affairs Piero Fassino, that the alliance should adopt a double-track policy: internal discussion among NATO members without external—that is, Russian—interference, and at the same time negotiations with Moscow to define the features of a "system of common security in Europe."[18] Several leading parliamentarians from both the majority and the opposition took a more assertive line. Chairman of the House Foreign Affairs Committee Occhetto concluded after a visit to Moscow that "the strategy of NATO enlargement is questionable and simply wrong on certain aspects."[19] Dario Rivolta, echoing criticism of the opposition Forza Italia, argued that "what is inappropriate is the mode and timing of enlargement," as they both fed Russian feelings of isolation.[20]

Foreign Minister Dini made his final statement before the vote on ratification by arguing that NATO enlargement was aimed at

- providing security for the most vulnerable countries in European history, which were applying for membership;
- setting the stage for further enlargements, on the basis of the "open-door" policy;
- avoiding a "renationalization" of security policies in Europe; and
- consolidating the Euro-American strategic link.

Dini also stated that, despite such ambitious goals, the enlargement process would be financially affordable, with limited costs for current members; would not be detrimental to relations with Russia; and would not be detrimental to a strengthened European role, as a larger number of European members in NATO would actually improve prospects for a common European defense.[21]

The foreign minister noted further that no member of the alliance had rejected the notion of "moving forward the frontiers of multilateral security." Ratification procedures had already been successfully completed in Canada, the United States, Germany, Greece, Norway, Denmark, Luxembourg, and Iceland—many of which were led by center-left governments.

Eventually, government assurances together with, above all, the understanding of the unpalatable repercussions of a negative vote proved sufficient to allow the ratification of the three accession protocols. The NATO decision was ratified by the Italian Parliament on 23 June 1998, with 310 votes in favor, 79 against, and 169 abstentions. Thanks to the unambiguously constructive role played on this occasion by the opposition—which refrained from threatening a mass abstention—it was unnecessary to ask for a vote of confidence on the ratification motion.

ITALIAN POLITICS AND THE RATIFICATION OF ENLARGEMENT

The center-left government had come to power in 1996 with an electoral platform that stated that "Italy will support a gradual expansion of NATO."[22] One of the main goals of the center-left coalition, led by the PDS, was to break down the old divisions between the political leaders, with their Atlanticist and anti-U.S. attitudes, and the public. The coalition continually stressed the growing role of the European component in the Euro-American alliance as well as the need to realize the full potential of the European Union as a long-term stabilizer. The medium-term adaptation of NATO was viewed within this greater context of Europe's global identity.

Of course, success in this project was far from assured, especially because the issue of enlargement ratification came to the fore in the wake of the experience of the Alba Operation, which had been a major embarrassment for the governing majority. The approval of the center-right opposition was required in order to launch the operation following the decision by the Refounded Communists to vote against a UN Security Council Resolution authorizing a "multinational protection force." On the one hand, it was clear to everyone that the coalition government was extremely vulnerable on foreign policy issues; on the other hand, the precedent of Alba demonstrated that uneasy bipartisanship could still prevail when important national interests were at stake.

Lingering ambiguity about the enlargement process limited the criticisms that could be launched against it. Financial concerns, for instance, played a minor role in the deliberations over ratification. This issue had been resolved at the alliance level—in part through the high-profile positions taken by both

Chancellor Helmut Kohl of Germany and President Chirac of France. Each leader explicitly advocated an essentially zero-cost first round. No serious attention was given to the prospect of an increase in the national defense budget as a consequence of NATO enlargement. Quite simply, the prospect was not even raised during the ratification debate. Like the other members of NATO also involved in the Euro project at the time, Italy considered compliance with the "Maastricht criteria" for economic convergence to be its foremost priority.

CONCLUSION

Just like the other European members of the alliance, Italy was confronted by a plan to enlarge NATO over which it could exercise little influence.[23] The possibility of expanding NATO eastward had been discussed seriously for some time, both in government circles and among opinion leaders. The tentative consensus resulting from that protracted debate was that enlargement would bring some benefit for Italy, but how the enlargement would be done would make all the difference. The principle of enlarging NATO was consistent with certain key pieces of Italian foreign policy—projecting stability to the east and southeast, reassuring a host of important EU applicants, and demonstrating the alliance's vitality—but the specific format of the enlargement process had to be crafted carefully. Even those opposed to or undecided about enlargement soon realized that Italy was in no position to forestall the process once it was set in motion by a determined U.S. government.

In hindsight, Italy's enlargement decision was just the harbinger of an open-ended and difficult debate—which is still under way—on Italy's role in the Euro-Atlantic security framework. In 1997 and 1998, Italian leaders did not take the opportunity to re-examine the ramifications of NATO in terms of long-range Italian interests. This second look could have been made in a relatively calm international context, rather than under the enormous pressures and complexities resulting from the subsequent military crisis in Kosovo. A more focused discussion of Italy's substantial interests in relation to NATO's actual functions would have clarified a number of issues, whatever the outcome of the specific enlargement debate.[24]

The chief reason for the lack of focus during the enlargement ratification debate can probably be found in the peculiar attitudes that still prevail among Italian leaders: "Instead of [favoring] critical support for NATO, [they are] divided into an official line of loyalty and various unofficial discourses of opposition."[25] That division was a result of the Cold War and its ideological underpinnings but remains relevant today, despite the changed international environment. The "exclusion syndrome" is the principal manifestation of the new challenges of the twenty-first century, as opposed to the Cold War challenges.

Overcoming this syndrome requires Italy to do everything possible to avoid being left outside the small core of European countries considered to be "significant powers" (a term that might be a reasonable successor to the more traditional but inapplicable notion of great powers). The significant powers in today's Europe are Great Britain, France, and Germany. Italy's fear of exclusion was a crucial element in the decision by the Massimo D'Alema government to support NATO's policy of "diplomacy backed by force" toward Belgrade regarding Kosovo in the spring of 1999.

Two years earlier, Italian officials had little choice but to ratify the enlargement decision taken by all sixteen NATO governments, especially in light of Italy's ambitions to be one of the significant powers. Supporting enlargement, after all, could be seen as a way to buy friends and perhaps clients on the cheap, by offering support for membership of this or that country in Central or Eastern Europe. This helps explain the low profile of the debate on Italian ratification of the first round of enlargement, as short-term financial costs would be kept at a minimum (on the basis of a broad Euro-American consensus), while longer-term risks could be simply dismissed as too distant and unlikely.

On the other hand, genuine concerns about the future of southeastern Europe and of Russia, coupled with a somewhat cynical appreciation of the stakes involved in the enlargement business, moved Italian political leaders to engage in a few substantial discussions during which the country's standing among the significant powers was a key consideration. What appeared to be a somewhat "virtual" debate by the time of ratification has now been transformed into a very real policy dilemma requiring hard choices. The enlarged alliance has been activated militarily on a massive scale against a sovereign country and its regime, just as NATO celebrated the first round of enlargement.

Italy's overall approach to the enlargement issue has been somewhat vindicated by recent events in the Balkans. It is hardly conceivable that NATO can play a constructive role in projecting stability beyond its frontiers unless a workable regional arrangement for stability is conceptualized, implemented, and enforced in the western Balkans. Italy's insistence that southeastern Europe should not be left out of NATO's plans, which previously was received with some skepticism even in European policy circles, is now simply a statement of the obvious.

NOTES

I wish to thank Marta Dassù, director of the Centro Studi di Politica Internazionale (CeSPI), for permission to draw extensively on a previous coauthored work on the same subject (published in the journal of the Istituto Affari Internazionali of Rome,

The International Spectator, July/December 1997). I am also grateful to the Center for Strategic and International Studies, Washington, D.C.—Dr. Simon Serfaty in particular—for offering an initial stimulus and a suitable opportunity to explore this issue in the course of 1997.

1. The Prodi government was a center-left coalition composed of the Partito Democratico della Sinistra (PDS, the former Italian Communist Party), the Partito Popolare Italiano (PPI, founded after the diaspora of the old Christian Democratic Party and representing largely its left wing), the Green Party, the movement of Lamberto Dini (the former prime minister and foreign minister in the government of Prodi and subsequently D'Alema), and other minor parties. The coalition is called the *Ulivo* [Olive Branch]. The opposition also is a coalition (called the *Polo delle Liberta'*), composed of *Forza Italia* (led by former Prime Minister Silvio Berlusconi), *Alleanza Nazionale* (the right-wing postfascist party), and other splinters of the former Christian Democrats. Prime Minister Romano Prodi, himself a Catholic centrist, was regarded almost as an outsider, although his ties with the Christian Democrats were known to everyone.

2. Even on the occasion of ratification of the Maastricht Treaty, parliamentary debate was oddly low-key, with few participants seemingly realizing the full significance of the treaty for EU integration and Italy's national policies.

3. The strict requirement of a specific UN Security Council mandate authorizing the use of force was somewhat relaxed under the D'Alema government through a process of pragmatic adjustments to the latest NATO out-of-area operation in Kosovo and Serbia. In an article that appeared in the *International Herald Tribune* on 22 January 1999, Prime Minister D'Alema stated that a key Italian interest is "[a] balanced solution to the question of providing international legitimacy to the Alliance's new functions in the so-called non-Art. V missions. This is a central requirement if NATO is to serve as one of the foundations of a more secure and just international order. A practical mechanism needs to be devised to guarantee the broadest possible level of legitimacy, in the spirit of the United Nations, while maintaining the Alliance's political and operational effectiveness" (8). This formulation has not resolved the issue, but it does show a deliberate attempt to develop a more mature and sophisticated view of multilateral security.

4. Foreign Minister Lamberto Dini, letter to the Chairman of the House Foreign Affairs Committee, made public on 12 February 1997 (*Giunte e Commissioni Parlamentari, 99, Resoconto*).

5. Ibid.

6. On the evolution of the enlargement policy, see Roberto Menotti, "U.S. Policy and NATO Enlargement: Clinton's 'Unspoken Agenda'—1993–1996," *International Politics* 36 (June 1999): 235–271.

7. ANSA Press Agency Report (Rome, 10 January 1994).

8. This basic evaluation would surface again during the parliamentary ratification debate in 1997.

9. The unique qualities of the Partnership for Peace framework are indirectly confirmed by the perplexity and even frustration with which the six Mediterranean "partners" have received NATO's Mediterranean Dialogue initiative, launched in December 1994 as a counterpart to Partnership for Peace. It can be argued that, as long as Partnership for Peace remained the key instrument developed by the alliance to open up new opportunities for cooperation with nonmembers in Europe and the former USSR, the Mediterranean Dialogue was a distinct and yet consistent and somehow comparable initiative. But once the enlargement process picked up speed, the relative usefulness of the dialogue was discredited.

10. U.S. Department of State, Office of the Spokesman, "Transcript of Press Briefing, Albright-Dini" (Rome, 16 February 1997).

11. Operation Alba involved about 6,000 troops and was conducted essentially by the "Club Med" of NATO and European Union countries: Italy, France, Spain, Portugal, Greece, and Turkey.

12. Office of the Spokesman, U.S. Department of State, "Press Briefing with Italian Foreign Minister Lamberto Dini" (Villa Madama, Rome, Italy, 16 February 1997). Available online at http://secretary.state.gov/www/statements/970216.html [accessed 24 January 2001].

13. "Foreign Minister Speaks Out on NATO" (Il Sole-24 Ore, 21 February 1997). Available online at http://www.ilsole24ore.com/.

14. Beniamino Andreatta, *Atti Parlamentari,* Camera die Deputati (11 February 1997).

15. See, for example: CeSPI, "L'Italia e l'allargamento dell'Unione Europea ai PECO" (paper prepared for internal circulation in the Italian Ministry of Foreign Affairs, April 1997).

16. Achille Occhetto, *Bollettino delle Giunte e Commissioni Parlamentari,* Camera die Deputati, XIII Legislatura, (14 January 1997): 17. See also Senator GianGiacomo Migone, Senate Foreign Affairs Committee, interview by Roberto Menotti (4 April 1997).

17. Saverio Porcari, "The European Union and NATO" (speech given at the Società Italiana per l'Organizzazione Internazionale, Rome, 4 April 1997).

18. Undersecretary Fassino, L'Unita', interview by Roberto Menotti (6 April 1997): 2.

19. "Mistakes in NATO Enlargement," *Corriere della Sera,* 5 April 1997: 5.

20. *La Stampa,* 5 April 1997: 2.

21. Lamberto Dini (speech given at the House, 22 June 1997). Available online at http://www.esteri.it/notizie/discorsi/d220698i.htm.

22. Quoted in *Italy Daily,* 24 June 1998: 2.

23. Germany was a possible exception. Earlier, it had acted as a stimulus in breaking a political-bureaucratic stalemate in Washington on NATO's future. See Roberto Menotti, "U.S. Policy and NATO Enlargement: Clinton's 'Unspoken Agenda'— 1993–1996," on the origins of the enlargement policy.

24. For example, a more focused debate could have shown that the Refounded Communists (RC) can hardly call for the dissolution of NATO while also demanding that massive military means should be promptly mobilized in response to impending humanitarian crises. Following NATO's air campaign against the Federal Republic of Yugoslavia that began in late March 1999, the RC has consistently refrained from calling for the dissolution of NATO precisely because of the alliance's potential role as a kind of emergency military arm of the United Nations—therefore insisting that a specific UN Security Council mandate is always indispensable for any military operations.

25. Patrick McCarthy, "D'Alema and the System," *Italy Daily,* 11 May 1999: 2. The quotation is from an opinion piece written during the Kosovo intervention and refers to the D'Alema government that succeeded the Prodi government. The argument applies to any center-left coalition, however.

PART 2
Securing New Realities

7

Poland: Returning to Europe

MARCIN ANDRZEJ PIOTROWSKI AND ARTHUR R. RACHWALD

The Round Table negotiations that took place in 1989 in Poland between the Communist Party and the Solidarity Party initiated political changes that have been accompanied by a revolution in geopolitics. Although the Round Table guaranteed post-Communists and their allies a majority in the lower chamber of Parliament, the Sejm, Solidarity took almost all of the seats in the new Senate. The first non-Communist cabinet since 1945 was thereby formed.[1]

Poland was in the midst of a catastrophic economic crisis when the cabinet of Tadeusz Mazowiecki took power. Although short-lived, this cabinet rapidly made permanent changes. Poland was in need of not only internal reforms, however, but solid foundations for its international security as well. In the meantime, the Solidarity Party, which had been internally fragmented, was consolidated after only a few years. Krzysztof Skubiszewski was the minister of foreign affairs in the Mazowiecki cabinet and retained this head diplomatic position for the next three cabinets during a period of turbulent changes in the international environment. As Poland gained independence from the Warsaw Pact structures, it gave priority to its relationships with the United States, France, and Germany, which was considered a strategic partner in the mission to integrate with Western Europe. Polish politicians recognized that NATO guarantees could provide Poland with a solid base for its security, but such goals seemed somewhat unrealistic. Until this point, Poland's relations with NATO had been limited to meetings in its North Atlantic Cooperation Council (NACC). Moreover, Soviet (and later, Russian) troops remained within Poland's borders (although the troops slowly have withdrawn since 1993). The bloody war in the former Yugoslavia and the division of Czechoslovakia demonstrated that Eastern and Central Europe were still in a state of flux, a condition that complicated Polish efforts to foster regional structures to facilitate future integration with the West.[2]

President Lech Walesa and the next two Solidarity cabinets also made regional relations a priority, pursuing international treaties and regulatory agreements with Poland's new neighbors. The new map of Europe and the collapse of communism created a "space" between the more integrated Western Europe and the now-disintegrated Soviet Union, often referred to in Poland as "the vacuum of security" or "the grey zone of security." With the collapse of the Soviet Union, Poland had to define clearly its national security interests and its strategic goals. Four neighbors had taken the place of a superpower, and access to NATO increasingly seemed a realistic goal in Warsaw. Accordingly, three years after the collapse of communism, President Walesa recommended an elaboration of the national security strategy with an eye toward integrating Poland into existing European and Atlantic structures.

Jan Olszewski's subsequent cabinet was short lived and had a tumultuous relationship with the president, but, in a document issued on 21 December 1991, Olszewski did declare officially his desire for Poland's membership in NATO. It was his belief that deeper ties to the United States could help bring about membership in NATO for Central European countries. NATO membership, he and others argued, would in turn lead to Poland's membership in the European Union.[3]

Like President Walesa, the next premier, Hanna Suchocka, endorsed this new defense strategy, stating that "Poland's membership in NATO . . . is one of the strategic goals of our foreign policy."[4] A series of documents that regulated and guided this defense policy in the transitional period stated that Poland did not recognize any specific state as a foe or a direct threat but also that the lack of formal Polish allies was a serious security concern, especially given the disturbances that had arisen in the region since the collapse of the USSR.

On 17 September 1993, President Walesa and Minister of Defense Janusz Onyszkiewicz sent to Brussels the official declaration of Poland's desire to join NATO. The leading parties supported this goal as a means of achieving national security. The completion of the withdrawal of Russian troops from Poland, together with Russian President Boris Yeltsin's declaration that Russia would not be opposed to Poland's strategic choice, bolstered Poland's confidence that the pursuit of NATO membership was the best course for its security policy.[5] NATO greeted Poland's declaration with an ambiguous reply, a move that unintentionally raised serious questions about the nature of civil-military relations in Poland. General Tadeusz Wilecki, the chief of the General Staff, publicly advocated the "defense-in-all-directions" strategy and opposed parliamentary control or influence over military issues.

The success of the left-wing coalition of the Democratic Left Alliance (SLD) and the Polish Peasant Party (PSL) further challenged governmental authority. The SLD-PSL opposed the president—an opposition that continued

until the end of Walesa's presidency in 1995. Walesa retained his highly recognized role in the international arena, however. The minister of foreign
affairs was a presidential ally, further limiting what SLD-PSL cabinets could
do to change the direction of security policy, especially regarding NATO.[6]
During this period, Minister Andrzej Olechowski laid out seven propositions
to guide Polish foreign policy:

1. A U.S. presence in Europe is key to Poland's security.
2. The security vacuum in Central Europe must be filled.
3. Poland must be anchored in Western institutions, including NATO,
   the Western European Union (WEU), and the European Union (EU).
4. Polish participation in NATO's Partnership for Peace program must
   be a process leading to integration with NATO.
5. Poland would be an asset as a NATO member, not a detriment.
6. A democratic Russia would bolster the European security system.
7. NATO and Western Europe, in general, need special relations with
   Russia and Ukraine.[7]

Both the SLD-PSL coalition and the opposition generally accepted these
points, though this agreement did not lead to total consensus on Poland's foreign policies. Controversies between the cabinet and the opposition arose frequently, especially regarding the army and diplomatic tactics in economic
relations with Russia.[8] Despite the controversies, Walesa continued to work
with the foreign ministers—first Olechowski, and then Wladyslaw Bartoszewski—toward the goal of inclusion in NATO. The president would
express publicly his disappointment at the modest range of the Partnership for
Peace program, and the ministers of foreign affairs would spearhead negotiations in Brussels regarding the details of integration.

Polish foreign policy helped lower the population's anxiety about
national security. In 1991 two-thirds of the Polish people believed that threats
to the state's independence existed, while from 1994 to 1996, almost two-
thirds believed no such threats loomed. Three different polls disclosed public
confidence about the intentions of Poland's neighboring countries. In a March
1992 focus group, a majority of participants stated that they did not see a real
threat of military aggression against Poland and gave a positive assessment of
the principles governing diplomacy and the durability of territorial borders
with Ukraine, Belarus, Lithuania, and Russia.

The Polish people remained anxious, though, about the prospect of German economic domination in Europe and about the direction and possible consequences of Russian relations with newly independent states.[9] In 1993 public
opinion polls, Poles cited Germany (58 percent) and Russia (33 percent) as the
states they thought to be political threats.[10] By 1998 concerns had shifted.

Cited as potential threats were Russia (71 percent), Germany (17 percent), and Ukraine (11 percent).[11] Poles favored a strategic partnership with Germany and Ukraine and perceived potential threats as nonmilitary, consistent with concerns raised by tragic experiences of the past.[12] Still, however, a prolonged crisis in Russia remained a significant concern of the Polish people.[13]

FROM CONTINUATION TO INTEGRATION: THE POLICIES OF CIMOSZEWICZ'S CABINET

With the dismissal of Premier Oleksy's cabinet (SLD) and the success of Aleksander Kwaśniewski (former leader of SLD) in the presidential election in 1995, some of the political leaders in Solidarity feared that the new ministers of foreign affairs and of national defense, Dariusz Rosati (SLD) and Stanislaw Dobrzański (PSL) would not be capable of conducting negotiations with NATO.[14] The cabinet of Premier Włodzimierz Cimoszewicz created new institutions for negotiation to make sure that Poland's relationship with NATO continued to be fostered. President Kwaśniewski, meanwhile, actively lobbied leaders of NATO countries to supplement the lackluster diplomacy of his ministers.[15] The behavior of ministers and the fact that these issues were discussed in public debates during the parliamentary campaign of 1997 may create the impression that there was only a weak consensus about NATO, but, in actuality, none of Poland's political parties questioned the matter of accession.[16] Indeed, support for NATO grew during this period, which was notable for efforts to clarify the state's constitution in terms of where responsibility for defense policy lay in the government.

The center-right parties derived from Solidarity—the Union of Liberty (UW) and the Electoral Action-Solidarity (AWS)—were hugely successful in the elections to the Sejm and the Senate in 1997. These elections ushered in a group of pro-NATO officials from UW and AWS, many of whom had advocated Poland's access to NATO in the early 1990s and then went on to direct parliamentary commissions or pro-Atlantic nongovernmental organizations (NGOs).[17]

The new political leaders also recognized the necessity of resolving unfinished issues, including the potential military service of Polish soldiers abroad. The law concerning the use of the Polish army abroad had been provisional and was approved after Bronislaw Geremek declared his desire to send some units to the Persian Gulf; it passed with objections.[18] The Sejm and the Senate passed a new law without any reservations at the end of 1998. According to this law, the Polish army would be used abroad in operations following from international agreements and other allied obligations, such as military training, exercises, and rescue; humanitarian efforts; or counterterrorist operations. Jerzy Szmajdziński (SLD), vice chairman of the Sejm's Commission of National Defense, suggested that Parliament would support government decisions by special statements, but he also noted that decisions about support for the alliance should not be subject to long disputes in the chambers of Parliament.[19] The government also agreed to provide extra payment to those soldiers serving in "hot-spots."[20] Moreover, the cabinet of UW-AWS has been working on the implementation of reforms within special services and the armed forces, which have been the subject of contentious debate since 1989.[21]

MILITARY OBSTACLES TO NATO INTEGRATION

After 1989, Poland cut deeply its military expenditures, leading to a growing technological gap between Poland's military and those of NATO members—visible even after Poland began to increase the efficiency of its forces, making broad reductions, eliminating an outdated military doctrine, and adapting the armed forces to deal with small conflicts and crises.[22] The goal of Polish political and military leaders was to maintain the best armaments and the best people in order to insure that Poland could defend itself, if necessary. The main goal has been a more mobile army, capable of defending Poland's territory during a period of adaptation to the character of Western armed forces.[23] Pursuit of this goal required changes in the form and structures of military service. Ground forces were reassigned to operational forces and territorial defense units. Rocket and flying units were integrated within the forces of air defense. The amphibious units of the navy, meanwhile, were liquidated.[24]

The vice minister of defense in the SLD-PSL cabinets, Andrzej Karkoszka, helped lead this reorganization and modernization effort. He focused on interoperability needs and the compatibility of the Polish army with NATO standards. He cited the needs for improved communication between Polish and NATO headquarters and commands; modification of infrastructure and logistics; modernization of air defense; and purchase of new radar, communications, and airborne warning and control systems.[25] The estimated costs of this reorganization varied from analysis to analysis. The Polish General Staff initially estimated that the cost of full integration and compatibility through the year 2010 would be between Zl 110 billion and Zl 220 billion (110–220 billion złoty, between approximately U.S.$31.5 and U.S.$63 billion), while interoperability would cost another Zl 8 billion to Zl 10 billion (or between U.S.$2 billion and U.S.$3 billion).[26] According to other estimates, a modest military budget equal to less than 3 percent of the gross domestic product would allow for full integration in the long run, with a low share of cost for interoperability.[27] During this time, the SLD-PSL cabinet rarely presented cost estimates, but one SLD ally predicted that interoperability would cost between U.S.$100 million and U.S.$150 million per year.

The Euro-Atlantic Association (SEA), an NGO known to reflect Polish public opinion, released its own report on the cost of the military transformation. The SEA criticized the scale of defense options and the methodology used by the U.S. Congressional Budget Office (CBO) and the RAND Corporation to determine cost estimates of this process. SEA cited the need for separate consideration of the direct and indirect costs of NATO membership. The direct costs of integration—compatibility and contribution to the alliance budget—would cost Polish taxpayers Zl 3.09 billion (U.S.$1.26 billion), almost Zl 206 million (U.S.$84 million) annually, equaling almost 4 percent of the yearly budget of the Polish Ministry of Defense. Indirect costs, notably the gradual modernization of the army and the nonmilitary infrastructure, would total more than 20–23 percent of the annual ministry budget.[28]

Another report, prepared by Minister Jerzy Kropiwnicki (AWS) and the Governmental Center for Strategic Studies (RCSS), focused on the nonmilitary aspects of integration and potential Polish profits from integration and as a result produced cost estimates higher than those in the SEA report. Minister Kropiwnicki stated that quicker achievement of compatibility and modernization would require a military budget of 4.5 percent of the Polish gross domestic product.[29] But the official report about integration, prepared by the Ministry of Defense, stated that contributing the common funds to NATO, maintaining Polish personnel in alliance headquarters, and achieving a minimal level of interoperability (total direct costs) would cost Polish taxpayers Zl 9.6 billion (U.S.$3 billion) for the period between 1998 and 2010, 5 percent of the ministry budget, while the costs of modernization and full interoperability would be another Zl 28.42 billion (U.S.$8.3 billion). After Jerzy Buzek became prime minister in 1997, his cabinet estimated that direct costs for Poland would amount to U.S.$50 million per year, and it was this estimate that was included in the ratification law.[30] These varying estimates seemed to have no influence on public opinion, according to which Polish citizens favored NATO membership, even if it meant higher costs.[31]

During the 1997 campaign for the Sejm, Polish newspapers brought up again the issues of army modernization and restructuring. Just before the NATO summit in Madrid, the opposition and the media offered Cimoszewicz's cabinet universal criticism for the delay in achieving military reforms.[32] Simultaneously, a majority of political leaders called for increased professionalism in the army and its adaptation to NATO standards as well as for a period of universal military service shorter than eighteen months.[33]

The outgoing SLD-PSL cabinet approved the Governmental Program of Modernization in the Armed Forces for the years 1997–2012. The fundamental goal of this document was to guarantee that the modification of the army required to meet the standards of the alliance would be consistent with Poland's economic capacities. The program assumed reductions in the army from 225,000 to 180,000 soldiers by the year 2002. Cuts would take place in the ground forces, logistic and administration services, and an obsolete infrastructure, which saw a 35 percent decrease. Other changes included alterations in the command system, increases in armaments and materiel purchases, and shorter terms for military service, with a higher concentration of both professional and noncommissioned officers (from 44 percent to 61 percent).[34] Moreover this program, called Army 2012, contained measures for financing technical modernization, which would rely on eleven "hi-tech" governmental strategic programs (SPRs). Between 20 and 30 percent of the SPRs would be purchased from foreign technology firms, as the necessary technology was neither designed nor produced in Poland.[35]

Political leaders from AWS and UW have persistently questioned this program since the time of its announcement. One prominent AWS official maintained it was based on incorrect strategic assumptions and that it therefore should be entirely rejected.[36] Others questioned the long, fifteen-year duration of the modification program.[37] Despite this initial criticism, the AWS-UW cabinet endorsed the Army 2012 program. Apart from the controversy surrounding some of the SPRs, the majority of the structural reforms were finished during 1998. Army 2012 contained optimal resolutions, and foreign experts responded positively to the program. As minister of defense, Janusz Onyszkiewicz was successful in reducing the length of military service to one year, cutting bureaucracy, and enlarging the planning goals in the General Staff. The number of military circles, or areas of command, has been reduced from three to two, and the Pomeranian and Silesian Circles were put under the command of ground forces, now composed of two mechanized corps and one air-mechanized corps.[38] Both the air force and Poland's small navy adopted changes consistent with allied requirements. Reorganization of state administration and local self-governments also reduced the number of territorial defense command structures to sixteen regional staffs. All of these changes made the Polish military more compatible with the task force goals of NATO.

The military also needed to purchase multirole fighters and antitank missiles for helicopters and for the infantry as well as the training-jet SPR for the army. Also, technical problems with some military equipment led to occasional criticism in the newspapers about the armament and skill levels.[39] And despite fundamental organizational changes, serious problems remain with air armaments, as demonstrated by a crash of military jets before the Independence Day parade on 11 November 1998.[40] These problems demonstrate the need to reconsider the modification plans for the air forces. Complex political forces, however, make further adjustments difficult to pursue.

PARLIAMENTARY DEBATES

The first reading of the government draft on the law concerning ratification of Poland's invitation to join NATO took place 20 November 1998. In a speech to introduce the Washington treaty to the receptive Seym, Minister Geremek stated, "Never before in the history of the Polish Parliament has such a short law led to such great and historical changes." He discussed Polish determination, the merits of diaspora, and the unusual consensus of political parties and the people.[41] Geremek recognized that it was logical and fitting that the AWS-UW cabinet complete this final act of accession to the alliance, a statement that evoked much applause from AWS and UW factions. Geremek also stressed that membership would secure Poland's deep-rooted culture and political environment: "This will not change with political fluctuations. . . . For Poland, after the turmoil of history in the last centuries, this means entering a safe port." Geremek also discussed Poland's new obligations, cooperation with Prague and Budapest, an open-door policy to NATO, and regional security in general.[42]

After Minister Geremek's speech, various parliamentary groups reacted, with many voicing common points. Jacek Rybicki (AWS) noted the historical meaning of changes initiated by Solidarity and the erosion of the Communist system: "We want to end the old divisions. We want to advocate the openness of NATO in regard to Central and East European states, but we also want to advocate good relations with a democratic Russia." Rybicki recognized the consensus about the Atlantic program and the evolution of post-Communist opinions as a "Polish wonder." An SLD representative also noted the continuity in the pro-Atlantic policy. Referring to Rybicki's statements, he said that the mature decisions made in Polish policy represent something other than "wonders." Tadeusz Syryjczyk (UW) expressed satisfaction about the enlargement of NATO, stating, "The cruel Balkan war waged a few hundred kilometers from our borders and the lack of respect for democratic procedures and the rights of the opposition exist[ing] just beyond our border, in Belarus, obliged us to ensure the continuance of the principles of liberty and democracy that exist in our part of Europe." Lesław Podkański of the PSL discussed cooperation between NATO and Poland and stressed the need for equal status among member states and the rule of "one for all, all for one." As a representative of the opposition he also insisted on a wider discussion of the concept and strategy of defense. Leaders of minor parties and the Sejm's Commission chiefs also reacted to the presentation of the treaty, raising such issues as the need for reconciliation with Russia, the importance of allied obligations, and the cohesion between the values of the Polish state and society and those expressed in the Washington treaty.

Longin Pastusiak and Wlodzimierz Konarski spoke for the opposition. Both SLD political leaders appealed for support of the open-door rule for the future enlargement of NATO. Pastusiak referred to Poland's membership in the alliance as an insurance policy against catastrophe. Konarski appealed to the AWS-UW coalition to draft a new defense doctrine that would be indispensable in case of changes in Poland's status or in the strategic concept of NATO for the twenty-first century.

When all the speeches were finished, Minister Geremek resumed. He expressed satisfaction with the support Polish society and Parliament had shown for the Washington treaty and voiced his hope that Poland's NATO membership would be such that even today's skeptics would be convinced of its merits in the future. He added, though, that "unanimity in the Parliament is not a good situation." President Kwaśniewski summed up this stage of the Seym's work: "Agreement between the coalition and the opposition on this issue establishes that our entrance into NATO is based on strong political consensus. . . . It means also [our readiness] to take on obligations."[43]

The last reading of the ratification law and the debate over it took place on 17 February 1999. Chief of the Commission of Foreign Affairs Czeslaw Bielecki (AWS) presented the recommendations of the Joint Commission of Foreign Affairs, National Defense, and Public Finances. The commission declared that Poland had three priorities connected to NATO membership: establishing the open-door policy, nuclear deterrence, and speedy modernization of the Polish army. At the end of the presentation, Bielecki stated, "While our accession to NATO is a great achievement, it must be remembered that this is a start—not a single test, but a constant task."[44] Jerzy Szmajdziński of the SLD thanked all the countries who supported Poland's access to NATO, and he added that Poland's next strategic goal would be membership in the European Union. Just before the vote, Premier Jerzy Buzek spoke. In a long speech, full of optimism, he stated that NATO membership represented the end of centuries of geopolitical rule over Poland's fate.

For the vote on ratification of the Washington treaty law, 420 members of the Sejm were present: 409 members from AWS-UW, SLD-PSL, the Movement for the Rebirth of Poland (ROP), and the Confederation of Independent Poland (KPN) voted for ratification while 7 representatives (all the members of the Nasze Kolo party) voted against ratification. Four abstained.

Later, in a special sitting of the Senate, individual senators debated the issue but added nothing new to the previous public and parliamentary debates. Senator Władysław Bartoszewski (UW), chief of the Senate's Commission of Foreign Affairs (and a former minister) stated his strong belief that voting in support of accession to NATO would serve future generations well. In the Senate, 92 senators (AWS, UW, SLD, and PSL) voted for ratification, 2 voted against ratification, and 1 abstained.[45] After the voting in the Sejm and the Senate, Premier Buzek and President Kwaśniewski signed the ratification law in a joint ceremony with Czech President Václav Havel. In his comments on the debates and the voting, Kwaśniewski stated, "Welcome to NATO. I am happy that the results were so straightforward—it is proof that Poland is a democratic power. . . . Poland is the leader of this region. And entry into NATO is for us an additional safeguard."[46]

PUBLIC OPINION AND LOBBYING ACTIVITY

References by members of Parliament to the consensus in Poland on accession to NATO were not just rhetorical, as evidenced by the many polls taken through-out the 1990s on this issue. As the Polish government began to articulate clearly its position, and as the West sent out the first signs that enlargement was a real possibility in the near future, popular support for NATO membership grew steadily from about 30 percent to 50 percent to almost 70 percent, according to the Public Opinion Study Centre (CBOS). A comparison of these polls demon-strates that the high level of support of a majority of Polish society for accession has been permanent and not imposed by external forces. Undoubtedly this sup-port has given Polish diplomacy a good foundation, compared to the public ambiguity displayed in neighboring countries regarding aspirations to NATO.[47] In repeated surveys, Poles recognized as very important the need to address European security. Support for integration with NATO did not just come from Poland's political right or its political left. Variation in position on membership was, in fact, more closely linked to the age and education of respondents than to their ideological leanings. Eighty-five percent of Poles concluded that member-ship in NATO would be a historical turning-point for Poland.[48]

The question of whether Polish soldiers should be used abroad was an especially relevant one related to this public debate. In two special polls, Poles responded negatively to the question of assisting the operation in the Persian Gulf. Thirty-nine percent of respondents thought that Polish soldiers should be sent while 47 percent thought they should not be sent.[49] Polish opinion was also quite mixed with regard to support for operations in Kosovo: 37 percent favored Polish involvement while 43 percent were against it. However, in the case of using Polish soldiers to help bring about a cease-fire in the struggle between Serbs and Albanians, Poles did recognize the need for a NATO air operation, despite their negative view of the U.S.-led operation against Iraq. According to a CBOS poll on Polish involvement in Kosovo, 11 percent were strongly in favor, 26 percent were probably in favor, 21 percent were proba-bly against, 22 percent were strongly against, 7 percent were indifferent, and 13 percent were undecided. At the same time, 51 percent recognized the necessity for some type of operation in Kosovo.[50] This range of views about military operations can certainly be found in most societies, but it was surprising that it was present in a country like Poland, which has only a few thousand soldiers involved in United Nations peacekeeping and peace-enforcement operations.[51] The polls may serve as an indicator of positions on future allied operations. If that is the case, political leaders must be careful in dealing with military activity outside the range of the collective defense of the NATO area.

The hesitancy to involve Polish troops in missions abroad was not the biggest controversy of the NATO integration debate, however. The lobbying activities of arms producers became an important element within the integration debate. In June 1998, the Solidarity trade unions in the Polish defense industry declared a strike emergency. Romuald Szeremietiew, the vice minister of defense, had argued that the defense industry was facing a difficult economic situation because SLD-PSL cabinets delayed introducing doctrine and procurement changes and, instead, authorized managers to deal with state subventions.[52] An interministerial team analyzed the industry and concluded that the defense community needed a program to restructure the industry's concentration in holdings, to be supported by laws and guarantees for fired workers in privatized firms.[53]

The problems of the industry were discussed during a separate, special debate in the Sejm. There were mutual accusations and especially sharp speeches by two chiefs of rival trade unions, who claimed, respectively, that the SLD-PSL cabinets had "done nothing" between 1993 and 1997, and that efforts of those coalition governments to annul the debts of the defense industry eclipsed the efforts of AWS leaders to remedy industry ailments. Lech Podkański (PSL) supported critics of the present government and connected the problems of the industry with disputes among ministries, while an ROP official reproached the Buzek cabinet for not guarding against rivalry in the arms markets resulting from Poland's active participation in NATO. At the end of the debate all factions demanded that the cabinet work more quickly on drafting laws to improve the prospects of the defense industry.[54]

During the first debate on ratification, trade unionists from Solidarity picketed in front of the Sejm building. After the protests, Ministers Onyszkiewicz and Szeremietiew agreed to the conditional purchase of eighteen modernized Iryda training jets from the firm WSK Mielec, which was in trouble as a result of poor management. Now, because of the cabinet's agreement to draft laws and devise programs, it could be assumed that most of the problems would be resolved in a relatively short time. Premier Buzek also promised trade unionists that 18,000 fired workers would be enrolled in special social programs. According to governmental drafts, twenty-two private firms and twelve state-owned firms would constitute the Industrial Defense

Potential.[55] Other lobbying efforts would be organized outside the group of arms producers.

The Ministry of Defense had declared, in 1993, the need for new attack helicopters and an advanced model of antitank missiles that can be used with both ground launchers and helicopters. The rocket SPR would cost up to $800 million. But in 1997 the media was informed that field tests had raised significant doubts about the effectiveness of long-range, Israeli-made NTD missiles. Despite this, the Army 2012 program confirmed the purchase of helicopters and rockets. And three days before the dismissal of Cimoszewicz's cabinet, Minister of Economy Wieslaw Kaczmarek (SLD) signed a memorandum of understanding with Israel regarding the Polish attack helicopter *Huzar,* eliminating Boeing-Rockwell and Euromissile from discussions on this project. Kaczmarek signed the agreement with Israel despite President Kwaśniewski's and Premier Cimoszewicz's declarations that the outgoing cabinet would not make a decision on using the NTD before the field tests had been done in Poland. Only Vice Minister of Industry Jan Czaja (SLD), who had previously worked for this Israeli enterprise, supported the memorandum of understanding.[56]

In a long article, Kaczmarek argued that he was concerned only with the needs of Polish industry, and that he did not want to incur protests from the U.S. Embassy.[57] After all, the Israelis had agreed to offset contracts, cooperate in the avionics of *Huzar*, open the production line, give Poland access to Elbit-Rafael technologies, and consent to the export of the Polish *Huzar* with the NTD.[58] The new cabinet of AWS-UW did not sign a contract, however, citing confusion in the documents as well as the lack of NTD field tests. Moreover, Israel did not agree to the new round of bidding, contending that the NTD memorandum constituted purchases of avionics from Elbit. Minister Onyszkiewicz confirmed the refusal to accept the planned contract but also confirmed the continuation of the SPR *Huzar*. In conversations of leaders of the SLD with the Israeli Labor Party, Kaczmarek described the new decisions of the AWS-UW cabinet as "dishonest."[59] Bronislaw Komorowski supported the government's decision in the Sejm's Commission of Defense, arguing that armament of the ground forces with portable missiles for infantry is of vital importance to Poland. Decisions about SPR's *Huzar* and its armament were transferred to a special interministerial commission, directed by Minister of Economy Jerzy Steinhoff (AWS).[60]

An equally urgent and unresolved issue is the so-called contract of the century—the purchase of 100 multirole fighters. It is expected that the Russian Su-22 and MiG-29 will be maximally used and then retired. Poland will buy new fighters starting in 2001, through a special program financed separately from the Ministry of Defense budget and the Army 2012 program funds.

In 1997 the Cimoszewicz cabinet announced the provisional leasing of a future fighter model in order to avoid duplication of training and infrastructure costs. These plans coincided with heightened consultations with the United States on armament issues. Vice ministers from SLD-PSL as well as military experts have visited the United States; both countries agree that cooperation among U.S. and Polish firms would be helpful for restructuring the Polish industry.

After the 1997 elections Vice Minister Szeremietiew called for the urgent leasing of the F-16 in order to allow Poland to maintain a high level of skill and combat readiness. Some officials denounced the idea, citing the negative effect it would have on Polish enterprises. Minister Szeremietiew's colleagues from AWS presented more moderate statements: Stanisław Głowacki, chief of the Defense Industry Section of Solidarity, suggested producing such a fighter in Poland in cooperation with others; meanwhile, the vice minister of industry encouraged plans for purchase, in addition to leasing, the fighters.[61] Programs for leasing and purchasing in Lockheed and the Hornet Group were accompanied by proposals that Warsaw's payments for service and Polish pilot training be offset by U.S. purchases in the Polish defense industry.[62]

An alternative proposal from the rival group of BAe-SAAB-DASA encouraged leasing and purchasing the JAS-39, cooperating with regard to the modernization of the MiG-29, and the training of Polish pilots. BAe also offered detailed, long-term proposals through the year 2016: first, a plan for leasing and training to be implemented immediately; after that, purchases and payments to the year 2007, purchases in Polish industry, production of the BAe Hawk, and the inclusion of Mielec in the Airbus Group.[63] During a visit to Poland, the Swedish minister of defense proposed six versions of JAS-39 leasing together with the joint offer of SAAB and BAe to sell the Hawk.

Despite—or perhaps because of—Poland's looming inclusion in NATO, Russian exporters also wanted a presence in Poland. During the tenure of Vice Minister of Defense Nikolai Mikhailov, Poland and Russia signed an agreement concerning engines for the Polish MiG-29s and modernization of fifteen Su-22Ms.[64] Following the Russian proposals, France's Dassault Aviation also made new proposals for modernization of the MiGs. According to the French company, the purchase of thirty-six Mirage 2000-5s, as well as cooperation in their production, would give Poland its least expensive new fighters.

Analyses have revealed that leasing was the most realistic solution to Poland's current needs. Minister Steinhoff, chief of a governmental commission for the purchase of armaments, stated, "I feel great pressure from arms producers' lobbies, but I am not going to permit foreign firms to 'play roles' in the Polish government."[65] It now appears, after the modernization of the MiG-29s by the German DASA and the Russian Sukhois, that the future Polish fighter will probably be a U.S. model.

ISSUES FOR THE FUTURE

After formally obtaining membership in NATO on 12 March 1999, Poland is still concerned about the technical aspects of its membership. First, by the year 2003 Poland must complete all sixty-five of the Task Force Goals of NATO—especially in terms of military interoperability, compatibility, and infrastructure modernization. It is not only a matter of Polish credibility; it is also a preamble to the future enlargement of NATO. Poland is focused on preparing units for entry into NATO's rapid reaction forces.[66] As a result of diplomatic discussions about the new NATO strategic concept, Warsaw must prepare a document that establishes the principles of Poland's defense policy. This will bring continuity to new alliance obligations and parameters of Polish security. It will also give a new structure to the armed forces. Poland's new status as a NATO member requires strategic changes, as well:

- Poland will work to maintain the continuity and effectiveness of the collective defense, participate in the common effort of the alliance to modernize the Conventional Forces in Europe (CFE) treaty, and engage in the wider tasks of NATO in the twenty-first century—especially in the geopolitical environment of Europe.
- Poland will support more full transatlantic cooperation, new programs of the Euro-Atlantic Partnership Council and Partnership for Peace, and perhaps a stronger role for the Organization for Security and Cooperation in Europe in preventive diplomacy.
- In the case of further NATO enlargement, Poland will give strong support for the candidacies of Slovenia, Slovakia, and Lithuania, while maintaining support for the open-door policy, with its positive influence on the internal modifications of all countries aspiring to membership in NATO.

Poland's membership in NATO could lead to quicker and easier integration into the European Union, which is important to Poland's economic interests. Membership in the NATO-EU communities would bring new political, security, and economic contacts, with the special benefit of coordinated cooperation with the countries of Western Europe, Ukraine, and Russia.

On the issue of a second and future enlargements, Warsaw continues to oppose the creation of a political fortress with divisions between Central and Eastern Europe. Poland's special concern is to promote the closest possible ties between NATO and Ukraine. Fully aware that for a variety of reasons, Ukraine could never join NATO, the Poles encourage a pro-Western orientation by Ukraine to check Russian influence over Kiev. In terms of support for possible membership, Poland has been clear in its backing of neighbor Lithuania, in particular, and also Estonia and Latvia if the Baltic states are able to meet NATO standards.

But the Russian opposition to NATO enlargement in the Baltic region could threaten the cooperation the Poles have tried to encourage in recent years. The enclave Kaliningrad poses additional difficulties on the Polish border and would require careful negotiations with Moscow. Another neighbor denied membership in the first round and now being closely watched for its progress on democratic, civil-military, and free market reforms is Slovakia, which, as a NATO member, could be expected to enhance even further Polish security. On the one hand, Poland has been open in its support for future enlargement, but, on the other hand, it recognizes that a hasty enlargement could also ultimately undermine exactly the stability it seeks in NATO as well as the EU if weak members are admitted to these organizations. Beyond the issue of which states will gain admittance to the alliance, Poland's role in the next round of enlargement discussions may indicate the direction its participation in NATO will take in the future.[67]

NOTES

1. For one year in 1989 the president of Poland was General Wojciech Jaruzelski, who was elected by the Seym. He resigned when the Seym decided to have free presidential elections. In December 1990 Lech Walesa was elected president. The presidential campaign was the first stage of the decomposition of the Solidarity movement into an array of parties.

2. Poland, Czechoslovakia (subsequently the Czech Republic and Slovakia), and Hungary created the Visegrad Group in 1990 and, in 1991, the Central European Free Trade Agreement (CEFTA). Both initiatives intended to prepare the states for integration with Western Europe and NATO.

3. K. Zielke, "Concept of Poland's and Central European Countries' Approach to Membership in NATO. Draft of Ministry of National Defense Bureau for Defense Policy from 27 July 1992" (reprint), *Central European Review*, no. 6 (1994): 30–36.

4. Hanna Suchocka, "Poland and European Security" (speech given at the Aspen Institute, Warsaw, 24 August 1993).

5. Following requests by Walesa and Skubiszewski for such a statement, on 25 August 1993, Yeltsin signed a declaration that Russia would not be against Poland's aspirations to NATO, during a visit to Poland.

6. For a review of the evolution of the SLD position on NATO, see: "Europe, NATO, Germany and Russia. Questionnaire Among Parties' Leaders," *Życie Warszawy* (14 August 1993); "PSL-SLD Coalition Agreement," *Rzeczpospolita* (14 October 1993); W. Pawlak, "Expose," *Rzeczpospolita* (9 November 1993); K. Groblewski, "Polish Raison d'etat Today," *Rzeczpospolita* (13 July 1994); and L. Pastusiak, "We Can Afford Consent," *Rzeczpospolita* (14 November 1994).

7. A. Olechowski, "Seven Principles of Polish Security" (speech delivered at the Center for Security and Information Studies, Washington, D.C., 24 December 1993); A. Olechowski, "How to Come Out from Grey Zone of Security," *Rzeczpospolita* (29

December 1993); A. Olechowski, "Toward One Safe Europe," *Rzeczpospolita* (14 November 1994).

8. A. Z. Kamiński, "Why Doesn't Poland Have an Eastern Policy?" *Rzeczpospolita* (8 March 1995).

9. Summary of Poles' Opinions About Poland's Security," CBOS Focus Group Interview (December 1992): 4–14. This analysis summed up results of the *Security for Europe Project,* commonly realized by the CBOS, the Institute of Political Sciences in the Polish Science Academy, and the Center for Foreign Policy Development, Brown University.

10. Public Opinion Study Centre, "State Security in Public Opinion," Report 137 (Warsaw: CBOS, November 1993).

11. Osrodek Badania Opinii Publicznej, "NATO, Army, and Poland's Security" (Warsaw: OBOP, March 1998): 5

12. A. Hajnicz, "The West's Betrayal: Fact or Obsession?" *Gazeta Wyborcza* (30–31 January 1999).

13. For a deeper analysis of the perception of Polish-Russian relations, see Public Opinion Study Centre (CBOS), "Is Russia a Threat for Us?" Report 87 (Warsaw: CBOS, April 1995); "Independence not Aggression," *Rzeczpospolita* (13 August 1998); and Public Opinion Study Centre (CBOS), "Poles Toward Crisis in Russia," Report 138 (Warsaw: CBOS, August 1998).

14. R. Bobrowski, "Outside Security of Poland," *Przegl'd Œrodkowoeuropejski,* no. 14 (1995); R. Sikorski, "Courage in Draw of Conclusions," *Rzeczpospolita* (20 November 1995).

15. D. Rosati, "Governmental Information About Poland's Foreign Policy Presentation of Minister of Foreign Affairs in the *Seym,*" Warsaw, 9 May 1996; D. Rosati, "Continuity, Progress, New Challenges," *Rzeczpospolita* (7 October 1996); D. Rosati, "Wider, Safer NATO," *Gazeta Wyborcza* (8 January 1997); and D. Rosati, "To Undertake a Risky Game," *Gazeta Wyborcza* (27 May 1997).

16. H. Szlajfer, "Common Concert on NATO," interview, *Gazeta Wyborcza* (2 April 1997).

17. Almost all the senior officials elected had been active members of the prointegration NGOs Euro-Atlantic Association and Atlantic Club.

18. "Our Blood, Their Oil!?" *Gazeta Wyborcza* (23 February 1998).

19. "Abroad and by Agreement," *Gazeta Wyborcza* (20 November 1998); and J. Szmajdziński, "Seym's About Defense," *Armia,* no. 3 (1998).

20. "Service of Soldiers Out of the State's Borders," *Rzeczpospolita* (13 November 1998).

21. In the 1997 elections one of the important points in the AWS program was changing regulations of clearing and counterintelligence to make them similar to the security standards in NATO countries.

22. See more in A. Madejski and J. Zieliński, *Poland's Armed Forces Toward New Challenges* (Warsaw: Polish Institute for International Affairs, December 1992), 13–16.

23. E. Przewódzki and J. Gogolewski, "Directions of Changes in Armed Forces of the Geopolitical Environment of Poland," *Analizy-Syntezy DBM MON,* no. 36 (1996).

24. For details on the ideas behind modernization, see "Report on State Security" (Warsaw: Polish Institute for International Affairs, 1993): 102–108.

25. A. Karkoszka, "Dilemmas of Partnership for Peace," *Sprawy Miedzynarodowe,* no. 2 (1994).

26. P. F. Nowak, "Price of NATO," *Nowe Życie Gospodarcze* (24 March 1996).

27. E. Firlej and P. Wieczorek, "Economic-Financial Aspects of Poland's Integration with Structures of NATO," *Sprawy Międzynarodowe*, no. 1 (1996): 43–46.

28. *Estimated Cost of Enlargement (a Contribution to the Debate)* (Warsaw: Euro-Atlantic Association, 1997), 9–30, 49–70.

29. "Costs of Integration with NATO," RCSS Paper (Warsaw: Governmental Center for Strategic Studies, January 1998).

30. This estimate includes U.S.$4.5 million for NATO's civil budget, U.S.$21 million for NATO's military budget, and U.S.$25 million for the NATO Security Investment Program. Poland will pay 2.48 percent of the allied budget. See "Costs of Integration with NATO."

31. In a poll with the question, "Should Poland try to gain access to NATO if it will increase military spending, even at the expense of other needs?" 8 percent of respondents answered, "absolutely yes"; 36 percent, "probably yes"; 32 percent, "probably not"; 9 percent, "absolutely not"; and 15 percent, "hard to say." See OBOP, "NATO, Army, and Poland's Security," 13–14.

32. M. Wigrowska, "Situation Without Precedent," *Rzeczpospolita* (16 June 1997); K. Dziewanowski, "Start of Second Stage," *Rzeczpospolita* (24 June 1997); P. Wroński, "Before Entrance of the Golf Club," *Gazeta Wyborcza* (2 July 1997); "Poland-NATO," *Rzeczpospolita* (7 July 1997); and P. Wroński, "When Poland Gives Us Order," *Gazeta Wyborcza* (9 July 1997).

33. Interview with M. Siwiec, "It Will Not Be So Easy," *Trybuna* (23 June 1997).

34. For details, see "Army of XXI Century," *Gazeta Wyborcza* (10 September 1997) and "Principles of the Governmental Program of the Armed Forces Modernization," *Polska Zbrojna* (12 September 1997).

35. B. Weglarczyk, "Army Will Pay to Polish Enterprises," *Gazeta Wyborcza* (29 October 1997).

36. For more about this concept, see "Universal Defense," paper of Programming Team of AWS for National Security (Warsaw, August 1997) and R. Szeremietiew, "Poland's Defense: Questions and Doubts," *Rzeczpospolita* (22 January 1998).

37. P. Wroński, "Strange Laze of the MND," *Gazeta Wyborcza* (13 June 1997).

38. "Year of the Army," *Gazeta Wyborcza* (15 November 1997); Z. Lentowicz, "Ground Power," *Rzeczpospolita* (2 December 1997); "Nominations and Dismissals," *Gazeta Wyborcza* (17 August 1998); and "Shorter, but Hard to Postpone," *Gazeta Wyborcza* (20 November 1998).

39. "There Will Be Money for Army," *Gzos* (27 October 1997); and "What Change in Polish Army After Accession to NATO?" *Wprost*, no. 41 (1998).

40. B. Komorowski, "Dream About Fighter," *Polityka*, no. 48 (1998).

41. Quotations from and details of this session are drawn from *Stenogram 35 posiedzenia Sejmu* (18–20 November 1998).

42. Quoted in "Agreement for NATO," *Rzeczpospolita* (21–22 November 1998).

43. Polish newspapers printed the transcripts of these debates. See "About Entrance to NATO," *Rzeczpospolita* (18 February 1999) and "It Is Our Alliance," *Gazeta Wyborcza* (18 February 1999). For commentary on the debate and the vote, see "Now Sign of President," *Rzeczpospolita* (18 February 1999); "Applause for NATO," *Gazeta Wyborcza* (18 February 1999); "Safe Port—NATO," *Życie* (18 February 1999); and "Finish," *Trybuna* (18 February 1999).

44. Senators Józef Kuczyński (SLD) and Jadwiga Stokarska (independent) voted against; Senator Ryszard Gibuła (SLD) abstained.

45. See wider relation from press conference of Kwaśniewski: "Seym: Hundred Words," *Trybuna* (18 February 1999).

46. To compare, see "Central and Eastern Eurobarometer," no. 7, March 1997.

47. Public Opinion Study Centre (CBOS), "Polls About Membership of Our Country in NATO," Report 27 (Warsaw: CBOS, July 1998).

48. According to OBOP results: 9 percent declared *strong support* for sending troops abroad; 30 percent recognized it as *correct;* 28 percent, *rather incorrect;* 19 percent, *opposed;* and 14 percent were undeclared. See "NATO, Army, and Poland's Security," 15.

49. Public Opinion Study Centre (CBOS), "Participation of Polish Soldiers Eventually in NATO's Mission in Kosovo," Report 151 (Warsaw: CBOS, November 1998).

50. M. Ostrowski, "Calculated Risk in the UN," *Polityka,* no. 31 (1998).

51. *"Huzar* as Crime," *Rzeczpospolita* (9 July 1998).

52. Eighteen firms out of forty-five in the industry were found to be in debt. See M. Henzller, "Army Without Rears," *Polityka,* no. 35 (1998); and W. Zuczak, "Rescue Circle for Defense Industry," *Raport,* no. 12 (1998).

53. This overview of the debate is adapted from *Stenogram 34 posiedzenia Sejmu,* 10 November 1998.

54. "Dobrzañski Leave," *Trybuna* (16 October 1997); and P. Wroñski, *"Huzar* of Disagreement," *Gazeta Wyborcza* (19 November 1997).

55. "Battle for Contracts," *Życie* (11 February 1999).

56. "Israeli *Huzar," Gazeta Wyborcza* (15 October 1997).

57. W. Kaczmarek, "With Clear Conscience: Why I Signed Agreement with Israel," *Gazeta Wyborcza* (1 December 1997).

58. "Army Without Israeli Rocket," *Rzeczpospolita* (9 December 1998).

59. *"Huzar* Landed," *Rzeczpospolita* (9 December 1998).

60. A decision is soon expected from Poland about production of some model of NATO's attack helicopter. See "Costly Lesson of the *Huzar," Rzeczpospolita* (9 December 1998); and "The End of the *Huzar?" Raport,* no. 1 (1999).

61. M. Henzller, "Hornet Is Coming," *Polityka,* no. 36 (1998).

62. Hornet Group wants to produce parts for the F-18 in Poland and provide facilities for engine service, installation of radio locators, and production of simulators. See M. Piskorski, "36 Planes for $100 Mln," *Rzeczpospolita* (15 December 1998).

63. D. Walewska, "Preposition for Mielec," *Rzeczpospolita* (17 November 1998); T. Moreland, "American Offer," and S. Carr, "British Offer," *Armia,* no. 3 (1998); and "European Alternative," *Raport,* no. 12 (1998).

64. Many of these contracts will allow Russia to repay some of the U.S.$20 million it still owes Poland. See: "Russians Want to Repair Polish Fighters," *Rzeczpospolita* (4 December 1998); and Pavel Graczev (interview), "Rosvooruzheniye," *Nowa Technika Wojskowa,* no. 12 (1998).

65. "New Peoples and Regulations," *Rzeczpospolita* (17 December 1998); J. Szczepañski, "Will Hornet Land?" *Rzeczpospolita* (26 January 1999); and "Who Will Give Us Wings?" *Rzeczpospolita* (2 February 1998).

66. During the first stage, 10 percent of Polish main forces will serve under NATO command: 16th and 18th Assault-Airborne Battalions, Airborne-Mechanized Corps with two divisions and three brigades, a squadron of MiG-29, and two squadrons of Su-22, *Kaszub* corvette and support units and ships. See "Copernican Change," *Rzeczpospolita* (17 February 1999).

67. For more on future directions from officials in Warsaw, see B. Geremek, "We, the West, with Roots in East," *Polityka,* no. 1 (1999); R. Mroziewicz, H. Szlajfer, and G. Kostrzewa-Zorbas, "What NATO for Us?" *Życie* (13 February 1999); and "Kwaśniewski About Open Door to NATO," *Rzeczpospolita* (19 February 1999).

8

Hungary:
Building National Consensus

CSABA TÖRŐ

In early 1989, Hungary was a member of the political and military structure of the Warsaw Pact and of the Council for Mutual Economic Assistance (COMECON), the Soviet bloc economic integration program. Soviet troops were stationed on the territory of Hungary. The Hungarian People's Army numbered approximately 160,000 in peacetime. The magnitude of Hungarian military expenditure exceeded 3.5 percent of gross domestic product (GDP), a figure that was not made public. The country bordered five neighbors, three of whom were members of the same alliance, the Warsaw Pact. Today, as the millennium begins, and after the fall of the Berlin Wall and the Iron Curtain on the Hungarian-Austrian border, Hungary is a full-fledged member of NATO and preparations for accession to the European Union are advancing at full speed.

For several years now the NATO-led peacekeeping operations in Bosnia-Herzegovina have included Hungarian soldiers performing their duties under a multinational command while U.S., Swedish, Danish, Norwegian, Finnish, and Polish soldiers carry out tasks on Hungarian soil. During the NATO air strikes against Yugoslavia to enforce human rights and stop genocide in Kosovo, Hungary as a new member of the alliance made its airspace and airports fully available to NATO forces.

The Hungarian Defense Forces now number 53,000 in peacetime, and defense expenditure is 1.61 percent of GDP. This figure is made public since the Hungarian armed forces are under strict democratic and civilian control. For the time being Hungary borders seven countries, of which five gained or regained their independent statehood during the course of the 1990s.

HUNGARIAN FOREIGN AND SECURITY POLICY AFTER 1990

The foreign policy priorities identified by the first freely elected government, the Joszef Antall administration, cut across political parties and included: (1) Euro-Atlantic integration, (2) good neighborliness ensuring regional stability, and (3) an active national policy to support Hungarian minorities living abroad primarily in neighboring countries (altogether a community of 3 million ethnic Hungarians). All Hungarian governments in office since that time have considered and continue to consider these goals of primary importance.

The first concrete steps taken by Hungarian independent foreign and defense policymakers aimed at regaining the country's sovereignty and freedom of action within the international realm. In the summer of 1990—in cooperation with other countries such as Czechoslovakia and Poland—Hungary suggested a review of the Warsaw Pact Treaty and subsequently its dissolution, which finally took place in 1991. Simultaneously, Hungary succeeded in bringing about the complete withdrawal of Soviet troops. In the same summer of 1991, COMECON was disbanded as well.

Parallel with the shift of emphasis in its foreign policy, Hungary started to reassess the possible sources of risk and danger in the more complex post–Cold War international environment in a region awash in the vicissitudes of a historic social and political change. Transitional differences between countries and groups stemming from diverging social developments as well as economic, financial, and social crises; ethnic and religious tensions; terrorism and organized crime; illegal drug and arms trafficking; mass migration; and large-scale environmental damages all constituted an ever-increasing risk. The proliferation of weapons of mass destruction (WMD) and of their means of delivery as well as the possibility of attacks on information systems portended ever-increasing challenges and threats. Meanwhile interstate and intrastate armed conflicts continued to occur in Europe. Finally, instability and unpredictability triggered by the political transformation of formerly communist societies and the frailty of the processes of democratization posed a particular risk typical of the region. The unique feature of the Central and Eastern European security environment, and Hungary as well, is that new and traditional kinds of risks often appear simultaneously, reinforcing each other. As a general feature it can be said that instability constitutes the biggest risk in the changing security and political environment.

Pál Dunay, of the Geneva Center of Security Policy, considers Hungarian foreign and defense policy

> a national prerogative and major attribute of sovereignty without which a state may not be considered independent. Non-Soviet members of the Warsaw Pact had only limited sovereignty and throughout Eastern Europe dur-

ing the Cold War substantive thinking on defense and security was oppressed. Security was a military issue and nonmilitary factors were seldom considered. Demilitarization of security was . . . one of the priority tasks in Hungary to deal more effectively with pressing security problems.[1]

It was clear to Hungarian officials that innovative thinking about approaches to national security interests assures a secure future for the country. The political, territorial, and ethnic conflicts and the turbulent changes of Eastern Europe were reflected in the rearrangement of threat perceptions and the "renationalization" of security and defense policies in Hungary after 1991.

In terms of Hungary's security, the Balkan conflict that broke out in 1991 and has continued with varying intensity ever since is of much greater relevance than any other risk or danger. The armed clashes taking place in Slovenia and Croatia (not far from the Hungarian border) and border incidents of lesser or greater scale (the most serious of which was the bomb that fell on the small southern border town Barcs, but luckily did not explode) highlighted the issue of Hungary's vulnerability in an alarming manner. Ethnic conflicts taking place in the immediate neighborhood of Hungary have not always taken the shape of armed conflicts. Nevertheless, the fact that in the course of not more than two years the number of Hungary's neighbors increased from five to seven, out of which only two (Romania and Austria) did not undergo a radical change of state territory, underscores the uncertainty of the region. László Kovács, member of Parliament and chairman of the Socialist Party (the largest opposition party), notes, "There was an agreement among the Hungarian political elite that the only possibility to break away from the disintegrating Central and Eastern European region was through accession and integration with the West."[2]

The Hungarian governments since 1990 have paid particularly close attention to aligning foreign policy priorities (mentioned earlier) with the security and defense policy priorities of the country and to assuring that none is subordinated or detrimental to another. The successful fulfillment of both sets of objectives makes them closely linked, indeed, interdependent.

The premise of Hungarian foreign and security policy is that a successful Euro-Atlantic policy and Hungary's own security as well require regional stability. The process of Euro-Atlantic integration not only enhances regional security and cooperation but also provides an opportunity to advance the settlement of Hungarian national communities living abroad in neighboring countries. As for foreign policy goals related to integration, all significant European and Atlantic institutions are defined by Hungarian national security interests as different elements of one and the same structure and as instruments of Hungary's security policy, which can mutually complement and reinforce the country's bilateral relations and unilateral measures.

The Hungarian intention to join NATO has been firmly grounded in the conviction that NATO membership is an essential part of Euro-Atlantic integration through which Hungary's national interests can be better represented and defended. The country's military and nonmilitary security alike would be guaranteed at a qualitatively higher level and at a lower cost. The indispensable reform of the armed forces and the establishment of genuinely effective democratic political and civilian control would be more efficient, less painful, and less costly as a part of the North Atlantic Alliance. Membership in NATO is necessary for Hungary as official governmental sources have reiterated on many occasions, not primarily as a reaction to military threat, though that could not be neglected either, particularly in light of possible threats posed by Yugoslavia during the NATO air campaign, but, rather, as a positive action to achieve the broader objective of peace, security, and stability in Central and Eastern Europe. In addition, Hungary wishes to become a member of the alliance because NATO is the proof and guarantee of the irreversibility and definitiveness of integration and the accession to the community of values that ties the two sides of the North Atlantic region together. If others consider Hungary a stable part of Europe, it will be much more attractive to foreign capital and investment. Hungary's NATO membership is a means of ensuring not only its physical security but the broadest possible economic and political security as well.

THE FORMULATION OF SECURITY AND DEFENSE POLICY BY NATIONAL CONSENSUS

The principle of "national consensus" in Hungarian foreign policy decision-making was finally accepted in 1992. As Zoltán Rockenbauer, senior foreign policy adviser to the prime minister (and now minister of National Cultural Heritage) observes,

> In its essence [the consensus] rested on a gentlemen's agreement by which the opposition would not openly criticize the activities of the government in foreign and security policy and, in exchange, the government would consult with the opposition before taking important steps in foreign policy. The system of so-called "six-party coordination" was established in the Parliament, as a consultative forum, which in contrast to the composition of the Foreign Affairs Committee of the National Assembly operates on the basis of parity.[3]

The Basic Principles of Security Policy adopted unanimously by the Parliament in 1993 and the Basic Principles of National Defense, which resulted from that document, reflected the efforts to develop a consensus process. The work on the elaboration of these two significant parliamentary resolutions started in 1990 but had been delayed with the constant changes in the international environment and the initial mutual distrust among the political parties. The government submitted and withdrew several draft versions until, at the beginning of 1993, the Ministry of Foreign Affairs invited one representative from each of the six parties represented in the Parliament to finalize the text of the draft resolution in cooperation with the Foreign Ministry. The Basic Principles of Security Policy adopted on 2 March 1993 defined the security of the country in harmony with the requirements of the changing international political environment and was the first official document setting the target of full-fledged Hungarian membership in NATO.

These Basic Principles of Security Policy demonstrated that one of the main endeavors of Hungarian security policy is the rapprochement and subsequent membership in the institutions of Western European integration. The subsequent Basic Principles of National Defense, adopted on 14 April 1993, on the other hand, confirmed that the country's security can, in the long run, only be ensured through the institutional framework of multilateral and multidimensional cooperation. Through these parliamentary resolutions Hungary expressed its goals to cooperate effectively with the existing international security organizations and to become a member of those institutions.

The fourth paragraph of the resolution of the Hungarian National Assembly on security policy in 1993 laid out the different factors and dimensions of security as well as the means to security:

> The acquisition of full-fledged membership in the European Communities will provide a fundamental guarantee of the security of the Republic of Hungary. The security policy of Hungary starts from the assumption that the EC, NATO, OSCE, the Western European Union (WEU), the North Atlantic Cooperation Council (now the Euro-Atlantic Partnership Council) and the Council of Europe will continue to play an active role in enhancing economic and political stability in the region, in supporting reforms to establish democracy and a market economy, in initiating defense reform, in developing effective mechanisms of crisis- and conflict-prevention, in restoring the system of international relations of the region and in integrating Hungary into the new European security structure.

The resolution then proposed for the future that

> These bodies will ensure the security of the country in the long run. Relying on the achieved level and institutional frameworks of co-operation in the fields of foreign and security policy and on military matters will gradually lead to the achievement of the conditions of full-fledged membership in NATO and WEU.[4]

The Principles of National Defense adopted a month later also by consensus used even more unambiguous terms. Paragraph 16 reads,

> The goal of the Republic of Hungary is to accede to the existing international security organizations such as NATO and WEU as a full-fledged member. Existing cooperation with NATO member states in the fields of security policy consultations, defense management, training of officers, defense industry and human conversion as well as science and environmental protection provide valuable support to the restructuring of the Hungarian defense forces according to our needs and capabilities as well as to the establishment of the practical requirements for NATO-accession.[5]

Further necessary steps followed the adoption of the above mentioned basic principles resulting in a constitutional amendment regulating national defense and the passing of the Act on National Defense later in the same year. The guidelines for the transformation of the Hungarian armed forces and for the clear definition of national security interests derived from these principles.

In the case of security policy, the national security interests of Hungary require a consistent line of policy that enables the country to guarantee the success of

- the independence, sovereign statehood, and territorial integrity of the country;
- the internal stability of Hungary including the undisturbed functioning of democratic institutions and the market economy;
- the conditions for the development of international economic, political, and cultural relations and cooperation; and
- the maintenance of international peace and stability in Central and Eastern Europe and on the whole continent.

As far as national defense policy is concerned, the practical implementation of Hungarian defense policy is based on the principles of international cooperation, containment, and defense. According to the parliamentary resolution in its efforts to maintain an appropriate defense capability, Hungary basically relies on its own strength, the capabilities and determination of its own defense forces, and on the support of its citizens. In the long run, the country can only expect a solid guarantee for its own security from an institutional framework of multilateral cooperation and from a strong political, economic, and military community with countries pursuing similar goals.

Even if it did not apply to the entire sphere of foreign policy, the principle of the consensus among parliamentary parties survived with respect to security policy. This included the system of six-party coordination. Such consultations preceded, inter alia, the elaboration of a Hungarian position aimed at settling the crisis in the former Yugoslavia, including: (1) the draft resolution on the temporary deployment and transit of troops of the Implementation Forces (IFOR), (2) the formal confirmation of the Status of Forces Agreement (SOFA) on the legal status of foreign troops (both points 1 and 2 were adopted on 1 December 1995), (3) the draft resolution related to the engineering contingent to participate in the framework of IFOR (adopted on 5 December 1995), and, a year later, (4) the reconfirmation of Hungarian participation in the Stabiliza- tion Forces (SFOR) (adopted on 9 December 1996).

Hungary's active participation in the Partnership for Peace program beginning in 1995, the establishment of a NATO base at Taszár in January 1996, and the mutual experience gained during the operation of the latter as well as the activities of the Hungarian engineering units transferred under NATO command in February 1996 all put the cooperation between the Hun- garian armed forces and NATO, which had formerly existed mostly at a theo- retical level only, to a practical test. All parties in Parliament accepted Hun- gary's accession to NATO as a fact sanctioned with a referendum in November 1997, so that, as with the basic principles of security policy and defense adopted in 1993, the elaboration of the "new principles of security and defense policy" took place on 29 December 1998 as a joint work of all parties represented in Parliament.

CHANGE IN DOCTRINE

In accordance with the new security situation, the 1998 resolution on the basic principles of security and defense policy extended the purposes and redefined the content of the fundamental principles. The document clearly indicated the additional dimensions of the main purpose of security policy as compared to the previous doctrinal definition. Some of the points are concerned with the more thorough protection of the internal aspects of security:

- To create appropriate conditions for the implementation of the princi- ples enshrined in the constitution, to promote the practice of the rule of law and the undisturbed functioning of democratic institutions and the market economy, and to contribute to the internal stability of the coun- try.
- To promote the full implementation of citizens', human as well as national and ethnic minority, rights in the Republic of Hungary.
- To create the necessary conditions for the safety as well as material and social security of all persons living on the territory of the Republic of Hungary and for the safeguarding of national wealth.[6]

As the resolution determines, the goals of the Hungarian security policy (among others) are to assure the security of its allies and the implementation of the terms of the North Atlantic Treaty and to contribute to the maintenance of international peace and the enhancement of security and stability in the Euro-Atlantic region, in Europe and its immediate neighborhood.[7]

With the document, policymakers made clear their intention that the Republic of Hungary base its security on two fundamental pillars: first, Euro-Atlantic integration and international cooperation and, second, national self-strength. Hungary considers the process of Euro-Atlantic integration in its entirety with NATO and EU accession as components separable only in terms of timing. Hungary's accession to those organizations will, on the one hand, complete the process of economic and social modernization taking place in the country while, on the other hand, providing the means for Hungary to become a constructive player in the creation of security and stability in Europe.

The security of the Republic of Hungary, as reflected in the resolution, is based on the principle of collective security and defense. Hungary asserts its determination to assume all the duties that will fall on the country as an equal and integral part of the political and military structure of the alliance. It considers constructive participation in NATO's consultative and decisionmaking system as the means to contribute to international security and to establish effective representation as well as protection of its national interests.

The decisions that prepared the basis for the legal, institutional, and political background of national defense following the change of Hungary's governmental system were mostly made in the years that immediately followed the exit from the Warsaw Pact. The basic philosophy behind this defense policy was therefore aimed primarily at departing from an undesirable alliance system in order to prevent the return of anything similar and establishing the renationalization of security and defense policies. From a domestic standpoint, this philosophy was designed to clarify the legal status of the armed forces, to ensure the maximum respect of the rights of citizens in uniform, and to confirm the civilian control of elected political bodies over the armed forces, while at the same time limiting day-to-day political interference. Limitations and regulations that were certainly legitimate and appropriate in the period of political and social change had to be replaced by new ones.

The most significant result of Hungary's accession to NATO is that, like other NATO members, Hungary will—as the resolution reflects its intention and commitment—ground its security not solely in a national but also in a collective framework. The 1995 NATO Study on Enlargement itself identified the expectations of promoting the "denationalization" of defense and security policies as one of its most important goals. In the course of accession talks, Hungary accepted the consequences deriving from NATO's collective security and military strategy. The adoption and implementation of NATO's common philosophy required a review and reassessment of Hungarian doctrine and constituted a task of fundamental significance for the country. Hungary identified itself with the principles of NATO's collective security and defense and made the transition from a national approach to a collective way of thinking.

The resolution clarifies the tasks of the Hungarian armed forces as a member of the alliance in the following threefold way:

- Assurance of the defense of Hungary's sovereignty and territorial integrity. The Hungarian armed forces must ensure that the capabilities required for defense relying on the country's national assets and resources prevent any possible attack and guarantee the conditions for the involvement of allied forces.
- Contribution to the collective defense of allied nations on the basis of Article 5 of the Washington treaty, participation in allied missions conducted on the basis of Article 4 of the Washington treaty, international peace support and humanitarian operations carried out under the auspices of other international organizations.
- In the final analysis, the Strategic Concept of the Alliance becomes the guideline, in the elaboration and further development of Hungarian security objectives.[8]

NATO ACCESSION AND THE HUNGARIAN DEFENSE FORCES

NATO accession meant an increased burden for the Hungarian armed forces. The establishment of armed forces capable of cooperation with NATO coincided with the intent of setting up a modern and effective army as well as air forces in the years following the change in political system. In September 1995, the alliance published its Study on Enlargement, which stressed that countries wishing to join would have to meet the requirements of interoperability (the ability to cooperate). This meant joint action, common thinking, and a coordinated application of principles and rules between the Hungarian armed forces and NATO partners.

Therefore, the first and foremost task and necessary precondition of accession was the establishment of interoperability in every sense of the word—technical and intellectual alike. The first requires significant investment but can be fulfilled in a short period of time if the financial conditions are provided. The second task, "intellectual compatibility," demanded the least funds and the longest time. Establishing the skills necessary for effective communication was clearly the most urgent task. Intellectual compatibility implies a similarity of doctrines, procedures, and principles and coordinated planning and decisionmaking as well as the adaptation of organizational, training, and operational methods.

The reform of the Hungarian Defense Forces accelerated with the possibility of NATO accession; the transformation gained momentum in the summer of 1996 with the first so-called quantitative phase ending in December 1997. Hungary concluded this first phase by restructuring and reducing its number of soldiers. In the ongoing, second "qualitative intellectual and technical phase," cooperation continues to be of primary importance with a strong emphasis on the intellectual. As Lajos Pietsch notes, "It is better to have people with a modern way of thinking and older equipment, than the other way round."[9]

The essence of this second phase is not the procurement of the latest military technology in great quantities. The alliance does not expect this from Hungary and the country could not afford it. Other important tasks are the reform of the command and control system; the training of officers; the development of air defense; the modernization of air-space control; the improvement of communication (particularly in English); and the procurement of modern communication, air surveillance, airspace sovereignty control, and radar equipment. These do not require excessive investment and are being implemented gradually step by step.

Hungary still has a long way to go to achieve full interoperability. Further problems need to be solved, and programs as well as plans elaborated in the course of operations must be implemented consistently. Hungary made its medium-term political and military commitment for the period from 1999 to 2003 to accomplish fully or partially forty-eight different Target Force Goals and to assign certain military units to the preparation of immediate as well as rapid reaction ground and air forces for the purpose of collective defense.

The long-term force development concept can be divided into two five-year cycles. Ferenc Végh, chief of staff of the Hungarian Defense Forces (and now ambassador to Turkey), explains: "Further advancement, qualitative aspects and full-fledged military integration into NATO will characterize the first cycle which will last from 2004 to 2008. In the second cycle, which will last from 2008 to 2013 we wish to put the emphasis on the qualitative aspects of the armed forces."[10] The qualitative aspects of modernization are going to be further advanced by the creation of highly motivated and efficiently equipped Hungarian Defense Forces, comprising both career and volunteer personnel, with a computerized command and control system operating at all levels according to common NATO principles. In addition, the Hungarian Defense Forces are expected to be able to send seventy-three officers to different positions at different NATO military commands. Hungary has already sent military representatives to Brussels, Mons, Naples, and other important posts.

In the course of preparing the country for NATO membership, Hungary paid special attention to stabilizing and improving relations between the Hungarian Defense Forces and the defense forces of neighboring countries. As a result of deliberate efforts, a regular dialogue was established with the military leaders of the countries adjacent to Hungary; several bilateral treaties were signed on military cooperation. One significant achievement is the establishment of a joint Hungarian-Romanian peacekeeping battalion. A remarkable role from the point of view of regional security and stability has also been played by the joint Italian-Slovenian-Hungarian brigade within the framework of the so-called Triangular Cooperation.

BUDGETARY ISSUES

During the debate on NATO enlargement, the cost of accession was a very important issue. Opponents argued short accession would impose an unbearable burden on the country. The supporters countered that participation in the alliance and sharing the costs of defense would be a much cheaper solution than ensuring national security alone. The debate in Hungary was heated and complicated by conflicting estimates of costs. The debate was further complicated by the significantly different (sometimes by order of magnitude) estimates published in the United States and in Western Europe by research institutes and governmental bodies.

Since the second round of accession negotiations in September 1997, it has become clear that the costs of accession to be borne by Hungary, as indicated by the alliance, are acceptable. According to the agreement, Hungary's contribution will amount to 0.65 percent of NATO's total budget, paid as Hungary's "membership fee." In 2000 this 0.65 percent would be slightly more than Ft 2 billion (2 billion Hungarian forint), which is 2 percent of Hungary's total defense budget.[11]

As a significant aspect of its commitment to the alliance, Hungary undertook to expand incrementally the defense chapter of the annual governmental budget in accordance with the responsibilities of NATO membership. Consequently, Hungary has attempted to contribute substantially but within the limits of its own possibilities and strengths to the efforts aimed at achieving NATO's common goals. The magnitude of Hungarian Defense Force expenditure illustrates the seriousness of these endeavors. As a result of the accession negotiations Hungary promised to devote appropriate budgetary resources to defense. In September 1997 a decision was made to increase the proportion of Hungary's defense expenditure from 1.44 percent of GDP in 1997 to 1.51 percent in 1998 and then to 1.81 percent in 2001.[12] With an expected 4 or 5 percent annual growth of GDP this budgetary expansion could mount up to an 8–10 percent increase in real value. But one crucial question remains: Will the budgetary resources made available for the modernization and upgrading of the Defense Forces be sufficient to fulfill the requirements determined by Hungary's membership in NATO?

ENLARGEMENT DEBATES IN PARLIAMENT

As discussed previously, the national consensus in defining national interests as they relate to national security and defense principles is critically important. One of the fundamental pillars on which the consensus was built was the high priority accorded to close cooperation with and eventual membership in NATO. Since democratic reforms were introduced, Hungarian parliamentary parties have agreed on the necessity of Euro-Atlantic integration. This agreement and the consequent lack of internal debates concerning accession in the National Assembly strengthened the position of the country and probably played a decisive role in NATO's decision to include Hungary in the first round of NATO enlargement.

The consensus was formed despite the fact that at the time of political and social change, the various political parties held different views on guaranteeing future security. The Hungarian political elite handled the issue of NATO accession very cautiously as long as the Warsaw Pact existed and Soviet troops were stationed in Hungary. According to Pietsch,

> This cautious approach characterized the debate in the National Assembly on the relationship between Hungary and the Warsaw Pact in June 1990. All government voices tried hard to avoid giving the impression that secession from the Warsaw Pact would automatically entail more intensive relations with NATO.[13]

In 1991, after the withdrawal of the Soviet troops from Hungary, the dissolution of the Warsaw Pact, the escalating conflict in Yugoslavia, and the coup d'etat in Moscow, the international security environment changed dramatically and offered the possibility of unlimited sovereignty for Hungary at the same time. All of these factors played a critical part in Hungary's discussion of possible NATO membership. The increasing Euro-Atlantic commitment was not questioned by the opposition either then or later. The subsequent period brought several important milestones in the process of integration: The North Atlantic Cooperation Council (NACC, now the European Atlantic Partnership Council) was established, the Partnership for Peace program was launched, the Treaty of Association with the European Union was signed, and the official Hungarian application for membership in the EU was submitted.

With the support of all political parties represented in the National Assembly, the country took a determined turn toward the West.

But despite the basic consensus, parliamentary parties had contending opinions on the requirements for acceding to NATO. Significant forces in the opposition felt that the basic treaties with neighboring countries should not be preconditions for the integration into the Western European and Atlantic institutions. The possible effect of Hungary's disagreement with neighboring countries was also viewed differently. Parties in the National Assembly fully agreed on the underlying policy of approaching the West and joining the institutions of the Atlantic community. However, consensus was undermined when this approach affected the sensitive and complex issue of the rights of Hungarian national minorities living in those countries surrounding Hungary. The debate was particularly acute when Hungary signed the Slovakian-Hungarian (1995) and the Romanian-Hungarian (1996) Basic Treaties. In both cases, the government argued that settling disputes and improving relations with its neighbors would definitely increase the chances of joining the Euro-Atlantic organizations. Any tense and fragile relations, they contended, would raise considerable obstacles and cause serious and undesirable delay in the process of accession.

While both the socialist-liberal coalition government and the opposition agreed that stable and harmonious bilateral relations with neighbors were a prerequisite for Western integration, several center-right opposition leaders questioned the necessity of such treaties.

Parliamentary consensus was absolute, however, on issues related to approaching NATO. In November and December 1995, following the conclusion of the Dayton Accord, when Hungary turned out to be an ideal location to back up the peacekeeping forces stationed in Bosnia-Herzegovina, the government and the opposition unanimously supported cooperation. All parties agreed that although Hungarian participation in IFOR did not mean automatic membership in NATO, it was a perfect occasion to demonstrate that Hungary was willing and able to establish the closest links with the alliance. This explains why the National Assembly voted unanimously to authorize the transit of IFOR troops and, not much later and with an overwhelming majority, the participation of a Hungarian engineering contingent in the IFOR mission. This contingent established Hungary in one of the most important new roles of NATO—conflict management.

The political forces represented in Parliament generally agreed on the necessity of NATO accession based on the following set of arguments:

- NATO membership is an indispensable element of Hungary's integration into the institutions of the Western community and therefore, that of the country's modernization.

- NATO membership provides a better framework for the representation and protection of national interests. Hungary would take part in the decisionmaking rather than simply be the subjects of that process as before membership.
- Hungary does not wish to accede to NATO because it feels threatened. The country looks for guarantees against security risks to avoid conflicts.
- Hungary's NATO membership would extend the area of stability.
- Neutrality is not a viable alternative since it has lost its traditional meaning and a small country could not afford the luxury of neutrality.
- Hungary would become the member of a military organization that implements the most modern military thinking, principles, and practices at the present.
- Hungary would be accepted and admitted as a mature member of a security community that represents the values of multiparty parliamentary democracy, rule of law, and market economy.[14]

The National Assembly implemented the legislative program related to membership in NATO in phases. It has been done in such a way that there would be no legal obstacles to Hungary's functioning as a NATO member. After the ratification of the protocol of accession of Hungary, with a view to ensuring full compliance with the obligations in Articles 3 and 5 of the Washington treaty, the Hungarian National Assembly had to pass a number of other acts of legislation. This package included an amendment of the laws on national defense and the service status of enlisted and military personnel. The amendments addressed primarily the issues of sending troops abroad and hosting foreign troops on Hungarian soil. The objective of the amendment was to transfer the decisionmaking authority from Parliament to the government under certain specific circumstances.

PUBLIC DEBATES: OPINIONS FOR AND AGAINST

The policy with respect to NATO has been opposed since the beginning by a few nonparliamentary parties and civil organizations of limited influence. Opponents include the Workers' Party (the communist party) and the Party of Hungarian Justice and Life (MIÉP, the extreme right). The loudest civil organization opposing NATO accession was the Alba Circle (Alba Kör).

The Workers' Party has argued from the beginning that Hungary did not need NATO; they proposed neutrality instead. Among its counterarguments, the party emphasized that acceding to the North Atlantic Treaty Organization would entail the stationing of nuclear weapons and foreign troops on Hungarian territory, and thus Hungary would lose most of its sovereignty. Another counterargument was that accession would place an unbearable economic and financial pressure on the country and would cause the bankruptcy of Hungary.

The Workers' Party did not confine itself to the usual form of public opposition. In the summer of 1995, they started a petition for a referendum to be held on NATO accession. The petition was successful with more than 180,000 signatures collected. In spite of this, the National Assembly decided on 19 December 1995 that no referendum would be held as a result of the initiative of the Workers' Party. The resolution of the National Assembly was based on the simple fact that the Hungarian population was not in the position to decide on this issue since the government had only recently expressed its intention to join NATO and NATO had not yet responded in any official way to it. Furthermore, the accession negotiations would have been greatly hindered if the population had given a negative vote on this issue, even if the referendum had been only a "consultative" (opinion-forming) procedure.

While opposition from the Workers' Party grew out of a communist platform, MIÉP opposition stemmed from extremist nationalism. MIÉP declared that it saw a national tragedy "in Hungary's fate being forced under a new military bloc." NATO membership entails only disadvantages, the party argued. It would force Hungary into another subordinate position. As MIÉP stated, "Hungary should maintain its commitment to neutrality by its history of 1,100 years and its Treaty of Trianon."[15]

Among the civil organizations opposing NATO, the most active and resourceful was the Alba Kör, a pacifist movement. Alba Kör warned that if Hungary joined NATO, it would take part in an organization in possession of nuclear weapons and thereby become a training field for both nuclear and conventional forces. The organization applied a variety of arguments ranging from ecological risks and immense economic burden to the loss of sovereignty and "political innocence." The anti-NATO sentiments of this and some other nongovernmental organizations spring from their romantic pacifist, antimilitarist, and moderately leftist schools of thought.

The Hungarian Atlantic Council (Magyar Atlanti Tanács) was clearly the most active civil organization supporting NATO accession. This nonprofit, nongovernmental think tank pursued an intensive campaign for Hungarian membership in NATO. The council engaged in a variety of activities abroad to coordinate the efforts of Hungarian organizations committed to the ideas of Atlantic cooperation. It represented Hungary's Atlantic movement in international bodies and informed the international public on Hungary and its objectives. The Hungarian Atlantic Council organized meetings and conferences, published materials, and supported research projects relevant to Atlantic integration.

The proportion of supporters slowly increased over the course of 1996, rising from 45 percent in May to 50 percent in December. Parallel to that, the weight of disapproval dropped from 32 percent to 28 percent. The overall success of the Bosnia IFOR operation, the participation of the Hungarian contingent, and the start of the bilateral Hungarian-NATO talks in April together with an actual timetable for NATO enlargement influenced public opinion in favor of accession in the second half of 1996.

In March 1997 a national dialogue about NATO began in earnest and by the time of a June survey, support had reached a high of 61 percent while opposition had dropped to 27 percent. As one observer commented, "The overwhelming majority of the public realized that accession to NATO was a fundamental national interest." The tide had seemingly turned in favor of NATO membership.[16]

According to a poll taken in October 1997, more than two-thirds of the population saw a relationship between European Union (EU) and NATO accession. At the same time and in light of the developments of the preceding year, those convinced that membership in NATO would help achieve EU membership rose from 20 percent in August 1996 to 37 percent in fall 1997.

As a senior coalition partner, the Socialist Party promised in its parliamentary election campaign in 1994 to hold a referendum on NATO membership; the government called the referendum for late 1997. While there was heated debate in Parliament over whether the results of the referendum should be decisive, and therefore binding, or merely consultative, there was agreement on the objective of the referendum and all the parties represented in the National Assembly at the time called for their supporters to vote in favor of accession. The referendum was in the end consultative; however, it played an important role in informing the public and forging consensus.[17]

The referendum took place on 16 November 1997 with the participation of 49.24 percent of all eligible Hungarian voters. Hungarian NATO accession received support from 85.33 percent of the voters; 14.67 percent voted in opposition. None of the polling institutes had forecast a favorable vote higher than 80 percent. Proponents found themselves pleasantly surprised. The result of the referendum unambiguously legitimized the efforts of successive Hungarian governments to attain membership in the North Atlantic community. Following the referendum public acceptance of NATO membership climbed to a peak of 63 percent by August 1998 while opposition dropped to 16 percent.

CONCLUSION

Only twelve days after the ceremonies admitting Hungary and the other two Central European states to NATO in Independence, Missouri, on 12 March 1999, NATO launched its first air strikes against the former Yugoslavia in Kosovo and Serbia. As public opinion surveys conducted by the Median Institute one week after the first strikes attest, these military actions triggered a perception of increased threat and uncertainty by Hungarians. According to polls, membership in an organization perceived as credible mitigated this fear. Public support registered 49 percent for the NATO air campaign on Serbian military targets.

In spite of a general public sense of tension and anxiety, particularly in the southern regions of the country adjacent to Yugoslavia, the attitude toward NATO remained high: 57 percent welcomed Hungarian membership, though 33 percent were dissatisfied by the country's new commitments to the alliance, and 10 percent were hesitant about the consequences of membership. The same pattern held true in responses to a question about whether NATO membership reduced the vulnerability of Hungary for a direct military attack.[18]

A public opinion survey taken by the Median Institute one month later, in April 1999, did not indicate any recognizable change in attitude toward NATO bombing. Nonetheless, Hungary sat geographically closer to the conflict than the other two new members and as a result had a direct interest in the course of the conflict. There were clearly serious concerns and considerable discussion about possible Serb repercussions for the Hungarian minority living in Vojvodina, the northern province of Serbia. There was fear over the potential for revenge on the minority by the Serb authorities or by extremists. Over 60 percent of those polled strongly rejected the deployment of Hungarian troops in the event of a ground offensive. Indeed, 60 percent opposed any form of direct Hungarian military involvement in NATO intervention. The public sense of insecurity remained at 55 percent in light of the enhanced probability of military attack against the country.

Fear of Serbian attack notwithstanding, 90 percent of the Hungarian public remained convinced throughout the air strikes that NATO would come to Hungary's assistance if any country committed aggression against the Hungarian state.[19] In sum, the conflict in Kosovo put on the Hungarian doorstep an immediate and unanticipated challenge within ten days of admittance to NATO. No other member country has had to confront such a challenge and confront it so unexpectedly and soon after membership. The fact that Hungary maintained its resolve to stand behind the alliance is a testament to its determination to be a reliable partner, willing to assume risks in exchange for the security and stability associated with NATO membership.

Despite a challenge to Hungarian security as a result of the NATO involvement in Kosovo, the continued high degree of public and official support for NATO membership demonstrates a consensus within the country that NATO membership is in the long-term national security interests of the country. That another outcome to the Kosovo and Serbian situation would have challenged the support would only be unsubstantiated speculation. But much clearer is that the conflict in the Balkan region at present has abated and the threat to Hungary greatly receded. While there is no official Hungarian position on a second NATO enlargement and the country continues to cement its own membership in the alliance, an enlargement at some point to include other Balkan countries would clearly reinforce Hungarian security and promote regional Balkan stability. Any such enlargement (to Slovenia, Bulgaria, or even other countries) would, however, only be in Hungarian interests if it could be pursued without challenging or undermining the ability of NATO to continue to provide security for all its members.

NOTES

1. Pál Dunay, "Adversaries All Around? The (Re)nationalization of Security and Defense Policies in Eastern Europe," *Clingendael Papers* (January 1994): 10–11.

2. László Kovács, "The Domestic Background Legitimizes Foreign Policy," *Magyar Hirlap* (11 March 1995).

3. Zoltán Rockenbauer, *The Hungarian National Assembly and European Integration in Hungary: A Member of NATO,* ed. Rudolf Jou (Budapest, 1999), 62.

4. Hungarian National Assembly, "Basic Principles of the National Security of the Republic of Hungary," Resolution No. 11/1993/III.12, paragraph 4.

5. Ibid., Resolution No. 27/1993/IV.23, paragraph 16.

6. Hungarian National Assembly, "Basic Principles of the Security and Defense Policy of the Republic of Hungary," Resolution No. 94/1998/XII.29, paragraph 3.

7. Ibid.

8. Hungarian National Assembly, Resolution No. 94/1998/XII.29, paragraph 14.

9. Lajos Pietsch, *Hungary and NATO* (Budapest: Atlantic Council, 1998), 42.

10. Ferenc Végh, "The Hungarian Defense Forces: From Preparation to Full Interoperability," in *Hungary: A Member of NATO,* ed. Rudolf Jou (Budapest: Ministry of Foreign Affairs of the Republic of Hungary, 1999), 49.

11. Janos Gombos, *MagyarorszAg Os a NATO [Hungary and NATO]* (Budapest: Star Pr Egynokseg, 1997).

12. Hungary, Ministry of Foreign Affairs, *Hungary and NATO: On the Road to Membership,* fact sheets on Hungary (Budapest: Ministry of Foreign Affairs, 1997).

13. Pietsch, *Hungary and NATO,* 42.

14. Pál Dunay, "Theoretical Debates in Hungary," in *The North Atlantic Treaty Organization: Studies and Documents,* ed. Pál Dunay-Ferenc Gazdag (Budapest: Srtatogiai Os Vodelmi Kutatuintozet [Institute of Strategic and Defense Studies], 1997).

15. Pietsch, *Hungary and NATO,* 58.

16. Ferenc Somogyi, "NATO Accession and the Hungarian Public Opinion," in *Hungary: A Member of NATO,* ed. Rudolf Joó (Budapest, 1999), 77.

17. There was also an attempt to link the referendum to a vote on land reform, which was not popular (with possible deleterious effects on the NATO vote). After a dramatic late-night parliamentary session early in November, this attempt was blocked.

18. Endre Hahn, "Bizakodó Félelem [Optimist Anxieties]," *Heti Világgazdaság [World Economic Weekly]* (3 April 1999): 9.

19. "Tartó Bizonytalanságérzet [Permanent Uncertainty]," editorial, *Heti Világgazdaság [World Economic Weekly]* (1 May 1999): 9.

9

Czech Republic: A Pan-European Perspective

Radek Khol

Following the events of 1989, establishing security and escaping the bitter history of the twentieth century have been common goals for many countries in Central and Eastern Europe, including Czechoslovakia, and later the Czech Republic. Debates on Czech security during the 1990s provided frequent reminders of the historical traumas of modern Czech statehood. The years 1938, 1948, and 1968, together with words such as "Munich," "Victorious February," and "international help" often came up in the debate. Political leaders who took power in 1989 returned, however, not only to the roots of the security legacy but also to the roots of modern Czech political thinking, associated primarily with the first Czech president, Tomáš Masaryk. President Masaryk viewed the Czech security question from a European perspective.[1]

The most pressing issue for the political leaders in 1989 was the presence in Czechoslovak territory of several hundred thousand Soviet troops, stationed there since the invasion by five Warsaw Pact countries on 20 August and 21 August 1968. The unlawful presence of foreign troops had to be addressed, and negotiations toward that end began on 15 January 1990. The Czechs rejected the original Soviet suggestions to hold talks within a multilateral framework and to connect this issue with reform of the Warsaw treaty. After surprisingly brief talks, an agreement was signed on 22 February 1990, in Moscow.[2] The withdrawal of Soviet troops was completed on 25 June 1991, but the impact of the presence of Soviet troops lingered and significantly influenced the general public's view of security, including the NATO debate in the Czech Republic. The Czech people were wary of alliances, a reasonable sentiment given the betrayal of the allies in the past.[3]

POST–COLD WAR NATIONAL SECURITY PERCEPTIONS AND EXPECTATIONS

Identification of Threats

The security policies of Czechoslovakia and later the Czech Republic did not identify any imminent or direct threats. Rather, these policies stressed a broad variety of potential risks stemming from multiple directions and sectors of life. The Czech perception of risk took into account the country's position at the geopolitical center of Europe—as a connection between the East and the West. All potential risks to European or global security also concerned the Czech Republic. While the general public originally considered the greatest potential threat to be from the East (the USSR and, later, Russia), political leaders were concerned as well about unstable parts of Europe and the Czechs' immediate neighborhood—namely the territory of the former Yugoslavia and the Caucasus.[4] In addition, the Czech people and a significant number of their leaders were concerned with possible developments in the recently united Germany, its influence on Central Europe, and the conduct of its foreign and economic policies. The establishment of a "standard" relationship between Germany and the Czech Republic was not an easy task, due to lingering issues concerning war compensation in general and the question of transfer of the Sudetenland after World War II.

Czechoslovak security policy encouraged the quick dissolution of the Warsaw Pact (especially its military structures) and suggested the creation of a pan-European security system based largely on an enhanced Conference on Security and Cooperation in Europe (CSCE, as it was then named) in an effort to avoid a return to the Cold War bloc confrontation. Officials elaborated on this initiative in a proposal to the European Security Council on 6 April 1990.[5] Its aim was to stabilize the East with the help of the countries of Central Europe.   Subsequently, President Václav Havel and Foreign Minister Jiří Dienstbier adopted a pan-European foreign policy in early postrevolution Czechoslovakia, stressing human rights and respect for universal values. Then, following the change of government in 1992, Foreign Minister Josef Zieleniec firmly set the course toward early membership for the country in major Western organizations without paying much attention to either regional coordination or alternative tracks. The Zieleniec approach was a one-way policy directed toward NATO and European Union memberships. It would either succeed completely or fail with significant consequences.

National Security Interests

The Czech Republic identified full-fledged membership in both NATO and the European Union (EU) as a long-term, unalterable national security aim following the 1993 division of Czechoslovakia. Foreign Minister Zieleniec stressed in his agenda-setting speech before Parliament that he would "oppose further institutionalization of the Visegrad group as well as efforts to create parallel integrative structures alongside EC and NATO."[6] Czech national interests would come before regional or international cooperation. Thus, the policy of the "champions in Central Europe," well established in economic spheres, was adopted also in the field of diplomacy.

Together with the basic goals to join NATO and the EU, the government further identified a set of national security interests. These goals included "maintenance of peace and conflictless international development in Europe and in the world, securing Czech independence and territorial integrity, and the development of democracy, internal political stability and economic prosperity."[7] Three events brought about only refinements of these general goals: government statements following the 1996 elections, the creation of a temporary government in 1997, and early elections in 1998. However, a wide set of tools were used to secure Czech influence within the heart of Europe, including good-neighbor relations and economic cooperation. The government of Josef Tošovský strengthened regional cooperation—especially with two other NATO candidates, Poland and Hungary. And in 1998 the new Social Democratic government of Miloš Zeman emphasized fostering the republic's special relationship with Slovakia as a way to pursue Czech national interests. The acts of anchoring the Czech Republic in NATO and in the European Union and establishing cordial relations with neighbors sat at the core of Czech security policy.[8]

CHANGES IN SECURITY PERCEPTIONS BY THE PUBLIC AND BY POLITICAL LEADERS

The Czech people clearly distinguish between internal security issues and those of "traditional" military and external security. While the former was of high concern as the Czech Republic developed its new security agenda, the latter was only a marginal concern. The division of the Czechoslovakian state further entrenched this ranking of issues. The new Czech Republic occupied a safer geopolitical situation than had Czechoslovakia, shifting the state's borders away from both Russia and the Balkan crisis area. The establishment of the Czech Republic led to an increased focus on internal economic, social, political, and even ecological concerns.[9] But, in contrast to the early 1990s, increased involvement in international affairs, including Czech participation in peacekeeping activities in the former Yugoslavia, led to a greater emphasis on threats to national security, including nontraditional security issues such as mass migration and civil emergency. Only the recent increase in unemployment brought renewed interest in domestic topics such as social security.[10]

MAJOR ISSUES ADDRESSED IN THE DEBATE

The NATO debate in the Czech Republic incorporated numerous issues, not just security. Beyond the issues directly related to NATO membership, the debate spurred discussions of civilizational roots, democracy, transition and its outcomes, and foreign and security policy in general. The major issues that arose in the debate were linked as much to domestic political life as to NATO.

Culture and Identity

For proponents of enlargement in the ruling right-wing coalition, membership for the Czech Republic meant being part of Western civilization and Western traditions, consistent with the Velvet Revolution slogan "Return to Europe." Similarly, many Czech political leaders viewed NATO membership as a first step—even a prerequisite—for acquiring European Union membership. The EU and NATO have been perceived as exclusive Western clubs. Membership would make the Czech Republic part of that elite.[11]

Democracy

Related to the cultural issues were arguments that NATO membership would uphold, strengthen, and even fix a democratic regime in the Czech Republic.[12] Enlargement represented a unique opportunity to join the group of countries rooted in democracy, freedom, and the rule of law. Many coalition leaders also regarded NATO membership as recognition of the country's successful transition process.[13] The political and economic qualifications of the three leading NATO candidates—the Czech Republic, Poland, and Hungary—were stressed as evidence of their "good fit" in NATO, although the political stability and economic success of the Czech Republic was often overstated. When the first real Czech political crisis brought down the government of Václav Klaus in December 1997, some anxious political leaders thought that the Czech Republic would thus be ruined and that early elections might seem irresponsible during the period of NATO ratification.

Paradoxically, opponents of NATO enlargement in the extremist Communist and Republican parties criticized the Czech government and later Parliament for a lack of democratic procedures on the issue of NATO membership. The ruling coalition strongly resisted any consideration of a public referendum on Czech membership in NATO. Public support of inclusion was lukewarm, at least partly because of insufficient information provided by the Czech government. The nature of the procedures involved in determining whether to join a democratic alliance in some ways tested the state of democracy in the Czech Republic.

Sovereignty

Closely connected to these democratic considerations was the fierce quarrel over Czech sovereignty and the referendum question. Opponents argued that NATO membership would substantially limit Czech sovereignty and should therefore be decided by consultation with the citizens via a referendum. Supporters of NATO membership countered this claim by underscoring the principle of equality in NATO decisionmaking: No decision can be taken against the will of a member country. They stressed that pooling resources with other Western countries actually would strengthen Czech sovereignty, as more options would be available to the state during a time of crisis.

The second objection stemmed from the questionable legitimacy of the Parliament and the government after Klaus's ruling coalition had been deposed. Adherents of this position believed that any decision about NATO membership should be made by a newly elected Parliament after early elections. Ultimately, these objections were overruled and all the democratic parties decided to go ahead with ratification before the next elections.

Within the entire debate, the most precarious position held was that of the Social Democrats of the Czech Republic (CSSD)—the main opposition party—which for a long time viewed referenda as essential tools in democratic decisionmaking. The party proposed this view at the time of the Czech-Slovak split and consequently criticized the ruling coalition for not consulting with citizens. During the NATO debate the CSSD divided into two camps: One insisted on holding a referendum, while the other was prepared to give up on the issue in favor of wider political and practical considerations (mainly the lack of a constitutional law on the use of referenda). When the CSSD came to power in 1998, it dropped all plans to hold a referendum on NATO. The responsibility of being the ruling party in a coalition outweighed the CSSD's earlier plans for holding at least a consultative referendum on the issue.

Security

The NATO debate essentially substituted for a general debate on security in the newly created Czech Republic. Members of Parliament discussed the advantages and disadvantages of various security arrangements in Europe, the viability of neutrality, and the utility of NATO in civil emergencies. But only one issue sparked emotional debate—the nuclear weapons status of new members, especially the question of whether allied nuclear weapons would be placed on Czech soil. Soviet nuclear weapons had been pulled out of the Czech Republic only a short time before. NATO had stated clearly that it had no plan, no intention, and no need to deploy nuclear weapons on the territory of new member states. Even so, the coalition parties immediately stated that they would support a deployment of nuclear weapons. This invigorated those opposed to nuclear weapons or substantial foreign units on Czech territory. The nuclear weapons question was an argument used by NATO opponents at every possible occasion.[14]

The fundamental security arguments made during the debate focused on whether membership would increase or decrease the security of the Czech Republic. Supporters argued that joining NATO would enhance significantly Czech security and stability because NATO is the most effective security alliance in history, still functioning after fifty years. They even saw NATO membership as insurance against Russia, should the democratic experiment there fail. NATO's inclusion of Central European states was seen as an opportunity to stabilize this historically unstable region. Some supporters even stressed the important role NATO could play in containing the second traditional heavyweight of the region, Germany. U.S. interests in NATO were seen to balance German interests in the region, limiting the possible threat of German political domination. Dealing with civil emergencies—a new dimension of security, though long established within NATO—was also considered to be important for the security of the Czech people, who had suffered through disastrous floods in 1997.[15]

Opponents of NATO membership also cited concern for security issues as a reason to reject inclusion in NATO, arguing that the Czech Republic would be drawn into distant conflicts to defend the interests of other countries, especially the United States and Germany. Such a commitment could lead to heavy casualties. Anti-NATO members of the Communist Party (KSCM) discussed alternative security structures, including strengthening the Organization for Security and Cooperation in Europe (OSCE).[16] At the same time Republicans advocated neutrality while conjuring images of foreign officers (again, especially U.S. and German) leading Czech troops. When the nuclear weapons question arose, some retired Communist generals suggested that membership could lead to the targeting of Russian nuclear weapons on Czech territory, exposing the Czech people to great danger.[17]

Economics and Cost

A favorite subject among the opponents of NATO membership was that of costs—both direct and indirect. Various foreign estimates, as well as calculations by pre-1989 Communist generals, contained especially high cost figures of hundreds of billions of Czech "crowns" (KC), based on studies by the RAND Corporation and the U.S. Congressional Budget Office. These figures were released at a sensitive time—immediately following budget cuts and the imposition of austerity measures by the Klaus government in 1997. "Bread or guns" was the cry of both extreme parties, which listed the social problems of contemporary Czech society and lamented the spending of billions of KC on NATO integration, modernization of the armed forces, and procurement of expensive Western-produced weapons. NATO opponents maintained that pursuing security through either the OSCE or a policy of neutrality would be cheaper and more appropriate at a time when the Czech Republic and its citizens faced no immediate threats.

NATO supporters argued that collective defense is the best economic option; in the long term, it is the cheapest one and still provides a high degree of assurance. These officials cited low-end cost estimates produced by various foreign studies, including an official study by NATO, a second RAND study, and the Clinton administration's study for the U.S. Senate. These reports presented the direct costs of membership, distinct from the costs related to modernizing the armed forces, and equaled a few billion KC per year rather than hundreds of billions.[18]

NATO supporters also asserted that NATO membership would generate indirect economic benefits. They frequently mentioned technology transfers, support for ailing Czech research and development programs, and even support for the Czech education system. Enhanced stability was also associated with increased hope for more foreign investment. The potential benefits of NATO membership were nevertheless much more difficult to calculate than the real costs to which the Czechs already subscribed (0.9 percent contribution toward the three NATO budgets) or those projected within the defense budget. It was certainly difficult to justify the government's commitment to increase the defense budget annually by 0.1 percent, reaching 2.0 percent of the gross domestic product by the year 2000, when all other ministries had to cut expenses for both the 1997 and 1998 fiscal years. It was therefore necessary to prove that these funds would be used effectively and would contribute toward building a small, modern, and efficient military.

Military Reform

A final major issue during the NATO debate centered around reform of the Czech armed forces. These discussions occurred mainly within the military community, with the inclusion of only a handful of political leaders and civilian security experts. For the armed forces, NATO membership promised them secured finances, support from politicians, and clear tasks such as fulfillment of the interoperability criteria—all of which had been absent in the past. Membership also would ensure the successful completion of reforms, would provide guidance for the main direction of Czech security policy, and could help attract talented individuals to pursue military careers in an institution that would no longer have low prestige.

Several analysts of civil-military relations pointed out that the promise of NATO membership was a significant incentive for progressive military reforms in Central Europe.[19] Inclusion of the Czech Republic in NATO would bolster reforms through regular exposure to Western practices, through a myriad of contacts on various levels, and through day-to-day practice of international cooperation. Consequently, professional military personnel were among the most enthusiastic supporters of NATO membership, despite their overall leftist political inclination. Unlike in the general press, exploration of the NATO debate in Czech military journals was factual and not dominated by ideological considerations.

Surprisingly, fundamental questions about the shift in Czech security policy and military doctrine arose only late in the debate. Until the final months of 1997, long-term security and military planning did not take into account the possibility of Czech membership in NATO, nor were its wider military and security implications considered. It was not until late 1998 that officials revised expensive procurement plans for the modernized T-72 battle tanks, for the future composition of the air force, and for other programs in order to accommodate NATO membership. This lack of early forward thinking no doubt cost the Czech government hundreds of billions of KC.[20]

GOVERNMENT SECURITY POLICY

The quest for NATO membership was one of the most stable features of Czech security policy—at least in the government's declarations. NATO membership appeared to be a cornerstone of official security policy even before NATO had decided to accept any new members. It continued as a priority after the creation by NATO of the Partnership for Peace program and through the evolution of NATO's enlargement policy. It became *the* Czech priority when NATO invited the Czech Republic to the Madrid summit. All of this would suggest that preparations for NATO membership were in progress in Prague, but a thorough examination shows that this was not the case.

Despite all official declarations, internal political struggles, primarily within the coalition itself, were the primary driver of security policy as well as defense reform and all related matters. The main coalition party, headed by Prime Minister Klaus, used the defense sector to pressure its smaller coalition partner—the Christian and Democratic Union–Czechoslovak People's Party (KDU-CSL), which headed the Ministry of Defense from 1993 to 1997 and presided over the transformation, reduction, and reform of the Czech armed forces. As security and defense issues were not of high priority for the government, the two Klaus governments adopted only a limited number of very general framework documents. Almost no fruitful government debate on

Czech security policy, its direction, or alternative armed forces reforms took place. Officials spent most of the time devoted to defense matters disputing procurement policies, including selling the T-72 to Algeria and procuring the L-159 for the Czech Air Force, investigating alleged fraud, notably with several staff information system tenders related to modernization of the T-72, and using defense issues as a ploy in intercoalition skirmishes.

Neither of the two Klaus governments was able to agree on a basic conceptual document defining Czech security interests, and the country went without one for six years. The government finally adopted both the National Defense Doctrine and the National Defense Strategy in 1997. Prime Minister Klaus later acknowledged that NATO pressure indirectly induced the government to approve these documents prior to the Madrid summit. Changes continued, and the Tošovský government adopted a new constitutional law on security in May 1998. The law re-established the National Security Council, which immediately began considering legislation and other measures needed to speed armed forces reform and inclusion in NATO in general. The Tošovský government began work on the principle long-term strategic document, and Zeman's government redrafted and completed the National Security Strategy of the Czech Republic in February 1999. Upon its approval, the government made this document available to the public in order to inform the citizens of its content, encourage open debate, and build as wide a public consensus on it as possible.[21]

In order to facilitate its relations with NATO and to prepare for NATO membership, the government created the Governmental Committee for Integration of the Czech Republic into NATO in 1997. The committee had three main bodies: a governmental body with an advisory function, a working committee representing all concerned ministries as well as the Office of the President, and a body of nine working groups to deal with the principal problems. In addition, these bodies also dealt with the accession talks between the Czech Republic and NATO that took place from 23 September to 10 November 1997 and led to the signing of the accession protocol on 16 December 1997 by foreign ministers of the three invited countries.

After the 1998 elections, the Zeman government continued to meet the agreed-to timetable for reforms. In October 1998 the government adopted a plan to secure the necessary resources for Czech integration into NATO and to launch a campaign to inform the public of the benefits of this important step. Despite the uneasy position of the minority government, which incurred some negative comments by right-wing parties, there were no major setbacks in the integration efforts. One of the most positive steps was the preparation of the long-overdue legal framework of the Czech armed forces, presented to the government on 1 February 1999. Among other things, these laws regulated the functions and the place of the armed forces within the state, the armed forces' relations with allied troops on Czech territory, and the participation of Czech units in missions abroad.

PARLIAMENTARY DEBATES

By the start of the parliamentary debate in 1998 all parties had taken a clear position on Czech membership in NATO. The coalition parties supported membership, and both the extreme left-wing and right-wing opposition parties staunchly opposed it, while the sole democratic opposition party desired a referendum on the issue as well as modified membership for the Czech Republic within NATO similar to that of Norway.[22]

The Civic Democratic Party (ODS), the major coalition partner from 1992 to 1997, supported the goals of membership in both NATO and the EU. However, the party did not actively pursue that security policy until forced to do so after the Madrid summit. The party had even blocked some vital steps toward full membership. One junior coalition partner, the Civic Democratic Alliance (ODA)—responsible for neither defense nor foreign policy—was regularly critical of the progress on military reform but fiercely supported NATO membership. KDU-CSL, the junior partner responsible for the defense ministry, also supported NATO membership. Nor did, in 1998, the newly created party Freedom Union (US) differ from ODS in foreign or defense matters.

All coalition parties were criticized for their inability to articulate to the general public the main reasons for seeking NATO membership. The members of the government believed that they had a mandate on NATO policy from the voters because they had featured this issue in their electoral platforms. Moreover, they considered the issue to be too complex for public debate; this was to be a matter for the "experts" in Parliament to decide. Some political leaders demonstrated their aversion to any sort of public information campaign about NATO issues, while others feared public debate could be divisive for society.[23]

The government's lack of clear arguments and serious debate gave rise to the policy of the CSSD party, which insisted on holding a referendum. The party hoped that a pending referendum would push the government to initiate an information campaign, as had occurred in Hungary. Opponents of NATO membership also pointed out similarities to the Communist approach, which also did not allow any discussions about choices. The "one choice only" thinking alarmed some officials and analysts, as it could have serious consequences for future security and foreign policy decisionmaking.

Parliament's low level of overall interest in security and defense matters changed only as the Madrid summit approached. Only a handful of political leaders were security and defense experts, a fact that became apparent both in parliamentary debates and in press or TV interviews. During 1997, the main topic of debate within foreign and security committees was the fight between the government and the opposition party CSSD about the need to have an information campaign about NATO at all. On 2 January 1998, interim Prime Minister Tošovský was appointed and began the ratification process in Parliament. Defense policy, the military, NATO membership, and foreign policy were among the ten most discussed issues during the 1998 pre-elections campaign.[24]

The two legislative blocs disagreed about the legitimacy of this Parliament to make the decision about NATO membership. The opposition parties (primarily KSCM and the Association for the Republic–Republican Party of Czechoslovakia, or SPR-RSC, but initially also CSSD) tried to postpone the decision until after the early elections and after agreement to call for a referendum. Opposition officials used the break-up of Czechoslovakia without popular consent as analogous to the refusal to call for a referendum on NATO.

The first reading of the Washington treaty started in the lower chamber on 11 February 1998 and lasted two days. Six committees were asked to give their views on the proposed treaty. A second reading was made in an extraordinary session of Parliament on 14–15 April 1998. The Chamber of Duputies ratified the treaty with a vote of 154 to 38; in the end, only KSCM and SPR-RSC members of Parliament opposed it. It was then sent to the Senate, which voted on it 30 April. An affirmative vote of 64 to 3 in the Senate left only the signature of the president to complete the ratification procedure. President Havel finally signed the ratification document, in coordination with the signing of Poland's ratification document in Warsaw, on 26 February 1999.

The character of the debate in the Chamber of Deputies and in the Senate differed strikingly. In the lower chamber the debate was conducted primarily by opponents of NATO membership from extremist parties; in the Senate the debate was relatively short and primarily directed by NATO supporters. In the lower chamber the most frequently discussed issues were the cost of NATO membership, alternative security schemes, the need for a referendum, expression of anti-German sentiments, and some Communist-era propaganda against world capitalism.[25] Democratic members of Parliament for the most part refrained from arguing with their opponents.[26] Positive constructive arguments appeared mainly in the opening and closing speeches of Prime Minister Josef Tošovský, Foreign Minister Jaroslav Šedivý, and Defense Minister Michal Lobkowicz.

PUBLIC DEBATES AND OPINION

The Czech general public had been kept in the dark about the issue of NATO accession for a long time. The public did not seem to take a strong interest in defense and foreign policy issues, although it felt strongly about the priority of internal security issues.[27] Until 1998 there was no real dissemination of information to the public because top political leaders believed these issues should be primarily dealt with by the government. The Czech public was therefore either apathetic or ambivalent about the issue. Public support for NATO membership peaked at about 50 percent, with the opposition at 30 percent and those who were ambivalent at 20 percent.[28]

Only in 1997 did political leaders begin to worry about the public's view—or lack of a view—on NATO issues. At that time, both domestic and foreign media began to criticize widely Czech political leaders for their failure to educate the public.[29] After the fall of the Klaus government, hasty preparation was made for a massive information campaign, which was launched in 1998.

By this time, other efforts to spread information about NATO, defense, and security issues were being made. The Ministry of Defense had prepared a communication plan in 1997, directed toward various policy and opinion groups, journalists, and academics. The Ministry of Foreign Affairs, especially under Jaroslav Šedivý, also supported an information campaign in the autumn of 1997. The major educational drive was nevertheless left to nongovernmental organizations (NGOs). Academic discussion was taking place on the pages of *Mezinárodní politika*.[30] The Czech Atlantic Commission published several booklets on NATO and the Czech Republic as well as a Czech translation of the *NATO Handbook*.[31] This NGO, together with the Ministry of Defense, organized several "Days of NATO" in various towns and initiated education programs for teachers to enable them to discuss security issues. In the military, the most interesting and articulate debate was concentrated on the pages of the theoretical military journal *Vojenské rozhledy (Military Outlook)*. Media coverage of NATO issues expanded generally between mid-1997 and mid-1998.

Unlike in Poland or Hungary, participation by the Czech public in the NATO debate originated in the nongovernmental sector rather than through the initiative of political leaders. Paradoxically, it was the camp of NATO opponents who started the education process with its "anti-campaign." A banner with the words "SPR-RSC against NATO" hung from the windows of the offices of SPR-RSC members of Parliament for a few days in February 1998. Stickers with a strong anti-German message were used by many NATO opponents. The stickers, containing an image of a skull with the Wehrmacht insignia, a helmet, and the NATO symbol appeared in many public places and drew much criticism. These statements triggered the involvement of otherwise nonpolitical figures such as actors, artists, priests, and athletes in the debate, but on the side of NATO proponents rather than opposed to membership.

The NATO debate peaked during the first four months of 1998 when Parliament was about to start the ratification process, and both main TV channels aired a series of short documentaries and interviews on the issue. *Nova TV*, a champion of nationwide commercial television in Central Europe with a large audience and much influence, aired flashy testimonials by popular public figures, all of whom took a pro-NATO position. Both series were shown during prime-time hours.

Opponents of NATO received foreign support to help energize existing NGOs. A Pan-Slavic Congress anniversary celebration turned into a forum for NATO opposition. The NGO Res Publica hosted several public events advocating the idea of Czech neutrality and published several books against NATO enlargement, including the comprehensive work of Oskar Krejcí, *NATO—na co? (NATO—What for?)*.[32]

NATO was a hotly debated issue during the 1998 election campaign, even though Parliament had made its decision by that time. Thereafter, NATO debate subsided. Since the summer of 1998, there has been only moderate discussion, focusing on the pace of successful preparation and how to deal with the problems connected with such a complex issue. Czech membership in NATO has now been granted, and the case is closed.[33]

The public information campaign in the Czech Republic had only a limited effect: Support increased from 34 percent in 1995 to slightly over 50 percent in 1998.[34] While the public continuously supported the idea of a referendum, the issue ultimately would be decided by Parliament, spurring a widely shared belief that the NATO membership issue was not of great importance to Czech citizens.[35]

The eventual bipartisan support from all democratic parties, the activity of the nongovernmental sector, and support obtained from influential figures from nonpolitical fields reflect the positive side of the debate. It is hoped that the political consensus of the majority parliamentary parties after the 1998 elections will be mirrored by support and understanding for NATO issues in society as a whole. Following the NATO debate, the opposition party SPR-RSC failed to pass the 5 percent threshold in the 1998 elections and lost its place in Parliament. This was one of the major surprises of the elections, as the SPR-RSC's secure electoral niche was generally taken for granted and might reveal heightened public consensus.

Less clear, still, is the general understanding of why the Czech Republic joined NATO. Polls on this question generate ambiguous results: Less than than 50 percent of respondents to an open question on why the Czech Republic should join NATO could provide arguments either for or against membership.[36]

Various opinion polls demonstrate that the Czech public increasingly believes that entry into NATO will have a positive impact on the Czech military and national security. According to questions posed in the polls, Czechs believe that entry into NATO will ensure rapid-force modernization, improved quality of career soldiers, better order and discipline, and increased budgetary expenditures for the military. At the same time, the public does not expect a rapid improvement of the quality and prestige of the Czech military, and it does not believe that Czech political leaders will pay increased attention to military issues. There is a growing perception that Czech admission into NATO will impose certain limitations on the sovereignty of the Czech Republic.[37]

ROLE OF OUTSIDE LOBBYISTS AND INTEREST GROUPS

In comparison to other candidate countries and also to some current NATO member countries, outside lobbying groups played a relatively limited role in the Czech Republic. There are several reasons for this. First, Czech citizens generally view Czech emigrants with suspicion, and their influence—if any— is quite limited. Relations between Hungary and its emigrants and Poland and its emigrants are much better than the Czech Republic's with its emigrants. While emigrants are quite influential in the sphere of economics, they have little direct political influence and, with some clear exceptions, do not play a crucial role in Czech political life. But at least one prominent emigrant had a discernible impact on the Czech NATO debate: U.S. Secretary of State Madeleine Albright. Her few but pertinent interventions in the Czech debate were influential, especially with top political leaders.[38]

An interest group that did have a great impact on the Czech NATO debate is the foreign arms industry—especially those companies bidding for contracts to supply supersonic aircraft to the Czech Air Force, those interested in investing in and coproducing the Aero-Vodochody (the future backbone of the Czech Air Force), and those interested in procurement of information systems.[39] The indirect influence of these companies—including Boeing/McDonnell-Douglas, Lockheed Martin, British Aerospace–Saab, Digital, IBM, and Matra— provided especially valuable support for the NATO information campaign and various pro-NATO events. At the same time, however, the policy of these firms became the subject of parliamentary debate about the firms' profiteering through modernization programs as well as through the use of offset packages, which will provide indirect economic benefits to the civilian sector, to promote industrial cooperation with the local defense industry and Czech firms' integration into the Western defense industry market.

FULFILLING REQUIREMENTS AND PREPARING FOR THE NEXT STAGE

Civil-Military Relations, Political and Civilian Expertise, Wider Responsibility, Good Preparation for EU Talks, and Integration

The NATO enlargement process proved to be a turning point in civil-military relations in the Czech Republic. It forced Czech political leaders to recognize the armed forces as an indivisible part of society and to acknowledge their role in the transformation process. And once the military was included as a key player in Czech integration into the West, its importance, prestige, and potential grew substantially. Entry into NATO has served as a starting point for a deeper awareness on the part of both society and political leaders of security and defense issues. The government has finally had to realize its responsibility to guide the military in a democratic society and to justify the military's role to its citizens.

Czech membership in NATO should result in healthy civil-military relations and democratic control of the armed forces. Political and civilian expertise gained during the NATO debate should not be wasted; sustained attention, systematic work on strategic planning, policymaking, and resource management will be needed. By entering the West's security community, the Czech Republic should widen its political horizon and provide local political leaders with a greater sense of responsibility, skills for building consensus, and a long-term vision.

These skills should be an essential aid in discussions about full-fledged accession to the European Union. The experience of the NATO debate, the process of preparing for integration, the illumination of major issues for the public, the participation of NGOs, and the potential for an open society will all be important for the much more complex task of integration into an entity of unprecedented complexity.

Regional Cooperation—Foreign and Military Dimension, Special Relationship with Slovakia and Perhaps the Baltics: The Need for an Open-Door Policy

The enlargement had a generally positive impact on foreign policy, especially in its later stages when the focus was on regional cooperation. The practice of consultation and coordination of the main steps with Poland and Hungary, the pooling of resources for joint lobbying in member countries, and an exchange of expert advice in dealing with similar problems of adaptation to NATO standards and practices consitute some of the most important long-term effects of this period. The Czech Republic should continue to enhance these revitalized relations, something the Zeman government identified as a foreign-policy priority. Joint activities during the NATO accession period have, to a certain extent, eliminated earlier rivalries among candidate countries.

Policy toward Slovakia remains a key issue in regional cooperation for the Czech Republic. For the past several years, Slovakian participation in the same Euro-Atlantic structures has been a clearly stated Czech interest and has been facilitated by political developments in Slovakia. Hungary and Poland also support Slovakia's integration into the West. Military cooperation with Slovakia has been among the most successful of all Czech international military cooperation efforts. Moreover, the Slovak minority in the Czech Republic has never caused controversy between the two states. Putting aside the complicated and volatile Gypsy question, this situation should improve even more once the Czech plan for granting dual citizenship to the Slovak minority is implemented.

Czech interest in keeping NATO's doors open does not, however, stop with Slovakia. The Czech Republic will probably try to help not only its closest neighbor but also the Baltic states and Slovenia. Sharing experiences about the NATO debate and integration process should foster close ties to all prospective candidate countries in the next round of NATO enlargement. Further enlargement of NATO finds broad support across the Czech political spectrum and should not become a source of internal political quarrels.

Czech Armed Forces Reform

NATO membership has had an enormous impact on the Czech military. While it struggled successfully to be ready for NATO integration, its adaptation and reform is by no means finished. Sustained progress is needed in several areas. First, all fifty-two agreed goals of interoperability must be met to ensure the effective functioning of Czech units within the NATO structure. This will require not only the investment of material, financial, and human resources but also careful planning.

The military requires internal restructuring and shrinking its overall size as well as an alteration of the ratio between noncommissioned officers, warrant officers, junior officers, and senior officers. Personnel problems have plagued the Czech military. Thousands of officers left the Czech military during the first few years of its existence because of concerns that the system was perpetually reorganized, without a clear objective. The situation grew even worse when many graduates of Western military courses, academies, and training programs were not given assignments commensurate with their qualifications. They became frustrated and soon resigned. Personnel policy thus became a top priority for Minister of Defense Lobkowicz in 1998 and continues to be one for his successor, Minister Vladimír Vetchý.

Finally, the Czech military faces the challenge that concerns all Western armed forces—attracting qualified and motivated personnel, offering them responsible and rewarding jobs, and allowing them to learn skills that enable them to rejoin civil society after leaving the military. There are several types of transition needed: from an authoritarian to a democratic military; from conscription to a combination of conscription and volunteer forces, or even an all-volunteer force; and eventually from the "profession for a life" to "profession like any other profession." The Czech armed forces will offer young people a relatively good prospect if it can establish itself as an effective Western-modeled institution. But if all these issues cannot be resolved successfully, then the optimism of current and future military personnel will be lost.

CONCLUSION

NATO was once again featured in news headlines in the Czech Republic in March 1999. On 12 March 1999, Czech Foreign Minister Jan Kavan, together with his Polish and Hungarian counterparts, presented the Czech ratification documents to U.S. Secretary of State Madeleine Albright at the Truman Memorial Library in Independence, Missouri. This presentation, along with speeches from top officials in the government, the Parliament, and the Czech armed forces, brought to a close the lengthy Czech debate on NATO membership.

While the intensive public phase of the debate was limited to about a year—from the time of the Madrid summit until the 1998 elections—the discussions of political leaders and experts spanned a more extensive period. The NATO debate revealed both positive and negative features of the contemporary Czech Republic. The process of NATO accession was one of the first tests of the country's ability to forge a consensus and to accomplish complex tasks within a set deadline. The country was able to meet these challenges—a good sign, indeed.

At the same time, the lack of a real information campaign—a consultative process vis-à-vis the public, complete with an illumination of the basic features of NATO—was problematic, as revealed by later development: The Czech public and their political leaders were extremely divided about NATO action during the Kosovo crisis. The reaction to this crisis revealed lingering questions about Czech membership in NATO, issues that had been glossed over during the earlier anxious debates.

For these reasons, the Czechs may be expected to focus more inwardly on their integration into NATO and the necessary restructuring of Czech military forces and equipment than on a second round of enlargement. However, it is clear that a broader umbrella of security in Central and Eastern Europe would enhance stability more generally in the region. In addition, there will be concern that such an enlargement not be undertaken with disregard for the Russians and other states not included in a next round, a move that could lead to heightened tensions rather than the desired stability. While no official position has yet been taken, the Czech Republic may be expected to want to lend official support to further enlargements that meet this objective.

NOTES

1. Jiří Šedivý, "From Dreaming to Realism—Czechoslovak Security Policy Since 1989," *Perspectives*, no. 4 (Winter 1994/95): 62–63.

2. Jiří Šedivý, "Pull-Out of Soviet Troops from Czechoslovakia," *Perspectives*, no. 2 (Winter 1993/94): 21–39.

3. During the interwar period France refused to fulfill its obligations to Czechoslovakia during the Munich crisis. There are also, of course, recriminations about an invasion by an official ally—referring clearly to the Soviet Union and the other five Warsaw Pact countries who took part in the 1968 suppression of the Prague Spring.

4. Ministry of Defense, *White Paper on Defense of the Czech Republic* (Prague: Ministry of Defense, 1995): 7.

5. Jiří Šedivý, "From Dreaming to Realism," 64–65.

6. Foreign Minister Josef Zieleniec (speech given at the 8th session of the House of Deputies of Parliament, 21 April 1993) in Ministry of Foreign Affairs of the Czech Republic, *Documents 1993* (Prague: 1994): 322–323.

7. See first official Czech document dealing with security and defense issues, adopted on 21 December 1994, "Military Strategy of the Czech Republic," in *White Paper on Defense of the Czech Republic*, 17.

8. Prime Minister Klaus, *Policy Statement of the Government of the Czech Republic—1996* (Prague: Office of the Prime Minister, 1996); Prime Minister Tošovský, *Policy Statement of the Government of the Czech Republic—1998* (Prague: Office of the Prime Minister, 27 January 1998); and Prime Minister Zeman, *Policy Statement of the Government of the Czech Republic—1998* (Prague: Office of the Prime Minister, August 1998).

9. Roman Blasek, "Perception of Security Risks by the Population of the Czech Republic," *The Journal of Slavic Military Studies* 11, no. 3 (September 1998): 89–96.

10. The unemployment rate doubled in less than two years, reaching 9 percent by early 1999. See Czech Statistical Bureau monthly statements.

11. The Senate debate on 30 April 1998 demonstrates this view of membership. See Jan Sliva, "Czech Senate Ratifies Accession to NATO," *AP Worldstream* (30 April 1998).

12. Ibid., especially the speeches by P. Sobotka, M. Žantovský.

13. Defense Minister Lobkowicz, interview, *Reflex* (23 April 1998).

14. Jiří Šedivý, "Czech Republic: Nuclear Controversy," *Perspectives*, no. 9 (Summer 1997/98): 77–88.

15. View presented shortly after the floods by Deputy Minister of Defense Novotný, in *Slovo* (23 September 1997).

16. See speeches of Senators Recman, Grebeníček, and Frank among others during the parliamentary debate, 14–15 April 1998. Available online at http//:www.senat.cz/index-eng.htm.

17. See parliamentary debate on 14–15 April 1998, especially the speech by M. Grebeníček. Available online at http//:www.senat.cz/index-eng.htm.

18. Stefan Sarvaš, *One Past, Two Futures? The NATO Enlargement Debate in the Czech Republic and Slovakia,* Harmonie Paper 4 (Groningen, The Netherlands: Center for European Security Studies, 1999), esp. 19–21.

19. Reka Szemerkényi, *Central European Civil-Military Reforms at Risk,* Adelphi Paper 306 (London: International Institute for Security Studies, 1996); Jeffrey Simon, *Central European Civil-Military Relations and NATO Expansion*, McNair Paper 39 (Washington: National Defense University, 1997).

20. Tomáš Hoøejší, *Týden* (23 November 1998).

21. Full text can be found at the Ministry of Foreign Affairs at http://www.mzv.cz/bezp_strategie/estrategie.html.

22. Sarvaš, *One Past, Two Futures?* 12–15; Jiří Šedivý, "Czech Republic," *Security in Central and Eastern Europe: Problems—Perceptions—Policies* (Vienna: Austrian Institute for International Affairs, 1999).

23. Václav Klaus stated that those who wanted information on NATO could find it; for those who didn't want to know, any information campaign would just be a waste of money. See Christine Spolar, "Aspiring to NATO: Ex-Communist States Steer Westward: Will Alliance Play in Posnan, Plzen?" *Washington Post,* 18 June 1997: A1.

24. Sarvaš, *One Past, Two Futures?* 15.

25. Communist and Republican MPs invoked the sensitive Czech-German relations and tried to raise the fear of Sudeten Germans, the German war-like nature, and possible domination or even direct German command over the Czech Republic within NATO. In addition, several Communist members of Parliament employed hard-line rhetoric about "world capitalism" and "imperialism."

26. See *Respekt,* no. 18 (19 April 1998).

27. Internal security has for a long time been among the top concerns of the Czech public; however, since 1993, the number of poll respondents seeing no external threat has steadily grown, reaching 83 percent in 1997. See Šedivý, "Czech Republic," 10.

28. When asked in June 1997 about their knowledge of Czech accession to NATO, 6 percent of poll respondents answered they were informed "in detail," 58 percent "partially," and 36 percent "not at all." Ibid., 14.

29. See Peter S. Green, "East Europe Fears EU Expansion Delay," *International Herald Tribune,* 19 June 1997: 13.

30. *International Politics Monthly,* published by the Institute of International Relations, is the only journal that covers international affairs and foreign policy of the Czech Republic each month.

31. The Czech Atlantic Commission is a relatively small NGO, not supported by a great number of politicians, academics, and entrepreneurs as in some other candidate countries.

32. Oskar Krejcí, *NATO—Na co?* (Praha: Alternativy, 1997).

33. See Jan Gazdík and Jiří Pergler, "Acceptance of Alliance," *Mladá Fronta Dnes,* 19 May 1998: 4.

34. Sarvaš, *One Past, Two Futures?* 32.

35. Long-term opinion polls asking for the public view on a referendum had sustained support at 75 percent. In the case of a NATO membership referendum, from March 1996 to December 1998, there was a range of support between 59 and 68 percent. A referendum for NATO membership was even supported by potential voters of right-wing parties. See Stefan Sarvaš, "Public Perceptions of Security and the Military in the Czech Republic," NATO Democratic Institutions Paper, available online at http://www.nato.int/acad/fellow/96-98/sarvas.pdf.

36. Czech Public Opinion Poll Institute, "Opinions on the Entry into NATO," (Prague: June 1997): 1.

37. Ibid., 78–81.

38. See collection of articles and interviews in *Lidové Noviny,* 7 December 1998.

39. See Tomáš Hoøejší, "Questions Arise About Agreements," *Týden* (20 July 1998): 17.

PART 3
Accepting New Realities

10

Russia: Facing the Facts

IRINA KOBRINSKAYA

It is not the struggle between the Communist past and a democratic future,
but between liberal and authoritarian concepts of modernization which
goes on in Russian society today.
  —V. Kuvaldiri, *Moscow News,* 19 July 1992

The expansion of NATO became the touchstone of Russian foreign policy in
the second half of 1993, and since that time, it has dominated debate. Recent
developments in NATO have had (and likely will have) little effect on Russia's military posture: NATO enlargement has had little impact on Russia's
military structures or on its military budget. Nevertheless, the issue of NATO
enlargement has become the basis of both domestic and foreign policy debates
in Russia. This development reveals profound changes in Russian political
life, notably, that it is now possible to debate and criticize official policy in
Russia. In addition, the high profile of NATO enlargement in public debate
during the initial period of post-Soviet history has played a role in the formation of a new national self-perception and identity in the international environment. Further, when NATO enlargement became a significant matter of
Russian *domestic* policy, it created a novel, dynamic linkage of foreign and
domestic matters in Russian political life. Finally, the issue of NATO enlargement has come to be seen as the embodiment—at least on the public policy
level—of Russian-Western, or rather Russian-U.S., relations. These phenomena make the analysis of the Russian perspective on and reaction to NATO
enlargement particularly interesting and important.

It is widely accepted both in the West and in Russia that Russia's future
place in the world depends to a significant extent on its domestic development—that is, whether Russia adopts democratic and market reforms or devi-
ates from those norms. Whether justified or not, Russia has treated other

countries' declared intention to join NATO as a criterion that identifies an enemy. This was especially true with regard to the former Warsaw Pact members, which are seen as carrying out foreign policies detrimental to Russian interests. Likewise, Russia generally regarded the criticism of NATO enlargement by a number of political leaders and influential political experts in the United States and Western European nations of NATO as a friendly gesture.

Exaggeration of the importance of NATO enlargement, and even the demonization of the process, has influenced significantly Russian foreign and domestic policies. The process of NATO enlargement placed perceived foreign threats among the principal concerns of foreign policy; however, in an indirect way, it simultaneously affected ongoing efforts to identify the new national interests of Russia.

The majority of both the elite and the people in Russia perceived the war in Yugoslavia as additional evidence of the threat to stability caused by NATO's enlargement and its extended zone of responsibility. The allies' decisionmaking processes and actions in the former Yugoslavia also demonstrated NATO's disregard for Russia. As a consequence, the need to identify and define Russian interests in international and regional security became even more acute.

Russia's heightened sensitivity to NATO enlargement is perceived by many in the West as an exaggeration or a legacy of imperialist thinking, but the sentiment is deeply rooted in the nation's history. Russia's seemingly "inappropriate" reaction to NATO enlargement emerges in reaction to several historical layers, each of which helped to shape present foreign policy–thinking in the country. At least three interconnected relationships complicate the picture of Russian foreign policy to an even greater degree: (1) Russia and the outside world; (2) Russians and non-Russians in Russia; and (3) the people and the Russian state. During the last three centuries—since the reign of Peter the Great—the dynamics of these three relationships have changed again and again, and each change has significantly influenced the thinking of the Russian people. Identification of the "Russian interest" is further affected by the relationship between the political thinking of the people and that of political leaders. Finally, the dramatic and yet unfinished changes in the Russian state itself, illustrated by the ambiguous status of Chechnya, greatly shape Russian perceptions of both internal and external developments.

But the historical and contemporary factors forming the context in which Russian domestic debates on NATO enlargement occur all revolve around one particular phenomenon: the progressive loss of Russia's status as a great power.

The domestic policy discussions on this controversial issue revealed a widening gap of perception and understanding between elites and the rest of society. Many experts believe that the elite class, with its more dynamic and easily adaptable mentality and behavior, deliberately initiated the destruction of Russia as a superpower as the 1990s began. Scholars consider this destabilizing push, motivated by a desire for power, to be one of the main causes of the dissolution of the Soviet Union. Both the new and the old elite in the post-Soviet era acquired extended economic and financial opportunities in the new state. Meanwhile, the majority of the population—conservative in its thinking and unprepared or unwilling to acknowledge or adapt to a new regime—suffered from the loss of the traditional state identity. This psychological crisis was complicated by the absence of any improvement in living conditions, which in fact worsened. People were deprived of both the state orientation and the state support for social, medical, and educational needs on which they had relied for years. The inconsequential economic reforms initiated by the ruling elite did nothing to improve the people's lot.

For the West, Russia's status as a "great power" has depended on the number of nuclear warheads it possessed and the potential damage it could inflict. For the Russians, however, this characterization had a broader meaning. "Great power" status has long been an ingredient in Russia's unique national history and culture. This partly (but only partly) explains the unwillingness of the elite to move away from the rhetoric of the popular myth of Russia's renown. For centuries, this myth has offered compensation to the people for their extreme poverty and for the violation of their civil and human rights. The main question remaining for the West is whether Russia's tradition as a great power necessitates Russian imperialism. Is a return to empire possible? There is no simple answer. Russia's domestic and foreign policy–making processes have not stabilized, nor has Russia even acquired definite policy goals. At present, Russian foreign policy is distinguished from that of the Soviet Union by the new function of the state and by a quest to achieve a new national identity.

Because the search for a new identity coincided with the formation of the new Russian state, foreign policy was destined to become a relevant factor in the state's struggle for identity. Russia has had to rethink and redefine its place in the world and its relations to the other nations and peoples that were once part of the Soviet Union. As a consequence, during the initial post-Soviet period (1991–1993), a divide between the concepts of "nation" and "state" began to emerge. The concept of national interests, which barely existed during the Soviet period, was formulated and declared preferable to those state interests that had dominated both Czarist and Soviet Russia. Pursuit of state interests involved the overwhelming domination of and disregard for citizens. One Russian historian expressed the situation well in the aphorism "The state got fat—the people got thin."[1]

Russian analysts in the beginning of the 1990s regarded the reformulation of Russia's foreign policy as a process involving both domestic and foreign considerations. The principal goals were to strike down the standard of "the state before the people," in order to establish control of the state by the people and to form a mechanism for the "transmission" of the interests of different social groups into the sphere of foreign policy.[2] At the end of 1997, the well-known Russian political expert and diplomat Aleksander Bovin stressed in a popular Russian daily newspaper that national identity reflects, and is reflected in, both domestic and foreign policy, with foreign policy being the more important realm:

> In the domain of foreign policy, national interests are tied to simple and concrete issues: whether and how to react to NATO enlargement? . . . The principle of the Danes—"we do not offend anyone and we let no one harm us"— is deserving and may appropriately govern the activities of the Ministry of Finance. . . . But Russia is and will remain one of the great powers; to accept the position "don't hurt me and I won't hurt you" means losing the status of a great power, not participating actively in world policy, thereby losing the ability to influence it, and, thus, striking a blow to our national interests.[3]

Russian foreign policy from 1991 to mid-1993 followed logically from Mikhail Gorbachev's Soviet foreign strategy. It was Gorbachev who withdrew troops from Afghanistan and introduced openness and transparency into foreign policy—not only for the West, but internally as well. He initiated the "new political thinking" and developed the idea of "the common European home." He revised attitudes toward Western European integration, rejected the "Brezhnev doctrine" in relations with the Soviet Union's Central and Eastern European neighbors, and voluntarily (and practically unconditionally) agreed to the unification of Germany. He also proposed the idea of a "new world order." In his remarkable address to the United Nations General Assembly on 7 December 1988, he said that "further world progress is possible only through a search for universal human consensus as we move forward to a new world order."[4]

Destruction of the old system signaled a new beginning, a time for international forums like the United Nations and the Conference on Security and Cooperation in Europe (CSCE), as it was then named. The Paris charter incorporated new democratic values as common grounds for the CSCE process "from Vancouver to Vladivostok." As security scholar A. D. Rotfeld noted, "A new phenomenon which has arisen since the 1990 CSCE Paris Summit meeting is that the system agreed to by the participating states is now addressed chiefly, if not exclusively, within the sphere of domestic rather than international relations."[5] Gorbachev introduced a new style of relations with Western leaders, again rejecting the usual standards. Introducing personal, nonofficial notes into summit-level meetings, he broke Cold War stereotypes and assumed more personal responsibility in foreign policy decisionmaking, rather than relying on the "politburo" collective approach.[6] All of this sub-stantially hastened the decay of post-totalitarianism. Gorbachev's famous *glasnost* brought an avalanche of democratization and liberalized the internal regime, leading inevitably to the massive destruction of Soviet ideology. For-eign policy–thinking was overwhelmed by this wave of "de-ideologization," which itself became a sort of new ideology. During his short tenure as minis-ter of foreign affairs, Boris Pankin proclaimed de-ideologization, together with economizing and observing human rights, to be the "three whales" of new Russian (Soviet) foreign policy.[7] Gorbachev's government aimed de-ide-ologization efforts inward and outward simultaneously: against totalitarian thinking within the country and against the Cold War regime that character-ized international relations. This campaign set out to undermine the ideology and psychology that perpetuated the idea of the "great power." Toward this goal, subsequent minister of foreign affairs Andrey Kozyrev argued that Western values and foreign policy principles made a suitable basis for Rus-sian policies. Because Russia had begun to undertake social democratic and market economic reforms, many considered partnership between it and the West inevitable. Some Western experts defined this stage of Russian foreign policy development as "unqualified Westernism."[8]

The Belovezhskie agreements of 1991 were a definite step toward the abandonment of superpower ideology and psychology. However, the unwill-ingness to acknowledge distinct realms of authority among former members of the Soviet Union—for example, in military affairs—constituted a step backward. Indeed, the dramatic period from 1991 to 1992 was a time of simultaneous attempts to both ruin and return to the structures of the past. Heated discussions about the nature of the new Russian state, largely rooted in three centuries of Russian history, began both in Russia and in the West. Cultural considerations were an essential part of this debate. Some believed that the Soviet Union had deprived its citizens of an identifiable culture. Con-sequently, they believed that upon the dissolution of the Soviet Union, no principles, rules, institutions, or even history would remain in Russia. No less popular were the rival interpretations, put forth by Henry Kissinger and Zbig-niew Brzezinski, which argued that the Soviet Union's superpower status would manifest itself in the new Russia, which would no doubt adopt an expansionist foreign policy. Expansionism, they argued, was a persistent his-torical tendency that would eventually reappear and characterize the new Russian state.

Parallel debates began in Russia, where stereotypes and ideologies proved no less tenacious. This debate took place between "Eurasianists" and "Westernizers." The Eurasianists, like their predecessors in the nineteenth century, insisted that Russian civilization was unique, that it should not be placed in the same category as either Western or Eastern culture. The imperial, superpower tendency, as well as the supremacy of political and ideological factors over economic ones, were features inherent to the Eurasian concept of the country. However, these positions did not affect the official foreign policy of "unqualified Westernism."

Cultural disputes took place in a geopolitical context when the problem of a cultural border between Central and Eastern Europe came into focus. These debates put on the agenda the issue of drawing new lines in Europe. Russian officials perceived this primarily as an attempt to revise the Yalta agreements and to separate the former Soviet republics—first and foremost, Ukraine—from the Russian sphere of influence. This served as another indicator of Russia's demise as a great power. Countries identified as candidates for NATO and European Union membership were referred to as part of "the other Europe." Political scientists stressed that these countries sought not merely a Central European identity but a European identity. Director of the Russian Institute of Strategic Studies Yevgeny Kozokhin, for example, maintained, "The democratic nationalism in most of these countries reveals their extreme western orientation. The borders of states are to be fixed along cultural borders. . . . The opposition of these countries to Russia serves the aims of self-identification and satisfies their unhealthy nationalist selfishness."[9] Consequently, Russia became an alien, a "constituting other" to Central Europe.[10] This tension manifested itself at the end of the 1990s, when the first wave of NATO enlargement drew a new "red line" through Europe, and the potential second round immediately became the topic of discussion and speculation.

Another, no less important, debate concerned the question of whether the West needs a weak Russia or a strong Russia. As early as 1992, many experienced diplomats stressed that Russians needed to articulate their interests soon in order to avoid Western efforts to define those interests for them.[11] Russian officials recognized that the interests of Western nations would be well-served by the disappearance of the Soviet Union and by the emergence of a weakened and vulnerable Russia. They also recognized, though, that they could not allow the West to determine the role that Russia would play in the world community in the future.

As may be expected, the theme of the Communist opposition has been that if Russian leadership works under Western tutelage, it would work against its own national interests. At the same time—though not in such a straightforward manner—the moderate conservative, or "realistic," part of the establishment began to question the expediency of following traditional Western recipes for governance. In the second half of the 1990s this issue and its slogans provided a convenient basis of attack for the left-wing opposition. For example, at the end of 1997 the "young reformers" (including Anatoly Chubais and Boris Nemtsov) were attacked in the newspaper *Nezavisimaja gazeta* (which was partly controlled by one of their political antagonists).

Printed on the front page, in huge letters, was the sentence: "Why does Russia need its own government? In Washington there are clever people, who not only know what our country needs but also give concrete instructions."[12] Thus, in substance, the criticism of the official foreign policy from the left and from the pragmatic and moderate part of the political elite did not differ greatly. While the opposition from the left accentuated the threat of Western intervention into domestic affairs, the moderates and pragmatists stressed the necessity of diversifying foreign policy in order to insure that it reflected Russian national interests.

Thus, from 1991 to 1993, the perception of Russia in the West and in Russia itself differed dramatically. Faced with economic crisis and the fear of further disintegration, the political elite had little hope that Russia would endure as great power. But Russia's military potential, its geopolitical relevance, and its natural resources led the West to continue to perceive Russia as a great power. These tenaciously held opinions helped delay the geopolitical expansion of Western influence eastward, to Central and Eastern Europe and the Commonwealth of Independent States (CIS). Meanwhile, this lengthy pause by the West created an illusion among some Russians about the possibility of maintaining or restoring Russian influence in the post-Soviet realm. The initial mutual misunderstanding made the return to a more realistic vision more painful to the Russian elite, which had nourished high expectations for a Russian-U.S. "strategic partnership" as the Cold War concluded. However, it is unfair to blame the Russian elite for its pro-Western illusions. They could hardly be avoided. The possibility of obtaining freedom of speech, communication, and movement; a market economy and entrepreneurship; Western culture; and, finally, full stores idealized the Western way of life and gradually undermined Communist ideology. These attitudes were most marked in the very thin, upper layer of Russian society, most notably in those citizens of Moscow and a few other big cities who had had the opportunity to visit the West during the 1970s and 1980s. However heated the discussions between Westernizers and Eurasianists became on the definition of a "Russian way" of development, the elite class, which included the main decisionmakers, was consistently and firmly pro-Western.

Meanwhile, the Western ideals proclaimed by the elite found little support among the vast majority of the people, who had experienced no material improvement in their situation. As has occurred many times throughout Russian history, the people reacted to hardships by searching for an "enemy," a scapegoat to blame. The public majority directed its dissatisfaction against the political elite on the one hand and against national minorities (*inorodtsy*), primarily from the Caucasus, on the other hand. The West, together with the pro-Western, antinational, "Zionist," political, and financial elite represented secondary enemies. But nostalgia for superpower status and national identity, aggravated by socioeconomic difficulties, fueled an even deeper hatred, manifested in nationalism and xenophobia. In the late 1990s, these tendencies were exposed in a wide-scale explosion of anti-Semitism.

Out of this context grew Russian criticism of NATO policy as "reactive" and lacking any coherent long-term strategy. NATO enlargement has been the most vivid example of integrated Western policy; as such it has come to represent all policies perceived as detrimental to Russian interests. During his tenure as minister of foreign affairs, Yevgeny Primakov comprehensively articulated this point of view:

> When the West sought the withdrawal of Soviet troops from the German Democratic Republic and asked us to swallow yet another bitter pill—the dissolution of the Warsaw Treaty Organization—we were told the same thing: NATO won't expand an inch eastward; don't worry, none of the countries that were Warsaw Treaty Organization members will ever be accepted into NATO. At that time none of these representations were set out in writing; whatever we might agree to remained spoken only. . . . If NATO, created to deter global threats, comes to include all former Warsaw Treaty Organization countries, Russia's geo-political situation will deteriorate. Why? Because in politics, intentions change; but potentials are constant. I do not believe that NATO will attack us. But hypothetically the situation may arise when we'll have to act against [NATO's] interests.[13]

Again, historical parallels surface. The Russian philosopher Nikolai Berdiaev wrote that, without the superpower status and deprived of order and protection, the Russian people reveal themselves as "people of the state." The intelligentsia, on coming into power, used the "great power" ideology in order to rally citizens behind its agenda.[14]

At the beginning of 1993 the regime began to correct its foreign policy as it tried to maintain power. Pro-Western, anti-Soviet, anti-imperial rhetoric gave way to the vague but well-sounding concepts of "national pragmatism," "real foreign policy" and "compelled limited great power." The government regarded these concepts, which served partly to build foreign policy consensus, sufficient to soothe public concerns. New rhetoric emphasized the temporary nature of things. It hinted that Russia could again claim an exclusive position in world politics, once the domestic situation changed. In this way, the new rhetoric kept Russian public expectations and aspirations alive.

As early as 1992, the Civil Union (*Grazhdanskij soiuz*), defense industry supporters influential with the political elite, put forward the concept of "compelled limited great power."[15] The most peculiar aspect of this concept was that the word *limited* referred to internal factors. The idea of "great power" was transformed from a characterization based predominantly on a country's outward relations into a concept based equally on foreign and domestic issues. Proponents of this ideology regarded the restoration of Russia as occurring not at the cost of its people but in their interests. Nevertheless the concept was controversial. The process of recovery presupposed the successful develop- ment of a democracy and a market economy, with their goal of overcoming "forced limitations." Moreover, fully regaining great-power status presup- posed a return to great-power foreign policy. Whether democratic institutions could become deeply rooted in Russia would determine whether Russia would again become a great power.

Another specific ingredient of the great-power conception of foreign pol- icy is Russian nationalism, which rhetoric helped to foster. Indeed, some ana- lysts regarded the traditional absence of nationalism a cultural peculiarity of the state of Russian and a source of its past weakness. However, the dissolu- tion of the Soviet Union and subsequent ethnic hostilities have spurred nation- alism, which has gradually penetrated the realm of significant foreign policy considerations.

Although the deep economic crisis made realization of great-power sta- tus a distant goal, the concept became more and more popular as a "national idea" within political leadership circles. In the meantime, though, Russia was conducting a realistic foreign policy on the Western flank, in line with the lim- its presented by the increasingly reduced resources and ineffective strategies of the former Soviet sphere. Thus, the gap between the rhetoric clamoring for a return to great-power status and the actual practice of foreign policy deep- ened. However, this discussion took place only at the elite level. As for the general public, they were concerned only with the ongoing economic crisis, which undermined all confidence in the elite and the ruling regime.

As the Russian people gradually adjusted to life in their new state, to new borders, and to the independence and sovereignty of the former Soviet republics, they also became increasingly concerned about Russia's position in the world. In the past, many Russians made their livings from the small-scale sale of consumer goods imported from abroad. The extension of visas by neighboring countries caused a decline in this import industry and has resulted in the loss of income for many thousands of Russians. Continued enlargement of NATO and the European Union will only intensify this problem. But con- cern about Russia's role in the world has arisen also from feelings of national—and personal—pride. The extreme weakness of the state and its institutions is tolerable as long as it is recognized only within Russia. When this situation becomes obvious outside national borders, Russians are humili- ated. Thus, strengthening the state, its institutions, and, therefore, its interna- tional prestige has become another goal that must be met in order for political leaders to stay in power.

In sum, Russia's history coupled with specific domestic developments have established the nature of domestic foreign policy debates. NATO enlargement became the most significant issue within these debates.

IDENTIFICATION OF THREATS

Most Russians regard NATO enlargement as a most serious threat to Russian culture and to its regional and international political position. Analyses of post–Cold War foreign policy debates in Russia show that the majority of the political establishment (excluding extreme nationalists) believe that NATO expansion will lead to Russian isolationism, and this, in turn, is thought to pose a danger to Russia's future. Despite the negative attitude, the realistic members of the elite reluctantly admit that in order to neutralize this threat, Russia—hampered by shrinking resources—has no choice but to cooperate with NATO. In the long term, this may even mean joining the reformed alliance. Even before NATO officials declared the intention to expand the alliance, Russian analysts stressed that "isolation may strengthen the argument for the enlargement of the western security structures (NATO, the Western European Union) to [include] the countries of Central and Eastern Europe [and exclude] Russia."[16] In 1994, for example, analysts for the influential Council on Foreign and Defense Policy concluded,

> There exists the danger of the third scenario—Cold War. The West may undertake . . . to restore the system of the military-political isolation of Russia, further diminishing its influence in the world and its ability to stand up for its interests. . . . Even without the serious worsening of relations there is a real threat of long-term strengthening of the geostrategic isolation of Russia and weakening of its international position, particularly in the case of Russia's exclusion from NATO enlargement.[17]

A year later, analysts added,

> The plans for NATO enlargement . . . may lead the West and the East to the first serious crisis in their relations after the Cold War. . . . The threat of being isolated or self-isolation is rather real. . . . Central and Eastern European proponents of NATO enlargement probably nourish vague hopes that NATO enlargement, by provoking a confrontation with Russia, will turn their states into a "front-line" with . . . adequate . . . political and economic support and aid.[18]

Russian political leaders and analysts used the threat of isolation as an effective lever in relations with the West. As early as December 1992, Minister of Foreign Affairs Kozyrev shocked NATO members in Stockholm by speaking with what he characterized as the "voice of reactive forces." Indeed, he actively used his position and authority to oppose NATO enlargement.

Kozyrev's position and actions provoked discussion in the West as well as in Russia. Pro-Western policy was already vulnerable to criticism from the right. It was opening the way to radical nationalism. The "great power" psychology penetrates into the mentality of the people and part of the intelligentsia, and their hopes will [certainly] be used in the parliamentary and presidential elections by the camp of nationalists. If the ruling regime doesn't correct its course, it will be smashed by the nationalist opposition.[19]

Once the decision to enlarge NATO was announced in the summer of 1995, neither the Ministry of Foreign Affairs nor the political elite articulated their positions clearly. Some Western anti-enlargement diplomats advised analysts in Moscow to formulate a clear Russian position on enlargement and to campaign against it in the mass media. This suggestion was accepted by some in the Ministry of Foreign Affairs, which at one point issued a letter to NATO headquarters stating, "We are convinced that [NATO enlargement] does not correspond to the interests of the national security of Russia, nor to the interests of European security as a whole."[20] Few officials were willing to move beyond this statement, though.

The threat of "restoration," of the resurgence of hard-line leaders and policies, was among the main reasons that the West did not make the final decisions on NATO enlargement until after the Russian presidential elections in 1996. After the elections, however, restoration lost its power of intimidation, although some continued to use it. The left-wing opposition, which constituted the parliamentary majority, established working contacts with the government of Victor Chernomyrdin and showed its openness to discussion and compromise, even in matters of foreign policy. Experts observed that the Communists and the moderate-left political forces close to them (such as the agrarians) gradually became a part of the political coalition defined as the "systemic opposition."

The next wave of nationalism, fascism, xenophobia, and anti-Semitism, which arose toward the end of 1998, had little to do with the world environment and was particularly unrelated to NATO enlargement. Rather it reflected the domestic political and financial crises of 1998, the worsening economic and financial situation, and a drastic decrease of confidence in the ruling elite.

This is not to say that Russians stopped perceiving NATO as threatening. This view was merely refocused. Toward the end of the 1990s, the elite grew especially concerned about the enlargement of the zone of NATO responsibility and about the creation of precedents for further unlimited enlargement. At the same time, the Russian political establishment was extremely unhappy about shifts in NATO's decisionmaking process aimed at eliminating the need for United Nations Security Council resolutions for military actions falling under Chapter VII of the United Nations Charter. Russian officials perceived these changes not only as a threat to the whole post–World War II order but also as an obvious attempt to exclude Russia from the decisionmaking process, thus further cutting its bargaining power in world politics. The war in Yugoslavia—and NATO's involvement there—lent credence to all of these concerns.

The political elite became increasingly anxious about the West's dealings with new independent states, notably, Ukraine, Azerbaijan, Georgia, and Uzbekistan. Cooperation, even on economic and security issues, was increasing, but with less and less consideration of the possible Russian reaction to such cooperation. NATO conducted military exercises under its aegis both in Ukraine and in the Black Sea. Ukraine agreed to rent its largest training ground to NATO. And a proposal to accept Azerbaijan into NATO so as to allocate radar on its territory was announced, though not confirmed. Russia perceived all of these events as open challenges to Russian security interests.

As such, the threats that were directly or indirectly connected to NATO enlargement attained a more concrete context toward the end of the decade. The pragmatic wing of the elite now admitted that deepening economic and financial problems, not to mention political struggles and instability, continue to limit Russia's maneuverability and leverage in former Soviet countries. Nevertheless, NATO involvement in the region is considered a hindrance to mutually profitable economic, political, and security relations between Russia and the newly independent states. For example, many Russian analysts considered the financial crisis of August 1998 a potential catalyst for closer cooperation within the CIS, but the activities of NATO, specifically, and the West, generally, in the new independent states continue to limit this potential.

While Russian resentment of NATO on cultural and political levels remains high, both the military and the political elite appear comfortable with the military implications of enlargement. The first wave of NATO enlargement was never considered a direct military threat. Opinions are divided concerning the impact of the planned second wave of enlargement, but for the first time in Russian history, most Russians, including the predominant part of the political elite, do not perceive NATO, or indeed, any country, as posing a military threat. NATO enlargement has not caused changes in the Russian security doctrine or the structure or allocation of its forces, budgetary decisions, or force levels. Obviously the increasing budget deficit virtually eliminates any chances of enhancing Russia's military structure. Economic considerations have, in fact, led to a shrinking of the Russian army. Announced cuts would have left the armed forces at 1.2 million personnel (less than 1 percent of the population, making Russia consistent with most democratic states, including the United States). Because of the subsequent August 1998 financial crisis, however, experts believe that the Russian budget can provide for a level of only about 550,000 to 600,000 personnel.

Actual budget allocations for national defense purposes decreased steadily from 1991 to 1998, as did Ministry of Defense budget requests, even in those years when NATO expansion had a high profile in policy debates.[21]

The military remains a powerful policy lobby in Russia. Had military leaders felt that a military threat to the state existed, the government would have made appropriate allocations. In addition, the announced cuts of forces in north-western Russia demonstrate the military's estimates of the low level of military threat to Russian security posed by NATO.

Public policy statements, however, did not reflect the absence of any significant military threat from NATO enlargement. Decisionmakers would address primarily domestic audiences on this topic, but the statements made by officials were mere rhetoric intended to bolster the images of specific officials. Among the best-known "scarecrows" was *Nezavisimaja gazeta*'s publication in September 1995 of an article stating that the General Headquarters of the Armed Forces of the Russian Federation decided that Russian nuclear missiles would be retargeted toward the Czech Republic and Poland in the event of actual enlargement of NATO to the East. A map accompanied the article and reportedly reflected data from anonymous sources at the headquarters. The map showed arrows pointing from Russia toward Central and Eastern Europe and the Baltic countries. Many Western publications reprinted this story and its vivid visual aid.

MINISTERIAL DEBATES AND DIFFERENCES

During the post-Soviet period the process of foreign policy decisionmaking has undergone drastic changes, generally coinciding with ideological changes and other substantial shifts in the country.

From 1991 to 1993, the traditional vertical hierarchy of decisionmaking was destroyed. The Soviet Union's ideological center, the Central Committee of the Communist Party, dissolved. There was no well-elaborated legal framework for the relations of Russia with the Newly Independent States (NIS), the former Council for Mutual Economic Assistance (COMECON), or with Warsaw Pact partners. As a consequence, the traditional hierarchy became imbalanced. The physical center of foreign policy–making moved from the Old Square (Central Committee) to Smolenskaya Square (the Ministry of Foreign Affairs), which was strongly driven by a pro-Western optimism that largely rested on illusions. But, for both objective reasons (such as the lack of adequate experience and appropriate laws) and subjective reasons, the Ministry of Foreign Affairs proved weak and unable to solve the urgent issue of conflict resolution and crisis regulation within the CIS. This led to severe criticism, causing the center of decisionmaking to shift again, to Arbatskaya Square (the Ministry of Defense). The Ministry of Defense took the initiative and elaborated a peacemaking code for the CIS corresponding to—or at least not contrary to—the United Nations' international standards.

The end of 1992 was a time of political crisis and struggle. When the first signs of re-ideologization ("compelled limited great power") emerged, foreign policy–making became even more dispersed and atomized. It became an instrument of political struggle. The lack of coordination in foreign policy decisionmaking bordered on chaos and raised serious concerns about Russian foreign policy in general. One well-known Russian diplomat wrote, "'Who speaks on behalf of Russia?'—the foreigners ask."[22]

The Security Council (in the Kremlin), a quasi–Central Committee with unarticulated ideological claims for political leadership and control, was established as a competing center of foreign policy decisionmaking. Later, the Defense Council balanced the power of the Security Council. Proximity to the president, though, was the ultimate source of power and influence in decisionmaking. The constitution provided the president with the highest prerogatives in the domain of foreign policy, a position bolstered by the Russian tradition of locating foreign policy–making authority in a single person. Below this level, as state control and vertical hierarchies weakened, numerous state and nongovernmental institutions made their own foreign policy decisions in line with their particular interests. Not infrequently, such interests conflicted with Russian foreign policy, increasing confusion and tensions about the intents and direction of policies.

The role played by the head of the Russian state in foreign policy decisionmaking has been enormous. Several phenomena led to this. The concentration of power is consistent with the practices of Czarist Russia and Soviet traditions and has been entrenched through constitutional norms. These factors were enhanced by the personality and political style of Boris Yeltsin. Political psychologists characterized Yeltsin as intrinsically inclined to solve problems only when they reached the critical stage. They also pointed to his habit of not relying consistently on the same circle of advisers. By changing the personal environment, by "shuffling" it, Yeltsin caused different institutions and personalities to clash as they struggled for presidential favor, while he remained above the battle and retained the freedom to maneuver. Given these conditions, efforts to systematize the decisionmaking process seemed doomed to failure.

It turn, the discord between the Ministry of Foreign Affairs and the Ministry of Defense, and the special position of the Security Council on foreign policy issues, precipitated severe criticism from experts, former officials, and the mass media. This prevented the elaboration of common identification or understanding of national and state interests. Both the institutions and the personalities involved in making foreign policy decisions were roundly criticized, further undermining the prestige of the political regime and its representatives and deepening indifference and frustration.

Meanwhile, the obvious physical weakness of Boris Yeltsin, specifically from the summer of 1998 until the end of his tenure in the spring of 1999, led to the disruption of several summits and the gradually reduced role of the "quasi-president" (that is, the presidential administration of policy making). This development demonstrated the necessity to revise foreign policy–making style and to lessen its "Byzantine," personified nature in favor of a more systematic and bureaucratic one. The prime minister adopted functions of the president for protocol in the foreign policy domain, de facto. Yevgeny Primakov, who had served as the foreign affairs minister, accepted these responsibilities as the prime minister under Yeltsin. Both Russians and officials abroad accepted the change as the best solution for the time being. The ascendancy of Vladimir Putin to the presidency will affect efforts to regulate the structure of foreign policy–making. Will he seek the central role that Yeltsin occupied? Or will Russian foreign policy be driven by institutions rather than by personality? It is still too soon to assess.

Events during the 1999 Kosovo conflict demonstrated the peculiarities of Moscow's foreign policy and security decisionmaking. During the first days of NATO air strikes, statements from Russian Ministry of Defense officials differed significantly from those made by the Ministry of Foreign Affairs. This disconnect and inconsistency caused serious concerns in the West about who would identify and guide the Russian position on the war in Serbia and Kosovo. Later, Boris Yeltsin used the Balkan conflict for domestic purposes, specifically to weaken the position of the prime minister. Yeltsin nominated Chernomyrdin, a former premier with little experience in national security issues, as the presidential representative to international negotiations concerning the settlement of the conflict. Many observers noted that Chernomyrdin could not and did not successfully do this job, and the conditions under which Russia initially participated in the Kosovo Peacekeeping Force (KFOR) clearly could have been less controversial and more favorable had policymaking been better coordinated. The intrigue of the order for Russian peacekeepers in Bosnia to march to Kosovo and take up positions at Pristina airport, against NATO orders, once more demonstrated that the military and the president can make decisions without coordinating or even consulting with the Ministry of Foreign Affairs in a timely manner.

Although foreign policy remains the constitutional prerogative of the central federation power, it has become the domain of the subjects of the Russian Federation, again on a legal basis. Russian regions have the freedom to engage in foreign economic activity, which, in turn, influences the situation in that region, the relations between the center and the region, and the international position and standing of Russia.

The role of leaders in both regional politics and in foreign and economic policy has increased, with a new distinction appearing between the "inland" regions (those bordering the newly independent states) and the regions bordering the "traditional" countries abroad. This last group may provide Russia with a foreign policy opportunity. Developing crossborder cooperation between these Russian regions and European states may help prevent the isolation of Russia from European integration and neutralize the negative effects of NATO and EU enlargement. At the same time, given the present economic and financial crisis in Russia, foreign neighbors have become increasingly crucial actors in the development of distant inland regions, such as the Russian Far East or the exclave in Kaliningrad.

Despite the chaotic nature of Russian foreign policy, attitudes in decisionmaking circles concerning NATO enlargement remain relatively constant—and negative. But it should also be noted that the attitude of high-ranking Russian military officers on this issue has gradually softened. While shrinking resources and severe financial conditions have forced some degree of pragmatism, this attitude shift was spurred by widening contacts with NATO, including participation in the multilateral, NATO-led Implementation Force (IFOR) and Operation Joint Guard and Joint Force (the Stabilization Force, or SFOR) missions in Bosnia. From this point of view, the Partnership for Peace program, in which Russia has scarcely participated due to financial and political problems, still represents a potential bridge to better and more informed understanding between Russian and NATO military organizations.

In the first half of the 1990s, national interests dominated state interests in Russia. Although the concept of national interests has not received much elaboration, it could return to the forefront, especially given the intensified disputes about the possible further dissolution of the Russian state that could result from controversies between the federal center and the regions about Russian domestic and foreign policy.

It is necessary to propose a mutually acceptable constructive alternative to the speedy enlargement of NATO. This alternative might include simultaneous, but delayed, enlargement of the EU and NATO; enlargement of just the EU first; or, as the last option, enlargement of the political, but not military, organization of NATO in Central and Eastern European countries.[23]

NOTES

1. Nikolai Berdiaev, *The Sources and Meaning of Russian Communism* (in Russian) (Moscow: Nauka, 1990), 8–9.

2. Ibid.

3. Aleksander Bovin, "Searching for a National Interest" (in Russian), *Segodniá*, 12 December 1997: 23.

4. Mikhail Gorbachev, "Address at the United Nations General Assembly" (speech given at the United Nations General Assembly, New York, 7 December 1998).

5. A. D. Rotfeld, "The CSCE: Toward a Security Organization," *SIPRI Yearbook 1993: World Armaments and Disarmament* (New York: Oxford University Press, 1993), 171.

6. Yeltsin inherited this "without ties" style, according to which overpersonification of foreign policy–making gradually became counterproductive, both for Russian and Western interests. In his memoirs ex–prime minister Yegor Gaidar wrote, "The wide Russian soul of Boris Nikolaevich is not always good for state affairs. . . . He often makes decisions *ad hoc* in the situations where patience and detailed study of all arguments, and unhasty solutions, are needed. In a number of cases it was detrimental to national interests." Yegor Gaidar, "Excerpts from *Days of Victories and Defeats*" (in Russian), *Itogi* (5 November 1996): 24. See also Yegor Gaidar, *Days of Defeat and Victory,* trans. Jane Ann Miller (Seattle: University of Washington Press, 1999).

7. Yevgeny Menkes, "Pankin on Soviet Delegations' Tasks at 46th G.A. Session" (ITAR-TASS Russian Information Agency, 20 September 1991).

8. N. Malcolm, A. Pravda, R. Allison, and M. Light, *Internal Factors of Russian Foreign Policy* (New York: Oxford University Press, 1996).

9. Yevgeny Kozokhin, "Gde nachinaetsia i konchaetsia Evropa?" *Otkrytaja politika* 14, no. 7–8 (1996): 74–79.

10. I. B. Neumann, "Russia as Central Europe's Constituting Other," *East European Politics and Societies* 7, no. 2 (Spring 1993).

11. See Ruslan Khasbulatov, "Speech by Chairman of the Russian Federation Supreme Soviet Ruslan Khasbulatov to the 7th Congress of the Russian Federation People's Deputies" (official Kremlin International News broadcast, Moscow, 1 December 1992).

12. Tatiana Koshkaryova, "What Does Russia Need Its Own Government For?" *Nezavisimaja gazeta*, 18 December 1997: 1–2.

13. Y. Primakov, "Russia, the West, and NATO," *Obscshaja gezeta*, no. 37, 21–27 September 1996: 18.

14. See N. Berdiaev, *The Russian Idea* (Herndon, Vir.: Anthroposophic Press, 1992).

15. Vladimir Desyatov, "Let's Meet and Decide to Live Separately," *Nezavisimaja gazeta,* 18 November 1992: 1.

16. "Strategy for Russia (Some Theses for the Report of the Council on Foreign and Defense Policy)," *Nezavisimaja gazeta,* 19 August 1992: 4–5.

17."Strategy for Russia—2 (Theses of the Council on Foreign and Defense Policy—Draft for Signing and Publication)." Available online at http://www.svop.ru/doklad_en1.htm.

18."Russia and NATO: Theses of the Council on Foreign and Defense Policy." Available online at http://www.svop.ru/doklad_en1.htm.

19. "Vneshniaja politika Rossii doizhna byf prezidentskoi. Prichiny i sledstvija porazhenia diplomatii Andreia Kozyreva," *Nezavisimaja gazeta,* 17 May 1995: 5.

20. See Paul Ames, "Vows to Push on with Enlargement, Despite Russian Warning," Associated Press Newswire, 30 May 1995.

21. "The Prognosis of the Financial-Economic Provision for the Structure of the RF Armed Forces for the Period up to the Year 2010," *Nezavisimoje voeenoje obozrenie,* no. 4 (1999): 12.

22. V. Logunov, "Society Must Know Where It Is Being Led," *Rossiiskaya gazeta,* 1 December 1992: 1, 6.

23. "Russia and NATO: Theses of the Council on Foreign and Defense Policy."

11

Ukraine:
Between NATO and Russia

MARIA KOPYLENKO

Today Ukraine is a country searching for its ultimate identity; it is mired in the traditions and structures of the past while trying to forge new institutions for the future. The issue of NATO enlargement puts these divergent trends in stark relief. On the one hand, there are Ukrainians drawn to the West and the values of democracy, free markets, and open societies that the West represents. On the other hand, there are those who continue to value the relationship with Russia, largely speak Russian, and feel strong ties to the north. This divergence in attitudes is reflected in contradictory pronouncements and policies over major issues. Thus, to understand Ukrainian policy on NATO, it is important to consider its current political structures.

The current president of Ukraine does not represent any particular political party. Consequently, neither the president nor the government feels responsible for fulfilling an electoral program or platform, for there are no such party-mandated programs. In addition, Ukraine has a Council for National Security and Defense, which, according to the Constitution of Ukraine, is responsible for national security and for guiding the formation of the foreign policy of Ukraine. When undertaking the development of foreign policy, the Ukrainian foreign office must take into account at least four centers of power—the presidential administration, the Council for National Security and Defense, the cabinet of ministers, and the Parliament (Verchovna Rada) of Ukraine, which has the constitutional right ultimately to define the foreign policy of the country.

In addition to institutions, political attitudes influence Ukraine's foreign policy. Initially, both the Ukrainian public and its political leaders adopted an almost romantic vision of European integration and NATO membership, considering such steps as key to Ukraine's self-identity in the world. Three goals of political groups reflect these earlier attitudes: The People's Rukh was determined to break through to the West; leftists hoped to continue traditional support of Russia and to integrate with the countries of the Commonwealth of Independent States (CIS); and both right-wing and left-wing political groups worked to create an independent and sovereign Ukraine that could be supported by the nuclear weapons it possessed.

Ukraine's subsequent decision to get rid of its nuclear weapons, however, encouraged a sober analysis of Ukrainian integration into European structures. To some extent, the existing political attitudes persisted—left-wing political forces still want to turn to the East, and the right-wing political forces continue to look to the West, as demonstrated during the discussion of Ukrainian participation in the Inter-Parliamentary Assembly of CIS. Those attitudes have evolved, though, as officials have been forced to consider the stark realities and difficulties faced by Ukraine. Political leaders now admit that independence does not serve as an automatic pass to European and world structures. For example, the optimistic illusions that accompanied the achievement of Ukrainian independence and sovereignty have been replaced by a clear understanding of the vital necessity of forming economic links to the East; the West cannot compensate for the absence of such links. Support for this position is growing into a powerful argument, bolstering the views of left-wing politicians.

Currently, the interests of much of the Ukrainian political elite—the majority of which is formed from the old Soviet political elite—are inclined toward cementing relations with Russia. But declarations regarding movement toward integration with Russia and with Belarus are populist attempts to win that part of the Ukrainian electorate, which cannot comprehend a Ukranian existence outside the Soviet sphere. Most likely, neither the Ukrainian political elite nor the mass public would ever want to come back under the thumb of "big brother" after tasting sovereignty.

The Ukrainian Foreign Ministry, which maintains a strong pro-Western position, has worked mightily toward European integration, while the political elite—holding the real reins of power—has adamantly opposed these efforts. Such structures as the Council for National Security and Defense attempt to moderate the radical and contrary views within Ukraine, but the division presents a significant obstacle to the formation of a consistent and unified foreign policy.

Ukraine's foreign policy institutions increasingly are concerned with national security, now that Poland, the Czech Republic, and Hungary have become NATO members. The Ukrainian Ministry of Defense took the position in 1996 that NATO expansion to the east would automatically shift NATO borders as far as the western border of Ukraine, and that this western border of Ukraine would be considered by NATO to be the western border of Russia.[1] Thus, NATO expansion would create a new dividing line in Europe—along the western border of Ukraine.

This situation would determine NATO's strategic and military plans as well as NATO's delineation of "enemy territory." That enemy could be called anything, but in reality it would be a very real country with a real military potential. Ukraine's western border would constitute the line of division between the East and the West and would be turned into a "strategic forefield," both for NATO and for Russia and its military alliance. If Ukraine tried to remain nonaligned in the midst of this situation, then military actions in Ukrainian territory, including those involving nuclear weapons, might be planned by either or both sides, without prior consultation with Ukraine.

It is also possible that strategic nuclear weapons could be deployed in the territory of the new NATO members, close to Ukrainian borders. Indeed, old Soviet military sites could be used for a convenient deployment of such weapons by NATO. This would reduce the general cost of the reorganization that must be done in Central and Eastern Europe to meet NATO standards. At the same time, the agreement signed by Russia and Belarus on 2 April 1996 allows Russia to deploy its tactical nuclear weapons in the territory of Belorussia, right at the future NATO borders. The eastward expansion of NATO provides Russia with a disincentive, yet even without this, the situation would be sufficiently threatening to stop the withdrawal of Russian nuclear weapons from the Belorussian territory.

The process of NATO enlargement would, in addition, lead to an imbalance in terms of conventional weapons. Already the balance of conventional weaponry between the East and West tilts heavily in the West's favor. The number of armored vehicles destroyed by CIS countries in accordance with international agreements is larger than the number destroyed by Western powers. NATO enlargement would exacerbate this skewed balance. Poland alone will bring into NATO 1,730 tanks; 1,250 armored vehicles; 1,610 artillery systems; and 460 military aircraft.[2]

Ukraine could feel increasing pressure if Russia were to move its forces from Siberia to the western borders, allocate more of its budget to defense, or form a new defensive alliance, Tashkent, that has until now been only a vague plan. Ukraine might have to deal with other problems, as well. Some neighboring countries have territorial claims against Ukraine. Inner political, economic, and social problems weaken the country and threaten stability. The Ukrainian army is weak and fragmented and would pose a weak challenge to an organized uprising.

The complexity of Ukraine's situation makes its future somewhat unpredictable. NATO enlargement will be acceptable only if Ukraine signs an agreement with NATO that guarantees the country's security. If Ukraine turns to either the West or the East, it will divide Europe into spheres of influence. Thus, a reasonable argument can be made that the policy of Ukraine should be that of cooperation with both the East and the West. Ukraine should remain a strategic partner of Russia in all realms—political, economic, and military—but it should be recognized that the stability of Ukraine is in the interests of both the East and the West.

The perception of the Ukrainian military of the process of NATO enlargement has not evolved much in recent years. Ukraine's three choices, determined by geopolitics and according to the Academy of Armed Forces of Ukraine, are military alliance with CIS countries; joining NATO; or maintaining a neutral status.[3] If Ukraine joined the CIS countries in some sort of military and defense alliance, it could lead to a repeat of the past. Ukraine might again perform a subordinate role in Russia's weapons production, while NATO enlargement as far as Poland, Hungary, and Romania turns Ukraine into a "front-line country" with all the consequences that would negatively affect the Ukrainian economy and military.

If Ukraine joined NATO, its armed forces would number about 170,000 to 190,000 soldiers, and Ukraine would gradually make the transition to a voluntary armed forces system. Weapons would be standardized to meet NATO requirements. Military equipment—that is, cargo aircraft, tanks, and missiles—would be produced in cooperation with Western allies.

Which choice Ukraine will make remains unclear. A great deal will depend on the foreign policy that Ukraine establishes. The country needs a standardized foreign policy in order to develop successfully its armed forces. However, the final decisions on both foreign policy and armed forces development rest with the Verchovna Rada.

The strategic perspective of Ukraine's national security remains tied to integration considerations. Consequently, many analysts say that the country should develop its relations with NATO as part of the European security system.[4] As early as 1995 some insisted that Ukraine seek integration into NATO political structures and cited the Partnership for Peace (PfP) program as the first significant step in that direction. They concluded that "NATO Eastern enlargement does not contradict the strategic plans of Ukraine."[5]

Ukrainian attitudes about a partnership with NATO are based on realistic appraisals, and there is no unanimity in the Ukrainian attitude on NATO enlargement. Some have adopted the perspective of former NATO Secretary General Willy Claes that NATO does not need consumers of security but seeks rather those countries that can bear full military responsibility and deal with the resulting financial matters and possible risks. Nonetheless, Ukraine, the only European country to voluntarily get rid of its nuclear weapons and allow NATO enlargement as far as its own borders, had reason to expect special considerations from NATO. The 1997 Charter on Distinctive Partnership Between NATO and Ukraine (discussed under the section Government Security Policy in this chapter) established such a relationship by institutionalizing consultative procedures between Ukraine and NATO.

Until 1995 no real discussion on NATO's potential role in the countries of the former Soviet Union had occurred. A May 1995 edition of the Ukrainian Parliament newspaper *Holos Ukrainy* noted that an official inclination toward NATO (and, consequently, away from Russia) would cause a split in society, which would overwhelm the significant conflicts over an official language and state symbols.[6] As time passed, Ukrainian officials increasingly realized that the country would not be able to meet the military, economic, or political standards expected for NATO membership. It also became clear that NATO was not ready to accept the burden of Ukraine. Some Ukrainian analysts hoped that the burden of other Central European countries would prove to be too heavy for NATO, as well, and that the alliance would ultimately maintain its original membership.[7] If NATO admitted no new countries, Ukraine, as a nonmember, would not be considered a "second-class" country in the region.

Ukrainian leaders kept the idea of integration into NATO in mind but never articulated plans for pursuing it. The Main Guidelines of the Foreign Policy of Ukraine, adopted by the Ukrainian Parliament in 1993, stated that Ukraine was striving to become a neutral, bloc-free country, but that this goal should not stand in the way of full-scale participation in an all-European security system.[8] Still, leaders acknowledged that accession to NATO for Eastern and Central European countries meant a guarantee against the "Russian threat" and represented the shortest path to integration with Western Europe, particularly into its economic structures. Yet Ukraine's multifaceted dependence on Russia made inclusion in NATO seem unfeasible and essentially impossible. Only in 1995, under President Leonid Kuchma, did Ukraine begin to shift foreign policy away from the East and CIS and toward the West and NATO.

By 1996 Ukrainian relations with the East and the West had a dual character. Ukraine persistently maintained that Russia was and would continue to be its main strategic partner, that its relations with Russia had a unique character, and that the relationship should be developed on an equal and friendly basis, in pursuit of a "strategic partnership." At the same time, Ukrainian officials believed that NATO enlargement should not be a revolutionary or accelerated process; on the contrary, it should be evolutionary and protracted. As such, Partnership for Peace represented an appropriate means of pursuing a steady development of relations between countries in the West and the East.[9]

Regardless of the pace, enlargement was considered to be an insufficient adaptation of NATO to the post–Cold War world. NATO needed to become the basis of a pan-European collective security system. The relationship between the alliance and those countries, like Ukraine, not striving for full NATO membership would be an important component of such a transformation. Moreover, stable relations throughout the continent would require both bilateral and multilateral cooperation throughout Europe. Most Ukrainian officials believed that the development and fostering of relations with NATO would provide an opportunity for new initiatives, with the eventual creation of a new system of European security that would include Russia.

MAJOR ISSUES ADDRESSED IN THE ENLARGEMENT DEBATE

Armed Forces

In 1996, Ukraine's military budget was U.S.$1.2 billion. Annual expenditure on the military is expected to increase to U.S.$2 billion by 2002. During this same period, the number of people in the Ukrainian armed forces is expected to drop from 350,000 to 100,000. The budget increase, then, is not intended to fund a larger military but rather a more technologically advanced one, in which soldiers receive more adequate compensation.[10] Although Ukraine has decided now not to join NATO, it is trying to adapt its armed forces to NATO standards in the hopes of inclusion into the new weapon markets of Central Europe.

Then–NATO Secretary General Javier Solana visited Ukraine in July 1998 to mark the first anniversary of the signing of the Charter on Distinctive Partnership Between NATO and Ukraine. While there, Solana visited the Dnepropetrovsk missile production plant "Juzhmash," then in the process of converting from a military operation to a civilian one. "Juzhmash" missiles are to be part of a joint Russia-Norway commercial satellite project, known as "Sea Launch." While there, Solana stressed NATO's support of the conversion of war instruments into peace instruments.[11] Consistent with Ukraine's previous efforts in this realm, it will play a significant role in the regional Science for Stability program.

Ukraine has been promoting its large military cargo aircraft Antonov-70 to countries throughout Europe. Developed in conjunction with Russia, the Antonov project has been monitored closely by Daimler-Benz Aerospace (DASA). It is still unclear whether Western manufacturers will make purchases, but Ukrainian political and military leaders are hoping for success with the cargo plane.

Ukraine is also offering to NATO its firing ground near Lviv for military training purposes. This ground is reputed to be one of the largest in Europe and has already provided space for training actions in the Partnership for Peace program.

Right now Ukraine is developing a special three-year program of cooperation with NATO. Forty ministries and other institutions will be establishing contacts with different departments at NATO Headquarters in Brussels.

The program will cover not only military matters but also emergency situations, organized crime, drug use, and a variety of other issues causing problems in Ukraine.

Economic Integration

Unfortunately, Ukraine's relations with NATO countries have proven less profitable in terms of economic cooperation. The country maintains a consistent positive trade balance with Turkey only, and in some years, with Greece. After CIS, NATO countries represent the second-largest collective source of Ukraine's negative foreign trade balance. At the same time, however, NATO countries have proven the main source of direct foreign investment in Ukraine. The United States has invested U.S.$381.2 million in Ukraine, representing 18.6 percent of all foreign investment in the state; the Netherlands has invested U.S.$214.9 million (10.4 percent of the total); and Germany has invested an additional U.S.$184.7 million (9 percent).[12]

Good relations with NATO will make it easier for Ukraine to communicate and work with international financial organizations, such as the World Bank and the International Monetary Fund. This incentive makes Ukraine reluctant to oppose openly NATO initiatives in any realm. Officials remain hopeful that cooperation with NATO will foster integration of Ukraine into the European and global economies, but also into the more general realm of world politics.

Government Security Policy

In 1994 Ukraine joined the Partnership for Peace program. Despite the decision to join leaders in Kiev still felt that Ukraine deserved something more than mere "partnership," given NATO's planned eastward expansion. The threatening implications of this expansion for Ukraine led to the drafting and adoption, in July 1997, of the Charter on a Distinctive Partnership Between Ukraine and NATO, intended to create stability and advance democratic values within the region. (See Appendix H.) Under Chapter II of the charter, Ukraine accepted the obligation to carry on its program of military reform by strengthening democratic and civil control over its armed forces and by ensuring the compatibility of Ukrainian forces with NATO forces. NATO confirmed its support of all these efforts. Under Chapter III, Ukraine promised to consult NATO on all issues concerning its own security—as well as that of Europe in general—including nonproliferation of nuclear and chemical weapons, disarmament, export of weapons, drug trafficking, and terrorism. NATO officials, in turn, agreed to organize joint seminars and conferences to discuss and advise on the problems of domestic emergencies, democratic control over armed forces, defense planning and budgeting, economic security, environmental security, air-traffic control, and aerospace cooperation. Special attention would be paid to military training and maneuvers in the territory of Ukraine.[13]

After signing the charter, the president of Ukraine issued a decree entitled "On Founding a Ukraine Mission at NATO." The mission would carry out Ukrainian policy in its relations with NATO and represent Ukraine at NATO Headquarters and at various bilateral and multilateral conferences.[14] This provided Ukraine with a means of institutionalizing its communication with NATO's political and military institutions.

A year later, on 4 November 1998, President Leonid Kuchma issued another decree, "On a State Program of Cooperation with NATO Until the Year 2001." The thirty-page document declared one of Ukraine's strategic aims: "a full-scale integration of Ukraine into European and Euro-Atlantic structures and equal participation in the system of all-European security."[15] The statement was seen by many as an expression of Ukraine's complete support for the process and nature of NATO enlargement. Despite the Ukrainian leadership's promises that Ukraine did not plan to join NATO and despite the multiple Russian declarations that NATO posed a threat to both it and Ukraine, these bilateral agreements and official documents represented a concerted effort by Ukraine not only to foster closer relations with NATO but also to exercise its main political principle—establishing a multidirectional foreign policy. Ukrainian leaders were trying, essentially, to serve two masters at the same time.

Parliamentary Debates with Respect to National Political Parties

The polarization of the Verchovna Rada into two almost incompatible camps reflects the complexity and tensions associated with NATO enlargement in Kiev. Communists and socialists favor complete cooperation with Russia, while the People's Rukh favors the quickest possible integration of Ukraine into NATO. However, the members of Verchovna Rada have never debated explicitly the nature of Ukraine's relations with NATO. Only in February 1999 did the Parliamentary Committee on Defense and National Security consider a special closed parliamentary session devoted to the relationship between Ukraine and NATO. Prior to this time, officials debated Ukrainian/NATO relations only in the context of other issues, for instance, during discussions about whether to join the Inter-Parliamentary Assembly of CIS. Those debates reflected positions on improving relations with the West: The Communists favored joining the CIS assembly, while the Rukh opposed membership. But the Communists and other left-wing forces could not garner a majority of votes during this debate without forming a coalition with other parliamentary factions. Parliamentary committees on foreign affairs also could not take a definite position on this question because, according to parliamentary rules, these committees are formed in accordance with proportional party representation. Consequently, committee staff fully reflected the Verchovna Rada's conflicted party structure.

Parliament members debated the question of whether Ukraine would join the CIS Inter-Parliamentary Assembly on five different occasions. Some of the discussions were so heated they led to physical fights between representatives. The legislators finally made the decision to join the assembly on 3 March 1999. Left-wing parliamentary forces were supported by Social Democrats, Greens, and some independent deputies. The president himself expressed his support for joining the assembly, but some representatives of the People's Democratic Party—which supposedly backs the president—supported the Rukh's unsuccessful attempts to withdraw the question on the ground that it contradicted the Constitution of Ukraine.

If we consider NATO enlargement in the context of Ukrainian membership in the Inter-Parliamentary Assembly, we can understand some of the questions introduced by Rukh representative Deputy Head of the Parliament Committee on Foreign Affairs Ivan Zajets. When the leader of the Communist faction, Petro Symonenko, introduced the issue of Ukrainian membership in the Inter-Parliamentary Assembly, Zajets responded by introducing a proposal to stop immediately all contacts with CIS and its institutions and urged the president of Ukraine to initiate discussions between Kiev and Brussels on joining NATO. When deputies of the People's Democratic Party voiced opposition to membership in the Inter-Parliamentary Assembly, they argued that membership would make it difficult to establish cooperative relations with the Council of Europe and NATO. But these arguments were disputed by proponents who argued that the Council of Europe is, in fact, concerned about Ukraine's delayed decision to join the Inter-Parliamentary Assembly, as the CIS assembly and the Parliamentary Assembly of the Council of Europe had secured an agreement on cooperation. Advocates of membership in the CIS assembly noted that the prospects of NATO membership for Ukraine were distant. That fact, advocates, argued, should not influence parliamentary debate regarding the assembly.

All parliamentary discussions of relations between Ukraine and NATO have been similarly couched in other, somewhat tangential, debates. For example, after the Verchovna Rada agreed that Ukraine should join the Inter-Parliamentary Assembly, the Rukh proposed to change the military policy of Ukraine in order to eliminate its bloc-free status, with an eye to joining NATO in the future.

Public Debates and Opinion

A national opinion poll on the question of an acceptable security structure for Ukraine taken in 1994 showed that 29 percent of respondents favored military and political alliance with Russia, 14 percent favored NATO membership, and

24 percent favored an alliance-free status.[16] These results seemed to show that the integration of Ukraine into NATO would be possible only after securing an agreement on cooperation between Russia and NATO. It is unrealistic to view the integration of Ukraine into NATO as a counterbalance to the influence of Russia in Ukraine. Such a balance would only be possible if the Ukrainian population were to turn against Russia, a highly unlikely development. Attempts to encourage such an attitudinal shift by means of a propaganda campaign would be just as pointless and unproductive as similar efforts by Moscow during the Soviet era.

In 1996, SOCIS-Gallup, together with the Democratic Initiatives Foundation, asked respondents whether Ukraine should join NATO: 45 percent of those asked could not answer the question, 15 percent favored the quickest possible integration into NATO, 21 percent favored the idea but thought it should be implemented later, and 19 percent were strictly against joining NATO.[17] The majority of those who supported joining NATO were young people, those with a university degree, and those who favor more private enterprise in Ukraine. Overall, though, the poll seemed to demonstrate general ambivalence among Ukrainians on the question of NATO membership. Polls asking Ukrainians about the level of trust they have in NATO generates equally mixed results.

According to Deputy Head of National Security and Defense Council of Ukraine Olexandr Razumkov, almost 60 percent of the population of Ukraine oppose integration of Ukraine into NATO.[18] Razumkov's position against integration, moreover, should be regarded as the official presidential position. The Security Council and its leadership are closely allied with the president—both officially and privately.

Officials offer several arguments in support of their opposition to NATO membership:

- Joining NATO is not feasible now, because it would mean a tenfold increase in the military budget, which Ukraine cannot afford.
- It is not the case that Ukraine's ties with Russia have become weaker. Russia remains Ukraine's most important partner.
- Drastic changes in foreign policy would accomplish little for Ukraine. Current relations with NATO are satisfactory.
- An application to join NATO might be discussed after ten years, but nobody can predict what NATO will be like in that time, so there is no reason for Ukraine to be in a hurry.[19]

Consideration of relations with NATO have divided the political landscape of Ukraine into two major groups—those who support integration with Russia and those who support integration with the West. The former lean left, the latter, right. Each branch possesses its own mass media (newspapers, TV channels, radio programs) that fully support, represent, and propagate its views.

Role of Outside Interest Groups

Interest groups have not lobbied in Ukraine because NATO enlargement has not yet affected the vital interests of any powerful groups. Economic and business interests are concentrated in the East, especially in Russia, which is why the powerful industrial elite of Ukraine encourages further development of close contacts with Russia. Naturally, one might expect this sector to oppose closer contacts with the West, particularly with NATO.

There is, however, a potential problem for some businesses in Ukraine. With Poland becoming a member of NATO and, at some point, an EU member, Ukrainians will lose visa-free entry into one of its neighboring countries. This will adversely affect a border trade that has become a source of livelihood for the majority of the population in the western regions of Ukraine. Such developments may yet cause the public and elite alike to change their opinions of the type of relationship Ukraine should foster with NATO and the West.

THE NEXT ROUND OF ENLARGEMENT?

Such uncertainty about the future is likely to entrench the sometimes contradictory view of Ukrainians toward the alliance. Until a clearer vision of the future of the East and West emerges, a consensus view of desirable Ukrainian relationships will prove to be elusive. For its own future, it is clear that Ukraine neither anticipates nor really desires at this time to join NATO. For that reason, its role in the discussions over enlargement will be muted, first, not to alienate the Russians who will not hesitate to weigh into the discussions and on whom the Ukrainians are heavily dependent for a range of natural resources, not least of which is energy. Second, Ukraine will also not want to be seen as an obstacle to a NATO decision, which would alienate current and potential economic and political partners. Finally, Ukrainian sovereignty will find support from countries such as the United States, Germany, and Poland in that these countries will not be isolated from both NATO and the EU. This consideration would argue for a future phased enlargement over a number of years and with only a few states admitted at a time.

NOTES

1. V. Tertychnyj, "Rozshyrennja NATO: vijskovi aspekty," *Polityka I Chas,* no. 8 (1996): 20–21.
2. Ibid., 21.
3. A. Pavlenko, "Zovnishnja polityka i zbroini syly Ukrainy," *Polityka I Chas,* no. 1 (1997): 36–39.

4. S. Pirozhkov and V. Chumak, "Ukraine and NATO," *Polityka i Chas,* no. 6 (1995): 17.

5. Ibid., 17.

6. "Vitse-Admiraly Pryishly do Uhody," *Holos Ukrainy,* 19 May 1995: 3.

7. V. Kulyk, "Rozshyrennja NATO i pozytsija Ukrainy," *Polityka I Chas,* no. 11 (1995): 54–60.

8. Ibid., 56.

9. S. Alpatov, "Bezopasnost Ukrainy i NATO," *Vlast,* no. 11 (1996): 65–67.

10. A. Pavlenko. "Zovnishnja polityka i zbroini syly Ukrainy," *Polityka I Chas,* no. 1 (1997): 39.

11. V. Budkin. "U ramkah osoblyvogo partnerstva," *Polityka I Chas,* no. 9 (1998): 26.

12. Ibid., 27.

13. The text of the charter is available online at http://www.nato.int/docu/basictxt/ukchrt.htm. See Appendix H for excerpts of the charter.

14. I. Kharchenko, "The New Ukraine-NATO Partnership," *NATO Review* 45, no. 5 (1997): 27–29.

15. Leonid Kuchma, "On State Programs for Cooperation Between Ukraine and the North Atlantic Treaty Organization (NATO) Up to the Year 2001," presidential decree, *Official Bulletin of Ukraine,* no. 45 (1998): 6–7.

16. A. Ponomarenko, "Ukraina—strana atlanticheskaja?" *Biznesinform,* no. 6 (1997): 9.

17. See I. Galin, "Mass Public Opinion in Ukraine About NATO and NATO-Ukraine Relationships: Analytic Report," *NATO Democratic Institutions Paper, 1996–1998.* Available online at http://www.nato.int/acad/fellow/96-98.

18. I. Ivzhenko, "Ukraine Will Not Join NATO Within the Next 10 Years," *Nezavisimaya gazeta,* 11 February 1999: 1–2.

19. Ibid.

12

Romania:
The Quest for Membership

MARIANA CERNICOVA-BUCA

At the beginning of the twenty-first century, Romania's main goal is to ensure its admission into the two most successful international organizations in Europe: the North Atlantic Treaty Organization and the European Union. Both of these organizations provide a framework for general success and stability. The countries that belong to them enjoy enviable security and have a leading position in the world economy. In contrast, as the Cold War has faded away, the structures within which Romania had exerted its influence have dissolved, leaving behind only debts, bitterness, and insecurity. Thus, the aspiration to join NATO and the EU is not the latest fashion of the fin de siècle, but rather the necessary choice for success and progress in coming decades.

BEHIND A CHINESE WALL

By 1989, Romania had severed all of its traditional, and even its nontraditional, ties: Nicolae Ceaușescu's abhorrent policies isolated Romania from the West, but it was also kept apart from the rest of the Communist bloc, where *perestroika* and *glasnost* policies had fundamentally altered the status quo. Romania essentially had built a Chinese Wall around itself. By 1989 Romania finished paying off its foreign debt (it paid heavily, at the pace of almost U.S.$3 billion per year over the course of seven years). With this payment program, Romania hoped to join the community of world creditors and set up a socioeconomic experiment of "development on our own, by our own resources, for our own benefit."[1] At the same time, the 14th Communist Party Congress re-elected Ceaușescu as secretary general, in an event that was nothing more than a ceremonial display announcing the beginning of Ceauşescu's twenty-fourth year of harsh rule.[2]

On the international front, important delegations stopped visiting Romania, as Ceauşescu lost the celebrity of being the "dissident" within the Soviet bloc. Mikhail Gorbachev, the Kremlin leader, emerged instead as the champion of change. Although Romanian leaders had been in office for a much longer time than the new leadership in Moscow, they could not compete for visibility in international affairs with the new leaders, and they did not grasp the signs of the dissolution of the Communist bloc.

Romania made desperate efforts to conceal its isolation. Barely participating in the Council for Mutual Economic Assistance (COMECON) exchanges of goods, adopting a policy of "cooperation but not subordination" with the Warsaw Treaty Organization, disallowing common military maneuvers with other Soviet states, and refusing the *perestroika* model urged by Gorbachev, Romania was like an iceberg trying to remain afloat in the warm waters of international events. It was seemingly unaffected by Hungary's shift to a multiparty system, by the collapse of the Berlin Wall under the hammers of change, and by Czechoslovakia's "velvet revolution." Even Bulgaria had accepted reforms. It was obvious that the USSR was no longer willing to play the part of guardian of communism in Europe. Romania's iceberg was melting slowly and perhaps invisibly for most eyes. The subsequent December 1989 explosion took everybody—including Romanians—by surprise.

Over ten years later, the signs of change that *were* there in the late 1980s seem obvious. The re-election of Ceauşescu as party leader in 1989 did not go as smoothly as it had in the past. Local organizations dared to question whether he should be nominated for this position. Some even voted against him. A dissident group of six prominent intellectuals sent a letter denouncing his regime to foreign media.[3] Restlessness among some policymakers and the members of society notwithstanding, it would still have been difficult to predict that only one month after the election, Romania would rise up against the uncompromising rule of Ceauşescu.

It was the persecution of a Hungarian reform pastor, Laszlo Tokes, that served as the spark that set Romania afire. By mid-December 1989 the government had exiled Tokes to a small village in northern Romania, while his defenders stood silently day and night in the streets of the city of Timisoara, candles in their hands, to protest the exile, despite the fact that public gatherings were forbidden in Romania. Rebuke of citizens together with a wave of arrests aroused the country transformed the peaceful protests. The army and political police (Securitate) were summoned to put down protests, a move that amplified dissension. Ceauşescu and his wife issued an order for the pacification of Timisoara at all costs, as a popular uprising ensued. When the army ultimately sided with popular opinion, the revolt spread to other cities, including the capital city of Bucharest. The last public appearance of Ceaușescu was a fatal one for him and his rule. As he called a meeting meant to reassert his power, Ceaușescu had to flee when the people of Bucharest openly turned against him. The event, broadcast on television, could not be hidden. The ad hoc National Salvation Front (NSF) took power and immediately set premises for major change: the abolition of the one-party system and the need for free elections, freedom of the press, economic liberalization, domestic policies to satisfy basic needs of the population, and a foreign policy oriented toward Romania's integration into the "common house of Europe."[4] Three days later, on Christmas, the Ceaușescus were briefly tried and sentenced to death. Romania then entered a transition period and has struggled ever since to meet the challenge of modernizing its government and policies.

Divergent tendencies and setbacks in reform, not to mention the international context in which Romania must work, make the outcome of this transition uncertain. Though optimistic by nature, Romanians find themselves more and more unsure when trying to forecast the future.

In its initial statement of purpose, the NSF stated that Romania would uphold its Warsaw Pact obligations but that the country would pursue greater integration with the West. None of the Romanian politicians could imagine that in less than a year and a half, the Warsaw Treaty Organization (WTO) would cease to exist. Ceaușescu had predicted repeatedly that the WTO would disappear one day but had reasoned that it would dissolve in unison with NATO. Events disproved his foresight, and NATO lived on.

NEW DANGERS IN A NEW WORLD

Praised so warmly after the 1989 revolution, Romania expected that the democratic world would quickly welcome it into the institutions of the West. Romania's new leaders applied for membership in the Council of Europe, NATO, and the European Union at the first opportunity. However, Romania soon learned that entry into these organizations is not easy and that memberships were not going to be passed out like entitlements.

Meanwhile, COMECON and the WTO disappeared, and the international balance became uncertain. The "common security" concept devised during the Cold War was no longer operable, and the future of the area became difficult to predict. Czechoslovakia divorced, albeit peacefully. The USSR fell to pieces, and Yugoslavia's efforts to keep its federation failed tragically. The wars in Yugoslavia and the separatist drive in Transnistria (in the newly proclaimed Republic of Moldova, formed after the disintegration of the USSR) represented the closest fighting, geographically, to Romania since World War II, and Romanians viewed both conflicts as national threats.

The revival of questions concerning the status of minorities in democratic countries greatly magnified the fear of possible spillover from these crises. Romania's significant Hungarian population—representing more than 7 percent of the total population and concentrated in the historical region of Transylvania—publicly requested more autonomy, going so far as to contest some of the constitutional provisions concerning the public use of the official Romanian language. Along Romania's western border, the right-wing Hungarian government of Joszef Antall claimed that it stood not only for the interests of the 10 million Hungarians in Hungary but for the people of that origin all over the world. Given this setting, Romanian officials often noted that the state had only two traditional friends along its border—Yugoslavia and the Black Sea. Although the official policy of the governing majority was rather cold when dealing with Belgrade during the Balkan conflicts, many Romanians have generally viewed Serbia as a regional ally.

It was essential for Romania to limit regional tensions by establishing new relationships with two important neighbors: Hungary and Ukraine. Nationalist parties openly voiced fears that Hungary would interfere with Romanian internal affairs, in terms of either minority rights or border issues.[5] Officials believed that joint projects between Romania and Hungary were the key to overcoming anxieties between the two states. Such confidence-building measures included forming a Romanian-Hungarian battalion, signing the Open Sky Treaty that provides each state with overflight rights, agreeing to historical reconciliation (following the Franco-German model), and, finally, negotiating a new basic treaty with firm stipulations regarding frontiers and the rights of ethnic minorities. Despite these collaborative efforts, many Romanians believed their country's foreign policy goals would be frustrated by the early accession of Hungary to the institutions in which Romania sought membership. A certain level of tension between the states remains.[6]

Romania's negotiations with Ukraine—a big, newly established country with no historical precedents to set patterns for future relations—would be more difficult. The Romanian-Ukrainian relationship was further strained by the inclusion within Ukraine of territory to which Romania believes itself traditionally entitled. The two countries agreed to a basic Romanian-Ukrainian treaty, presented to the public as a "necessary, historical sacrifice." Leaders in Bucharest and Kiev signed and ratified the treaty in a hurry, in time for the July 1997 NATO summit in Madrid. Romanian policymakers, especially President Emil Constantinescu and Foreign Minister Adrian Severin, believed that the treaty bolstered Romania's argument in favor of accession to NATO. Members of opposition parties and many nongovernmental organizations, however, accused the government and its leaders of having unnecessarily forced Romania into a disagreeable and disadvantageous treaty under the pressure of NATO enlargement.

A treaty to establish relations between Romania and Russia has proven more elusive. The countries have discussed such an agreement, but it remains nothing more than an ongoing dialogue. Romanian concerns about the absence of such a treaty are compounded by the presence of the Russian 14th Army, stationed in the Republic of Moldova, which could pose a significant threat to the region. Yet, as President Constantinescu stated—amid objections from some in Romania who considered such a declaration unlucky—"for the first time in a multi-century history, Romania is not bordering with Russia."[7] Russia does not pose the immediate threat it did for so long, but its concept of "close vicinity," which defines its sphere of influence, does raise a concern for Romanian officials: Will Russia try to re-establish its satellite and buffer-zones system, which would again entrap Romania in a gray area of Russian control?

Bulgaria, another of Romania's neighbors, also offered elements of disquietude, though on different matters than other states. Bulgaria did not raise special problems politically, militarily, or historically. However, during the late-1990s crisis in Bulgaria, Romanians started using the term *Bulgarization,* meaning something that led to economic collapse. Bulgaria demonstrated to Romania that internal insecurity can threaten a state's international leverage and prestige and, as such, could undermine efforts to integrate into desirable international institutions (including NATO).

After the revolution of 1989 a wide range of issues influenced Romania's stability and its international status. As President Ion Iliescu noted, the potential spillover of conflicts in Romania's neighborhood represented an immediate, short-term concern. Meanwhile, old rivalries with neighboring states, especially relating to disputed border and minority rights, posed a "medium-term" threat to Romania's domestic conditions and international standing. And the possible reassertion of an ideology of imperialism and domination by Russia presented a serious, long-range concern. All of these factors complicated Romania's situation as it tried to define its new foreign policy direction.[8]

Romania can pursue either one or both of the following strategies in order to address these problems: (1) reform on the domestic level, including the democratization of the country, the stabilization of the political situation, and economic growth or (b) accession to those organizations and institutions that would provide the "umbrella" to shield Romania from external threats. In the current debate in Romania, this latter approach is generally called "integration into European and Euro-Atlantic structures." Most often, Romanians identify NATO as the true source of security, although, from time to time, the Western European Union (WEU), the military component of the EU, is mentioned but with lower expectations than people have for NATO.

The public (and the great majority of politicians) considers integration a matter of "when will they take us?" rather than "should we join them?"[9] Thus, as soon as NATO and the EU announced that they were ready to accept members from the former Communist bloc, Romania submitted its applications. Romania takes pride in being the first state to enroll officially in NATO's Partnership for Peace (PfP). Romania participates actively in all PfP conferences and exercises and considers its PfP membership to be a first step toward inclusion in NATO. While Romania's campaign for inclusion in NATO did not earn the country an invitation during the first round of enlargement, officials in Bucharest remain confident that Romania will be included as a second-round invitee. While Romania's integration into NATO was the theme of a tremendous national campaign, discussion of EU was confined mainly to the level of parliamentary parties, never reaching the dimensions of authentic public debate.

GETTING READY FOR INTEGRATION

How Much Will It Cost?

All post-1989 Romanian governments and Parliaments have pursued a common foreign policy. No official or party has contested the strategic goal of integration into NATO and the EU. This universal support makes integration a unique issue in the divisive realm of Romanian politics. Agreement has extended to even the details of integration—namely, the speed of approach and the legislative, financial, and diplomatic efforts needed. As early as 24 July 1990, Romanian Prime Minister Petre Roman invited Secretary General of NATO Manfred Wörner to pay an official visit to Romania, just months after the collapse of the Ceaușescu regime. At that time, Roman requested the accreditation of a Romanian ambassador to NATO Headquarters in Brussels. One year later, Wörner came to Bucharest. The secretary general was so supportive of Romanian integration efforts that the Manfred Wörner Foundation, a nongovernmental organization (NGO) with the mission of researching and encouraging debate on security policy, opened in Bucharest. In February 1992, the government established the Euro-Atlantic Center in Bucharest with a similar mission. Romania made its official application for NATO membership in 1993, joined the Partnership for Peace in 1994, and made an appeal to the legislatures of all NATO countries to support Romania's candidacy in 1996. Each step was accompanied by debates concerning the criteria of admission on economic, political, and military levels.

Many in Romania argued that NATO membership would be economically wise: The financial costs of Romania standing on its own would be far greater than the costs of integration. According to the Ministry of Foreign Affair's *White Book on Romania and NATO*, integration into NATO would cost the country a total of U.S.$3.8 billion. U.S.$1.6 billion of that total would be spent on upgrading or acquiring equipment for those forces earmarked for NATO missions; U.S.$1.2 billion would be dedicated to improving the military infrastructure, including airfields and sea and river naval bases and harbors; U.S.$800 million would be used for implementing a new military command, control, and communication system compatible with NATO systems; and U.S.$200 million would go toward achieving interoperability of Romanian units assigned to carry out NATO missions. In a study of the costs of restructuring the Romanian army, Secretary of State Constantin Dudu Ionescu estimates that, regardless of Romania's admission into NATO structures, the army would swallow up to U.S.$1.866 billion (U.S.$122 million annually through 2009) in order to make the Romanian armed forces sufficient to fight in a war. His estimates point at lower costs than the ones presented by the Ministry of Foreign Affairs, although he includes in the overall expense an annual contribution of U.S.$30 million made by Romania to NATO's common budget (about 1.2 to 1.5 percent of the current NATO budget). Ionescu argues that the costs were, indeed, "affordable for Romania." He continues, "As the economic reform progresses, greater financial flexibility to fund [the] NATO integration program is expected in the years ahead."[10]

However, Romania's optimistic prediction that the defense budget would reach 3 percent of its gross domestic product (GDP) in 1999 has proven unrealistic. Romania was able to maintain a defense budget over 3 percent from 1990 through 1992, but this situation could not last. In 1995 the defense budget dropped to 2.28 percent of GDP; in 1996, it was 2.34 percent; in 1997, 2.27 percent; in 1998, 2.23 percent; and, in 1999 it dropped below the 2 percent mark. Defense Minister Victor Babiuc has pled for a more generous defense budget, warning that the 1999 funding level freezes current activity, compromises future reforms, and ruins Romania's chance to be considered a NATO candidate. The budget allotment was enough only to fund current salaries, partial maintenance of equipment, and a limited amount of minimal investments.

Actions by the international community have had an indirect but traumatic effect on Romania's economy. Embargoes on Iraq and on Yugoslavia have cost Romania approximately U.S.$3 billion and U.S.$10 billion, respectively. Prior to the upheavals of 1989, both Iraq and Yugoslavia had been reliable markets for Romanian products, and the level of economic exchange with these partners had been high. The loss of Iraqi markets was painful, but the loss of Yugoslavian markets was severe. Early in 1990, small-scale foreign investment and joint venturing thrived along the Romanian-Yugoslav border. Romania has had no choice but to uphold the costly international sanctions against these two states. To do otherwise—that is, to violate the embargoes—

would likely hurt its chances of being invited into NATO and the EU, both of which have played essential roles in enforcing these embargoes.

Forces Involved

The Conventional Forces in Europe (CFE) treaty—negotiated in the midst of the Cold War—still stipulates the size of the Romanian armed forces and the weaponry they use. Consistent with this treaty, Romania slashed the size of its conventional army between 1992 and 1995. By 1995, the forces had been reduced by a full 40 percent, including 1,667 tanks, 1,053 armored vehicles, 2,453 artillery pieces, and 72 combat aircraft. Romania launched its own reduction program, Armed Forces–2000, starting in 1995, in which Romania established standards for its armed forces comparable to those of NATO requirements, including downsizing the army to 195,000 by the year 2000.

Romania is not just cutting the size of its forces, but it is adapting the forces to today's threats. The state has organized a rapid reaction force (RRF), which includes specially trained and modernized units of infantry, armor, paratroopers, mountain troops, reconnaissance, and artillery, supported by air force and navy units. The main features of the RRF units, which will involve between 20,000 and 30,000 troops, are flexibility, interoperability with NATO forces, and storage capacities on the national territory.

At the same time, Romania is modernizing its defense industry in cooperation with Western companies through technology transfers.[11] Although a lack of funding has hampered the transfer of technology, the level of training within the armed forces has increased consistently. Romania takes pride in two major achievements in this realm: training the military in the spirit of the NATO doctrine and institutionalizing civilian control of the military. Over 450 officers have attended courses organized in NATO countries in order to learn about specific missions such as peacekeeping, search and rescue, and delivery of humanitarian aid.[12] According to the *White Book on Romania and NATO*, participation in multinational exercises within the PfP (or in the spirit of PfP), in peacekeeping missions in the Middle East and Africa, in the Joint Endeavor exercise, and in the peace implementation mission in Bosnia have considerably improved the level of officer, command, and troop training in the Romanian military.[13]

The government created the College of National Defense in 1992, the first such institution in Central and Eastern Europe. Its direct goal was to provide needed training to the military and defense communities and to expose military personnel to civilian expertise. The government also hoped, however, that the presence of the institution would bolster its chances for an invitation to join NATO. The college became the source of the highest level of education in the military system and brought about a tremendous change in field culture and practice.[14]

Reshaping the Doctrine, Changing the Mentality

Along with the church, Romanians express a higher degree of trust in the army than in any other institution or structure in Romanian society.[15] This prestige results not only from Romanian tradition, but also from the fact that the army has never attempted to play a political role in the country (except for a brief period during World War II). During the 1989 revolution, the army could easily have taken over control of the country after Ceausescu briefly fled Bucharest. Despite shooting and quasi-warfare in the capital and major cities, the military did not consider itself an alternative regime or a replacement for civilian political authority and readily accepted subordination to the new authorities, as soon as these were formed.

The government was able to enhance civilian control over the armed forces without much resistance from the military. The first civilian was appointed to a leading post within the Ministry of Defense, as head of the newly created Department for Defense Policy and International Relations, in 1993. One year later, a civilian—Gheorghe Tinea, a diplomat with experience in international security—was appointed minister of defense; his successor was also a civilian, Victor Babiuc. He had served as the first civilian minister of internal affairs from 1990 to 1991.

The democratization process helped to involve different parts of the government in security matters. Today the Defense and Internal Affairs Committees of the Senate and Chamber of Deputies not only meet with and question candidates for defense-related ministries but also debate specific elements of policies and make amendments to the yearly budgets of the Ministry of Defense and the Ministry of Internal Affairs.

The Supreme Defense Council, established in 1991, is now the highest authority over the military. The council is headed by the president of Romania (who also serves as the commander in chief of the armed forces) and the prime minister (who is deputy commander in chief). The council is made up of the principals responsible for the security of the country, including the ministers of defense, foreign affairs, internal affairs, and industry—as well as the directors of the foreign and domestic intelligence services, the chief of the general staff, and the presidential counselor for military affairs. The Supreme Defense Council is responsible for all matters relating to security; its decisions are implemented by the government and local administrations.[16]

In the fall of 1998, the Supreme Defense Council decided on a new military strategy for Romania, stating explicitly the necessity of the country's more rapid accession into NATO. The new strategy reflected the changes that had occurred in the international milieu since 1989. The council stressed collective defense, interoperability with NATO forces, and multinational operations, with specific reference to the institutions and allies newly friendly to Romania, including the United Nations, NATO, the Western European Union, and the Organization for Security and Cooperation in Europe (OSCE, previously the Conference on Security and Cooperation in Europe). Romania's leaders no longer perceived rivalry among states to be the main source of danger in the realm of international relations. Instead, they identified myriad emergent problems as potential threats to Romania: the saturation of weapons and military equipment in the former Soviet sphere; the proliferation of weapons of mass destruction, including terrorist groups' access to this class of weapons; crossborder terrorism and organized crime activities; the collapse of multiethnic states; intercommunity violence driven by demands for recognition of ethnic and cultural identity and for self-determination; migration and forced displacement of populations due to terror or violence; economic disparities; and religious disputes.[17] The strategy reflects Romania's traditional aversion to aggressive foreign policy and emphasizes the strictly defensive character of national defense. Also, in keeping with tradition, Romania has tried to assert its role as a stabilizing element in the region and as a security provider. Indeed, official military strategy advocates strongly for negotiated political solutions for the conflicts in neighboring areas (especially Yugoslavia and Moldova). The thorough debates that accompany any decision to include Romanian troops in an active military mission abroad reflect the state's desire for a moderate foreign policy.

NATO Accession as a Government Priority

When the Warsaw Treaty Organization sang its swan song in 1991, most members of the organization set the course toward NATO membership. Successive Romanian governments have pursued this course with especially strong determination. Each cabinet has worked toward the goal of membership, both directly—through cooperation with and participation in PfP programs—and indirectly—by trying to stabilize relations with neighbors and fostering Western institutions within Romania.

By 1996, Romania had become an associate member of the EU and of the WEU (an organization with which cooperation increased during the observation of the embargo against Yugoslavia), a full member of the Council of Europe, and an active participant in UN and OSCE activities. When Victor Ciorbea became prime minister in 1996, he stated openly that the previous government had not made enough effort in pursuit of NATO membership. The cabinet during Ciorbea's tenure worked to highlight the benefits for NATO of

Romanian membership, presenting Romania—together with Poland—as an anchor of stability in the area. It also tried to secure support for membership from likely first-round candidate states like Hungary, in addition to lobbying the capitals of NATO countries.

The Ciorbea government platform approved by the Parliament—its Basic Program—emphasizes that Romania is part of European civilization and culture and supports the common values of democracy, rule of law, human rights, and market economy. Regarding NATO, the program states,

> In keeping with Romania's vocation of peace and regional stability, the Government views accession to NATO from a double perspective: on one hand, ensuring national security, and, on the other hand, fostering confidence and cooperation in the region. The Government shall act with a view to determining the simultaneous admission into NATO of all countries belonging to the same strategic area and having expressed their wish to become members in the North Atlantic Alliance.[18]

The platform also stated that Romania's military would undergo whatever modifications and modernization necessary to meet NATO standards.

The government formed an Inter-Ministerial Committee for Integration into NATO to guide the complex integration effort. This committee gathers representatives from all executive levels—the presidency, ministries, departments directly subordinate to the prime minister, and related governmental agencies for monthly sessions. It provides expertise to Romanian delegations on all NATO issues and works in ad hoc subcommittees to carry out specific tasks. Forwarding its conclusions and results to the Council of National Defense, the committee makes proposals for bringing Romania closer to achieving the membership it so ardently pursues.

The mid-1997 Madrid summit, during which alliance members did *not* invite Romania to join NATO, coincided with a change in ministerial staff. The new leadership team of Radu Vasile continued efforts toward integration. Dialogue between Romania and NATO intensified. Bucharest further developed its bilateral and multilateral relations with neighboring countries and with NATO countries. And the government signed treaties—including agreements on military cooperation—with both NATO and non-NATO countries.

Romania's post-Madrid strategy for accession to NATO is a predictable plan that emphasizes securing the support of Western governments and "the fortunate three" new members, Hungary, Poland, and the Czech Republic. The Vasile government hoped that Romania would receive a specific promise from NATO on admission during the 1999 Washington summit, but the alliance extended no additional membership invitations at that time. Romanian leaders have begun to question the accuracy of labeling NATO's enlargement strategy an open-door policy.

Parliamentary Diplomacy in Action

All parliamentary parties have agreed that Romania should continue to pursue integration into NATO. Even nationalistic parties such as the Great Romania Party have agreed that the best security arrangement for Romania is the collective defense umbrella provided by NATO. Opinions differ, however, regarding how best to comply with NATO criteria. Displacement of foreign military bases within the national territory of Romania, participation by Romanian forces in missions abroad, and the costs associated with NATO admission are issues that continue to cause concern. Dissension on these issues has led some in Parliament to advocate a national public referendum to determine whether the Romanian people sincerely desire membership.

In the session of the National Consultative Council for Euro-Atlantic Integration held at the end of 1994, the first important year in relations between Romania and NATO, most parliamentarians expressed concern over accession procedures. Their worries included whether NATO really would expand eastward, the potential negative consequences for Romania of a multistep admission process, the extent of the threat posed to Romania by Russia and Moldova, and the feasibility and desirability (or lack thereof) of Romanian neutrality in Europe. The conclusion of the session did not reveal any significant disagreement. In the final declaration it was

> noted with satisfaction that the participants were in consensus regarding the concept of Euro-Atlantic integration and agreed with all the steps undertaken by the legislative body, by the Presidency and the Government of Romania, by other governmental and non-governmental institutions to reach the goal of integration.[19]

The Romanian Parliament tried to back up governmental efforts concerning the country's admission into NATO, using delegation exchanges as opportunities to call for the support of NATO countries. On 5 June 1996, the legislature in Bucharest adopted the Appeal of the Parliament of Romania to the parliaments of NATO member states, which states that

> Romania's entire activity within Partnership for Peace, the North Atlantic Assembly[,] as well as its quest for NATO admission is based on the will of the people, backed by all parliamentary parties, [with the] view of becoming, as soon as possible, a full-fledged member of NATO structures. . . . Romania understands [that it would] assume the rights, commitments and obligations that are inherent to a NATO member. The Parliament of Romania conveys to the Parliament of [the member state] the assurances of its highest consideration and requests support for its endeavor as a free, independent, sovereign and democratic country, in compliance with article 10 of the Washington Treaty, in view of becoming a full-fledged NATO member.[20]

A new appeal was launched in October 1998 by the subsequent Parliament but did not make significant changes to the first.

The leader of the Democratic Party, Petre Roman, in his capacity as a delegate to the North Atlantic Assembly (NAA) and special rapporteur, kept the issues linked to NATO enlargement alive in Romanian political and public debates during the pre-Madrid period. He emphasized controversial issues among the NATO member states concerning the steps and speed of enlargement and the position that Russia took regarding NATO membership for former WTO countries. In reports presented to the Political Committee of NAA in 1994 (Washington) and 1995 (Budapest), Roman made a strong plea for NATO enlargement and a new European security system to which all countries could contribute.[21]

This idyllic hope for the future faded somewhat during the critical situation that arose in Kosovo. Through the spring of 1999, Romanian participation in NATO activities had been limited to either humanitarian missions (such as peacekeeping in Bosnia) or military exercises. The Kosovo crisis demanded a more nuanced position. President Emil Constantinescu asked Parliament to pass a decision that would allow NATO aircraft to survey Romanian territories on the way to Kosovo, and Minister of Defense Babiuc suggested that Romanian troops might take part in a stabilization force in Yugoslavia. The parliamentary session devoted to discussion of the Kosovo crisis was a lively one. Major disagreements arose for the first time in matters concerning security and military action, but the National Council for Defense adopted an unequivocal position. According to the council, Romania should put the airports in Timisoara, Craiova, Constanta, and Bucharest at NATO's disposal; should permit NATO aircraft to use Romanian airspace if necessary; and should send a mission of humanitarian aid to the population in the Yugoslav province, while refraining from putting troops in the conflict area.

Opposition parties were outraged: They had not been consulted, even informally, prior to this decision on Romania's position. Members of Parliament held press conferences and public declarations, engaging the citizenry in the debate. While the governing majority believed that Kosovo provided Romania with an opportunity to prove its commitment to NATO, the opposition—especially the Party of Social Democracy in Romania (PDSR), led by the former Romanian President Ion Iliescu—considered the council's plans as violating Romania's security interest and contradicting Romania's traditional foreign policy. PDSR withdrew from the final vote on the declaration, energetically contesting its necessity. The Yugoslavian embassy in Bucharest soon expressed its concern over the visible change in Romanian policy toward the Yugoslav Federation, but an anti-Milosevic position, consistent with that of NATO, had already been established. Romanian policymakers chose Western solutions to the Kosovo crisis.

In the Name of the People

Public support in favor of NATO membership has been consistently very high, but Romanians have grown impatient over time. Public opinion polls reveal that from June to November 1998 the number of Romanians who favored an increased effort to join NATO and the EU had gone up 9 percent—from 48 to 57 percent. Only 7 percent opposed speeding up efforts, while 21 percent were neutral on the question.[22] Most analysts interpret the enthusiasm for NATO membership as reflecting a general pro-Western attitude in Romania rather than an understanding of this military and political organization. Romanians want their country to have the prosperity, success, and security found in NATO countries.

In the period prior to the NATO Madrid summit, the private TV station "Pro-TV" spearheaded a pro-NATO campaign, which had started earlier in the country's newspapers. The military newspaper, *Observatorul militar,* dedicated pages to explaining the new military strategy, changes in doctrine, the weaponry Romania should expect to use, the elements of interoperability with NATO structures, and Romania's procedure for lobbying for Romania. The Pro-TV campaign, though, took to a new level efforts to inform and excite the public about NATO. For the first six months of 1997, Pro-TV ran special programs to explain NATO to Romanians and interviewed domestic and foreign specialists, policymakers, and military experts on the topic. The station asked prominent politicians in member states about the likelihood of Romanian membership in the first wave of enlargement. During one program, Pro-TV linked leaders in the capitals of six countries in a simultaneous transmission, a performance no other Romanian television was able to achieve. In addition, the station sponsored the participation of twelve private Romanian citizens at the NATO summit in Madrid to ensure the presence of civilians in a conference otherwise dedicated only to political and military decisionmakers. According to polls conducted by Pro-TV, 69.9 percent of Romanians completely supported NATO membership, 20.2 percent favored the idea, and 4.2 percent were opposed. Only 38 percent of the public, however, believed that the Madrid summit would bring Romania the desired membership.

Romanian Efforts Thwarted

The activity of the Romanian government in the first half of 1997 had been solely oriented to Madrid. Prime Minister Ciorbea had asked for the people's patience and promised that NATO membership would come as a reward for their sacrifices. Most ministers in his cabinet talked about "catching the first wave." The population has accepted the sacrifices required for creation of a market-oriented economy, a prerequisite for admission.

These sacrifices did not pay off at Madrid, nor did additional efforts prove sufficient during the 1999 Washington summit. NATO has not yet decided when the next wave of enlargement will occur. Until then, efforts by officials in Bucharest to secure the position of Romania as favorite for the next round of invitations continue, but they are making this case without many new ideas. At the same time, the divide between the government and the opposition is growing, and the public seems disenchanted. While recent Romanian governments have ranked NATO admission efforts among their top priorities, only 2 percent of Romanians believe that admission into NATO should be the most important concern of the government, with only 3 percent ranking the same goal as the second-highest priority.[23]

Lobbies for Romania

The National Consultative Council for Euro-Atlantic Integration recommends that all political parties and organizations in Romania openly endorse the integration effort, which continues to be a crucial objective of foreign policy. Outside of the government, the Manfred Wörner Foundation and the Euro-Atlantic Center organized debates to foster public awareness about joining NATO. A much smaller NGO based in Timisoara, the General George Pomutz Association for Commemorating Heroes of Romanian Origin Abroad, has meanwhile endeavored to make the United States more aware of the long traditions of military cooperation between Romania and the United States in order to encourage U.S. acceptance of Romania's application to NATO.[24]

Apart from domestic efforts, groups have tried to mobilize whatever support Romania can get from abroad. A primary target has been the people of the Romanian diaspora. Romanians represent the seventeenth-largest ethnic group in the United States, and many Romanian-Americans wrote letters to members of Congress and to President Bill Clinton requesting support for Romania. Even the exiled former king of Romania, Michael I, became involved. He traveled to the capitals of those NATO countries that are still monarchies, encouraging support for the Romanian candidacy. The former king demanded that responses be given to Romania's main concerns, including whether a next wave of enlargement would occur, when it might occur, and if NATO could guarantee that Russia would not hinder future expansion of the alliance. Inasmuch as NATO did not respond to the royal lobbying, which seemed to make clear that European monarchs are merely symbols of power, King Michael's diplomatic tour seemed useless, if not paradoxical: It demonstrated that Romania was a democratic country with a republican majority that nonetheless needed the aid of an aged, exiled monarch to achieve its primary foreign policy goals.

France has supported Romania's inclusion in NATO since the early 1990s and has volunteered to continue advocating the Romanian cause in all international matters. Teodor Melescanu, the Romanian minister of foreign affairs from 1992 to 1996, explained that French support came not only from France's desire to regain its leverage in European affairs but also from recognition of traditional ties between France and Romania, such as common Latin origin and strong friendship. Melescanu said that nobody else offered to do this.

Ultimately, French support did not turn out to be of much help during the NATO summit in Madrid. Germany, which had problems of its own, showed little interest in Romania. Great Britain seemed to withdraw from its traditional role as arbitrator in the Balkans. Lastly, the United States supported Romania, but it was difficult to transform this benevolence into a tangible position.

Romania encouraged the defense industries in NATO states to lobby for its accession by purchasing military equipment from them and exploring the chances of future purchases. It was argued that a contract with Bell Helicopters, for instance, might help bring about NATO membership. Romania's financial woes, however, limited the effectiveness of this course of collaboration.

CONFIDENCE FOR THE FUTURE

Romanian policymakers and the public share the conviction that there are few alternatives when it comes to finding an umbrella of protection and security. Romania is trying its best to foster a European identity and to bolster coherent institutions that reflect this identity. These efforts account for painful reforms and for the determination with which Romanian policymakers pursue strategies of accession to the EU. Whatever type of development the EU finds suitable—economic, political, or defense related—Romania will try to join the effort.

At the same time, in broader Euro-Atlantic affairs, Romania continues to seek membership in NATO, the main source of security for the wide region. After the Madrid and Washington summits, foreign analysts began to suggest that Romania look for non-NATO options or for other security arrangements. But Romanian Minister of Defense Babiuc made it clear that, regardless of postponements, "Romania's choice will still be NATO."[25] It has been argued that Romania cannot count solely on a European solution to its security problems and cannot make membership in NATO its only goal. Former Minister of Foreign Affairs Adrian Severin urged Romania not to seek membership so desperately. He also suggested that, even while pursuing NATO, Romania should make regional and subregional security arrangements as a complement to NATO membership, that is, the country should make "stand-by" arrangements until the ultimate goal is achieved. Given the lukewarm reception NATO has thus far offered to Romania, officials in Bucharest should consider thoughtfully Severin's warnings. Otherwise, Romania may be left with no coherent foreign and security policy mission.

NOTES

1. In the early 1980s, Ceauşescu decided to pay back over U.S.$11 billion (plus interest) in foreign debt by slashing imports and enforcing an austerity program on the country. After the triumphant announcement that the foreign debt had been paid back in the spring of 1989, Ceauşescu continued the same policy, hoping that the savings would be enough to proclaim Romania a great economic power. By December 1989 the government had more than U.S.$2.7 billion and over 900 million rubles stashed away, in addition to huge investment projects at home and abroad. At the same time, though, Romanians were starving and suffering from lack of basic necessities.

2. By 1989, Ceauşescu had accumulated the positions of party secretary general, president of Romania, president of the State Council, general commander of the armed forces, and several other less important positions, securing total personal control over all political, military, and civil institutions Romania had at the time.

3. "The letter of the six" was a novelty, since all the initiators belonged to the Communist elite and remained in the country while criticizing Ceauşescu 's policy. In it, the authors denounced the lack of citizen liberties, aberrant agricultural policy, famine, and isolation of Romania.

4. The NSF was a group of former Communist leaders, military commanders, and citizens. Ion Iliescu, well known for his opposition to Ceauşescu's dictatorship, was its clear leader. Iliescu remained president throughout the transition period.

5. The two parties that most often take this stand are the Party for Romanian National Unity (PUNR) and the Great Romania Party (PRM). Both parties have had parliamentarian representation since 1992 and supported the government in power from 1992 to 1996.

6. The 1997 *White Book on Romania and NATO*, edited by the Ministry of Foreign Affairs prior to the NATO Madrid summit, states one element of the political cost of Romania's nonadmission (and Hungary's inclusion in the enlargement process):

> [T]he process of rapprochement and partnership-building between Romania and Hungary could be slowed down, if not compromised altogether. The impact on all the political Romanian-Hungarian relations could be serious, even devastating. Thus, the ground would be prepared for those nationalistic and extremist politicians who opposed all along the development of normal partnership relations between Romania and Hungary to acquire renewed credibility and audience. . . . A differentiated treatment of Romania and Hungary in their drive to be admitted into NATO would be contrary to the fundamental purpose of NATO enlargement, i.e., to enlarge the area of democracy, security, and stability in Central Europe. (Public declaration, made by President Emil Constantinescu, Bucharest, February 1997)

See Romania, Ministry of Foreign Affairs, *White Book on Romania and NATO* (Bucharest: February 1997), 18. Available online at http://mae.kappa.ro/wbrn/contents.html.

7. Valetin Stan, "The Government of Failure/Guvernul esecului," *Sfera politicii* 4 (1998): 6.

8. Iliescu argued that integration into NATO, WEU, the EU, and the Council of Europe would counterbalance all of these threats. See Ion Iliescu, "Romania—An Outlook on Europe or How Europe Is Seen from Bucharest" (speech given at the French Institute for International Relations, Paris, 16 November 1994).

9. This perception is openly stated in regard to NATO, among the principles underlying the defense policy in Romania's military strategy. See Ministry of Defense, "Romanian Armed Forces—A Partner for the Future," *White Book*, no. 3 (1997): 38.

10. Constantin Dudu Ionescu, "Financial Costs of Romania's Integration into NATO," *Central European Issues*, no. 2 (1997): 29. His conclusions are that "some of the previous estimations for Romania's integration into NATO were overestimated, while the potential that Romania is actually able to support the costs was underestimated." Ionescu argued that money from NATO Common Funds and from special cooperation and assistance programs provided by NATO would pay for up to 60 percent of the needed infrastructure investments.

11. During the Soviet era, Romania produced most of its technology and equipment domestically, in an effort to avoid dependence on its Warsaw Treaty partners, but the domestic defense industry is undergoing the general process of privatization and is, at the same time, shrinking, as Romania's economy as a whole contracts.

12. After 1989, although there have been limited amounts of money for training (for example, only twelve hours of flight per pilot are possible in the Romanian air force), enhancing the general training of personnel has been considered a basic need—and a feasible task.

13. See Ministry of Foreign Affairs of Romania, *White Book on Romania and NATO*.

14. The College of National Defense started with a student body composed of two-thirds military personnel and one-third civilians. Now, this has reversed. The civilians are parliamentarians, policymakers, and journalists, and some from other European states. Each group undergoes six months of training.

15. According to the Soros Foundation's "Barometer of Public Opinion," between 69 and 84 percent of Romanian society has expressed support for and trust in the army since 1996. In comparison, 77 percent of the Romanian people *distrust* political parties in the state. Data compiled by Soros's Open Society Institute, available online at http://www.osf.ro/English/programe/Barometru/public/bop.htm.

16. Gheorghe Diaconescu, Floarea Serban, and Nicolae Pavel, "Democratic Control Over the Army in Romania," *Editura Enciclopedica* (Budapest: Editura Enciclopedica, 1996).

17. Constantin Dudu Ionescu, "Integration in European and Euro-Atlantic Structures—A National Goal," *Romanian Civilization* (special NATO issue), Center for Romanian Studies, 6, no. 1 (Spring/Summer 1997): 61–63.

18. For "Basic Programme for Macro-Stabilization and Development of Romania Until the Year 2000" (1996), see "Speeches of the Minister" available online at http//:www.domino.kappa.ro/mae/presa.nsf/InformatiiDePresaEng.

19. Vladimir Rodina, "Romania to Go Ahead with European Integration," United Press International, 28 December 1994.

20. For "Appeal to the Parliament of Romania to the Parliaments of NATO Member States" (Bucharest, 5 June 1996), see Ministry of Foreign Affairs of Romania, *White Book on Romania and NATO*, Annex VII. Available online at http://mae.kappa.ro/wbrn/a/a7.html.

21. National Peasant Party parliamentarian Ion Ratiu was another avid advocate of integration, but his public speeches are less focused than Petre Roman's and did not stir debates. Roman's activity always attracted public reaction. For Roman's speeches, see, for example, Petre Roman, *The Spirit of Democracy and the Fabric of NATO—The New European Democracies and NATO Enlargement,* Draft Special Report (Sub-Committee on NATO Enlargement and the New Democracies, NATO Parliamentary Assembly, Brussels, 2 October 1996). Available online at http://www.naa.be/publications/comrep/1996/an246pc.html.

22. Soros's Open Society Institute, available online at http://www.osf.ro/English/programe/Barometru/public/bop.htm.

23. Apud Ioana Avadani, "Madrid—esec sau success [Madrid—Failure or Success]," *Politica externa* 2, no. 3–4 (Fall 1997): 35.

24. The organization presented U.S. President Bill Clinton with letters noting that Romanian-American ties date back to the nineteenth century. General Pomutz, of Romanian origin, was an officer in the United States Army in the late 1800s.

25. "Romania Determined to Enter NATO," Associated Press Newswire, 10 October 1997.

13

Estonia:
Confronting Geostrategic Limits

BERND SCHÜRMANN

Baltics is commonly used as a collective name for the three Baltic republics of Estonia, Latvia, and Lithuania at the southeastern rim of the Baltic Sea. It is common practice to lump these countries together not only in the media but also in scholarly publications. The result has been an image of the Baltic states as a diffuse but single entity. This widespread habit originated from the similarity of the development of the three Baltic republics during the twentieth century in the shadow of Russia and the Soviet Union. Finally, after becoming independent simultaneously in 1918 and occupied by the Soviets in 1940, these states jointly regained their independence in August 1991. Since then, all three have adopted a goal of integration into the Western world, especially Western institutions like NATO and the European Union. This will require the Baltic states to overcome their Soviet past and transform their societies and their economies into democratic, free-market systems. The Baltics have also had to settle relations with Russia by negotiating the withdrawal of former Soviet troops still deployed on their territory until 1994. Until the withdrawal was complete, border treaties could not be negotiated.

Analysis of the national debates over enlargement of NATO must look beyond certain commonalities in the modern history of the Baltic states, including similar strategies regarding future roles in the European state system. Obviously, superficial similarities overshadow important differences in the political systems that affect societal and economic recovery. Looking beyond official rhetoric, which repeats more or less the goal of Western integration and the necessity of close Baltic cooperation, observers will note that the three Baltic states have differing foreign policy tactics. Lithuanian decisionmakers, not only for historical but also cultural reasons, are more oriented toward Poland and Central Europe, while politicians in Latvia stress the

Nordic character of their country and emphasize relations with Denmark, Sweden, and Germany. Facilitated by its geographic situation as well as linguistic affinity, meanwhile, Estonia turns even further north to close relations with Finland. Lithuania, unlike Latvia and Estonia, does not have to cope with a large Russian-speaking population, which came to the region during Soviet rule. This influences Lithuania's foreign policy, especially toward Russia.

Because of the similarities and differences, I will examine one country, Estonia, in detail, looking at the domestic conditions caused by internal reform as well Estonia's political constellations and foreign policy. The evaluation of Estonia's domestic policy toward NATO can serve as a case study of the Baltics, the only countries on the territory of the former Soviet Union applying for NATO membership. This procedure allows a detailed analysis of the stumbling blocks faced by small nations of the former USSR on their way toward partnership with the West.

NATIONAL DEFENSE IN ESTONIA

Building an Army from Nothing: Estonia's Defense Forces

Like the two other Baltic countries, Estonia started from scratch to establish its own defense structures. Unlike Ukraine and other successor states of the Soviet Union, the Baltics insisted on the immediate withdrawal of Russian troops from their territory. They feared that these large and heavily armed forces could pose a threat to the domestic stability of the young states, especially to their sovereignty.

National defense in Estonia is based on two pillars, the regular defense forces and the volunteer national guard, called Kaitseliit, or Defense League. Both operate under the command of the chief of general staff. The regular armed forces consist of the main services—army, navy, and air force. At present, the conscription period lasts twelve months. During peacetime, one of the army's main tasks is to train a sufficient number of reservists for territorial defense. According to current figures, this planning aims for a wartime strength of 45,000 personnel. But to reach this size, Estonia's armed forces still have a long way to go.

Since 1994 and especially since 1996, Estonia has made considerable progress toward reliable defense, having bolstered its basic organizational and training schemes and command structures. There is considerable rivalry, though, between the regular army and the Kaitseliit. Observers call the years 1992 and 1993 the "time of the two armies."[1] Although such problems have, by and large, been eliminated, important difficulties, especially financial shortfalls, persist. The government and the Parliament have to weigh carefully military expenditures against social and economic demands. In the short and medium term, only increased efficiency and an effective planning process can diminish this problem.

Foreign advisors have diagnosed an inconsistent "hand-to-mouth policy," wherein the defense budget was used as a quarry in case of budget problems in other areas.[2] Lack of money for defense leads to difficulties in recruiting. From the very beginning, Estonia with its 1.6 million inhabitants has suffered from scarce availability of personnel in absolute numbers. Furthermore, the personnel available have received training and military socialization mostly in the Red Army. Their personal qualifications, ways of thinking, command and training methods, and language skills were to a large extent not up to the standards of armed forces in democratic, Western countries.[3]

The second-largest difficulty with which the military has had to cope was a tremendous lack of equipment. Under the conditions of a severe economic crisis in the early 1990s, the defense forces were more or less dependent on worn-out equipment, donated by the United States and Western and Northern European countries. Because of the very unstable situation in the Baltics, especially with regard to the armed forces and the remaining Russian forces in the country, Western countries were reluctant to supply Estonia with even light armaments. Only when a certain degree of stabilization became obvious and some basic decisions concerning the structure and the goals of the national defense system had been made, was the path to greater material support opened. Until now, the armed forces not only in Estonia, but in all three Baltic states, rely more or less on the assistance of Western countries. For example, in 1998 Finland laid the ground for an Estonian artillery platoon by donating nineteen discarded mortars for the symbolic price of one Estonian Kroon.[4]

MILITARY COOPERATION WITH NATO

Considering the various problems mentioned above, the support from NATO has had, in addition to a number of bilateral initiatives, especially by Finland, an important impact on the increase of defense forces in Estonia. The main instrument promoting the relations between NATO and all Baltic states has been the Partnership for Peace Program (PfP), initiated in 1994. The Baltic states were among the first participants. As a result their security and defense policies are the success story of Baltic cooperation. Despite various repeated controversies in different areas, ranging from trade relations to border issues to the competition for EU accession, a considerably close and smooth cooperation on security and defense has been initiated with the assistance of NATO.

The Baltic Battalion (BALTBAT) constitutes a core element of PfP. This trilateral platoon of Estonian, Latvian, and Lithuanian infantry companies boasts 141 servicepeople from each country with a total authorized strength of 721. Denmark functions as the lead nation on the NATO side. BALTBAT operates headquarters in Adazi, Latvia, and takes part in the Implementation Forces (IFOR) and Stabilization Forces (SFOR) missions in Bosnia and Herzegovina. It is complemented by BALTRON, a joint minesweeping squadron, and BALTNET, a joint air surveillance system, both of which are operated in cooperation with Norway.

These joint Baltic forces serve mainly four purposes. First, they are considered the core of the future Estonian armed forces. Officers and the enlisted of these units will later be used as multipliers in the training of ordinary conscripts and reserve officers. Second, the joint forces are a means to train for interoperability with NATO structures, especially on the level of command, control, communications, and intelligence. The adoption of NATO's Planning and Review Process (PARP) by the Baltic states is just one example.[5] Third, they are the contribution of the Baltic states to the peacekeeping missions of NATO and other international organizations. The psychological effect in all three Baltic republics of not only consuming but also contributing to the overall stability of Europe should not be underestimated. Participation in the IFOR and SFOR missions in Bosnia-Herzegovina is often mentioned in this respect. Lastly, BALTBAT enhances Baltic and regional cooperation, including that among militarily nonallied states like Sweden and Finland.

NATIONAL SECURITY PERCEPTION IN ESTONIA

The Impact of History

In Estonia, historical experience has a manifold effect on the security perceptions of decisionmakers and on public opinion as well. Most decisive in this respect have been the years between 1940 and 1991, when Estonia belonged to the Soviet Union. The collective Estonian memory recalls the loss of independence, the displacement of extensive segments of national elites in the 1940s, and the nationalization and integration of the Estonian economy into the Soviet planned economy, together with forced industrialization and an influx of mainly Russian-speaking citizens.[6] In conjunction with a strict policy of Russification, these events caused widespread anxiety over extradition and a fear of losing the Estonian language and cultural heritage under Russian pressure. This perception of threat played a key role in the independence movement in the late 1980s, which led in turn to the re-emergence of a sovereign Estonian state in 1991.[7] Additionally, Estonians remember their weak resistance against the Soviet occupation in 1940; this memory also motivated independence.

National security interests are influenced mainly by two lessons from history. First, it must be the principal security policy goal to maintain the territorial integrity and sovereignty of Estonia. Constant democratic development must be ensured. The country must avoid a repetition of the events of 1940, when the country fell victim to external Soviet pressure due to its weak international standing and domestic instability. Second, Estonia must maintain a certain distance from its neighbor Russia in order to counterbalance Russian unpredictability and attempts to influence the domestic politics of Estonia.[8]

According to Estonian politicians, security policy has two main aspects. Domestically, stable political development and dynamic economic growth are the preconditions for sufficient public support for the young state. Furthermore, a successful transformation of political and economic systems is seen as a long-term instrument for the integration of Russian-speaking inhabitants of the country. Externally, the country has to be anchored in the European state system by membership in the leading Western institutions, especially NATO and the European Union. Also Estonia must normalize its relations with Russia.[9]

The primary conclusion Estonia draws from historical experience in foreign policy is the idea of Western integration and regional cooperation.[10] This idea is based on Estonia's desire not only to distinguish itself from Russia in pure practical or ideological terms but also to seek deliberate incorporation into a security community in a Deutschian sense.[11] Obviously, Estonia has learned from the failure of a policy of neutrality during the 1930s and the inability to create a more supportive environment through at least loose forms of regional cooperation.[12] Furthermore, like many other states in Central and Eastern Europe, the Baltic states are looking for unambiguous and lasting symbols of their belonging to the Western world. Therefore, NATO and the European Union have quickly been identified as the main sources of "hard security" in a traditional sense and as some sort of comprehensive "soft" security as well.

ESTONIAN VIEWS ON CURRENT RISKS AND THREATS

In the current situation, neither the Estonian political elites, that is, the people professionally concerned with preparing and making political decisions, nor the Estonian public perceives an immediate Russian threat to their country's sovereignty by military or political means. Various vague risks from an unstable development of Russian internal affairs are instead perceived. These risks include the safety of Russian nuclear facilities, environmental devastation in general, migration of larger groups of Russians from the border regions because of an ongoing economic and social deterioration, and finally insubordination of local Russian army platoons along the border, which may lead to further tensions.[13]

In this respect, the perceptions of risk in Estonia and the other Baltic republics have gradually changed during the last five or six years. They now come close to the Finnish understanding of "comprehensive security" with a broader conception of possible dangers to national security.[14] This development can be traced back to different sources. The final withdrawal of the remaining Russian forces in 1994 and the sometimes tense, but nevertheless stable, relations with Russia eased existing perceptions of threat.[15] The successful integration process into the European Union with Estonia as one of the first membership candidates was another important step. Moreover, domestic developments like the onset of economic recovery since the end of 1993 and the calming down of questions concerning minorities and citizenship also contributed to this overall stabilization.[16] At last, especially in foreign policy but also in defense policy, political and administrative personnel suffered from a severe lack of diplomatic experience in the first years after independence. This lack of professional training produced some annoyance and tension at the outset of the decade.[17]

However, keeping this general tendency of political détente in security matters and a minimized perception of threat in mind, different schools of thinking inside the Estonian foreign policy elite can be identified. Similar observations apply to Latvia and Lithuania. The gradual differentiation of elite perceptions of risk results from individual opinion, namely attitudes toward Russia. Elite conceptions of security policy will be directly influenced by developments in Russian domestic and foreign policy.[18]

The goal of quick NATO accession is usually not questioned. However, different perceptions of risk lead to different expectations concerning the character and objectives of NATO membership. Furthermore, accession affects not only the future role of NATO in the Baltic states but also the relationship between NATO and the European Union. This includes different opinions about the importance of membership in both organizations in the long term.

Like most other Central and Eastern European countries, Estonia makes a distinction between a traditional understanding of NATO on the one hand and a more progressive one on the other.[19] Exponents of a traditional understanding of security tend to lay emphasis on the military capacities of NATO and the importance of Article 5 of the Washington treaty. In their view, NATO membership serves as a means to gain solid security guarantees from the transatlantic community against possible Russian threats. Usually, advocates of traditional security policy do not consider a close link between NATO and EU necessary for achieving security and regional stability.

Meanwhile, the progressive position, which can be described as the "cooperative-political concept" of Estonia's national security policy, has gained support during the past years and is represented by a growing number of decisionmakers in the administration. Advocates of this understanding of NATO emphasize elements of the so-called new NATO, which is in the process of shifting from an organization of collective territorial defense to an instrument of joint European or perhaps even global crisis management, including peacekeeping and peace-enforcing capabilities.[20] In principal, they do not expect a dramatic deterioration of Baltic-Russian relations in the future. This more relaxed view to the East enables policymakers to broaden their concept of security. Their vision of the future security system in Europe combines NATO, EU, and other institutions and stresses the need to integrate Russia into such a security network.[21] They try to combine the idea of a Baltic NATO membership with Nordic concepts of comprehensive and cooperative security.[22]

Security concepts oriented around the cooperative-political model are on the upswing, especially in Estonia, primarily for two reasons. First, an ongoing process of learning is obviously taking place. The changing character of NATO and its adaptation to the overall political situation in Europe after the end of the Cold War is being observed closely. Second, however, the Estonian elite pay tribute to reality. They are more or less forced to adapt to their country's security situation. Despite negative experiences and the desire to establish some distance from the big Russian neighbor, it becomes more and more obvious that if not good, regular and normal relations with Russia are nevertheless indispensable for a successful integration into the West. This understanding encourages a concept of security beyond strictly military terms[23] but also beyond the goal of NATO membership, which is, especially in the case of the Baltic states, a red flag to most Russian politicians.

Reality also intervenes when Estonia considers the prospect of joining the transatlantic alliance in the near future.[24] Instead of waiting idly for NATO membership, Estonia has made significant progress in promoting its accession to the European Union. In 1997 Estonia was the only Baltic state starting concrete negotiations on the terms necessary for full EU membership. Subject to the EU's own preparedness to enlarge eastward, Estonia now has a well-grounded position for reaching the first of its main foreign policy goals in 2003 or 2004. This scenario, having developed since the end of 1996 and the beginning of 1997, has led to an unofficial adjustment in Estonia's integration strategy: the success of the EU's Luxembourg summit in December 1997.[25] Foreign Minister Toomas Henrik Ilves deserves credit for seizing the opportunity to get at least one invitation to join a European organization.[26]

This development has been accompanied by a further strengthening of the cooperative-political understanding of Estonia's national security. Since 1997 Estonia has paid more attention to the possible effects of EU membership on security policy, the strengthening and further development of the

Common Foreign and Security Policy (CFSP) of the EU, and the future role of a "new NATO." Again, a certain rapprochement to "Nordic" ideas of comprehensive or cooperative security became obvious, even if the perceptions of threat and traditional conceptions of NATO as an organization of collective defense against the USSR are still deeply rooted for historical reasons.

DEBATE ON NATIONAL SECURITY AND NATO MEMBERSHIP

The Constitutional Basis of National Defense

The official national security and defense policy of Estonia is based on two pillars. The first pillar comprises the constitution as well as the Regular Armed Forces Services Act, the Peacetime National Defense Act, and the Wartime National Defense Act. These pieces of legislation embed the national defense into the overarching political system and also lay the foundation for the basic structures of Estonian defense. The Constitution of the Republic of Estonia was adopted 28 June 1992 by a referendum. Chapter X of the constitution is devoted to national defense.[27] Articles 124 and 125 declare "the duty to participate in national defense" for all Estonian citizens and describe the democratic rights and duties of individuals in the defense forces. Articles 126 and 127 deal with questions of responsibility and command. Finally, Articles 128 to 131 contain the procedural questions for declaring a state of emergency and a state of war. These constitutional provisions are further elaborated in the acts treating the Regular Armed Forces Service, Peacetime National Defense, and Wartime National Defense.

With respect to its legal basis, the national defense system and the defense forces meet relevant Western standards. The civil political leadership and control of the armed forces is laid down in the constitution and completely internalized by the political and military elite. The protection of human and civil rights of military personnel is ensured by the constitution and the Regular Armed Forces Service Act. In practice, single incidents of illicit treatment of conscripts and cases of disobedience have become public during the last years, but there are no regular or systematic violations of human rights on a larger scale.

As usual in a Western parliamentary democracy, the armed forces are under the command and control of elected political institutions. In Estonia the Riigikogu, or Parliament, the president of the republic, and the minister of defense are the main actors on security and defense policy issues. The Riigikogu is responsible for budgetary issues and legislation dealing with the nation's defense. It also decides on the participation of Estonia's armed forces in international peacekeeping operations. The president of the republic, since 1992 the former writer and historian Lennart Meri, also serves as supreme commander of national defense. According to Article 127 of the constitution, the commander of the armed forces is appointed by the Riigikogu on the recommendation of the president. In wartime this person is allowed to declare a state of war. The government, meanwhile, especially the Ministry of Defense, is responsible for the implementation of national defense policy and the day-to-day business of command and control. These three national authorities are linked by the National Defense Council, "an advisory body in the questions of National Defense for the President of the Republic," which brings together defense policy leaders from the Riigikogu, the government, and the armed forces.[28]

An important structural problem has occurred in recent years with regard to Article 127 of Estonia's constitution. Again, the Riigikogu approves the chief commander based on the recommendation of the president. Despite expectations that the ruling majority in the Riigikogu would guarantee a process of consultation and negotiation between the president and the government on the choice of the chief commander, the system has caused severe friction between the political administration and the military.

The main problem is the lack of direct subordination of the chief commander to the minister of defense. Instead, the military commander answers only to the president, who then becomes involved in the daily management of defense policy. This creates a permanent friction between the political and military commands. Because of the small number of political elite and the weakness of ideological, party-based relations, the political system in Estonia relies somewhat heavily on personal connections. As a result, personal disputes affect defense policy.

In the late 1990s, for example, strained relations between Minister of Defense Andrus Öövel and Chief Commander Johannes Kert surfaced in official decisionmaking. Because of the constitution, Öövel could not fire Kert on his own, while the president hesitated to dismiss him. With the new government elected in March 1999, Jüri Luik became defense minister, and Admiral Tarmo Kouts was named chief commander in fall 2000. The personal friction abated. It is clear, however, that the system contains inherent problems. It is up to future leaders to make this tension productive and, in the end, beneficial for the armed forces themselves and the citizens they defend.

The second legal pillar for security policy is the National Defense Plan, adopted by the Riigikogu on 30 May 1996, which defines the security needs and interests of the country and details its defense policy goals.[29] It is an Estonian peculiarity that the Riigikogu has adopted the so-called Guidelines of the National Defense Policy of the Estonian State (DPG) without any legally binding security policy guidelines. Thus the DPG has to fulfill not only the task of formulating defense policy, but moreover it has to deliver some basic definitions of Estonia's security interests and strategic goals.[30]

The DPG is a traditional set of defense policy tasks. Basically, it guarantees the "preservation of independence and sovereignty of the state, the indivisible integrity of its land area, territorial waters, and airspace, its constitutional system, and the vitality of its people."[31] Further, it describes as key factors to Estonian independence the guiding principles of international law and the maintenance of neighborly relations. To achieve these goals, Estonian defense relies on an independent national defense and an "international defense related cooperation" in the European context.[32] In its basic provisions, the DPG entails the usual formulations, as they may be found in similar documents of various Western democracies.

But the DPG does elaborate the instruments of national defense policy in more detail than other countries' documents might. In particular, it recognizes Estonia's status as a small nation with restricted defense capabilities and the importance therefore of international cooperation in the security of the country. Explicitly spelled out is the goal of full membership in NATO and the Western European Union (WEU). It calls for full participation in NATO's PfP and the associated partner status of WEU.[33] Other platforms for regional defense cooperation, according to the DPG, are close relations with the two other Baltic states and active participation in regional Baltic Sea security efforts. The participation in "international peacekeeping, peace implementation, humanitarian aid and rescue operations" is also explicitly designated.[34]

Russia is not mentioned in the document explicitly. Relations with Russia are addressed only in general, namely that good neighborly relations are an important precondition to Estonia's national security and defense. Russia does appear in an indirect and even negative way in a point about possible dangers for Estonian security: "The main sources of the dangers threatening the security of the state are aggressive imperialist aspirations and political and/or military instability" can only be understood as directed against Russia.[35]

A series of legal acts and government procedures regulating technical aspects of Estonia's national defense complements the DPG. The Military Service Act organizes the procedures of conscription and other related aspects. A system of defense planning procedures, the Planning and Accountancy Process (PAP), ranges from the General Defense Plan (GDP) and the Medium Term Development Plan (MTP) to annual defense planning. While the GDP presents a long-term perspective on military planning, focused on a period of ten to fifteen years, the MTP delivers a guideline for the development of defense forces during a five-year period. The PAP is compatible to NATO's PARP process and is carried out by the Ministry of Defense in cooperation with the chief commander of the regular armed forces. It is mainly a practical guideline for the administrative and technical procedures of Estonia's military build-up during the first decade of the twenty-first century.

Political Parties and NATO: The 1999 Parliamentary Elections

NATO membership was not a main topic of the parliamentary election of 7 March 1999 or of the preceding election campaign. This was due to a broad consensus in foreign policy issues among the leading political parties. There is also a relative lack of interest in a society more concerned with problems of economic development and social welfare than with foreign or security policy.

Still, the integration into Western European and transatlantic structures, especially accession to the European Union and NATO, has been the top foreign policy priority of every Estonian government since 1992. This broad consensus results from a peculiarity of the Estonian party system, which shows much less right-left division than most other Western and also Eastern European countries. Most parties, especially the leading ones, define themselves as neither left nor right, and they vary only by the degree to which they emphasize social or market-economic elements in their platforms.

In sum, foreign policy issues have a low profile within Estonia's political parties. As the 1998–1999 election campaign underscored, the formula of Western integration has been repeated again and again without intense discussion.[36] This analysis applies even more to NATO than to the European Union. NATO membership is recognized as a purely political problem with no direct influence on the everyday situation of Estonian citizens, while the economic and social effects of EU accession are perceived as more severe. Furthermore, the electorate does not necessarily identify with certain parties or programs. Voting decisions are much more influenced by the personality and charisma of the respective party leaders. As long as elected officials maintain the consensus on integration with the West while refraining from public comment on the issue, a controversial debate about NATO or even EU membership cannot be expected. Even if they did speak to the press, it seems the public would not show concern. Edgar Savisaar, speaker of the leading opposition Center Party, carefully tried to initiate a debate on Estonian foreign policy by launching a series of newspaper articles in 1999, but he did not succeed to any degree.[37]

As far as NATO membership is concerned, the only conceivable debate could arise from the necessity of an increased defense budget.[38] The tense financial situation of the Estonian state budget is an apparently insurmountable obstacle to sufficiently financing the defense sector.[39] The margins are further narrowed because of the legal obligation of the government and Riigikogu to adopt a balanced budget and avoid credit-based deficits. Under these circumstances, social expenditures, pensions and wages, and economic policy have attracted the overwhelming amount of state money. The government in office at the time repeatedly encouraged raising the defense budget to a level of 2 percent of the gross domestic product (GDP), in accordance with the average level of NATO member states. This goal failed during the late 1990s because of financial constraints. Instead, defense expenditures ranged from only 0.8 percent to 1.2 percent of GDP.

The right-center government elected in 1999 consists of the Pro Patria Union (Isamaaliit), the Reform Party (Reformierakond), and the Moderates (Möödukad), with Foreign Minister Toomas Henrik Ilves (Moderates) and Minister of Defense Jüri Luik (Pro Patria Union), former Estonian NATO ambassador in Brussels.[40] Observers expect this administration to follow a comparatively active and efficient foreign and security policy. Despite Estonia's best intentions, in fact defense spending increased to only 1.6 percent of GDP in 2000, 1.8 percent GDP in 2001, and will only hit the targeted 2.0 percent in the projected budget for 2002. Despite gradual increases, defense will remain secondary in Estonian policy concerns.[41]

Public Opinion and NATO

Low public interest in foreign policy is not a phenomenon unique to Estonia but a tendency in many former socialist societies in Central and Eastern Europe. Due to the tremendous impact of social and economic changes on the people's daily lives, comparatively abstract issues like national foreign policy receive little attention.[42]

Yet a second overarching tendency in foreign policy and public opinion in Central and Eastern Europe is a high esteem for national independence. This may be explained by the suppression of such ideas by socialist rule since World War II. Because the USSR held Estonia and the two other Baltic states within its empire, socialist ideology had an especially stifling influence. The violent incorporation of these states into the Soviet Union and their long struggle for independence in its best sense, instead of "just" getting rid of Soviet influence, led to according a high value to sovereignty as well as national political and cultural identities.

The widespread feeling that Estonia should not risk its newly gained independence or curtail its sovereignty by entering new integration processes becomes obvious in public opinion polls. These polls hint at a romantic idea of Estonian statehood, but they also address the realistic conviction that Estonia, as a small nation-state, has no alternative to integration with the West in the long term. A large majority of Estonians favor disassociation, leaving EU and NATO far behind.[43]

But assuming a public referendum, NATO is usually valued higher than the European Union. At the end of 1998, 35 percent of the Estonian population favored NATO membership, but only 27 percent favored EU accession, the lowest level in all EU candidate countries of Central and Eastern Europe.[44] The results change when respondents are asked to *prioritize* forms of integration. The European Union ranks higher for Estonia's further development than NATO. Also in 1998, 41 percent of all Estonians responded that Estonia should join the EU, with 17 percent ranking NATO as the most important organization for Estonia and 3 percent supporting Eastern integration with membership in the Commonwealth of Independent States (CIS).[45]

It is interesting to note that 51 percent of all Estonians are convinced that Estonia's independence and sovereignty can best be guaranteed by ongoing *economic* success, while only 6 percent consider military strength most important. This figure is particularly informative because of the low number of undecided respondents to this question, compared with the referendum question and the popularity question discussed earlier.[46] The usually high degree of undecided citizens may indicate a lack of information and knowledge but also a general lack of interest in foreign policy, and it would appear that Estonians pay more attention to economic issues than to security issues.

Compared to the European Union, NATO is considered a more popular but less important organization by the public. This confirms the conclusion that perceptions of military threat from Russia have diminished since the completion of the Russian withdrawal in 1994. They have been replaced by more vague feelings of different risks, caused by unstable and unpredictable economic and social development in Russia.

The popular view that accession to the EU is more important than NATO is shared by the foreign policy elite. But there are also important differences between these perspectives, which cause a certain gap between the political and administrative elite and the Estonian public. First, foreign policy experts often complain about the public's lack of knowledge about NATO, EU, and the whole process of Western integration. Policymakers often blame ignorance for the romantic way in which many people view Estonia and its sovereignty, ideas that often go hand in hand with the self-perception of Estonia as a small society in a difficult stage of political, social, and economic recovery. This need to identify Estonia as a sovereign nation with unique needs is not generally shared by the political elite. Again, most foreign policy professionals do not see any alternative to Western integration.

According to public opinion polls, security forces enjoy a high esteem in Estonian society. This generally positive attitude is directed in a similar way to the armed forces as well as to the border guard and police. In rankings of confidence for single political, societal, and official state institutions, security forces earn high marks.[47] On the other hand, young men often try to avoid military service, viewing it as inconvenient. Furthermore, the country cannot afford to pay its military personnel well, and service usually means deployment in remote areas of the country. In sum, the positive attitudes toward the armed forces reflect the strong urge for security in times of great change and uncertainty. People generally worry not only about their country's external security but also about organized crime, symbolized by "the Russian mafia" and illegal immigration. On the practical and personal level, however, most young people have an ambiguous sense of personal duty to national security. Obviously, many doubt the importance of military service and question the practical value of defense forces under current conditions.

The differences in opinions between ethnic Estonians and the Russian-speaking population form another important aspect of attitudes toward national security. Regardless of whether the Russian-speaking Estonians have gained citizenship, ethnic Estonians are mainly more positive toward NATO and less positive toward the European Union than Russian speakers. On the one hand, this difference results from the opposition of the Russian government to NATO enlargement, which affects Estonia's Russian-speaking population. On the other hand, Russian-speaking inhabitants seem more concerned by the negative effects of Estonia's economic reforms. Formerly employed mainly in less competitive branches of Estonian industry, Estonians of Russian descent were more affected by the conditions of a liberal market economy. They now hope for EU membership, anticipating that economic and social improvements will result. Furthermore, they expect that Estonia's policy on citizenship, which is very often perceived as discriminating, would be modified under pressure from the EU. In contrast, the rural population, mainly formed by ethnic Estonians, is more skeptical toward EU membership because the Common Agricultural Policy (CAP) of the European Union has some influence at the polls.[48]

THE WASHINGTON SUMMIT AND PERSPECTIVES FOR NATO ACCESSION

After the disappointing experience with NATO enlargement in the past, expectations about the Washington summit and celebrations on the fiftieth anniversary of the alliance have been comparatively low in Estonia. This differed from Lithuania, where a slight hope of NATO membership had been entertained early in the process. Estonia held no such illusions. The leading state representatives and the foreign ministry mainly attempted to assure language in official NATO declarations concerning further enlargement.[49] It is nearly impossible to anticipate whether the Kosovo conflict or NATO's long-term structural reassessment and further enlargement will have a positive or negative effect on Estonia's goals.[50] It might be that NATO wants to avoid further deterioration of relations with Russia. That could result in a very cautious next stage of enlargement and a concentration on countries like Romania and Slovenia.

Such a development would correspond to the worst-case scenarios of Estonian officials. In their opinion, a clear acknowledgment of Estonia as a possible future member would constitute the minimum amount of momentum needed by Estonia to move forward. Anything less than this would not indicate progress on the 1997 Madrid declaration and would be understood as a clear lack of Western interest. Additionally, the Estonian government is still waiting for NATO's proposals for further practical steps in an enhanced rapprochement strategy. The Ministry of Defense continues to discuss the possibility of permanent joint units of Baltic and NATO forces. These forces could follow the example of the Danish-German-Polish battalion in the German-Polish border town Szczecin or the attachment of BALTBAT to the Danish SFOR contingent in the former Yugoslavia.[51]

Looking at the results of the Washington summit with respect to an ongoing enlargement process, Estonians have been disappointed, even though the worst case has been avoided in the short term. NATO acknowledges Baltic progress in creating reliable defense systems and mentions the Baltic states by name in the summit declaration, albeit behind Romania and Slovenia.[52] The impression of a definite refusal has been avoided, but not much more.

To assist the applicants in preparing for a possible future accession, the 1999 Washington NATO summit adopted its Membership Action Plan (MAP). The MAP defines the requirements the applicant countries have to meet before accession and invites them to negotiate Annual National Programs. On this basis, the current Estonian government plans to be ready for membership in 2005 or 2006. Lithuania, which has the most advanced defense structure of the three Baltic states, has hopes for inclusion in a second enlargement round, possibly in 2002.

Of greater importance for Estonia's NATO chances in the medium term will be the impact of the war in Kosovo and the lessons NATO and Russia will draw from it.[53] Since the war in Kosovo, NATO's attention has focused mainly on the Balkans and the need for stabilizing southeastern Europe. One result may be that greater importance is laid on NATO membership for the countries of the Balkan region. In contrast, the Baltic states are stable and calm.

Russia will draw a number of lessons from the Kosovo crisis, which may affect its relations with NATO in the future. First, NATO was not reluctant and probably will not be reluctant in the future to use its military capabilities under certain circumstances. Second, the Kosovo conflict required NATO to draw heavily on deployments in the immediate neighborhood of Yugoslavia, and NATO depended on close cooperation with countries such as Albania and the Former Yugoslavian Republic of Macedonia (FYROM). Third, Russia perceived that it achieved respect from NATO based primarily on its remaining military potential.[54] For all these reasons, NATO enlargement to the Baltics both threatens Russia at its borders and intensifies the already uneasy position of Kaliningrad, a Russian enclave rumored to have nuclear weapons and a devastated economy. If the NATO-Russia relationship continues to deteriorate, it could lead to even stronger Russian resistance to enlargement of NATO to the Baltic states and NATO hesitation to enlarge in the face of that resistance.

NOTES

1. Marcis Gobins et al., "Außen und Sicherheitspolitik," in *Handbuch Baltikum,* ed. by Heike Graf and Manfred Kerner (Berlin: Nomos, 1998), 113–147.

2. "Estonia on the Threshold of NATO," *The Final Report of the International Defense Advisory Board to the Baltic States* (24 February 1999), 7.

3. Ibid., 7.

4. On the consequences on operational and military aspects of these problems, see the Kievenaar Report, the Executive Summary of Estonian Defense Assessment, conducted by the Office of the Secretary of Defense of the United States of America as part of U.S. assistance to the Baltic states in 1998. U.S. European Command (USEUCOM), "Executive Summary of Estonian Assessment" (Brussels: U.S. Department of Defense, 1998).

5. Estonia, Ministry of Defense, "Vienna Document: Annual Exchange on Defense Planning 1999" (Tallinn: Ministry of Defense, 1999), 13, note 1.

6. See Romuald J. Misiunas and Rein Taagepera, *The Baltic States: Years of Dependence 1940–1990* (Berkeley: University of California Press, 1993) or Dietrich Loeber et al., *Regional Identity Under Soviet Rule: The Case of the Baltic States* (Hackettstown, N.J.: Published for the Institute for the Study of Law, Politics, and Society of Socialist States, University of Kiel, 1990).

7. See the extensive literature on this topic, for example Anatol Lieven, *The Baltic Revolution: Estonia, Latvia, Lithuania, and the Path to Independence* (New Haven and London: Yale University Press, 1993); in German: Marianne Butenschön, *Estland, Lettland, Litauen: Das Baltikum auf dem langen Weg in die Freiheit* (München: Piper, 1992); Andrejs Urdze, ed., *Der baltische Weg: Das Ende des Sowjetkolonialismus* (Hamburg: Rowohlt 1991).

8. For example Lennart Meri, "Eesti Julgeolekupoliitilistest Aspektidest" [On security policy aspects of Estonia] (speech given at the Security Policy Forum in St. Gallen, Switzerland, 25 January 1995, in "Presidendikõned" [Speeches of the President], ed. by Lennart Meri (Tartu: Ilmamaa, 1996), 424–431.

9. To consider the influence of Russia on the security perception in the Baltic states, Buzan's concept of a "security complex" with simultaneous presence of cooperative and competitive elements seems to be helpful. Barry Buzan, *People, States, and Fear: An Agenda for International Security Studies in the Post–Cold War Era* (Boulder: Lynne Rienner, 1991), 188–218.

10. See for example former Estonian Minister of Defense Hain Rebas, "Barriers to Baltic Cooperation—Opportunities for Surmounting Them" (Kiel: unpublished manuscript, 1997), 9.

11. Karl W. Deutsch et al., *Political Community and the North Atlantic Area* (Princeton: Princeton University Press, 1957), 5.

12. Olav F. Knudsen, "The Foreign Policies of the Baltic States: Interwar Years and Restoration," *Cooperation and Conflict* 28, no. 1 (1993): 47–72.

13. Robert Dalsjö, "Baltic Self-Defense Capabilities—Achievable and Necessary, or Futile Symbolism?" *Baltic Defense Review,* no. 1 (1999): 17–23.

14. Unto Vesa, "Back to Deutsch: Integration, Peaceful Change, and Security Communities," in *Changes in the Northern Hemisphere*, ed. by Jyrki Käkönen (Tampere: Tampere Peace Research Institute, Research Report No. 52, 1993), 159–164; Susanna Perko, ed., *Nordic-Baltic Region: New Actors, New Issues, New Perspectives* (Tampere: Tampere Peace Research Institute, Research Report No. 75, 1996).

15. Sergei Medvedev, "Geopolitics and Beyond: The New Russian Policy Towards the Baltic States," in *The European Union and the Baltic States: Visions, Interests, and Strategies for the Baltic Sea Region*, ed. by Mathias Jopp and Sven Arnswald (Helsinki and Bonn: Programme on the Northern Dimension of the CFSP, Vol. 2 by UPI Helsinki and the Institut für Europäische Politik Bonn, 1998), 235–269.

16. As Kristi Raik shows, the EU contributed to this development. Kristi Raik, *Towards Substantive Democracy? The Role of the European Union in the Democratisation of Estonia and the Other Eastern Member Candidates* (Tampere: Tampere Peace Research Institute, Research Report No. 84, 1998), 54–96.

17. Marcis Gobins, "Möglichkeiten und Grenzen der Baltischen Zusammenarbeit" (Graduate Thesis, the Free University of Berlin, 1996), 27–29; see also Peeter Vares, "Dimensions and Orientations in the Foreign and Security Policies of the Baltic States," in *New Actors on the International Arena: The Foreign Policies of the Baltic Countries*, ed. by Pertti Joenniemi and Peeter Vares (Tampere: Tampere Peace Research Institute, Research Report No. 50, 1993), 3–31.

18. Hildegard Bedarff and Bernd Schürmann, "NATO und EU aus der Perspektive Ostmitteleuropas: Meinungsbilder der Eliten in Polen, der Tschechischen Republik, Estland und Lettland," *Forschungsberichte Internationale Politik* 24 (Münster: Lit, 1998), 84–85.

19. Ibid., 116–118.

20. See "The Alliance's Strategic Concept," approved by the Heads of State and Government participating in the meeting of the North Atlantic Council in Washington, D.C., 23–24 April 1999, NATO Press Release NAC-S (99) 65 (24 April 1999).

21. This view has been very clearly expressed by Estonia's President Lennart Meri, "Eestile on Euroopa Liit ja NATO ühe mündi kaks külge [For Estonia the European Union and NATO Are Two Sides of the Same Coin]," *Eesti Päevaleht*, 17 March 1999: 2.

22. See overview, provided by Kari Möttölä, "Security Around the Baltic Rim: Concepts, Actors, and Processes," in *The NEBI Yearbook 1998: North European and Baltic Sea Integration*, ed. by Lars Hedegaard and Bjarne Lindström (Berlin: Springer, 1998), 363–404. See also Olav F. Knudsen, *Cooperative Security in the Baltic Sea Region*, Chaillot Paper 33 (Paris: Institute for Security Studies WEU, 1998).

23. See for example K.G.H. Hillingsø, "Defensibility," *Baltic Defense Review*, no. 1 (Tartu: Baltic Defense College, 1999): 36–40.

24. Steven C. Johnson and Rebecca Santana, "Balts Bite the Bullet, Hope for NATO by 2002," *The Baltic Times*, 29 April 1999: 1, 8.

25. European Commission, *Agenda 2000—Summary and Conclusions of the Opinions of Commission Concerning the Applications for Membership to the European Union by the Candidate Countries*, DOC 97/8 (Strasbourg and Brussels: EU-COM, 15 July 1997); Luxembourg European Council, "Conclusions of the Presidency," *Agence Europe*, no. 7121 (14 December 1997).

26. The concentration on EU accession "just in time" in Estonia's foreign policy has been reported in discussions by the author with various officials of the Estonian Ministry of Foreign Affairs between 1997 and 1999.

27. The Constitution of the Republic of Estonia, Chapter X, "National Defense," in Estonian Translation and Legislative Support Center, *Estonian Legislation in Translation—Legal Acts of Estonia,* No. 1 (Tallinn: Estonian Translation and Legislative Support Center, 1996), 53–55.

28. Vienna Document (1994), 5, note 1.

29. Government of the Republic of Estonia, "Guidelines of the National Defense Policy of the Estonian State" (Tallinn: draft presented to the Riigikogu, 1996).

30. As reported by officials in the Ministry of Defense to the author in 1999.

31. Government of the Republic of Estonia, "Guidelines," 1, note 30.

32. Ibid., 1.

33. Ibid., 3.

34. Ibid.

35. Ibid.

36. Compare for example the various party platforms in the 1999 election campaign. "Milliseid ohte näete Eesti liitumisel Euroopa Liiduga? [Which Risks Have to Be Expected from Joining the European Union?]" in *Aripäev*, 10 February 1999: 30; untitled article, *Postimees,* 6 March 1999: 7.

37. For example Edgar Savisaar, "Skepsis Euroopa Liidu suhtes levib [Skepticism Concerning the European Union Is Spreading]," *Postimees*, 16 January 1999: 7.

38. See Neeme Raud, "Trumani sõnad NATOst saavad täna teoks [Truman's Words About NATO Are Becoming Reality Today]," and Kadri Liik, "NATO laienemine ja Venemaa [NATO Enlargement and Russia]," *Postimees*, 12 March 1999: 12.

39. On Estonia's current budgetary problems see Denise Albrighton, "Kallas [Estonian minister of finance] Outlines Plans to Trim State Budget," *The Baltic Times,* 29 April 1999: 4.

40. See Kärt Karpa, "Kolmikliit suutis kohad jagada [Three-Party Coalition Agrees on Sharing Posts]," *Eesti Päevaleht*, 17 March 1999: 3.

41. See the government schedule, *Eesti Päevaleht,* 18 March 1999: 4.

42. Andrus Saar, director of the Estonian opinion research institute Saarpoll, interview by the author, 16 March 1999.

43. Saarpoll, "Euroopa Liit: Elanikkonna Monitoring, Küsitlusperiood: 02–09.09.1998 [European Union: Citizen's Survey, Period 2–9 September 1998]" (Tallinn: Saarpoll, 1998), 4.

44. Jaanus Putting, "Suhtumine euroliitu on Eestis patiseisus [Attitude Toward EU Falters in Estonia]," *Postimees,* 15 January 1999: 3.

45. Saarpoll, "Uuringu 'Euroopa Liit, Eesti ja rahvas' [Study 'European Union, Estonia, and the People']" (Tallinn: Saarpoll, 1998), 17.

46. Andrus Saar, interview by the author, 16 March 1999. Saar is director of the Estonian opinion research institute Saarpoll.

47. Ibid.

48. Saarpoll, "Uuringu 'Euroopa Liit, Eesti ja rahvas,'" 3, note 48.

49. Rebecca Santana, "Baltic Presidents: Time for NATO to Name Names," *The Baltic Times,* 25 February 1999: 1–2; Daniel Silva, "Washington's Mixed Messages," *The Baltic Times,* 25 February 1999: 2.

50. Rokas M. Tracevskis, "Baltics Back NATO, Anxious About Russia," *The Baltic Times,* 1 April 1999: 1, 6.

51. Officials of the Ministries of Defense and of Foreign Affairs, interviews by the author, March and April 1999.

52. North Atlantic Council, *An Alliance for the 21st Century,* Washington Summit Communiqué (meeting of the North Atlantic Council, Washington, D.C., 24 April 1999), NATO Press Release NAC-S (99)64 (24 April 1999), 7.

53. Steven C. Johnson, "NATO Bombs, Russian Rhetoric and the Baltics," *The Baltic Times,* 22 April 1999: 1, 10.

54. This opinion is also expressed by Peer Lange, "Die ausgeklammerte Sicherheit in der Nördlichen Dimension" (lecture given at the seminar "Die Nördliche Dimension der Europäischen Union," the Finnland-Institute Berlin, 24 April 1999), 5.

PART 4

Conclusion

14

New Realities, New Challenges

GALE A. MATTOX

If one conclusion stands out in reviewing the foregoing chapters, it is that the transformation of the European geopolitical realities has had a deep impact on the continent and continental security. Europe is only now beginning to adapt to the changes initiated by Polish workers in the late 1970s and early 1980s and symbolized by the fall of the Berlin Wall in 1989. One of the most substantial adaptations to those major societal changes has been the enlargement process of NATO, begun formally in 1994 and resulting in membership for three new states in 1999. The authors of this volume have looked at the national debates within several countries to determine the factors that informed the debates, the positions taken by country elites and publics, the role of interest groups, if any, and the action taken both at executive and legislative levels in the formal and informal processes of ratification.

In reviewing the similarities and divergences among the debates taking place in the twelve countries included in this volume, a number of issues and questions emerge. What was the strategic context within which each of the national debates took place? What were the various domestic influences on the decision to admit new members or the decision to seek or not seek admittance to NATO? To what extent and at what point were the respective publics involved and to what extent was the decision an elite one? What was the nature of the parliamentary debates? Are there conclusions to draw in any of these areas?

The answers to these questions will differ from country to country, but does comparison permit conclusions about the potential success or failure of the first phase of enlargement or provide a signpost to possible future enlargements? In sum, what if any generalizations might be made based on the past several years of the enlargement process, and are there any lessons from the first enlargement for potential future enlargements? Will there be pressure to admit a second group of countries? Which countries? And how will those not chosen be expected to react? What role will the Russians play, and how will the alliance change and evolve with enlargement? What impact has enlargement and other factors had on the evolution of the European common foreign and security policy?

NATO enlargement has not occurred in a vacuum. Its success or failure will lie not only in the national debates, but also in the ability of NATO as an alliance to adapt to the changes of the post–Cold War era and to the challenges of enlargement to the organization. While this book focuses on the national debates, it would be remiss not to address those debates from the perspective of the alliance more generally, including a description of NATO reforms paralleling enlargement. This final chapter addresses and reviews those reforms and the potential future direction of NATO. The 1999 Washington summit, the first for the three new members, laid out an ambitious program of reform and transformation for NATO.

What form will the transformation take? Will NATO remain the primary defense organization in Europe or will an organization like the Organization for Security and Cooperation in Europe (OSCE) or another of the many continental institutions step in as the Cold War institutions are discarded? Will a new reinvigorated European elite commit to increased defense funding and pursue its security through an EU common foreign and security process? In addressing these issues, the final section considers the NATO program of reform articulated in its 1999 strategic concept and its potential future impact as well as the broader strategic context of European security.

THE NATIONAL DEBATES

The Strategic Context

By the end of the Cold War, the strategic context in Europe was strikingly similar throughout the continent—it was defined by the East-West divide with threat perceived clearly from the Warsaw Pact led by the Soviet Union or NATO led by the United States, depending on which side of the divide a country fell. Indeed, for many of those states in the Warsaw Pact, the memory of Soviet intervention in Czechoslovakia in 1968 heightened a sense of threat from both sides. Some analysts have cynically expressed a yearning for that era in which friend and foe were easily identified and consensus was quickly built. Reality has changed. The real and symbolic fall of the Berlin Wall and the subsequent revolutions culminating in the disintegration of the Soviet Union in 1991 dramatically altered the easily defined strategic landscape of the Cold War.

As the preceding chapters indicate, the search for stability within the new strategic realities began almost immediately after the governments of the former Eastern bloc changed. NATO included among its new missions in the 1991 New Strategic Concept peacekeeping and conflict management. The success of the Gulf War together with the emergence of democracies in Europe, moreover, convinced the West of its rightful mission as leader of the democratizing world. At the same time, the East took the opposite turn and become increasingly unsure of its appropriate direction. When rebuffed by the West from immediate accession to its institutions, the more assertive of the states—Poland, Czechoslovakia, and Hungary—banded together as the Visegrad states only eventually to determine that they were less than effective and that their security remained limited.

Here the differences in threat perception became strikingly visible. For the West, instability outside its borders was a potential threat, but the alliance was as strong as it had ever been and no longer under direct threat. The United States drew down its forces from over 300,000 (actually over 800,000 personnel, including dependents and civilians, at the height of the Cold War) to 100,000, as promised by President Bill Clinton even as the number continued to decrease. So-called Western Europeans also began to divert resources away from their forces, and most countries abolished the draft with only a few exceptions, including Germany and Italy. For the East, the domestic situation was by and large tenuous and the former Soviet Union a persistent danger. Even as the Soviet troops left Eastern Europe and the Baltics, the nervousness about a resurgence of the Northern Bear persisted.

NATO enlargement exposed the differences among these different perceptions of the threat. A number of the states of the East pushed for enlargement both to shore up domestic, internal development and to assure that their country did not fall again under the influence and control of Russia. The West, meanwhile, responded with structures designed to embed the East into the Western framework essentially without fear of the former Soviet Union, most prominently the North Atlantic Cooperation Council (NACC). While the NACC satisfied many of the former Soviet republics and may even have sufficed for some of the states most closely tied to the Soviet Union such as Romania and Bulgaria, it did not address the security concerns of the states that had during the Cold War perceived themselves at the frontline: Poland, Czechoslovakia, Hungary, and the Baltic states. As a Visegrad group, the former three (then four with the Czech-Slovak split) by 1993 were approaching the West for closer military ties. But as Poland, the Czech Republic, and Hungary moved clearly toward asserting their democratic reforms and undertaking market reforms, Slovakia fell behind in these areas. Reform also came more slowly to the Baltic states as it took longer to force out the Russians and gradually define their identities apart from Russia.

For the West, the move to bring Poland, Hungary, and the Czech Republic closer to NATO was first attempted militarily with the establishment of

Partnership for Peace (PfP) in January 1994 to intensify cooperation and reduce tensions more generally on the continent through military-to-military exercises and coordinated programs. This was followed by a decidedly political decision in December 1994 to encourage democratic and economic reforms in the former communist states by holding out the prospect for full membership in NATO. In both of these undertakings, the reaction of Russia raised concern, and provisions to bring Russia into these structures as well were made. In May 1994, the Russians became PfP members. The door to NATO membership presumably remains open to them even today, though many observers think the likelihood of Russian membership slight. Russia itself seems skeptical if not disdainful of this discussion.

From the NATO Enlargement Study in September 1995 outlining objectives for those states interested in membership to the naming of Poland, the Czech Republic, and Hungary during the Madrid summit in 1997 to the signing of the accession agreements to the Washington treaty in March 1999, NATO and Russia have sparred over a number of issues. In fact, Russia made a concerted and vocal effort to derail the process. Chapter 10 demonstrates the continuing friction in Russia over NATO enlargement, but there is no denying that the 12 March 1999 treaty accession by the three new members may be said to have sealed the changes to the strategic context begun in 1989 and 1991.

Domestic Influences

While the enlargement issue was elite-focused in most countries, there were also public influences. In the three candidate member states, the public supported links to the West that would move the former Warsaw Pact states away from the former East bloc. Those segments of the population who saw their future economic and political success in free markets and democratic institutions were clearly supportive of either European Union (EU) or NATO membership, often in that order, but they were also pragmatic in that they considered NATO membership the most feasible solution. In the case of Poland, Polish emigrants in NATO member countries (especially in the United States where those groups had remained active abroad and maintained home links) mobilized on this issue, as did representatives of the arms industry (who would benefit greatly). But the strong sense that Poland had always really belonged to the Western community and was, as one parliamentarian put it, "returning to its roots" was less of a factor in the Czech Republic and Hungary.

In these two countries, the public questioned both the potential cost of alliance membership from a budgetary perspective and the impact on its Cold War relationships. Would the Atlantic alliance really be able to guarantee their security should Russia seek to secure its outer borders? Among significant segments of the population, the perception of Western threat countered by

Soviet protection was hard to overcome. In the Czech Republic, in fact, there was an active debate whether nuclear weapons would be introduced on Czech soil if NATO enlarged. These concerns were calmed only with assurances by U.S. Secretary of State Madeleine Albright, a popular figure in a country traditionally suspicious of foreigners. It was the condition of the economy, however, that motivated the region's turn to the Western system of governance and free markets. Put simply, Czechs sought higher standards of living, and the EU, not NATO, seemed to offer more in this respect. Despite these objections, though, as the prospect of EU membership faded, the push to "return to Europe," as coined during the Czech Velvet Revolution, was intensified, shifting the focus to NATO membership.

Of the current members of NATO, the United States had some of the most vocal advocates of enlargement through its émigré communities as well as its multinationals, interested in trade and markets. Among the political elite, there was a clear sense of "righting a wrong," that is, the West had been forced to abandon these countries due to the circumstances of World War II. Most notably, high State Department officials and President Clinton himself argued persuasively that the United States should seize the opportunity to tie populations as close and as quickly as possible to the Western community of values. For Republicans, the issue was clear and understood both in the Contract with America and in Republican-sponsored congressional legislation. Meanwhile the Defense Department was initially more cautious due to added commitments and argued for a longer "waiting period," a government position officially solidified by mid-1994. By the time of Senate ratification, U.S. opposition to enlargement was concentrated on the extreme left and right and in the community of scholars concerned about the impact of enlargement on the direction of Russia and Russian relations with the West generally.

In contrast, the French, Italian, and German debate was largely intragovernmental with the public discussion considerably muted. In these countries, there were high levels of support by the public who saw the opportunity to stabilize the continent and secure standards of living achieved over the previous decades. However, the initial euphoria over revolutions in these countries and the open borders had been followed by a fear of the impact of liberalized trade relations in the case of EU membership, which could lead to a loss of jobs to countries with a much lower cost of production. For this reason, quick admittance to the EU was perceived as a potential threat to standards of living, and NATO membership seemed a more logical first step given these considerations. In the case of Germany, this translated into a Defense and Foreign Ministry split at the early stages of consideration on pace and timing of membership.

For many of the smaller and less prosperous EU members not included in this volume, the issue was even more acute—their rising standards of living could be directly attributed to the high infusions of subsidies (this was also an

Italian concern) from the wealthier EU countries. New members could threaten this valuable assistance. Finally, the EU was in the midst of its own enlargement to Austria, Finland, and Sweden as well as focused on implementation of the Maastricht Treaty. A further enlargement to the East would divert resources and attention.

The domestic and interest group influences in the states not asked to be members were also muted, but for a different reason—the focus was on the traumas of daily life and the economic situation. It is also the case that the nongovernmental sector was underdeveloped in countries such as Romania and Bulgaria or countries such as Albania. In the Baltic states the debate differed. In Lithuania, the discussion had been intense and left many undecided about NATO membership, but the Polish decision and the location of Lithuanian had been decisive—membership in NATO would have to take precedence over EU. In contrast, the Estonians determined that their interests were best served by giving primacy to the pursuit of EU membership. The large Russian minority there and the even larger one in Latvia meant that Russian concerns played a more prominent role in the decision both by the elite and the public.

Similarly, Russian and Ukrainian domestic influences came more from the challenges of the political fringes such as Vladimir Zhirinovsky rather than the less organized interest groups and private sector. In the Russian arguments against NATO enlargement, officials pointed both to the potential to strengthen the hand of the rightist nationalists and maintained that sentiment against NATO enlargement would play a determining role in the outcome of the elections. The polling data did not support this contention; rather, the economic situation outweighed all other issues for the public. That did not stop official use of this argument, and the rhetoric was sharp against enlargement. Despite selected comments about potential NATO membership (trial balloons, perhaps?), it was clear to Ukraine that, one, its economic and political reforms were not sufficiently progressed to justify the country's membership, and, two, the reaction in Russia would be severe and potentially threatening to the yet fragile emerging democracy. The persistent struggle for control over Sebastopol was the most pronounced manifestation of this concern. The large Russian segments of the population clearly opposed definitive ties to NATO although there was substantial support for establishing Ukrainian independence from the Russian dominance of the Cold War and consequently little opposition to the NATO-Ukrainian Charter.

Parliamentary Debates

The differences in political systems marked the parliamentary debates as well as the public discussions surrounding NATO enlargement. For the United States, the signature of the president on the alteration to the NATO treaty to include three new members was still subject to two-thirds Senate advice and consent under the U.S. Constitution. This prompted the requisite hearings and thus public debate, which had not accompanied many earlier NATO reforms. While dissension to enlargement was primarily an issue of experts from the community of Russian scholars, joined by some arms control communities worried by the potential impact on U.S.-Russian cooperation in arms reductions, there was challenge on the left from senators concerned about the United States not being as forthcoming to the Russians as necessary in a tenuous time for democracy in Russia. (These senators might have preferred simply dissolving NATO as an outdated Cold War relic.) Those on the right also expressed concern about the potential for a renewed Russian threat to a weakened NATO. But in the face of more moderate Senate attempts to halt consent or slow it by tying it to EU enlargement, the legislation passed easily.

The European parliamentary system meant that for Germany, France, Great Britain, and Italy, the debate played out almost exclusively among the foreign and defense policy elite. By the time of the parliamentary debate, the vote was a foregone conclusion. In fact, the actual French count did not even appear in the media. While the issue was debated in all of these parliaments, the outcome had been determined within the governing coalitions before the vote, with only fringe groups directly opposed. Italy's vote diverged from this pattern, with 310 favorable votes and 169 abstentions (and 79 extremist votes against), in part reflecting the state's reluctance to share NATO and EU resources.

In selected cases, there were clear differences in positions on the details of timing, particularly with respect to EU enlargement, but otherwise only marginal differences largely settled out of the public scrutiny. With few exceptions, for example the Italian Communist party, there were no major parties, on the governing or opposition side of the fence, opposed to enlargement in these four countries or in the smaller countries. This was even true in Germany by the time of the debate despite sharp Green opposition to NATO. There was a clear sense that the NATO enlargement debate was perceived in part as a litmus test for responsible Green partnership in a governing coalition.

For the entering states, the votes were primarily also a question of elite decisionmaking. But the stakes were high and there was much more involvement at the public level than in current member states. For the Polish, one member of Parliament even joked about avoiding mention abroad of the high level of membership support (98 percent in some polls) for fear it would raise the specter of earlier communist voting! The support was high, substantial, and sustaining. There was very little question of Polish public and elite support for enlargement.

In contrast, for the Hungarians the public education effort was substantial and the referendum nonbinding only in order to assure that the considerable elite support was not undermined. In fact, it was with considerable effort that the NATO vote was separated from a property vote, which might have meant its defeat had it not been saved with a late-night parliamentary session.

The Czechs were even more skeptical and the public not easily convinced. Unlike the Hungarian educational campaign, there was scant government effort in the Czech Republic to educate the public, leaving nongovernmental organizations with the task. The final large parliamentary majorities did not necessarily reflect a broad public enthusiasm. Instead they reflected political support by decisionmakers and officials who focused more on the vote as a signal of willingness to adopt Western values of free markets and democracy than as an enthusiastic embrace of NATO as a defense institution.

For the states not admitted to NATO, there was obviously no parliamentary debate for ratification, but NATO enlargement has had the unfortunate effect of polarizing the states not admitted, including Romania, Bulgaria, and the Baltic states. This has both hardened their resolve to be accepted into NATO and accelerated their push for EU membership. Estonia has, for instance, been named by the EU among those earmarked for "faster-track" entry should reforms continue and broaden—together with Slovenia, Poland, Hungary, the Czech Republic, and Cyprus. The door to the EU, as to NATO, has presumably been left open; and more are now slated for future membership, including Latvia and Lithuania.

Likewise, no parliamentary debate took place in the states unlikely to be included in the near future, such as Russia and Ukraine. This is not, however, to say that parliaments had nothing to comment on the issue. To the contrary, a number of Russian parliamentarians were vocal in their opposition to enlargement, criticizing the extension of NATO membership to the three selected former Warsaw Pact states. During this entire period, pressure from the Duma slowed the Russian signature on PfP, hardened the negotiating stance of Russia over the Russia-NATO Founding Act, and blocked arms control treaty ratification. The debate was intense, vigorous, and almost universally critical. There were assertions by policymakers traveling to the United States that NATO enlargement was a major election issue but no substantiating evidence that it was a public concern of any magnitude.

In Ukraine, the issue had a much lower profile. There were limited comments about possible membership for the country, but, by and large, the focus was on forging a closer NATO-Ukraine consultative mechanism. Recognizing the sensitivities of the Russians who envisioned a sixteen-plus-one NATO structure, the Ukraine charter with NATO was signed in Madrid after the NATO-Russia Founding Act. (See Appendix G.)

Future Enlargement

There is no clear agreement on future members of the alliance. The Madrid summit in 1997 suggested that states such as Romania and Slovenia might be acceptable if they continue to reform. France and Germany respectively provided firm backing for their membership. But while these two are specifically named in the final communiqué from Madrid, NATO made no firm commitment at the time. In fact, there were specific disagreements over the feasibility of such a future expansion of membership, particularly after the slowing of reforms in many of the potential candidate countries. Support for Slovenia, specifically, waned when the Austrians officially declared that they would not for the foreseeable future seek membership, but it remains a strong contender.

In one of the most contested and awaited paragraphs (for the order in which prospective members were listed) at the 1999 Washington summit, the alliance stated,

> Today we recognize and welcome the continuing efforts and progress in both Romania and Slovenia. We also recognize and welcome continuing efforts and progress in Estonia, Latvia and Lithuania. Since the Madrid summit, we note and welcome positive developments in Bulgaria. We also note and welcome recent positive developments in Slovakia. We are grateful for the co-operation of the Former Yugoslav Republic of Macedonia with NATO in the present crisis and welcome its progress on reforms. We welcome Albania's co-operation with the alliance in the present crisis and encourage its reform efforts.[1] (See Appendix J.)

But despite listing these nine potential candidates by name, NATO has offered no firm commitment to a timetable or specific criteria. There is, however, a Membership Action Plan adopted by the 1999 summit laying out general criteria and an offer to review the progress made by states in 2002.

There are three major objections voiced in the alliance debate over enlargement: (1) The impact of another enlargement on Russia might be sufficient to even or reverse the slow movement toward free markets and democratic reform. (2) In addition to the internal impact, it is feared that such a reversal could have dramatic implications for the security of the region more generally. Opposition built on this fear appears in the German and British debates as well as in influential segments of U.S. debate. This opposition is particularly stiff with respect to Baltic candidates or other states contiguous to Russia. (3) There is concern about the ability of the Atlantic alliance to absorb additional states. Although there has been considerable effort to ensure that new members are "both producers as well as consumers of security," the fact is that it is expensive to bring new states up to NATO standards. Additionally, new members have the potential to disrupt existing relationships and finely tuned decisionmaking processes. An alliance of sixteen differs from that of nineteen and certainly that of twenty-two plus. This third concern is widely shared but most acute among the smaller NATO countries who fear that their security will be reduced.

NATO: FUTURE TRANSFORMATION AND CHALLENGE

The 1999 New Strategic Concept

The NATO fiftieth anniversary summit in April 1999 may certainly be seen as a watershed for the alliance. First, NATO was in the midst of its first conflict since its establishment. This proved a larger undertaking than anticipated. Second, the alliance had just admitted three new members who at the time of NATO founding had represented the enemy; their admittance was an achievement and a challenge. Third, NATO agreed to an ambitious course for the twenty-first century, one that would prepare it for future challenges. Perhaps even more significantly, non-NATO members attended the summit. Members of Partnership for Peace and the European Atlantic Partnership Council (EAPC) appeared, though Russian representatives were glaringly absent. There were other difficulties: Alliance actions in Kosovo had detractors, the three new members had a long road in front of them before they would meet the expected standards, and the agreed documents faced the same shortfalls that such documents usually face. Still, the summit was historic. The assembly of forty-eight states, many of which had been communist and looking gun-to-gun at the other side for forty years, was possibly the most impressive event in the week of Washington meetings.

What will NATO mean for the future? If pronouncements give any indication, the alliance will undertake future enlargements, albeit with uncertain invitees and timing. Even more important, the 1999 meeting appeared to solidify the determination to develop an alliance of inclusion and not exclusion. Even for those states not wanting or failing to achieve full membership, the alliance demonstrated commitment to bringing the PfP and EAPC countries into a partnership for broader security. Initiatives such as Combined Joint Task Forces (CJTF), in essence used in Bosnia and Kosovo operations under a different name, could include "interested states" and allow those not directly affected to choose not to participate.

There were also very specific commitments made in the NATO documents signed at the summit. The Defense Capabilities Initiative (DCI) committed members to improvements in forces and armaments. Other documents established a greater level of cooperation in nonproliferation, defense industries, scientific undertakings, and other areas. There was an attempt to deepen the cooperation as well with the EAPC countries and to enhance the PfP. While not all the pronouncements will yield what their earnest signatories may have had in mind—even at the time of signing, the conflict in Kosovo was challenging some of the original intentions of the authors—the existence of the documents will have a mobilizing effect in many areas.

At the same time, however, other considerations posed countervailing pressures. The difficulties of working within the alliance with the Russians despite the promises of no Russian veto over NATO decisions became obvious during the standoff at the Pristina airport in Kosovo and during the policy process at NATO Headquarters. As NATO adopts new priorities and restructures with the changing demands of new geopolitical realities, there is clearly a need for other organizations to undertake efforts in areas not addressed by NATO. For this reason, a number of regional corps have formed with overlapping interests to address problems that might not necessarily involve all of NATO, that is, the German-Polish-Danish corps, the Italian-Hungarian-Slovenian Brigade, the Baltic Battalion, and the Eurocorps, which now includes Spain and Belgium in addition to Germany and France.

The Evolving European Security and Defense Policy

The crisis in Kosovo confronted the alliance with its first military conflict since its founding in 1949. While Serbian leader Slobodan Milosevic did not pose a direct threat to the national interests of any NATO member, the human rights abuses and reported mass killings of Kosovo Albanians caused a public outcry and NATO response. The events in Kosovo represented the new type of threat spawned by the end of the Cold War and rise of ethnic hatreds that initially divided Yugoslavia and led to the events as well in Bosnia-Herzegovina and elsewhere. The Kosovo action taken by NATO was without UN mandate and required substantial and impressive cooperative support by the alliance. NATO maintained this support throughout the conflict, but success became threatened as the days passed and Milosevic did not back down. It is not the intent in this volume to recount the details of the conflict. But in terms of impact on the alliance, Kosovo was significant for a number of reasons.

The most significant reason with respect to the future direction of NATO is the European reaction to the overwhelming U.S. superiority in military capabilities during Kosovo. This caused a major rethinking of the ability of Europeans to take action in response to their next challenge, particularly if the United States does not perceive a need to act. As a consequence, the EU agreed in Cologne in 1999 (at the time of the Kosovo air strikes) and again in more detail in December 1999 to a European force of 60,000 by 2003 that could respond to contingencies of interest to Europe. In February 2000, they further agreed to set out headline goals for meeting that force requirement; progress on those goals received scrutiny in November 2000.

The potential impact of the EU goal for a conflict-ready force remains unclear. But there are those in the United States who argue that the further development of a European Security and Defense Policy (ESDP) would be inimical to the objectives of NATO and would threaten continued U.S. support of the alliance. This does not have to be the case. In fact, it is possible that this new EU force could operate in areas where no alliance consensus for sending NATO forces exists but where there is a clear need for conflict prevention measures or peacekeeping efforts. Coordinated with NATO and the United States, the new European defense force would not necessarily threaten alliance stability or longer-term European security. But such a high degree of coordination would require substantial political will. The EU decision in Nice in December 2000 was a step in the direction of coordination between the envisioned 60,000-person European force and NATO.

A truly functional and financed European Security and Defense Policy could as well impact national positions on future NATO enlargement. On the one hand, it might reassure current EU members in that countries with only EU membership such as Austria would see no need to become NATO members. A fast pace on EU enlargement might suffice for current nonmembers to feel secure. On the other hand, if the EU does not itself enlarge to include NATO nonmember states, NATO might find itself under pressure for a second round of enlargement and more. In another scenario, a turn away from democratic and economic reform by Russia and a subsequent increase in instability could also cause pressure on NATO to enlarge. In all these scenarios, the ability of the EU and NATO to coordinate their efforts will affect the handling of any conflicts in Europe and thus also the comfort level of former Warsaw Pact members with regard to their own security.

Broadening the Framework for Security

Possibly the most important lesson of the enlargement process is the need for a broader framework for security, one that addresses the multifaceted challenges of the post–Cold War era. It is important that other organizations, such as the Organization for Security and Cooperation in Europe and the United Nations, have also taken on tasks outside the purview of NATO, but involving NATO members. Given the uncertainty of future NATO enlargements and the necessarily gradual and extended pace of any enlargement decisions, these organizations provide a basis for a broader concept of security. This sharing of responsibilities in the future will take on added importance in the case of cross-border challenges outside of the NATO area.

In addition, the OSCE, Council of Europe, and other international and regional organizations are often better suited to address issues than NATO, with its orientation to resolution of acute conflict. This is particularly true in the case of conflict prevention, arms control, and a wide array of human rights issues. The instruments available to NATO often simply do not suffice.

Despite considerable NATO efforts in the pursuit of closer ties through NACC (now EAPC), the NATO-Russia Founding Act, and the Ukraine Charter as well as through military-to-military cooperation via PfP, there remain areas where NATO cannot be as effective as the EU, OSCE, or Council on Europe, for example in the early resolution of ethnic tensions, election oversight, economic cooperation, state rebuilding, or even environmental restoration. Whereas NATO and Russia have yet to agree on the nature and breadth of Permanent Joint Council consultations, Russian participation as an OSCE member, including the United States, Canada, and all European states, permits ongoing discussion. Seen from this broader perspective, NATO enlargement eastward is less important than the broadening of security using the full array of available tools and institutions.

CONCLUSION

The process of NATO enlargement prompted national debates by NATO members as well as the candidate states. In addition, those countries not accorded membership, even those not seeking membership but affected by enlargement, engaged in vigorous discussion over how to respond to the challenges of an enlarging alliance. The debates explored in this volume provide important insight into the varying perceptions of security, policy directions, and levels of public and governmental support on the issue of enlargement. While disparate in their intensity and focus, they proved interesting barometers of major security concerns for each country.

Perhaps one of the most significant conclusions of the sum total of these debates is that NATO enlargement represents part of a more comprehensive NATO reform, a response to the requisites of the new order in Europe, including security needs drastically different since the end of the Cold War. NATO reforms, including enlargement, are most effective when seen as part of an effort to provide the United States and Europe with a comprehensive framework to assure all aspects of European security. The national debates provide a view of emerging issues in the individual countries along with expectations prompted by enlargement for alliance members, new members, states hoping to join soon, and those that might not join in the foreseeable future.

The issue of future NATO enlargements remains a topic of heated debate, but behind closed doors. Behind those doors there are differences between countries, but the pressure for consensus dictates quiet diplomacy. President George Bush was not silent on the issue during the 2000 presidential campaign; he advocated moving ahead on enlargement, as did his opponent albeit somewhat more cautiously. Certainly there is Republican support in Congress for enlargement and the chairman of the Senate Foreign Relations Committee Senator Jesse Helms has spoken in favor of moving on to a second round. There may emerge a difference with the Clinton administration over the issue of open-door policy (although not with high expectations of that door actually being entered) for Russia. It is on this issue that the Europeans also disagree and have in the past pressed for a more realistic policy that acknowledges that Russia and even Ukraine are long-shots for NATO membership. For the next round of discussion, which is anticipated for 2002, France is expected to support Romania again, and Germany and Italy will weigh in for Slovenia. Romania will be more difficult than in 1997 at the Madrid summit as a result of its recent poor record on reform. Although there are not yet official positions on the next round, Slovakia's elections have reversed opinion and that country's membership is expected to have strong advocates—possibly on both sides of the Atlantic.

It is agreed that the Baltic states pose the most contention because of the expected Russian opposition to their membership. There are strong views—as in Europe, the United States, and Canada—that naming the Baltics for membership will push the Russians potentially into extremist hands and even threaten the modest progress Russia has made in its reforms. Particularly difficult will be the issue of Kaliningrad, the Russian enclave bordering Poland, although Poland has openly expressed its support for membership for its other neighbor Lithuania. All three Baltic states are expected to encourage their admittance simultaneously, and this might be an argument to delay until after EU enlargement.

The other contentious issue will be over the viability of an alliance that could become both unwieldy and expensive to bring new members up to NATO standards. After its first conflict in Kosovo, the larger European states who found themselves overly dependent on the United States particularly will need to be assured that additional members do not degrade the NATO defense guarantee. The smaller NATO members will also share the concern that NATO may become stretched too thin to react in a crisis. For this reason, the former Yugoslav states, with the possible exception of Slovenia, might find support elusive. This may also apply to Bulgaria, Albania, and even Romania.

In terms of the states named in the 1999 Washington Declaration, all have at some point publicly mentioned their desire to join NATO, but their diplomacy has been low-key and often bilateral. It has also had two fronts—toward the EU and toward NATO. But despite the argument that EU enlargement makes more sense, the pressures may increase from Washington as well as from European capitals to move ahead with NATO enlargement.

For all of these countries, the highest imperative is to secure the continent from economic and political instability. At present the threat of further Balkan conflict has replaced enlargement on the agenda. The Membership Action

Plan has also occupied potential candidate members while NATO monitors closely the progress of the three new members in meeting the standards promised in 1999. NATO must be inclusive, not exclusive, whether through enlargement or other avenues (such as through PfP or EAPC). Reaching out to those countries not formally members, it has the ability to stabilize and secure peace on the continent. Any future enlargements will need to build on the lessons of the first round to assure continued stability.

NOTE

1. "The Washington Declaration, 23–24 April 1999," Special Insert: Documentation, *NATO Review* 46, no. 3 (May-June 1999): 5.

Chronology of NATO Enlargement, 1989–2000

1989

October 26: Secretary General Manfred Wörner declares NATO's responsibility to support reforms in Eastern Europe: "As the midwife of change, we have a special responsibility in ensuring that it becomes both permanent and universal throughout Eastern Europe." NATO should provide, he maintains, "a framework of stability in an era of great change," and be "an instrument of that change, . . . [and] a solid anchoring point."

October 30: For the first time, Warsaw Pact officials participate in the North Atlantic Assembly (NAA), NATO's parliamentary wing.

November 9: The Berlin Wall opens, and U.S. Secretary of Defense Dick Cheney warns against a reduced U.S. commitment to NATO, which he refers to as "a rock in the sea of change."

November 13: West German leaders assure allies of NATO's importance.

November 28: U.S. Secretary of Defense Cheney assures Europe that the United States will not unilaterally withdraw, despite reduced Soviet threat. After the Malta summit with Mikhail Gorbachev, President George Bush repeats the promise to Europe.

December 14: U.S. Secretary of State James Baker suggests NATO should expand into the political realm to build contacts with Eastern Europe.

December 18: Soviet Foreign Minister Eduard Shevardnadze meets at NATO Headquarters with Secretary General Wörner; the Cold War is over, but NATO/Warsaw Pact should maintain stabilizing roles in the region.

1990

February 2: West German Foreign Minister Hans-Dietrich Genscher meets U.S. Secretary of State Baker; according to Genscher, Germany has "no intention to extend the NATO area of defense and security towards the East. . . . This holds true not only for GDR [East Germany], which we have no intention of simply incorporating, but . . . for all Eastern countries."

February 11: U.S. President Bush agrees with Secretary General Wörner that NATO should adopt new political roles. Bonn announces that unified Germany will remain in NATO, but troops will not be stationed in East Germany.

April 9: Czech President Václav Havel proposes European security commission to replace NATO and Warsaw Pact.

June 29: U.S. Secretary of State Baker announces that NATO leaders might agree at the upcoming summit to invite individual Warsaw Pact countries to sign nonaggression agreements.

July 5–6: Mikhail Gorbachev offers friendly relations based on nonaggression pacts with Warsaw Pact states. U.S. President Bush opposes their membership at NATO London summit. Instead, NATO offers the states official diplomatic relations.

July 18: Soviet officials approve unified German membership in NATO. Hungary and USSR accept NATO offer to establish diplomatic relations.

November 19–21: In Paris, CSCE adopts the CFE treaty, raising hopes that CSCE will replace NATO and the Warsaw Pact as Europe's new security institution.

December 8: NATO foreign ministers' meeting concludes it must stabilize external conditions to protect members; defense ministers cite Iraqi and Eastern European economic trouble as potential sources of instability for NATO.

December 18: NATO foreign ministers declare end of "outright [USSR] aggression," but military presence is still necessary.

1991

February 12: USSR announces Warsaw Pact is to dissolve by April 1991; USSR is to maintain bilateral defense treaties with Eastern Europe.

February 15: Romanian Foreign Minister Adrian Nastase declares his country's desire for NATO "associate member" status.

February 16: NATO insists it has no plans to expand into Eastern Europe.

February 25: Warsaw Pact members (USSR, Czechoslovakia, Poland, Hungary, Bulgaria, and Romania) announce dissolution of security alliance and the end of Soviet military control on 31 March 1991.

March 20: NATO says it will not alienate USSR by expanding into Eastern Europe.

March 21: On first official visit to NATO by leader of former Warsaw Pact state, Czech President Havel encourages NATO membership for Czechoslovakia and other states in the region.

April 25–26: In Prague, NATO conference focuses on Eastern Europe. Czech and Hungarian officials reject a Romanian proposal for separate Eastern security bloc; Secretary General Wörner assures USSR these states will not be ushered into NATO but says NATO will not abandon them either.

May 28: NATO defense ministers agree to a rapid reaction force under UK command and fewer allied forces in Central Europe by at least one quarter.

June 6: NATO warns against "any form of coercion or intimidation" to thwart democratization in Eastern Europe; NATO calls on USSR restraint in response to Baltic uprisings.

July 3: Polish President Lech Walesa calls for tighter NATO and Polish links to prevent "East-West buffer zone" and warns against isolating USSR but does not request membership in the alliance.

August 8: Eastern Europe and USSR military leaders attend NATO military schools in Rome and Germany.

August 19: Coup to oust Gorbachev fails but sparks collapse of Moscow's power over Soviet Union.

October 3: United States and Germany propose North Atlantic Cooperation Council to allow exchanges and contact among NATO, Eastern Europe, and USSR.

October 4: Visiting U.S. President Bush and Hungarian Prime Minister Jozsef Antall urge NATO to take responsibility for the security of Eastern Europe.

October 23: Following President Bush's affirmation of U.S. rejection of plans to grant NATO membership to former Warsaw Pact states, Czech President Havel tells U.S. congressmen his country is "interested in having the fullest possible cooperation with the North Atlantic alliance, a cooperation that could [lead to] some form of institutional link or associate membership."

November 8: At Rome summit, despite reservations by French President François Mitterrand, USSR, Hungary, Poland, Czechoslovakia, Romania, Bulgaria, Lithuania, Estonia, and Latvia are invited to join newly formed North Atlantic Cooperation Council (NACC), to include cooperation on defense planning, air traffic management, and enhanced democratic civil-military relations.

November 12: NATO opens diplomatic links with Estonia.

December 20: NATO and Warsaw Pact foreign ministers meet in Brussels for "unprecedented" talks at first NACC session. The discussion focuses on disintegration of USSR and its impact on European security. During meetings, Russian President Boris Yeltsin announces Russia's long-term goal of joining NATO.

1992

March 10: Ten former Soviet republics join NACC and discuss ethnic conflict in Nagorno-Karabakh.

March 12: In Warsaw, NATO Secretary General Wörner raises hopes of former Eastern bloc states: "Although we are not today considering whether to increase the membership of NATO, this does not mean that we exclude additional membership in the future. . . . We keep this option open."

April 1: NATO and former Communist states defense ministers discuss arms control and nuclear management.

April 10: NATO military leaders meet former Warsaw Pact states on defense matters.

May 16: The NAA includes four former Warsaw Pact delegations and six former Soviet republics and discusses potential break-up of NATO.

December 16: Albanian President Sali Berisha announces Albania's goal to join NATO.

December 18: Senior NATO officials meet with NACC to discuss peacekeeping missions in Europe.

1993

January 1: The Czech Republic and Slovakia peacefully become two independent states.

March 4: Former U.S. National Security Advisor Zbigniew Brzezinski encourages leaders of Poland, Hungary, Czech Republic, and Slovakia to apply jointly for NATO membership.

March 5: After meeting with Poland's defense minister, Supreme Allied Commander Europe (SACEUR) General John Shalikashvili announces that it is still too soon for NATO to debate eastward expansion.

May 21: During NAA meeting, German Defense Minister Volker Rühe says NATO expansion into Poland, Hungary, Czech Republic, and Slovakia is inevitable.

June 4: Czech officials urge clear NATO membership criteria.

June 11: U.S. Senator Richard Lugar encourages NATO to extend membership to Poland, Hungary, Czech Republic, and Slovakia and to consider Russia and Ukraine for future membership.

August 21: Polish Prime Minister Hanna Suchocka criticizes NATO's "wavering attitude" on expansion, warning that additional delays might force Central and Eastern European countries to form an independent security organization.

August 25: After meeting with President Walesa, President Boris Yeltsin declares "respect" for Poland's pursuit of NATO membership, signaling a change in Russia's opposition.

September 10: For first time NATO Secretary General Wörner publicly calls for NATO debate on membership: "The time has come to open a more concrete perspective to those countries . . . which want to join NATO and which we may consider eligible for future membership."

German Foreign Minister Klaus Kinkel announces plans for gradual integration of Eastern European states into NATO, but he advises potential members to protect ethnic minority rights and end border disputes with neighbors.

October 1: President Yeltsin now cautions NATO on expansion, insisting it will isolate Russia, and under clear pressure from his own military leaders, he offers a plan for joint NATO-Russian protection of Eastern Europe.

October 5: Meeting with U.S. officials, German Foreign Minister Kinkel suggests Eastern Europe would be more secure if the United States and Russia would cooperate; he does not call for expanded membership but encourages more cooperation.

October 12: German Chancellor Helmut Kohl supports NATO membership for Poland, Hungary, and Czech Republic.

October 16: To soothe divisions, Secretary General Wörner suggests associate membership for Eastern Europe, leading to greater consultations, joint planning, and eventual full membership in NATO.

October 20–21: During meeting of NATO defense ministers, U.S. Secretary of Defense Les Aspin announces NATO Partnership for Peace (PfP) for twenty-two former Warsaw Pact states, including Russia, and four neutral countries. The program provides no NATO guarantee on border defense, and it includes peacekeeping, disaster relief, crisis management, joint military exercises, and information exchanges. PfP membership is to be a prerequisite, but not a guarantee, of NATO membership. NATO members unanimously approve U.S. plan.

October 22: Hungary and Romania accept PfP plan; Poland and Czech Republic prefer full membership.

November 11: Russian military officials warn that NATO expansion contradicts Russian national interests; an expanded NATO will disrupt regional parity and pose economic, political, and psychological threats to Russia.

November 25: Russian intelligence officials call NATO expansion "a blow" to Russian security and argue that PfP represents NATO's Cold War attitudes.

December 10: Russian Foreign Minister Andrei Kozyrev encourages a Russian-NATO "partnership, not membership." But says Russia will not violate Eastern European sovereignty by dictating whether or not a state can join NATO.

December 14: Polish officials cite strong 1993 showing of nationalists, led by Vladimir Zhirinovsky, as indication of Russian unpredictability, necessitating Polish membership in NATO. Romania echoes. Baltic leaders call on NATO to "fill a [regional] security void" by admitting Latvia, Estonia, and Lithuania.

1994

January 4: U.S. officials resist expedited expansion and favor evolutionary plans to avoid instability in Europe.

January 5: Lithuania applies for NATO membership as the first former Soviet republic. Russia announces "the haste with which a number of countries including the republic of Lithuania are seeking to become members of the military-political alliance cannot but cause anxiety."

January 10–11: PfP plan is introduced at NATO's Brussels summit. President Bill Clinton says PfP "sets in motion a process that leads to the enlargement of NATO." No guarantees for enlargement are given.

January 12: Clinton meets former Communist leaders about joining PfP. Hungary, Czech Republic, Slovakia, and the Baltics endorse; Polish President Walesa is critical, calling the program "a step in the right direction, but a small step."

January 13: President Yeltsin says Russia supports PfP.

January 26: Romania is officially the first PfP enrollee.

January 27: Lithuania is first former USSR republic to join PfP.

February 2: Prime Minister Waldemar Pawlak enrolls Poland in PfP.

February 3–23: Estonia joins PfP, calling on Russia to withdraw its 18,000 troops from the Baltics; Slovakia, Hungary, Ukraine, Bulgaria, and Albania enroll in PfP.

February 25: NATO begins mission to persuade President Yeltsin to enroll Russia in PfP.

March 6: Despite NATO's refusal to accept Russia's request for special treatment as a superpower within the group, Russian officials signal their intention to join PfP.

March 10–30: Czech Republic, Moldova, Georgia, and Slovenia join PfP.

April 8: After weeks of Russian indecision on enrollment, President Yeltsin argues Russian membership should be rewarded with G-7 membership, a "club" of the world's wealthiest nations.

April 14: U.S. Representative Ben Gilman, ranking Republican of the House Foreign Affairs Committee, offers bill for full NATO membership by 1 January 1999 to

Poland, Hungary, Czech Republic, and Slovakia, based on economic and political reforms.

May 4: Azerbaijan accepts PfP membership and asks for assistance in Nagorno-Karabakh.

May 9: Sweden and Finland enroll in PfP as the first non–formerly Communist states.

May 10–30: Turkmenistan becomes the first Central Asian country to join PfP—eighteenth overall.

May 18: NATO offers Russia a "special relationship" after it joins PfP and closer consultations on security and nuclear issues.

June 22: After delays, Russia announces it will join PfP, asserting its special role. Legislation in Russia to block enrollment falls short of the required 225 votes by 9 votes. Russia agrees to sign the PfP documents in December 1994 but delays until May 1995.

July 7: President Clinton meets with President Walesa, reaffirms U.S. commitment to NATO enlargement and calls PfP membership a vehicle for integration into European security institution.

September 8: Senior U.S. foreign policy official announces a "growing understanding" by Russia that NATO expansion is not directed against Moscow; enlargement seems possible within four years.

December 1: NATO foreign ministers endorse U.S. proposal for an internal study on enlargement within one year. Leaders agree that new members should be protected under NATO's nuclear umbrella but offer no timetable, membership criteria, or list of potential new members.

Russian Foreign Minister Kozyrev refuses to sign two accords addressing NATO and Russian relations, including Russian entry into PfP.

December 5: During Budapest CSCE (OSCE) meeting, President Clinton and President Yeltsin clash on enlargement issue. While Yeltsin endorses a CSCE pan-European security arrangement, Clinton reaffirms that no single state should be allowed to veto NATO enlargement. Yeltsin charges NATO desire to "sow the seeds of mistrust." Meanwhile, French President Mitterrand criticizes rapid expansion for failing to regard Russia's historic fear of being isolated and surrounded.

December 12: U.S. official says Russia's inclusion in NATO is inevitable.

December 14–15: Meeting of NATO defense ministers in Brussels affirms that Article 10, the Washington treaty, is to be "open to membership of other European states in a position to further the principles of the Treaty and to contribute to the security of the North Atlantic area." Ministers also reiterate the importance of PfP in "development of co-operation between NATO and its Partners." (See Appendix E.)

1995

January 11: Belarus joins PfP; Tajikistan remains the only former Soviet republic in Asia outside of PfP.

February 2: NATO Secretary General Willy Claes says NATO will not permit Russia to veto membership applications.

February 8: Testifying before a House of Representatives committee, U.S. Secretary of Defense William Perry and U.S. Chairman of the Joint Chiefs of Staff General Shalikashvili admit many new PfP members will not qualify for NATO membership—and any NATO member can veto an application.

March 13: During Estonian visit, U.S. Vice President Al Gore assures the Baltics of their consideration as potential NATO members but says enlargement must be coupled with deeper ties to Russia.

April 3: Russian Defense Minister Pavel Grachev and General Alexander Lebed threaten to reassert Russian military presence in the former USSR if NATO expands eastward.

May 31: Russia formalizes its PfP commitment, "an unprecedented program of cooperation" in military training, joint military exercises, officer exchanges, and consultations on defense budgeting.

June 8: As part of PfP program, four NATO members (Italy, Greece, Turkey, Netherlands) and two PfP countries (Bulgaria and Romania) participate in NATO-sponsored naval maneuvers in the Black Sea.

June 28: NATO and PfP military leaders conclude a three-day joint exercise to improve coordination in future peacekeeping operations, highlighting problems of integration, communication, incompatible technology, and differing philosophies.

July 10: Despite Clinton's support of rapid NATO enlargement, criticism emerges in United States. Senator Sam Nunn warns of a "serious negative impact on political and economic reform" in Russia and advocates EU admittance as prerequisite to NATO membership.

September 1: NATO releases an internal study of enlargement that includes no set criteria for membership; applications are to be assessed case-by-case. As a concession to Russia, new members are not required to house foreign troops or nuclear weapons and are not obligated to join integrated military command. (See Appendix F.)

September 8: President Yeltsin says expansion is a "big mistake" that will lead to war in Europe.

September 22: U.S. Secretary of Defense Perry outlines five standards to join NATO: democratization, progress toward a market economy, civilian control of military, NATO force compatibility, and stable, peaceful relations with bordering states.

November 29: NATO and Russian military officials agree on Russia's participation in NATO-led peacekeeping operations in Bosnia. This arrangement maintains the decisionmaking power of NAC but involves Russia in troop movement decisions.

December 21: Russian intelligence director warns that NATO may place nuclear weapons on Russia's western border if NATO expands.

December 27: Russian Foreign Minister Kozyrev says Russia will likely become a NATO member one day.

1996

January 13: On a Southern European visit, President Clinton notes the high level of cooperation in Bosnia peacekeeping—60,000 troops from NATO, Russia, Poland, the Czech Republic, and Hungary.

January 18: Belarus president says nuclear weapons will be placed in Belarus if threatened by enlarged NATO.

February 6: Ethnic groups in United States accuse Clinton of giving in to pressure from Russia and backsliding on NATO enlargement issue (20 million Americans are of Eastern European descent).

March 20: NATO Secretary General Javier Solana visits Russia to ease NATO enlargement fears but rejects Russia's suggestion that new states be offered French-style nonmilitary membership.

May 14: During Warsaw visit, German Defense Minister Ruehe predicts Poland will be first new member of enlarged NATO by 1999.

June 3: Ukraine hosts ten-day joint PfP military exercise with Russia, the United States, and ex–Warsaw Pact states.

July 17: U.S. State Department notes Romania's political, economic, and military reform and suggests they merit early consideration for NATO membership.

July 26: U.S. Senate passes bill, earmarking U.S.$60 million to expectant members for meeting NATO criteria.

August 8: A Pentagon-sponsored RAND study concludes that NATO enlargement is affordable and poses no threat to Russian interests.

August 29: Secretary of Defense Perry announces 1997 summit meeting to select NATO member candidates.

September 24: Russian security chief says U.S. and German economic interests will suffer with enlargement.

October 6: At NATO defense ministers' meeting, U.S. Secretary of Defense Perry announces that Lithuania, Estonia, and Latvia will not be given first-round membership due to their small militaries and ongoing border disputes with Russia.

October 12: Russian Security Chief Lebed calls for a more significant PfP role for Russia to insure its influence over the progress and evolution of NATO.

December 1: OSCE leaders forge summit consensus that all states have the right to join a security alliance.

December 10: Russian presidential spokesman rebuffs claims that Russia softened stance on NATO expansion, warning it is not a "foregone conclusion." He argues it creates a security threat by squeezing Russia from Europe. To ease Russia, U.S. Secretary of State Warren Christopher vows that no nuclear weapons will be placed in Eastern Europe if NATO expands.

Neutral Switzerland joins PfP but rules out NATO membership.

1997

January 8: Russian Foreign Minister Yevgeny Primakov says Moscow's acceptance of NATO enlargement depends on renegotiating the Conventional Forces in Europe (CFE) treaty and limiting military deployments to Eastern Europe.

February 24: U.S. officials predict that the United States will pay 10 percent of NATO's enlargement costs, or U.S.$2 billion.

March 4: Kazakh president says NATO expansion will hinder Russia's democratic transition.

March 15: To ease Russian fears, NATO leaders declare there are no plans to deploy large forces to former Warsaw Pact states.

March 20: United States emphasizes NATO enlargement will not change U.S. military role in Europe.

March 22: At U.S.-Russian summit, Yeltsin agrees to talks on a new partnership between Russia and NATO.

April 17: Chancellor Kohl meets with Yeltsin to convince him that NATO expansion is no threat to Russia.

May 14: NATO Secretary General Solana and Russian Prime Minister Primakov negotiate the Founding Act on Mutual Relations, Cooperation and Security between NATO and the Russian Federation, establishing the Permanent Joint Council to guarantee Russia's voice, not a vote, in NATO discussions. (See Appendix G.)

May 27: President Yeltsin signs the Founding Act, but Russian officials warn that if membership is extended to any former Soviet republics (namely, the Baltics), the agreement is void.

June 12: During meeting of NATO defense ministers, Secretary General Solana says naming of countries to be considered during first round is still open, despite U.S. call that only Poland, the Czech Republic, and Hungary be considered. Germany supports Slovenia's accession, while France supports Romania.

July 7–8: At Madrid summit, membership invitations extended to Poland, the Czech Republic, and Hungary. While NATO remains open to future members, no details are given on second round. (See Appendix I.)

July 9: In Madrid, NATO and Ukraine sign the Charter on a Distinctive Partnership. (See Appendix H.)

August 26: Chinese Foreign Minister Qian Qichen says NATO expansion will undermine regional stability.

October 7: The U.S. Senate Committee on Foreign Relations begins NATO enlargement hearings, debating cost and threats.

December 16: In Brussels, leaders of NATO, Poland, the Czech Republic, and Hungary sign the Protocols to the North Atlantic Treaty, stating "the security of the North Atlantic area will be enhanced" by their inclusion. Each member state must ratify protocols and pass legislation to complete membership requirements.

1998

February 4: Canada becomes first NATO member to ratify the treaty to admit Poland, the Czech Republic, and Hungary into the alliance.

February 15: Denmark's Parliament approves the Protocols to the North Atlantic Treaty.

March 3: The U.S. Senate Foreign Relations Committee votes 16 to 2 to approve NATO enlargement, sending the measure to the full Senate for vote. Norway's Parliament votes to approve enlargement.

March 27: The German Bundestag and the Bundesrat ratify accession protocols.

April 30: U.S. Senate votes 80 to 19 in favor of extending membership to Poland, the Czech Republic, and Hungary, exceeding the required two-thirds vote. Several amendments to the legislation, however, are defeated. Russian officials say ratifying the accession treaty is a "fatal mistake," which might derail START II negotiations.

May 14: The Parliament of Greece approves NATO enlargement.

May 27: Luxembourg's Parliament approves NATO enlargement.

June 4: Iceland's legislators ratify NATO's protocols on accession.

June 10: The French National Assembly and Senate approve the protocols.

June 23: Plea from Italy's premier overcomes standoff in Chamber of Deputies to endorse NATO enlargement. Italy's powerful Communist party opposes enlargement.

The Spanish Senate ratifies the accession protocols; the Parliament had approved it in May.

July 16: Belgium's House of Representatives votes to support NATO enlargement; the Senate encourages NATO to include Bulgaria, Romania, Slovenia, and Slovakia in July 9 vote.

July 31: The UK House of Lords ratifies enlargement two weeks after the House of Commons.

September 2: President Clinton offers President Yeltsin the opportunity to "upgrade" Russia's partnership with NATO, increasing military-to-military contacts.

September 4: Lithuanian officials criticize the "unacceptably slow rate" of NATO enlargement, saying Russia is dictating the pace of expansion.

September 16: Portugal's Parliament approves NATO enlargement.

October 21: Turkey approves NATO enlargement.

November 19: At a U.S.-Nordic conference, U.S. officials say enlargement would be more prudent after NATO's fiftieth anniversary. Poland, Hungary, and the Czech Republic are poised to join at that time. Lithuania (not Estonia or Latvia) is also a likely candidate, despite Russian warning that Baltic inclusion would be treated as an act of hostility.

December 1: Netherlands is last NATO member to ratify enlargement.

December 4: Russian officials demand a revision of the CFE treaty before NATO enlarges.

December 9: NATO and Russia agree to Joint Permanent Council meetings on weapon proliferation, strategic doctrines, military infrastructure, assistance for soldiers adjusting to civilian life, and help with the "millennium bug" (a potential threat to computers controlling the nuclear arsenal).

1999

January 19: In State of the Union address, U.S. President Clinton says NATO enlargement is the key to European security.

February 16: Czech officials confirm that Poland, Hungary, and the Czech Republic will join NATO on 12 March in Independence, Missouri, where U.S. President Harry Truman had announced NATO's formation in 1949.

March 10: Zhirinovsky, Russia's Liberal Democratic leader, threatens economic blockade, end of trade and oil deliveries to the Czech Republic, and Russian troop deployment to Belarus, Ukraine, and Serbia as a counter to NATO's eastward expansion.

March 12: At ratification ceremony, U.S. Secretary of State Madeleine Albright says "NATO enlargement is not an event; it is a process."

NATO enlargement is greeted with Russian wariness as well as by threats from Belarus that it will strengthen its army out of fear of NATO aggression.

March 26: As NATO begins bombing Serbia, a historic Russian ally, Russia expels NATO representatives from Moscow. Foreign Minister Igor Ivanov calls for a "freeze in relations" until the campaign ends.

April 24–25: At fiftieth anniversary summit in Washington, Poland, the Czech Republic, and Hungary debut as NATO members. This meeting focuses on the air campaign against Serbia. NATO formalizes its transformation from defensive alliance to security institution. NATO and PfP members also meet. (See Appendix J.)

August 19: Slovakia's new president states his desire to pursue democratization and lead the second round of NATO enlargement.

November 9: On the tenth anniversary of the fall of the Berlin Wall, Russia criticizes the "inadmissibility of drawing new dividing lines . . . and reviving thinking based on bloc affiliation."

November 22: Senior U.S. official announces that the next round of NATO expansion appears likely in 2001.

December 22: The Russian Upper House of Parliament approves long-delayed Russia-Belarus treaty, ensuring military and economic cooperation between the two countries.

2000

January 14: Acting Russian President Vladimir Putin signs new national security doctrine to use nuclear weapons against enemies if confronted. Military experts view the move as a reaction to diminishing conventional forces. One Russian document attributes the changed doctrine to "U.S.-led effort to dominate the world," a popular Russian sentiment after NATO's eastward enlargement and its actions against Serbia.

APPENDIX B

North Atlantic Treaty,
4 April 1949 (excerpts)

The Parties to this Treaty reaffirm their faith in the purposes and principles of the Charter of the United Nations and their desire to live in peace with all peoples and all governments.

They are determined to safeguard the freedom, common heritage and civilisation of their peoples, founded on the principles of democracy, individual liberty and the rule of law. They seek to promote stability and well-being in the North Atlantic area.

ARTICLE 1

To settle any international dispute . . . in such a manner that international peace and security and justice are not endangered, and to refrain . . . from the threat or use of force in any manner inconsistent with the purposes of the United Nations.

ARTICLE 2

Will contribute . . . by strengthening their free institutions, by bringing about a better understanding of the principles upon which these institutions are founded, and by promoting conditions of stability and well-being. They will seek to eliminate conflict in their international economic policies and will encourage economic collaboration between any or all of them.

ARTICLE 3

Will maintain and develop their individual and collective capacity to resist armed attack. . . .

ARTICLE 5

The Parties agree that an armed attack against one or more of them in Europe or North America shall be considered an attack against them all and consequently they agree that, if such an armed attack occurs, each of them, in exercise of the right of individual or collective self-defence recognised by Article 51 of the Charter of the United Nations, will assist the Party or Parties so attacked by taking forthwith, individually and in concert with the other Parties, such action as it deems necessary, including the use of armed force, to restore and maintain the security of the North Atlantic area.

ARTICLE 10

The Parties may, by unanimous agreement, invite any other European State in a position to further the principles of this Treaty and to contribute to the security of the North Atlantic area to accede to this Treaty. Any State so invited may become a Party to the Treaty by depositing its instrument of accession with the Government of the United States of America. . . .

APPENDIX C

Declaration of the Heads of State and Government Participating in the Meeting of the North Atlantic Council (excerpts)

NATO HEADQUARTERS, BRUSSELS, 10–11 JANUARY 1994

1. We . . . have gathered in Brussels to renew our Alliance in light of the historic transformations affecting the entire continent of Europe, . . . the new climate of cooperation . . . with the end of . . . global confrontation embodied in the Cold War. However, we must also note that other causes of instability, tension and conflict have emerged. We therefore confirm the enduring validity and indispensability of our Alliance . . . based on a strong transatlantic link, the expression of a shared destiny. It reflects a European Security and Defence Identity gradually emerging as the expression of a mature Europe. It is reaching out to establish new patterns of cooperation throughout Europe. It rests . . . upon close collaboration in all fields.

Building on our decisions in London and Rome and on our new Strategic Concept, we are undertaking initiatives designed to contribute to lasting peace, stability, and well-being in the whole of Europe, which has always been our Alliance's fundamental goal. We have agreed:

- to adapt further the Alliance's political and military structures to reflect both the full spectrum of its roles and the development of the emerging ESDI, and endorse the concept of Combined Joint Task Forces;
- to reaffirm that the Alliance remains open to the membership of other European countries;
- to launch a major initiative through a Partnership for Peace, in which we invite Partners to join us in new political and military efforts to work alongside the Alliance. . . .

2. We reaffirm our strong commitment to the transatlantic link, which is the bedrock of NATO. The continued substantial presence of United States forces in Europe is a fundamentally important aspect of that link. All our countries wish to continue the direct involvement of the United States and Canada in the security of Europe. . . . This is also the expressed wish of the new democracies of the East, which see in

the transatlantic link an irreplaceable pledge of security and stability for Europe as a whole. The fuller integration of the countries of Central and Eastern Europe and of the former Soviet Union into a Europe whole and free cannot be successful without the strong and active participation of all Allies on both sides of the Atlantic.

3. Today, we confirm and renew this link between North America and a Europe developing a Common Foreign and Security Policy and taking on greater responsibility on defence matters. We welcome the entry into force of the Treaty of Maastricht and the launching of the European Union, which will strengthen the European pillar of the Alliance and allow it to make a more coherent contribution to the security of all the Allies. . . . The Alliance is the essential forum for consultation among its members and the venue for . . . policies bearing on the security and defence commitments of Allies under the Washington Treaty. . . .

9. [We] direct the North Atlantic Council . . . with the advice of the NATO Military Authorities, to examine how the Alliance's political and military structures and procedures might be developed and adapted to conduct more efficiently and flexibly the Alliance's missions, including peacekeeping, as well as to improve cooperation with the WEU and to reflect the emerging ESDI [and] endorse the concept of Combined Joint Task Forces as a means to facilitate contingency operations, including operations with participating nations outside the Alliance. . . .

12. We are committed to enhancing security and stability in the whole of Europe. We . . . wish to strengthen ties with the democratic states to our East. . . . The Alliance . . . remains open to membership of other European states in a position to further the principles of the Treaty and to contribute to the security of the North Atlantic area. We expect and would welcome NATO expansion . . . to democratic states to our East, as part of an evolutionary process, taking into account political and security developments in the whole of Europe.

13. We have decided to launch an immediate and practical programme . . . [to] transform the relationship between NATO and participating states, . . . a Partnership for Peace. We invite the other states participating in the NACC, and other CSCE countries able and willing to contribute to this programme. . . . Active participation in the Partnership for Peace will play an important role in the evolutionary process of the expansion of NATO.

14. PfP, which will operate under the authority of the North Atlantic Council, will forge new security relationships between the North Atlantic Alliance and its Partners for Peace. Partner states will be invited . . . to participate in political and military bodies at NATO Headquarters with respect to Partnership activities. The Partnership will expand and intensify political and military cooperation throughout Europe, increase stability, diminish threats to peace, and build strengthened relationships by promoting the spirit of practical cooperation and commitment to democratic principles that underpin our Alliance. NATO will consult with any active participant in the Partnership if that partner perceives a direct threat to its territorial integrity, political independence, or security. At a pace and scope determined by the capacity and desire of the individual participating states, we will work in concrete ways towards transparency in defence budgeting, promoting democratic control of defence ministries, joint planning, joint military exercises, and creating an ability to operate with NATO forces in such

fields as peacekeeping, search and rescue and humanitarian operations, and others as may be agreed. . . .

16. Since its inception two years ago, the North Atlantic Cooperation Council has greatly expanded the depth and scope of its activities. We will continue to work with all our NACC partners to build cooperative relationships across the entire spectrum of the Alliance's activities. . . .

20. We . . . welcome the adoption of a new constitution and the holding of democratic parliamentary elections by the people of the Russian Federation. This is a major step forward in the establishment of a framework for the development of durable democratic institutions. We further welcome the Russian government's firm commitment to democratic and market reform and to a reformist foreign policy, . . . important for security and stability in Europe. . . . An independent, democratic, stable and nuclear weapons–free Ukraine would likewise contribute to security and stability. We will continue to encourage and support the reform processes in both countries and to develop cooperation. . . .

26. Our Alliance has moved to adapt itself to the new circumstances, and today we have taken decisions in key areas. We have given our full support to the development of a European Security and Defence Identity. We have endorsed the concept of Combined Joint Task Forces as a means to adapt the Alliance to its future tasks. We have opened a new perspective of progressively closer relationships with the countries of Central and Eastern Europe and of the former Soviet Union. . . .

Appendix D

Partnership for Peace: Invitation (excerpts)

Issued by the Heads of State and Government participating in the Meeting of the North Atlantic Council held at NATO Headquarters, Brussels, 10–11 January 1994

We . . . wish to strengthen ties with the democratic states to our East. We reaffirm that the Alliance, as provided for in Article 10 of the Washington Treaty, remains open to the membership of other European states in a position to further the principles of the Treaty and to contribute to the security of the North Atlantic area. We expect and would welcome NATO expansion that would reach to democratic states to our East, as part of an evolutionary process, taking into account political and security developments in the whole of Europe.

An immediate and practical programme . . . will transform the relationship between NATO and participating states . . . beyond dialogue and cooperation to forge a real partnership—a Partnership for Peace. We invite the other states participating in the NACC and other CSCE countries able and willing to contribute to this programme, to join. . . . Active participation in the Partnership for Peace will play an important role in the evolutionary process of the expansion of NATO.

The PfP, which will operate under the authority of the North Atlantic Council, will forge new security relationships between the North Atlantic Alliance and its Partners for Peace. . . . States will . . . participate in political and military bodies at NATO Headquarters with respect to Partnership activities [and] intensify political and military cooperation throughout Europe, increase stability, diminish threats to peace, and build strengthened relationships by promoting the spirit of practical cooperation and commitment to democratic principles that underpin our Alliance. NATO will consult with any active participant in the Partnership if that partner perceives a direct threat to its territorial integrity, political independence, or security, . . . work in concrete ways towards transparency in defence budgeting, promoting democratic control of defence ministries, joint planning, joint military exercises, and creating an ability to operate with NATO forces in such fields as peacekeeping, search and rescue and humanitarian operations, and others. . . .

APPENDIX E

NATO Defense Ministerial:
Final Communiqué (excerpts)

BRUSSELS, 14–15 DECEMBER 1994

. . .

2. We underscored the central role of NATO and the determination of our Alliance to maintain its unity and cohesion, as well as to enhance stability throughout the transatlantic area in a manner that strengthens the security of all. We attach particular importance to the transatlantic relationship, which is fundamental to the stability of Europe. . . . Our security continues to depend on an integrated military structure and collective defence arrangements which enable the Alliance to act in the common defence as well as to fulfil its new missions, including peacekeeping. . . .

4. We support . . . the emerging ESDI and the role of the WEU. . . . We welcomed the rapid progress in implementing the Partnership for Peace, which now has 23 Partners.

5. At the Summit last January, our Heads of State and Government reaffirmed that the Alliance, as provided for in Article 10 of the Washington Treaty, remains open to membership of other European states in a position to further the principles of the Treaty and to contribute to the security of the North Atlantic area. . . . Enlargement will be an integral part of the more general development of co-operative security relationships in the entire Euro-Atlantic area. We therefore welcomed the decision taken at the recent meeting of NATO Foreign Ministers to initiate a process of examination inside the Alliance to determine how NATO will enlarge, the principles to guide this process and the implications of membership. . . . We have invited our Permanent Representatives, with the advice of NATO's Military Authorities, to ensure that these implications are addressed as a contribution to the work of the North Atlantic Council. . . .

6. It is an effective mechanism to develop the essential military capabilities required to operate effectively with NATO and to encourage interoperability between NATO and Partners which is of value to Partner countries whether they aspire to NATO membership or not. We confirmed that active participation in the Partnership for Peace will also play an important role in the evolutionary process of the expansion of NATO. . . .

9. [We] affirmed the importance of NATO's relations with Russia, including practical co-operation both inside and outside the Partnership for Peace. We also affirmed

the importance of an independent, democratic, and stable Ukraine, and our interest in developing further practical co-operation with it.

10. CJTFs will significantly enhance the effectiveness of contingency operations, whether undertaken by the Alliance or by the WEU, and our ability to involve non-NATO countries. We affirmed our view that implementation of the concept should be consistent with the principle of developing separable but not separate military capabilities for use by NATO or the WEU. We also underlined the importance of this work to the further evolution of the European Security and Defence Identity and to closer co-operation between NATO and the Western European Union, based on the principles of transparency and complementarity. . . .

19. We reviewed the status of the Alliance nuclear forces and reaffirmed their fundamental contribution to preserving stability and security. We received a presentation by the United States on the results of its Nuclear Posture Review, which was conducted in consultation with the Alliance, and expressed our deep satisfaction for the reaffirmation of the United States' nuclear commitment to NATO. . . .

APPENDIX F

NATO Study on Enlargement (excerpts)

BRUSSELS, SEPTEMBER 1995

Chapter 1: Purposes and Principles of Enlargement.

Chapter 2: How to ensure that enlargement contributes to the stability and security of the entire Euro-Atlantic area, as a part of a broad European security architecture, and supports the objective of an undivided Europe.

Chapter 3: How NACC and PfP can contribute concretely to the enlargement process.

Chapter 4: How to ensure that enlargement strengthens the effectiveness of the Alliance, preserves its ability to perform its core functions of common defence as well as to undertake peacekeeping and other new missions, and upholds the principles and objectives of the Washington treaty.

Chapter 5: What are the implications of membership for new members, including their rights and obligations, and what do they need to do to prepare for membership?

Chapter 6: Modalities according to which the enlargement process should proceed.

A. Purposes of Enlargement

1. With the end of the Cold War, there is a unique opportunity to build an improved security architecture in the whole of the Euro-Atlantic area, . . . to provide

increased stability and security for all in the Euro-Atlantic area, without recreating dividing lines. NATO views security as a broad concept embracing political and economic, as well as defence, components, . . . built through a gradual process of integration and cooperation brought about by an interplay of existing multilateral institutions in Europe, such as the EU, WEU and OSCE, each of which would have a role to play in accordance with its respective responsibilities and purposes. . . .

2. When NATO invites other European countries to become Allies, as foreseen in Article 10 of the Washington Treaty and reaffirmed at the January 1994 Brussels Summit, this will be a further step towards the Alliance's basic goal of enhancing security and stability throughout the Euro-Atlantic area, within the context of a broad European security architecture. NATO enlargement will extend to new members the benefits of common defence and integration into European and Euro-Atlantic institutions. The benefits of common defence and such integration are important to protecting the further democratic development of new members. By integrating more countries into the existing community of values and institutions, consistent with the objectives of the Washington Treaty and the London Declaration, NATO enlargement will safeguard the freedom and security of all its members in accordance with the principles of the UN Charter. Meeting NATO's fundamental security goals and supporting the integration of new members into European and Euro-Atlantic institutions are thus complementary goals of the enlargement process, consistent with the Alliance's strategic concept.

3. Therefore, enlargement will contribute to enhanced stability and security for all countries in the Euro-Atlantic area by:

- Encouraging and supporting democratic reforms, including civilian and democratic control over the military;
- Fostering in new members of the Alliance the patterns and habits of cooperation, consultation and consensus building which characterize relations among current Allies;
- Promoting good-neighbourly relations, which would benefit all countries in the Euro-Atlantic area, both members and non-members of NATO;
- Emphasizing common defence and extending its benefits and increasing transparency in defence planning and military budgets, thereby reducing the likelihood of instability that might be engendered by an exclusively national approach to defence policies;
- Reinforcing the tendency towards integration and cooperation in Europe based on shared democratic values and thereby curbing the countervailing tendency towards disintegration along ethnic and territorial lines;
- Strengthening the Alliance's ability to contribute to European and international security, including through peacekeeping activities under the responsibility of the OSCE and peacekeeping operations under the authority of the UN Security Council as well as other new missions;
- Strengthening/broadening the transatlantic partnership

5. New members, at the time that they join, must commit themselves, as all current Allies do on the basis of the Washington Treaty, to:

- Unite their efforts for collective defence and for the preservation of peace and security; settle any international disputes in which they may be involved by peaceful means in such a manner that international peace and security and justice are not endangered, and refrain in their international relations from the threat or use of force in any manner inconsistent with the purposes of the United Nations;
- Contribute to the development of peaceful and friendly international relations by strengthening their free institutions, by bringing about a better understanding of the principles upon which these institutions are founded, and by promoting conditions of stability and well-being;
- Maintain the effectiveness of the Alliance by sharing roles, risks, responsibilities, costs and benefits of assuring common security goals and objectives.

6. States which have ethnic disputes or external territorial disputes, including irredentist claims, or internal jurisdictional disputes must settle those disputes by peaceful means in accordance with OSCE principles. Resolution of such disputes would be a factor in determining whether to invite a state to join the Alliance.

7. Decisions on enlargement will be for NATO itself. Enlargement will occur through a gradual, deliberate, and transparent process, encompassing dialogue with all interested parties. There is no fixed or rigid list of criteria for inviting new member states to join the Alliance. Enlargement will be decided on a case-by-case basis and some nations may attain membership before others. New members should not be admitted or excluded on the basis of belonging to some group or category. Ultimately, Allies will decide by consensus whether to invite each new member to join according to their judgment of whether doing so will contribute to security and stability in the North Atlantic area at the time such a decision is to be made. . . . No country outside the Alliance should be given a veto or *droit de regard* over the process and decisions. . . .

STUDY ON NATO ENLARGEMENT

A. Introduction—NATO Enlargement in Its Broad Context

10. The current discussion on enlargement is taking place in very different circumstances than those which prevailed during the Cold War. In this context, the decision to admit new members must reflect the fact that the security challenges and risks which NATO faces now are different in nature from those faced in the past. In 1991, the Strategic Concept stated, "The threat of a simultaneous, full-scale attack on all of NATO's European fronts has effectively been removed. . . ." Since then, the risk of a re-emergent large-scale military threat has further declined. Nevertheless, risks to European security remain, which are multi-faceted and multi-directional and thus hard to predict and assess. . . .

12. The architecture of European security is composed of European institutions (such as the European Union [EU] and the Western European Union [WEU]) and transatlantic institutions (NATO). It also includes the OSCE, whose membership comprises all European as well as North American countries and is thus the most inclusive European

security institution, in whose framework agreements of particular importance for European security (the CFE treaty and the Pact on Stability) have been concluded. For its part, NATO has developed cooperation arrangements: the NACC and PfP. NACC/PfP cooperation will continue to play an important role in the European security architecture. . . .

13. Enlargement will have implications for all European nations, including states which do not join NATO early or at all. It will be important to maintain active, cooperative relations with countries which do not join the Alliance, in order to avoid divisions or uncertainties in Europe and to ensure broad, inclusive approaches to cooperative security. The Alliance should underline that there can be no question of "spheres of influence" in the contemporary Europe. NATO's relations with other European states, whether cooperation partners or not, are important factors to consider in taking any decision to proceed with the enlargement process as is building security for states which may not be prospective NATO members. . . .

Implementation of Russia's Individual Partnership Programme under the PfP and of our dialogue and cooperation with Russia beyond PfP will together renew and extend cooperation between the Alliance and Russia which we believe will enhance stability and security in Europe, as part of our broad approach to developing a cooperative security architecture in Europe. Equally, we want to develop further our relations with all newly independent states, whose independence and democracy constitute an important factor of security and stability for Europe. In this context, we attach particular importance to our relations with Ukraine which we will further develop, especially through enhanced cooperation within the PfP.

B. NATO Enlargement and Other European Security Institutions, in Particular, the OSCE, EU and WEU

18. Through the conclusion of Euro-agreements, the EU has given a number of European states a perspective of eventual EU membership and integration into EU structures.

The enlargement of the two organizations will proceed autonomously according to their respective internal dynamics and processes. This means they are unlikely to proceed at precisely the same pace. But the Alliance views its own enlargement and that of the EU as mutually supportive and parallel processes which together will make a significant contribution to strengthening Europe's security structure. . . .

19. European Union members are committed to a Common Foreign and Security Policy which shall include all questions related to the security of the Union, including the eventual framing of a common defence policy, which might in time lead to a common defence compatible with that of the Atlantic Alliance. . . .

C. Relations with Russia

27. NATO-Russia relations should reflect Russia's significance in European security and be based on reciprocity, mutual respect and confidence, no "surprise" decisions by either side which could affect the interests of the other. . . . NATO decisions, however, cannot be subject to any veto or *droit de regard* by a non-member state, nor can the Alliance be subordinated to another European security institution. . . .

D. Effects of the Decision-making Process on European Security and Stability

29. Each invitation will be decided on its own merits, case by case, and in accordance with the principles identified in this study, taking into account political and security related developments in the whole of Europe. It will be important, particularly in the meantime, not to foreclose the possibility of eventual Alliance membership for any European state in accordance with Article 10 of the Washington Treaty.

30. Countries could be invited to join sequentially or several countries could be simultaneously invited to join, bearing in mind that all Allies will decide by consensus on each invitation, i.e. new Allies must join consensus for subsequent invitations. There could be two or more sets of simultaneous invitations. Sequential accession could reduce the implication that others might be excluded and make it easier to begin with one or more countries but could also risk extending the calendar of accessions and thereby diverting attention from other important Alliance business. Simultaneous accessions would avoid the possibility of veto by new members on others joining at the same time; any decision on simultaneous accession should take into account relations among the prospective new members concerned and the impact on other states, including their relationship with NATO. Legislative/ratification considerations in Allied countries related to the accession of new member(s) to the Washington Treaty should also be taken into account.

Concerns have already been expressed in the context of the discussion of the enlargement of NATO that a new member might "close the door" behind it to new admissions in the future of other countries which may also aspire to NATO membership. Such a situation must be avoided; the Alliance rests upon commonality of views and a commitment to work for consensus; part of the evaluation of the qualifications of a possible new member will be its demonstrated commitment to that process and those values. . . .

CHAPTER 3: HOW NACC AND PFP CAN CONTRIBUTE CONCRETELY TO THE ENLARGEMENT PROCESS

C. The Role of PfP in Preparing for Membership

38. PfP activities and programmes are open to all partners, who themselves decide which opportunities to pursue and how intensively to work with the Alliance through the Partnership. This varying degree of participation is a key element of the self-differentiation process. Active participation in PfP will play an important role in possible new members' preparation to join the Alliance, although it will not guarantee Alliance membership. Active participation in NACC/PfP will provide the framework for possible new members to establish patterns of political and military cooperation with the Alliance to facilitate a transition to membership. Through PfP planning, joint exercises and other PfP activities, including seminars, workshops and day-to-day representation in Brussels and at Mons, possible new members will increasingly become acquainted with the functioning of the Alliance, including with respect to policymak-

ing, peacekeeping and crisis management. Possible new members' commitment to the shared principles and values of the Alliance will be indicated by their international behaviour and adherence to relevant OSCE commitments.

39. PfP will help partners undertake necessary defence management reforms. . . .

CHAPTER 4: HOW TO ENSURE THAT ENLARGEMENT STRENGTHENS THE EFFECTIVENESS OF THE ALLIANCE, PRESERVES ITS ABILITY TO PERFORM ITS CORE FUNCTIONS OF COMMON DEFENCE AS WELL AS TO UNDERTAKE PEACEKEEPING AND OTHER NEW MISSIONS, AND UPHOLDS THE PRINCIPLES AND OBJECTIVES OF THE WASHINGTON TREATY

. . .

43. On joining the Alliance, new members must accept the full obligations of the Washington Treaty. This includes participation in the consultation process within the Alliance and the principle of decision-making by consensus, which requires a commitment to build consensus within the Alliance on all issues of concern to it. New members must also be prepared to contribute to collective defence under Article 5, to the Alliance's new evolving missions and to Alliance budgets. This may include appropriate contributions to the Alliance's military force and command structures and infrastructure. . . .

44. NATO must ensure that all Alliance military obligations, particularly those under Article 5, will be met in an enlarged Alliance. This will require a case-by-case assessment of the military factors, including preparation time for NATO to take on new Article 5 commitments, for each prospective new member, taking into account the strategic environment, possible risks faced by potential new members, the capabilities and interoperability of their forces, their approach and that of the allies to the stationing of foreign forces on their territory, and the relevant reinforcement capabilities of Alliance forces, including strategic mobility. The Alliance will also have to ensure the accessibility of its forces to new members' territory for reinforcement, exercises, crisis management and, if applicable, stationing. This issue will need to be considered in the context of deciding individual new members' accession.

45. The Alliance will have to take a number of elements into account to ensure that NATO maintains its military credibility when it enlarges. . . .

Nuclear Forces

The supreme guarantee of the security of the Allies is provided by the strategic nuclear forces of the Alliance. New members will share the benefits and responsibilities from this in the same way as all other Allies in accordance with the Strategic Concept. New members will be expected to support the concept of deterrence and the essential role nuclear weapons play in the Alliance's strategy of war prevention as set forth in the Strategic Concept.

Force Structure

It is important for NATO's force structure that other Allies' forces can be deployed, when and if appropriate, on the territory of new members. The Alliance has no a priori requirement for the stationing of Alliance troops on the territory of new members. New members should participate in the Alliance's force structure. How this will be achieved may require additional considerations to include: whether new members should develop specially-trained units capable of reinforcing NATO forces and of being reinforced by NATO units; the prepositioning of materiel in critical areas; how to ensure that infrastructure is adequate to meet planned missions; and whether there is a need to increase strategic and intra-theatre mobility. . . .

48. There are currently three forms under which Allies contribute to NATO collective defence: full participation in the integrated military structure and the collective defence planning process; non-membership of the integrated military structure but full participation in the collective defence planning process together with a series of coordination agreements providing for cooperation with the integrated military structure in certain defined areas; and non-participation in the integrated military structure and collective defence planning but cooperation with the integrated military structure in more limited defined areas under agreements between the Chief of Defence and the Major NATO Commanders (MNCs). . . .

55. Individual Allies' policy on the stationing of other Allies' forces on their territory in peacetime varies considerably, taking into account a range of national and broader factors. For new members, the peacetime stationing of other Allies' forces on their territory should neither be a condition of membership nor foreclosed as an option. Decisions on the stationing of Allies' conventional forces on the territory of new members will have to be taken by the Alliance in the light of the benefits both to the Alliance as a whole and to particular new members, the military advantages of such a presence, the Alliance's military capacity for rapid and effective enforcement, the views of the new members concerned, the cost of possible military options, and the wider political and strategic impact. All Allies must of course be prepared in times of crisis or war to allow other Allies' forces to enter and operate on their territory, and to provide essential host nation support as mutually agreed, to enable NATO to provide effective common defence.

56. Individual Allies' policy on stationing their forces outside their borders in peacetime also varies considerably. Some Allies are, for example, legally constrained from doing so. For new members the peacetime stationing of forces on other Allies' territory should neither be a condition of membership nor foreclosed as an option. . . .

(iv) Nuclear Forces

58. The coverage provided by Article 5, including its nuclear component, will apply to new members. There is no a priori requirement for the stationing of nuclear weapons on the territory of new members. In light of both the current international environment and the potential threats facing the Alliance, NATO's current nuclear posture will, for the foreseeable future, continue to meet the requirements of an enlarged Alliance. . . .

CHAPTER 5: WHAT ARE THE IMPLICATIONS OF MEMBERSHIP FOR NEW MEMBERS, INCLUDING THEIR RIGHTS AND OBLIGATIONS, AND WHAT DO THEY NEED TO DO TO PREPARE FOR MEMBERSHIP?

68. New members will be full members of the Alliance, enjoying all the rights and assuming all the obligations under the Washington Treaty. There must be no "second tier" security guarantees or members within the Alliance and no modifications of the Washington Treaty for those who join. Possible new members should prepare themselves on this basis. . . .

A. What Will Be Expected Politically of New Members?

. . .

Conform to basic principles embodied in the Washington Treaty:

Democracy, individual liberty and the rule of law; Accept NATO as a community of like-minded nations joined together for collective defence and the preservation of peace and security, with each nation contributing to the security and defence from which all member nations benefit; Be firmly committed to principles, objectives and undertakings included in the Partnership for Peace Framework Document; Commit themselves to good faith efforts to build consensus within the Alliance on all issues, since consensus is the basis of Alliance cohesion and decision-making; Undertake to participate fully in the Alliance consultation and decision-making process on political and security issues of concern to the Alliance; Establish a permanent representation at NATO HQ; Establish an appropriate national military representation at SHAPE/SACLANT; Be prepared to nominate qualified candidates to serve on the International Staff and in NATO agencies; Provide qualified personnel to serve on the International Military Staff and in the Integrated Military Structure if and as appropriate; Contribute to Alliance budgets, based on budget shares to be agreed; Participate, as appropriate, in the exchange of Allied intelligence, which is based entirely on national contributions. . . .

71. The Alliance expects new members not to "close the door" to the accession of one or more later candidate members. . . .

B. What Prospective New Members Will Need to Do Politically to Prepare Themselves for Membership

Demonstrate a commitment to and respect for OSCE norms and principles, including the resolution of ethnic disputes, external territorial disputes including irredentist claims or internal jurisdictional disputes by peaceful means. . . . Show a commitment to promoting stability and well-being by economic liberty, social justice and environmental responsibility; Establish appropriate democratic and civilian control of their defence force; Undertake a commitment to ensure that adequate resources are devoted to achieving the obligations. . . .

C. What Will Be Expected Militarily of New Members

73. New members of the Alliance must be prepared to share the roles, risks, responsibilities, benefits, and burdens of common security and collective defence. They should be expected to subscribe to Alliance strategy as set out in the Strategic Concept and refined in subsequent Ministerial statements.

74. An important element in new members' military contribution will be a commitment in good faith to pursue the objectives of standardization which are essential to Alliance strategy and operational effectiveness. New members should concentrate, in the first instance, on interoperability. As a minimum, they should accept NATO doctrine and policies relating to standardization and in addition aim at achieving a sufficient level of training and equipment to operate effectively with NATO forces. . . .

D. What Prospective New Members Will Need to Do
Militarily to Prepare Themselves for Membership

75. The ability of prospective members to contribute militarily to collective defence and to the Alliance's new missions will be a factor in deciding whether to invite them to join the Alliance.

76. New members will need to adapt themselves to the fact that NATO's strategy and force structure are designed to exploit multinationality and flexibility to provide effective defence at minimum cost. NATO policy is therefore heavily dependent on standardization, particularly in the areas of operations, administration and material. Current NATO standardization priorities include commonality of doctrines and procedures, interoperability of command, control and communications and major weapon systems, and interchangeability of ammunition and primary combat supplies.

CHAPTER 6: MODALITIES ACCORDING TO WHICH THE
ENLARGEMENT PROCESS SHOULD PROCEED

79. The modalities for enlargement flow from Article 10 of the Washington Treaty. Previous accessions in accordance with Article 10 need not be considered precise models for future accessions, since the general political and security context of future accessions will be different as well as the number, individual circumstances and characteristics of new acceding members. In this context, a process which is predictable and transparent with respect to new accessions may be required to provide reassurance to public and legislative opinion in existing member states. The modalities for future accession should avoid any suggestion of different classes of membership.

80. While each invitation to join the Alliance will be decided on its own merits, case by case, the timing of future accessions could be sequential or in one or more simultaneous sets. In any case, it will be important to make clear that the Alliance remains open to further accessions by countries not among the earliest to be invited to join. A declaration at the time of the first invitation(s) being issued which clearly stated this would both reassure those countries that would not be among the first to be invited

and reduce the likelihood of some of those countries submitting unsolicited applications to join the Alliance.

81. The precise timing, sequence and content of the accession process need to be considered carefully, particularly with respect to talks and negotiations with countries to be invited to join. . . . The NAC will decide on beginning any necessary exploratory contacts, after which the following steps would be required for any future accession to the Washington Treaty:

- A decision by the NAC (at an appropriate level) to authorize the Secretary General to inform a country/countries that the Allies are favourably disposed to its/their accession, and to enter into talks with it/them;
- A formal notification from the country/countries to the Secretary General of its/their firm commitment, in accordance with domestic legal requirements, to join the Alliance;
- Detailed consultations with the country/countries concerned about the protocol of accession;
- Formulation by the Allies of the protocol of accession;
- Approval and signature of the protocol by the NAC;
- Ratification, acceptance or approval of the accession protocol by the Allies and entry into force;
- Formal invitation to the country/countries to accede to the North Atlantic Treaty. . . .

It may not be feasible for countries invited to join to provide assurances that all domestic requirements for it/them to do so have been met together with formal notification of its/their desire to join. Precision may therefore be required on this point. It will be important, however, to avoid legislative ratification procedures for new accessions going forward in existing Allied countries without assurance that the country concerned wants to and will accede.

82. Consultations regarding accession with any country concerned should not delay those with any other, i.e. the pace of movement towards accession by a number of invited countries should not be dictated by that of the slowest.

Founding Act on Mutual Relations, Cooperation and Security Between NATO and the Russian Federation (excerpts)

PARIS, 27 MAY 1997

The North Atlantic Treaty Organization and its member States, on the one hand, and the Russian Federation, on the other hand, . . . based on an enduring political commitment undertaken at the highest political level, will build together a lasting and inclusive peace in the Euro-Atlantic area on the principles of democracy and cooperative security.

NATO and Russia do not consider each other as adversaries. They share the goal of overcoming the vestiges of earlier confrontation and competition and of strengthening mutual trust and cooperation [and] reaffirm the determination of NATO and Russia to give concrete substance to their shared commitment to build a stable, peaceful and undivided Europe, whole and free, to the benefit of all its peoples. Making this commitment at the highest political level marks the beginning of a fundamentally new relationship between NATO and Russia. They intend to develop, on the basis of common interest, reciprocity and transparency a strong, stable and enduring partnership. . . .

I. PRINCIPLES

Proceeding from the principle that the security of all states in the Euro-Atlantic community is indivisible, NATO and Russia will work together to contribute to the establishment in Europe of common and comprehensive security based on the allegiance to shared values, commitments and norms of behaviour in the interests of all states. NATO and Russia will help to strengthen the OSCE, including developing further its role as a primary instrument in preventive diplomacy, conflict prevention, crisis management, post-conflict rehabilitation and regional security cooperation. . . .

NATO and Russia will seek the widest possible cooperation among participating States of the OSCE with the aim of creating in Europe a common space of security and stability, without dividing lines or spheres of influence limiting the sovereignty of any state. NATO and Russia start from the premise that the shared objective of strengthening security and stability in the Euro-Atlantic area for the benefit of all countries requires a response to new risks and challenges, such as aggressive nationalism, proliferation of nuclear, biological and chemical weapons, terrorism, persistent abuse of human rights and of the rights of persons belonging to national minorities and unresolved territorial disputes, which pose a threat to common peace, prosperity and stability. . . .

To achieve the aims of this Act, NATO and Russia will base their relations on a shared commitment to the following principles:

- Development, on the basis of transparency, of a strong, stable, enduring and equal partnership and of cooperation to strengthen security and stability in the Euro-Atlantic area;
- Acknowledgment of the vital role that democracy, political pluralism, the rule of law, and respect for human rights and civil liberties and the development of free market economies play in the development of common prosperity and comprehensive security;
- Refraining from the threat or use of force against each other as well as against any other state, its sovereignty, territorial integrity or political independence; . . .
- Respect for sovereignty, independence and territorial integrity of all states and their inherent right to choose the means to ensure their own security, the inviolability of borders and peoples' right of self-determination; . . .
- Mutual transparency in creating and implementing defence policy and military doctrines;
- Prevention of conflicts and settlement of disputes by peaceful means. . . .

II. MECHANISM FOR CONSULTATION AND COOPERATION, THE NATO-RUSSIA PERMANENT JOINT COUNCIL

The central objective of this Permanent Joint Council will be to build increasing levels of trust, unity of purpose and habits of consultation and cooperation between NATO and Russia, in order to enhance each other's security and that of all nations in the Euro-Atlantic area and diminish the security of none. If disagreements arise, NATO and Russia will endeavour to settle them on the basis of goodwill and mutual respect within the framework of political consultations. . . .

The Permanent Joint Council will meet at the level of Foreign Ministers and at the level of Defence Ministers twice annually, and also monthly at the level of ambassadors/permanent representatives to the North Atlantic Council.

The Permanent Joint Council may also meet, as appropriate, at the level of Heads of State and Government. . . . Under the auspices of the Permanent Joint Council, military representatives and Chiefs of Staff will also meet; meetings of Chiefs of Staff will take place no less than twice a year, and also monthly at military representatives level. Meetings of military experts may be convened, as appropriate. The Permanent Joint Council will be chaired jointly by the Secretary General of NATO, a representative of one of the NATO member States on a rotation basis, and a representative of Russia. . . .

III. AREAS FOR CONSULTATION AND COOPERATION

In building their relationship, NATO and Russia will focus on specific areas of mutual interest. They will consult and strive to cooperate to the broadest possible degree in the following areas:

Conflict prevention, including preventive diplomacy, crisis management and conflict resolution taking into account the role and responsibility of the UN and the OSCE; ... joint operations, including peacekeeping operations, on a case-by-case basis, under the authority of the UN Security Council or the responsibility of the OSCE, and if Combined Joint Task Forces (CJTF) are used in such cases, participation in them at an early stage; participation of Russia in the Euro-Atlantic Partnership Council and the Partnership for Peace; exchange of information and consultation on strategy, defence policy, the military doctrines of NATO and Russia, and budgets and infrastructure development programmes; arms control issues; nuclear safety issues, across their full spectrum; preventing the proliferation of nuclear, biological and chemical weapons, and their delivery means, combating nuclear trafficking and strengthening cooperation in specific arms control areas, including political and defence aspects of proliferation; possible cooperation in Theatre Missile Defence; enhanced regional air traffic safety; ... increasing transparency, predictability and mutual confidence regarding the size and roles of the conventional forces of member States of NATO and Russia; reciprocal exchanges, as appropriate, on nuclear weapons issues, including doctrines and strategy of NATO and Russia; coordinating a programme of expanded cooperation between respective military establishments. . . .

Other areas can be added by mutual agreement.

IV. POLITICAL-MILITARY MATTERS

The member States of NATO reiterate that they have no intention, no plan and no reason to deploy nuclear weapons on the territory of new members, nor any need to change any aspect of NATO's nuclear posture or nuclear policy—and do not foresee any future need to do so. This subsumes the fact that NATO has decided that it has no intention, no plan, and no reason to establish nuclear weapon storage sites on the territory of those members, whether through the construction of new nuclear storage facilities or the adaptation of old nuclear storage facilities. Nuclear storage sites are understood to be facilities specifically designed for the stationing of nuclear weapons, and include all types of hardened above or below ground facilities (storage bunkers or vaults) designed for storing nuclear weapons. . . .

This enhanced military-to-military dialogue will be built upon the principle that neither party views the other as a threat nor seeks to disadvantage the other's security. This enhanced military-to-military dialogue will include regularly-scheduled reciprocal briefings on NATO and Russian military doctrine, strategy and resultant force posture and will include the broad possibilities for joint exercises and training [and] will establish military liaison missions at various levels on the basis of reciprocity and further mutual arrangements.

To . . . ensure this partnership is grounded to the greatest extent possible in practical activities and direct cooperation, NATO's and Russia's respective military authorities will explore the further development of a concept for joint NATO-Russia peacekeeping operations. This initiative should build upon the positive experience of working together in Bosnia and Herzegovina, and the lessons learned there will be used in the establishment of Combined Joint Task Forces. . . .

APPENDIX H

Charter on a Distinctive Partnership Between the North Atlantic Treaty Organization and Ukraine (excerpts)

MADRID, 9 JULY 1997

I. BUILDING AN ENHANCED NATO-UKRAINE RELATIONSHIP

. . .

- Building on a political commitment at the highest level;
- Recognizing the fundamental changes in the security environment in Europe which have inseparably linked the security of every state to that of all the others;
- [Determining] to strengthen mutual trust and cooperation in order to enhance security and stability, and to cooperate in building a stable, peaceful and undivided Europe;
- Stressing the profound transformation undertaken by NATO since the end of the Cold War and its continued adaptation to meet the changing circumstances of Euro-Atlantic security, including its support, on a case-by-case basis, of new missions of peacekeeping operations carried out under the authority of the UN Security Council or the responsibility of the OSCE;
- Welcoming the progress achieved by Ukraine and looking forward to further steps to develop its democratic institutions, to implement radical economic reforms, and to deepen the process of integration with the full range of European and Euro-Atlantic structures;
- Noting NATO's positive role in maintaining peace and stability in Europe and in promoting greater confidence and transparency in the Euro-Atlantic area, and its openness for cooperation with the new democracies of Central and Eastern Europe, an inseparable part of which is Ukraine. . . .

II. PRINCIPLES FOR THE DEVELOPMENT
OF NATO-UKRAINE RELATIONS

2. NATO and Ukraine will base their relationship on the principles, obligations and commitments under international law [and] reaffirm their commitment to:

- The recognition that security of all states in the OSCE area is indivisible, that no state should pursue its security at the expense of that of another state, and that no state can regard any part of the OSCE region as its sphere of influence;
- Refrain from the threat or use of force against any state in any manner inconsistent with the United Nations Charter or Helsinki Final Act principles guiding participating States; . . .
- The rule of law, the fostering of democracy, political pluralism and a market economy;
- Human rights and the rights of persons belonging to national minorities. . . .

3. Ukraine reaffirms its determination to carry forward its defence reforms, to strengthen democratic and civilian control of the armed forces, and to increase their interoperability with the forces of NATO and Partner countries. NATO reaffirms its support for Ukraine's efforts. . . .

5. Reaffirming the common goal of implementation of a broad range of issues for consultation and cooperation, NATO and Ukraine commit themselves to develop and strengthen their consultation and/or cooperation in the areas described below. In this regard, NATO and Ukraine reaffirm their commitment to the full development of the EAPC and the enhanced PfP. This includes Ukrainian participation in operations, including peacekeeping operations, on a case-by-case basis, under the authority of the UN Security Council, or the responsibility of the OSCE, and, if CJTF are used in such cases, Ukrainian participation in them at an early stage on a case-by-case basis, subject to decisions by the North Atlantic Council on specific operations. . . .

11. Consultation and cooperation as set out in this Charter will be implemented through:

- NATO-Ukraine meetings at the level of the North Atlantic Council at intervals to be mutually agreed; NATO-Ukraine meetings with appropriate NATO Committees as mutually agreed;
- Reciprocal high level visits; mechanisms for military cooperation, including periodic meetings with NATO Chiefs of Defence and activities within the framework of the enhanced Partnership for Peace programme. . . .

V. COOPERATION FOR A MORE SECURE EUROPE

14. NATO Allies will continue to support Ukrainian sovereignty and independence, territorial integrity, democratic development, economic prosperity and its status as a non-nuclear weapon state, and the principle of inviolability of frontiers, as key

factors of stability and security in Central and Eastern Europe and in the continent as a whole.

15. NATO and Ukraine will develop a crisis consultative mechanism to consult together whenever Ukraine perceives a direct threat to its territorial integrity, political independence, or security.

16. NATO welcomes and supports the fact that Ukraine received security assurances from all five nuclear-weapon states parties to the Treaty on the Non-Proliferation of Nuclear Weapons (NPT) as a non-nuclear weapon state party to the NPT, and recalls the commitments undertaken by the United States and the United Kingdom, together with Russia, and by France unilaterally, which took the historic decision in Budapest in 1994 to provide Ukraine with security assurances as a non-nuclear weapon state party to the NPT.

Ukraine's landmark decision to renounce nuclear weapons and to accede to the NPT as a non-nuclear weapon state greatly contributed to the strengthening of security and stability in Europe and has earned Ukraine special stature in the world community. NATO welcomes Ukraine's decision to support the indefinite extension of the NPT and its contribution to the withdrawal and dismantlement of nuclear weapons which were based on its territory.

18. Ukraine welcomes the statement by NATO members that "enlarging the Alliance will not require a change in NATO's current nuclear posture and, therefore, NATO countries have no intention, no plan and no reason to deploy nuclear weapons on the territory of new members nor any need to change any aspect of NATO's nuclear posture or nuclear policy—and do not foresee any future need to do so."

Appendix I

Madrid Declaration on Euro-Atlantic Security and Cooperation: Issued by the Heads of State and Goverment (excerpts)

MADRID, 8 JULY 1997

1. We . . . have come together in Madrid to give shape to the new NATO as we move towards the 21st century. Substantial progress has been achieved in the internal adaptation of the Alliance. As a significant step in the evolutionary process of opening the Alliance, we have invited three countries to begin accession talks. We have substantially strengthened our relationship with Partners through the new Euro-Atlantic Partnership Council and enhancement of the Partnership for Peace. The signature on 27th May of the NATO-Russia Founding Act and the Charter we will sign tomorrow with Ukraine bear witness to our commitment to an undivided Europe. We are also enhancing our Mediterranean dialogue. Our aim is to reinforce peace and stability in the Euro-Atlantic area.

A new Europe is emerging, a Europe of greater integration and cooperation. An inclusive European security architecture is evolving to which we are contributing, along with other European organisations. Our Alliance will continue to be a driving force in this process. . . .

2. The vitality of the transatlantic link will benefit from the development of a true, balanced partnership in which Europe is taking on greater responsibility. In this spirit, we are building a European Security and Defence Identity within NATO. The Alliance and EU share common strategic interests. . . .

5. At our last meeting in Brussels, we said that we would expect and would welcome the accession of new members, as part of an evolutionary process, taking into account political and security developments in the whole of Europe. . . . The time has come to start a new phase of this process. The Study on NATO Enlargement—which stated, inter alia, that NATO's military effectiveness should be sustained as the Alliance enlarges—the results of the intensified dialogue with interested Partners, and the analyses of relevant factors associated with the admission of new members have provided a basis on which to assess the current state of preparations of the twelve countries aspiring to Alliance membership.

6. Today, we invite the Czech Republic, Hungary and Poland to begin accession talks with NATO. . . .

8. We reaffirm that NATO remains open to new members . . . in a position to further the principles of the Treaty and contribute to security in the Euro-Atlantic area. The Alliance expects to extend further invitations in coming years. . . . Those nations that have previously expressed an interest in becoming NATO members but that were not invited to begin accession talks today will remain under consideration for future membership. The considerations set forth in our 1995 Study on NATO Enlargement will continue to apply with regard to future aspirants, regardless of their geographic location. *No European democratic country whose admission would fulfill the objectives of the Treaty will be excluded from consideration.* Furthermore, in order to enhance overall security and stability in Europe, further steps in the ongoing enlargement process of the Alliance should balance the security concerns of all Allies.

To support this process, we strongly encourage the active participation by aspiring members in the EAPC and PfP, which will further deepen their political and military involvement in the work of the Alliance. We also intend to continue the Alliance's intensified dialogues with those nations that aspire to NATO membership or that otherwise wish to pursue a dialogue with NATO on membership questions [to] cover the full range of political, military, financial and security issues relating to possible NATO membership, without prejudice to any eventual Alliance decision. We will review the process at our next meeting in 1999. With regard to the aspiring members, we . . . take account of the positive developments towards democracy and the rule of law in a number of southeastern European countries, especially Romania and Slovenia. . . .

9. The EAPC will be an essential element in our common endeavour to enhance security and stability in the Euro-Atlantic region [to] provide the overarching framework for all aspects of our wide-ranging cooperation and raise it to a qualitatively new level. . . .

10. The Partnership for Peace has become the focal point of our efforts to build new patterns of practical cooperation in the security realm. Without PfP, we would not have been able to put together and deploy so effectively and efficiently the Implementation and Stabilisation Forces in Bosnia and Herzegovina with the participation of so many of our Partners.

We welcome and endorse the decision taken in Sintra to enhance PfP by strengthening the political consultation element, increasing the role Partners play in PfP decision-making and planning, and by making PfP more operational. . . .

11. The Founding Act on Mutual Relations, Cooperation and Security between NATO and the Russian Federation, signed on 27th May 1997 in Paris, is a historic achievement. It opens a new era in European security relations, an era of cooperation between NATO and Russia, . . . reflects our shared commitment to build together a lasting and inclusive peace in the Euro-Atlantic area on the principles of democracy and cooperative security. Its provisions contribute to NATO's underlying objective of enhancing the security of all European states. . . .

12. We attach great importance to tomorrow's signing of the Charter on a Distinctive Partnership [to] move NATO-Ukraine cooperation onto a more substantive level, offer new potential for strengthening our relationship, and enhance security in the region more widely. We are convinced that Ukraine's independence, territorial

integrity and sovereignty are a key factor for ensuring stability in Europe. We continue to support the reform process in Ukraine as it develops as a democratic nation with a market economy. . . .

18. We reaffirm, as stated in our 1994 Brussels Declaration, our full support for the development of the ESDI by making available NATO assets and capabilities for WEU operations. With this in mind, the Alliance is building ESDI, grounded on solid military principles and supported by appropriate military planning and permitting the creation of militarily coherent and effective forces capable of operating under the political control and strategic direction of the WEU [to] serve the interests of the Alliance as well as of the WEU. . . .

21. We reaffirm our commitment to further strengthening the OSCE as a regional organisation according to Chapter VIII of the UN Charter and as a primary instrument for preventing conflict, enhancing cooperative security and advancing democracy and human rights. The OSCE, as the most inclusive European-wide security organisation, plays an essential role in securing peace, stability and security in Europe. . . . Our goal is to create in Europe, through the widest possible cooperation among OSCE states, a common space of security and stability, without dividing lines or spheres of influence limiting the sovereignty of particular states.

APPENDIX J

The Washington Declaration: Signed and Issued by the Heads of State and Government Participating in the North Atlantic Council Meeting (excerpts)

WASHINGTON, D.C., 23–24 APRIL 1999

1. We, the Heads of State and Government of the member countries of the North Atlantic Alliance, declare for a new century our mutual commitment to defend our people, our territory and our liberty, founded on democracy, human rights and the rule of law. The world has changed dramatically over the last half century, but our common values and security interests remain the same. . . .

5. We must be as effective in the future in dealing with new challenges as we were in the past. We are charting NATO's course as we enter the 21st century: an Alliance committed to collective defence, capable of addressing current and future risks to our security, strengthened by and open to new members, and working together with other institutions, Partners and Mediterranean Dialogue countries in a mutually reinforcing way to enhance Euro-Atlantic security and stability. . . .

8. Our Alliance remains open to all European democracies, regardless of geography, willing and able to meet the responsibilities of membership, and whose inclusion would enhance overall security and stability in Europe. NATO is an essential pillar of a wider community of shared values and shared responsibility. Working together, Allies and Partners, including Russia and Ukraine, are developing their cooperation and erasing the divisions imposed by the Cold War to help to build a Europe whole and free, where security and prosperity are shared and indivisible.

9. Fifty years after NATO's creation, the destinies of North America and Europe remain inseparable. When we act together, we safeguard our freedom and security and enhance stability more effectively than any of us could alone. Now, and for the century about to begin, we declare as the fundamental objectives of this Alliance enduring peace, security and liberty for all people of Europe and North America.

BIBLIOGRAPHY

"About Entrance to NATO." *Rzeczpospolita*. 18 February 1999.
"Abroad and by Agreement." *Gazeta Wyborcza*. 20 November 1998.
"Agreement for NATO." *Rzeczpospolita*. 22 November 1998.
Albrighton, Denise. "Kallas Outlines Plans to Trim State Budget." *The Baltic Times*. 29 April 1999.
Alpatov, S. "Bezopasnost Ukrainy i NATO." *Vlast,* no. 11 (1996): 65–67.
"Americans Yet to Be Sold on Need for Larger NATO." *Washington Post*. 3 July 1997, sec A: 26.
ANSA Press Agency. Report. Rome. 10 January 1994.
"Applause for NATO." *Gazeta Wyborcza*. 18 February 1999.
"Army of XXI Century." *Gazeta Wyborcza*. 10 September 1997.
"Army Without Israeli Rocket." *Rzeczpospolita*. 9 December 1998.
Ash, Timothy Garton. "Germany's Choice." *Foreign Affairs* 73, no. 4. (July/August 1994): 65–81.
Asmus, Brown, et al. *NATO's Transformation: The Changing Shape of the Atlantic Alliance*. Lanham, Md.: Rowman and Littlefield, 1997.
Asmus, Kugler, et al. "What Will NATO Enlargement Cost?" *Survival* (Autumn 1996): 5–26.
Avadani, Apud Ioana. "Madrid—esec sau success (Madrid—Failure or Success)." *Politica externa* 2, no. 3–4 (Fall 1997): 35.
Bach, Jonathan. *Between Sovereignty and Integration: German Foreign Policy and National Identity After 1989*. New York: St. Martin's Press, 1999.
"Battle for Contracts." *Życie*. 11 February 1999.
Beniamino Andreatta. *Atti Parlamentari*. Camera die Deputati. 11 February 1997.
Berdiaiev, N. *The Sources and Meaning of Russian Communism* (in Russian). Moscow: Nauka, 1990.
Bérégovoy, Pierre. "L'Amérique, l'Europe, la France." *Le Monde*. 6 January 1993. 1.
Berger, Thomas. *Cultures of Antimilitarism: National Security in Germany and Japan*. Baltimore, Md.: Johns Hopkins Press, 1998.
Bertram, Christopher. *Europe in the Balance: Securing the Peace Won in the Cold War*. Washington, D.C.: Carnegie Endowment, 1995.
Besset, Jean Paul. "Á Denver, Américains et Européens s'opposent sur l'environment." *Le Monde*. 24 June 1997. 2.
"Bigger NATO, Big U.S. 'Mistake.'" *Washington Post*. 21 February 1997, sec A: 24.
Bilinsky, Yaroslav. *Endgame in NATO's Enlargement: The Baltic States and the Ukraine*. London: Praeger Publishing, 1999.

"Bislang Sagten die Bündnisgrünen nein zur NATO." *Die Taz.* 9 April 1997.

Blair, Tony. *Letter to Sir John Killick.* 8 June 1998. United Kingdom Ministry of Defense. Available online at http://www.mod.uk.

Blasek, Roman. "Perception of Security Risks by the Population of the Czech Republic." *The Journal of Slavic Military Studies* 11, no. 3 (Sept 1998): 89–96.

Bobrowski, R. "Outside Security of Poland." *Przegl'd Œrodkowoeuropejski,* no. 14 (1995).

Boniface, Pascal. "The NATO Debate in France." *NATO Enlargement: The National Debates over Ratification.* Ed. Simon Serfaty and Stephen Cambone. Washington, D.C.: CSIS, 1 October 1997.

Bresson, Henri de. "Les contentieux s'alourdissent entre Paris et Bonn." *Le Monde.* 4 December 1996. 2.

———. "Jacques Chirac espére voir la Roumanie intégrer l'OTAN en 1999." *Le Monde.* 24 February 1997. 2.

Bruce, Erika V.C. "NATO's Public Opinion Seminar Indicates Continuing, but Not Unshakable Support." *NATO Review* 40, no. 2 (April 1992): 1–8.

———. "The Image of the Alliance: Public Opinion Seminar Gauges Support." *NATO Review* 41, no. 6 (December 1993): 6–11.

Bruce, Leigh. "Europe's Locomotive." *Foreign Policy,* no. 78 (Spring 1990): 68–90.

Budkin, V. "U ramkah osoblyvogo partnerstva." *Polityka I Chas,* no. 9 (1998): 26.

Butcher, Tim. "Defense Chiefs Warn Against Enlarging NATO." *Daily Telegraph.* 6 May 1998. 9.

Butenschön, Marianne. *Estonia, Lettland, Litauen: Das Biltikum auf dem langen Weg in die Freiheit.* München: Piper, 1992.

Buzan, Barry. *People, States, and Fear: An Agenda for International Security Studies in the Post–Cold War Era,* 2nd ed. Boulder: Lynne Rienner, 1991.

Carr, S. "British Offer." *Armia,* no. 3 (1998).

Central and Eastern Eurobarometer, no. 7 (March 1997).

"Charter on a Distinctive Partnership Between NATO and Ukraine." *NATO Review,* Special Insert: Documentation, 45, no. 4 (July-August 1997).

Chirac, Jacques. "Discours devant l'IHEDN." Institut Hautes Etudes de Defence Nationale. Paris: 8 June 1996.

Christopher, Warren. Statement. Washington, D.C.: Senate Committee on Foreign Relations, 30 June 1994.

Chumak, V., and S. Pirozhkov. "Ukraine and NATO." *Polityka I Chas,* no. 6 (1995): 17.

Cook, Robin. Speech. 22 January 1999. London: Ernest Bevin Memorial Lecture.

"Copernican Change." *Rzeczpospolita.* 17 February 1999.

"Costly Lesson of the *Huzar.*" *Rzeczpospolita.* 9 December 1998.

"The Costs of Expanding the NATO Alliance." *CBO Papers.* Washington, D.C.: Congressional Budget Office, March 1996.

"Costs of Integration with NATO." RCSS Paper. Warsaw: Governmental Center for Strategic Studies, January 1998.

Czech Republic. Ministry of Defense. "Military Strategy of the Czech Republic." *White Paper on Defense of the Czech Republic.* Prague: 21 December 1994. 17.

———. Ministry of Defense. *White Paper on Defense of the Czech Republic.* Prague: 1995.

Dalsjö, Robert. "Baltic Self–Defense Capabilities—Achievable and Necessary, or Futile Symbolism?" *Baltic Defense Review,* no. 1 (1999): 17–23.

Davidson, Ian. "In the Fast Lane." *Financial Times.* 19 February 1997. 12.

Deutsch, Karl W., et al. *Political Community and the North Atlantic Area.* Princeton: Princeton University Press, 1957.

Diaconescu, Gheorghe, et al. "Democratic Control Over the Army in Romania." *Editura Enciclopedica.* Budapest: 1996.

Dienstbier, Jiri. "Central Europe's Security." *Foreign Policy,* no. 83 (Summer 1991): 119–127.

Dini, Lamberto. "Letter to House Foreign Affairs Committee Chairman." 12 February 1997.

————. Speech to House of Parliament. 22 June 1997. Available online at www.esteri.it/notizie/discorsi/d220698i.htm.

"Dobrzañski Leave." *Trybuna.* 16 October 1997.

Drozdiak, William. "U.S. Role in Aegean Revives Doubts on EU: Holbrooke's Criticisms." *Washington Post.* 8 February 1996, sec A: 17.

Dunay, Pál. "Theoretical Debates in Hungary." *The North Atlantic Treaty Organization: Studies and Documents.* Ed. Pál Dunay and Ferenc Gazdag. Budapest: SVKI, 1997.

————. "Adversaries All Around? The (Re)nationalization of Security and Defense Policies in Eastern Europe." *Clingendael Papers* (January 1994): 10–11.

Dutkiewicz, Piotr, and Slawomic Lodzinski. "The Grey Zone: Poland's Security Policy Since 1989." *NATO Looks East.* Eds. Piotr Dutkiewicz and Robert Jackson. Westport, Conn.: Praeger Publishing, 1998.

Dziewanowski, K. "Start of Second Stage." *Rzeczpospolita.* 24 June 1997.

Ek, Carl. "NATO Expansion: Cost Issues." Report. 97–668F. Washington, D.C.: Congressional Research Service. 2 July 1997.

"The End of the *Huzar*?" *Raport,* no. 1 (1999).

Erler, Gernot. "NATO Zwischen Einbindung und Ausgrenzung." *Blatter für Deutsche und Internationale Politik.* August 1997. 927–936.

"Estimated Cost of Enlargement (A Contribution to the Debate)." Warsaw: Euro-Atlantic Association, 1997. 9–30, 49–70.

Estonia. Ministry of Defense. "Guidelines of the National Defense Policy of the Estonian State." Tallinn: Presented to the Riigikogu, 1996.

————. "Annual Exchange on Defense Planning." *Vienna Document 1994.* Tallinn: Ministry of Defense, 1999.

"Estonia on the Threshold of NATO." International Defense Advisory Board, 24 February 1999. 7.

"Europe, NATO, Germany, and Russia. Questionnaire Among Parties Leaders." *Życie Warszawy.* 14 August 1993.

"European Alternative." *Raport,* no. 12. 1998.

European Commission. "Agenda 2000—Summary and Conclusions of the Opinions of Commission Concerning the Applications for Membership to the European Union by the Candidate Countries." DOC 97/8. Brussels: EU–COM, 15 July 1997.

European Union. "Chirac News Conference After NATO Summit." Report, Foreign Broadcast Information Service, Washington, D.C. FBIS–WEU–97–192. 17 July 1997.

————. *EU View on IGC Issues.* Report, Foreign Broadcast Information Service, Washington, D.C. FBIS–WEU–96–052. 15 March 1996. 11.

————. "Jospin's Foreign Policy . . ." Report, Foreign Broadcast Information Service, Washington, D.C. FBIS–WEU–97–108. 5 June 1997. 9.

————. "US Bids to Keep 'Absolute Control' over NATO." By Thierry de Montbrial. Report, Foreign Broadcast Information Service, Washington, D.C. FBIS–WEU–97–170. 19 June 1997.

Fassino, Piero. Interview. *L'Unita'*. 6 April 1997. 2.
"Finish." *Gazeta Wyborcza*. 18 February 1999.
Firlej, E., and P. Wieczorek. "Economic-Financial Aspects of Poland's Integration with Structures of the NATO." *Sprawy Miêdzynarodowe*, no. 1 (1996): 43–46.
"Founding Act on Mutual Relations, Cooperation and Security Between NATO and the Russian Federation." *NATO Review*, Special Insert: Documentation, 45, no. 4 (July-August 1997).
Frachon, Alain. "La France peine à impose sa conception de sécurité en Europe." *Le Monde*. 4 Dec 1996. 2.
"France Attacks U.S. Cruise Strike on Baghdad." *Financial Times*. 21 January 1993. 1.
"France Increases Its Participation in the Transformation of the Alliance." *NATO Review*. January 1996.
France. Senate. *Débat au Sénat sur la CIG: Intervention du Ministre des Affaires Entrangéres M. de Charette*. Paris: 14 March 1996.
"Für Oder Gegen die Ost–Erweiterung der NATO?" *Frankfurter Allgemeine Zeitung*. 8 March 1997.
Gaidar, Yevgeny. "The Days of Victories and Defeats." *Itogi*. 5 November 1996. 24.
Gallis, Paul. "NATO Enlargement: The Process and Allied Views." Report 97–666F. Washington, D.C.: Congressional Research Service. 1 July 1997.
Geremek, B. "We, the West, with Roots in East." *Polityka*, no. 1 (1999).
Germany's Geopolitical Maturation: Public Opinion and Security Policy. Santa Monica: RAND Corporation, 1994.
Gobins, Marcis. Graduate Thesis. "Möglichkeiten und Grenzen der Baltischen Zusammenarbeit." Berlin: Free University of Berlin, 1996.
———. "Auben und Sicherheitspolitik." *Handbuch Baltikum*. Ed. Heike Graf and Manfred Kerner. Berlin: Nomos, 1998.
Gogolewski, J., and E. Przewodzki. "Directions of Changes in Armed Forces of the Geopolitical Environment of Poland." *Analizy–Syntezy DBM MON*, no. 36 (1996).
Gombos, Janos. *MagyarorszAg Os a NATO [Hungary and NATO]*. Budapest: Star Pr Egynokseg. 1997.
Graczev, Pavel. Interview. "Rosvooruzheniye." *Nowa Technika Wojskowa*, no. 12. 1998.
Groblewski, K. "Polish Raison d'etat Today." *Rzeczpospolita*. 13 July 1994.
"Grüne Schliessen NATO–Erweiterung nicht aus." *Frankfurter Allgemeine Zeitung*. 12 June 1996.
Hahn, Endre. "Bizakodó félelem (Optimist Anxieties)." *Heti Világgazdaság (World Economic Weekly)*. 3 April 1999. 9.
Hajnicz, A. "The West's Betrayal: Fact or Obsession?" *Gazeta Wyborcza*. 31 January 1999.
Hampton, Mary. "Poland, Germany, and NATO Enlargement Policy." *German Comments*, 49 (January 1998): 85–94.
Hastings, Elizabeth Hann, and Philip K. Hastings. *Index to International Public Opinion*. Westport, Conn.: Greenwood Press, 1994–1995.
Hatschikjan, Magarditsch. "Foreign Policy Reorientations in Eastern Central Europe." *Aussenpolitik* 45, no. 1 (1994): 52–60.
Hellmann, Gunther. "The Sirens of Power and German Foreign Policy: Who Is Listening?" *German Politics* 6, no. 2 (August 1997): 29–57.
Henzller, M. "Army Without Rears." *Polityka*, no. 35 (1998).
———. "Hornet Is Coming." *Polityka*, no. 36 (1998).
"A Higher Priority: Early Enlargement of NATO Spells Danger for Europe." *The Times*. 17 February 1997, sec E: 19.

Hillingsø, K.G.H. "Defensibility." *Baltic Defense Review*, no. 1 (1999): 36–40.

"How to Come Out from Grey Zone of Security." *Rzeczpospolita*. 29 December 1993.

Hungary. Ministry of Foreign Affairs. *Hungary and NATO: On the Road to Membership*. Fact Sheets. Budapest: 1997.

Hungary. National Assembly. *Basic Principles of the Security and Defense Policy of the Republic of Hungary*. Resolution no. 94/1998/XII.29. Budapest: 1998.

———. *Basic Principles of the National Defense of the Republic of Hungary*. Resolution no. 11/1993/III.12. Budapest: 1993.

———. *Principles of the National Defense of the Republic of Hungary*. Resolution no. 27/1993/IV.23. Budapest: 1993.

"*Huzar* as Crime." *Rzeczpospolita*. 9 July 1998.

"*Huzar* Landed." *Rzeczpospolita*. 9 December 1998.

Iliescu, Ion. Speech. "Romania—An Outlook on Europe or How Europe Is Seen from Bucharest." November 1994. Paris: French Institute for International Relations.

"Independence Not Threaten." *Rzeczpospolita*. 13 August 1998.

Ionescu, Constantin Dudu. "Financial Costs of Romania's Integration into NATO." *Central European Issues*, no. 2 (1997): 29.

———. "Integration in European and Euro-Atlantic Structures—A National Goal." *Romanian Civilization* (special NATO issue), Center for Romanian Studies 6, no. 1 (Spring/Summer 1997): 61–63.

Isnard, Jacques. "La France est déjà contrainte d'agir dans un cadre interallié." *Le Monde*. 24 August 1995. 3.

———. "Le budget militaire sera réduit de 100 milliards de francs en cinq ans." *Le Monde*. 24 February 1996. 6.

———. "La Force d'extraction au Kosovo sera un test pour la France." *Le Monde*. 12 December 1998. 3.

"Israeli *Huzar*." *Gazeta Wyborcza*. 15 October 1997.

"It Is Our Alliance." *Gazeta Wyborcza*. 18 February 1999.

Italy. Camera dei Deputati. Commissioni Riunite Esteri (III) e Difesa (IV). 11 February 1997.

Italy. Ministry of Foreign Affairs. "L'Italia e l'allargamento dell'Unione Europea ai PECO." Rome: CeSPI, April 1997.

"Italy Will Support a Gradual Expansion of NATO." *Italy Daily*. 24 June 1998. 2.

Janning, Josef. "A German Europe—A European Germany? On the Debate over Germany's Foreign Policy." *International Affairs* 72, no. 1 (1996): 33–41.

Johnson, Steven C. "NATO Bombs, Russian Rhetoric and the Baltics." *The Baltic Times*. 22 April 1999. 1.

Johnson, Steven C., and Rebecca Santana. "Balts Bite the Bullet, Hope for NATO by 2002." *The Baltic Times*. 29 April 1999. 1.

Jonquieres, Guy de. "Russia Softens NATO Stance." *Financial Times*. 4 February 1997.

Kaczmarek, W. "With Clear Conscience: Why I Signed Agreement with Israel." *Gazeta Wyborcza*. 1 December 1997.

Kaiser, Karl. "40 Years of German Membership in NATO." *NATO Review* 43, no. 4 (July 1995): 3–8.

———. "Reforming NATO." *Foreign Policy*, no. 103 (Summer 1996): 128–143.

Kamiński, A. Z. "Why Doesn't Poland Have an Eastern Policy?" *Rzeczpospolita*. 8 March 1995.

Kamp, Karl–Heinz. "The Folly of Rapid NATO Expansion." *Foreign Policy*, no. 98 (Spring 1995): 116–131.

———. "NATO Entrapped: Debating the Next Enlargement Round." *Survival* 40, no. 3 (Autumn 1998): 170–186.

Karkoszka, A. "Dilemmas of Partnership for Peace." *Sprawy Miêdzynarodowe, no. 2 (1994).*

Karpa, Kärt. "Kolmikliit suutis kohad jagada (Three–Party Coalition Agrees on Sharing Posts)." *Eesti Päevaleht.* 17 March 1999. 3.

Kastl, Joerg. "European Security Without Russia." *Aussenpolitik* 48, no. 1 (1997): 31–38.

Kelleher, Catherine McArdle. "The Future of European Security: An Interim Assessment." *Brookings Occasional Papers.* Washington, D.C.: Brookings Institution, 1995.

Kinkel, Klaus. "Peacekeeping Missions: Germany Can Now Play Its Part." *NATO Review* 42 (October 1994): 3–7.

Kissinger, Henry. "NATO: Make It Stronger, Make It Larger." *Washington Post.* 14 January 1997, sec A: 15.

Klaus, Václav. *Policy Statement of the Government of the Czech Republic.* Prague: 1996.

Knudsen, Olav F. "The Foreign Policies of the Baltic States: Interwar Years and Restoration." *Cooperation and Conflict* 28, no. 1 (1993): 47–72.

———. "Cooperative Security in the Baltic Sea Region." *Chaillot Paper 33.* Paris: Institute for Security Studies WEU, 1998.

"Kohl: Bei Ost Erweiterung der NATO Muessen Russlands Sicherheits Interessen Beachtet Werden." *Frankfurter Allgemeine Zeitung.* 5 February 1996.

Komorowski, B. "Dream About Fighter." *Polityka, no.* 48 (1998).

Kostrzewa–Zorbas, G., et al. "What NATO for Us?" *Życie.* 13 February 1999.

Kovács, László. "The Domestic Background Legitimizes Foreign Policy." *Magyar Hirlap.* 11 March 1995.

Kozhokin, Ye. "Gde nachinaetsia i konchaetsia Evropa?" *Otkrytaja politika* 14, no. 7–8 (1996): 74–79.

Krejčí, Oskar. *NATO—Na co?* Praha: Alternativy, 1997.

Kulyk, V. "Rozshyrennja NATO I pozytsija Ukrainy." *Polityka I Chas,* no. 11 (1995): 54–60.

Kuźniar, R. "Tygodnik Solidarność." *Year of Europe,* no. 8 (1991).

"Kwaśniewski About Open Door to NATO." *Rzeczpospolita.* 19 February 1999.

Lange, Peer. Lecture. "Die ausgeklammerte Sicherheit in der Nördlichen Dimension." Berlin: Finnland–Institute, 24 April 1999.

Legge, Michael. "The Making of NATO's New Strategy." *NATO Review* 39, no. 6 (December 1991): 9–14.

Lentowicz, Z. "Ground Power." *Rzeczpospolita.* 2 December 1997.

Lieven, Anatol. *The Baltic Revolution: Estonia, Latvia, Lithuania and the Path to Independence.* New Haven, Conn.: Yale University Press, 1993.

Liik, Kadri. "NATO laienemine ja Venemaa (NATO Enlargement and Russia)." *Postimees.* 12 March 1999. 12.

Link, Werner. "Integration and Balance." *German Comments* 41 (January 1996): 17–23.

Livingston, Robert Gerald. "United Germany: Bigger and Better." *Foreign Policy,* no. 87 (Summer 1992): 157–174.

Lobkowicz, Michal. Interview. *Reflex.* 23 April 1998.

Loeber, Dietrich, et al. *Regional Identity Under Soviet Rule: The Case of the Baltic States.* Hackettstown, N.J.: Institute for the Study of Law, Politics, and Society of Socialist States, 1990.

Luczak, W. "Rescue Circle for Defense Industry." *Raport,* no. 12 (1998).

Luxembourg European Council. "Conclusions of the Presidency." *Agence Europe,* no. 7121. 14 December 1997.

"M. Chirac, l'Europe et l'Est." *Le Monde*. 20 January 1997. 13.
"M. Jospin craint les tendances 'hégémoniques' des Etats–Unis." *Le Monde*. 26 June 1997. 34.
"M. Jospin critique la réintégration de la France dans l'OTAN." *Le Monde*. 5 February 1997. 5.
Madejski, A., and J. Zieliński. *Poland's Armed Forces Toward New Challenges*. Warsaw: Polish Institute for International Affairs, December 1992. 13–16.
Madrid Declaration on Euro-Atlantic Security and Cooperation (Press Release). Madrid: North Atlantic Council, 8 July 1997.
Malcolm, N., et al. *Internal Factors of Russian Foreign Policy*. New York: Oxford University Press, 1996.
Mandelbaum, Michael. *The Dawn of Peace in Europe*. New York: Twentieth Century Fund, 1996.
McCarthy, Patrick. "D'Alema and the System." *Italy Daily*. 11 May 1999. 2.
Medvedev, Sergei. "Geopolitics and Beyond: The New Russian Policy Towards the Baltic States." *The European Union and the Baltic States: Visions, Interests, and Strategies for the Baltic Sea Region*. Ed. Mathias Jopp and Sven Arnswald. Bonn: Institut für Europäische Politik, 1998.
"Meinungsseite (Opinion Poll)." *Frankfurter Allgemeine Zeitung*. 2 July 1993.
"Meinungsseite (Opinion Poll)." *Die Zeit*. 30 July 1993.
Menotti, Roberto. "U.S. Policy and NATO Enlargement: Clinton's 'Unspoken Agenda' 1993–1996." *International Politics*, no. 36 (June 1999): 235–271.
Meri, Lennart. Speech. "Eesti Julgeolekupoliitilistest Aspektidest (On Security Policy Aspects of Estonia)." 25 January 1995. St. Gallen, Switzerland: Security Policy Forum.
———. *Presidendikõned*. Tartu: Ilmamaa, 1996.
Migone, GianGiacomo. Interview. *Bollettino delle Giunte e Commissioni Parlamentari*. Rome: Camera dei Deputati, XIII Legislatura, 14 January 1997.
Misiunas, Romuald J., and Rein Taagepera. *The Baltic States: Years of Dependence 1940–1990*. Berkeley: University of California Press, 1993.
Mitchell, Alison. "Clinton Urges NATO Expansion in 1999." *New York Times*. 23 October 1996, sec A: 20.
Mitterrand, François. "Speech Warning Against Hasty Unification." Spring 1990. Bonn, Germany: Bundestag.
Moeller, Richard R. "The Ambivalence of the SPD and the End of Its Ostpolitik." *German Politics* 5, no. 1 (April 1996): 121–136.
Moreland, T. "American Offer." *Armia*, no. 3 (1998).
Möttölä, Kari. "Security Around the Baltic Rim: Concepts, Actors, and Processes." *The NEBI-Yearbook 1998: North European and Baltic Sea Integration*. Ed. Lars Hedegaard and Bjarne Lindström. Berlin: Springer, 1998.
Mushaben, Joyce Marie. *From Post-War to Post-Wall Generations*. Boulder: Westview Press, 1998.
NATO (North Atlantic Treaty Organization). *Background Briefing on U.S. Mission to NATO*. Brussels: 1 December 1994.
———. *Final Communiqué*. Ministerial Meeting of the North Atlantic Council. Brussels: NATO Headquarters, 1 December 1994. M NAC 2(91)116.
———. *NATO Enlargement Study*. Brussels: NATO Press, September 1995.
———. "NATO Enlargement: The National Debates over Ratification." *NATO Academic Forum*. Brussels: October 1997.
———. Press Release NAC-S (99) 64. "An Alliance for the 21st Century." Washington, D.C.: North Atlantic Council Communiqué, 24 April 1999.

————. Press Release NAC–S (99) 65. "The Alliance's Strategic Concept." Washington, D.C.: North Atlantic Council, 24 April 1999.

Nelson, Daniel N. "Europe's Unstable East." *Foreign Policy*, no. 82. Spring 1991. 137–158.

Neumann, I. B. "Russia as Central Europe's Constituting Other." *East European Politics and Societies* 7, no. 2 (Spring 1993).

"New Peoples and Regulations." *Rzeczpospolita*. 17 December 1998.

Noblecourt, Michel. "M. Jospin se place dans la perspective d'une cohabitation non-conflictuelle." *Le Monde*. 20 May 1997. 5.

"Nominations and Dismissals." *Gazeta Wyborcza*. 17 August 1998.

Novotný, Jaromir. Statement. *Slovo*. 23 September 1997.

"Now Sign of President." *Rzeczpospolita*. 18 February 1999.

Nowak, P. F. "Price of NATO." *Nowe Życie Gospodarcze*. 24 May 1996.

Nunn, Sam. *The Future of NATO in an Uncertain World*. Norfolk, Vir.: 22 June 1995.

O'Hanlon, Michael. "Transforming NATO: The Role of European Forces." *Survival* 39, no. 3 (Autumn 1997): 5–15.

Occhetto, Achille. Interview. *Corriere della Sera*. 5 April 1997. 5.

Olechowski, A. Speech. "Seven Principles of Polish Security." 24 December 1993. Washington, D.C.: Center for Security and Information Studies.

"Optimismus Über NATO–Ost–Erweiterung." *Frankfurter Allgemeine Zeitung*. 13 June 1996.

Osrodek Badania Opinii Publicznej (OBOP). "NATO, Army, and Poland's Security." Warsaw: OBOP. March 1998. 5–15.

Ostrowski, M. "Calculated Risk in the UN." *Polityka*, no. 31 (1998).

"Our Blood, Their Oil!" *Gazeta Wyborcza*. 23 February 1998.

Pastusiak, L. "We Can Afford Consent." *Rzeczpospolita*. 14 November 1994.

Pavlenko, A. "Zovnishnja polityka I zbroini syly Ukrainy." *Polityka I Chas,* no. 1 (1997): 36–39.

Pawlak, W. "Expose." *Rzeczpospolita*. 9 November 1993.

Payne, Keith B., and Michael Ruhle. "The Future of the Alliance: Emerging German Views." *Strategic Review* (Winter 1991): 37–45.

Perko, Susanna, ed. *Nordic–Baltic Region. New Actors, New Issues, New Perspectives: Research Report no. 75*. Tampere: Tampere Peace Research Institute, 1996.

Pfeiler, Wolfgang. "NATO in the East." *German Comments* 42. April 1996. 38–42.

Pierre, Andrew J., and Dmitri Trenin. "Developing NATO-Russian Relations." *Survival*. Spring 1997: 5–14.

Pietsch, Lajos. *Hungary and NATO*. Budapest: Hungarian Atlantic Council, 1998.

Piskorski, M. "36 Planes for $100 Mln." *Rzeczpospolita*. 15 December 1998.

Poland. Ministry of Defense. *Principles of Polish Security Policy* and *Security Policy and Strategy of Defense of the Polish Republic*. Warsaw: November 1992. 6–13.

Poland. "Universal Defense." Warsaw: Programming Team of AWS for National Security, 22 January 1998.

"Poland-NATO." *Rzeczpospolita*. 7 July 1997.

Ponomarenko, A. "Ukraina—strana atlanticheskaja?" *Biznesinform,* no. 6 (1997): 9.

Porcari, Saverio. Speech. "The European Union and NATO." 4 April 1997. Rome: Società Italiana per l'Organizzazione Internazionale.

"Pour un modéle européen." *Libération*. 25 March 1996. 1.

"Principles of the Governmental Program of the Armed Forces Modernization." *Polska Zbrojna*. 12 Sept 1997.

"The Prognosis of the Financial–Economic Provision for the Structure of the RF Armed Forces for the Period Up to the Year 2010." *Nezavisimoje Voeenoje Obozrenie*, no. 4 (1999).

"PSL–SLD Coalition Agreement." *Rzeczpospolita.* 14 October 1993.

Public Opinion Study Centre (CBOS). "State Security in Public Opinion." Report 137. Warsaw: CBOS. November 1993.

———. "Polls About Membership of Our Country in NATO." Report 27. Warsaw: CBOS. July 1998.

———. "Participation of Polish Soldiers Eventually in NATO's Mission in Kosovo." Report 151. Warsaw: CBOS. November 1998.

Putting, Jaanus. "Suhtumine euroliitu on Eestis patiseisus (Attitude Toward EU Falters in Estonia)." *Postimees.* 15 January 1999. 3.

Raik, Kristi. *Towards Substantive Democracy? The Role of the European Union in the Democratization of Estonia and the Other Eastern Member Candidates:* Research Report no. 84. Tampere: Tampere Peace Research Institute, 1998.

Raud, Neeme. "Trumani sõnad NATOst saavad täna teoks (Truman's Words About NATO Are Becoming Reality Today)." *Postimees.* 12 March 1999. 12.

Rebas, Hain. "Barriers to Baltic Cooperation—Opportunities for Surmounting Them." Kiel, Estonia. Unpublished manuscript, 1997.

"Report on the State Security." Warsaw: Polish Institute for International Affairs. 1993. 102–108.

Rice, Condoleezza. "Now, NATO Should Grow." *New York Times.* 8 July 1996, sec A: 13.

Rice, Condoleezza, and Philip Zelikow. *Germany Unified and Europe Transformed.* Cambridge: Harvard University Press, 1995.

Rivolta, Dario. Interview. *La Stampa.* 5 April 1997. 2.

Robertson, George. Interview. *Financial Times.* 4 June 1997.

Rockenbauer, Zoltán. *The Hungarian National Assembly and European Integration in Hungary: A Member of NATO*, Ed. Rudolf Joó. Budapest: 1999.

Roman, Petre. Speech. "Romania—Where To?" 1995. Bucharest.

Romania. Ministry of Defense. "Romanian Armed Forces—A Partner for the Future." *White Book*, no. 3 (1997): 38.

Romania. Ministry of Foreign Affairs. *White Book on Romania and NATO.* Bucharest: 1997.

Rosati, D. "Governmental Information About Poland's Foreign Policy. Presentation of Minister of Foreign Affairs in the *Seym.*" Warsaw: 9 May 1996.

———. "Continuity, Progress, New Challenges." *Rzeczpospolita.* 7 October 1996.

———. "Wider, Safer NATO." *Gazeta Wyborcza.* 8 January 1997.

———. "To Undertake of Risky Game." *Gazeta Wyborcza.* 27 May 1997.

Rotfeld, A. D. "The CSCE: Toward a Security Organization." *SIPRI Yearbook 1993: World Armaments and Disarmament.* New York: Oxford University Press, 1993.

Ruehl, Lothar. "European Security and NATO's Eastward Expansion." *Aussenpolitik* 45, no. 2: 115–122.

"Russia and NATO: Theses of the Council on Foreign and Defense Policy." *Nezavisimaja Gazeta.* 21 June 1995.

Russia. Ministry of Economy. "Economy of Russia." *Development* (special issue), no. 48. December 1992.

"Russian Demons." *Financial Times.* 8 October 1996.

"Russians Want to Repair Polish Fighters." *Rzeczpospolita.* 4 December 1998.

Saar, Andrus. Interview. 16 March 1999.

Saarpoll. "Euroopa Liit. Elanikkonna Monitoring, Küsitlusperiood: 02—09.09.1998." Tallinn: Saarpoll, 1998. 4.

———. "Uuringu 'Euroopa Liit, Eesti ja rahvas' (European Union, Estonia and the People)." Tallinn: Saarpoll, 1998. 17.

"Safe Port—NATO." Życie. 18 February 1999.

Santana, Rebecca. "Baltic Presidents: Time for NATO to Name Names." The Baltic Times. 25 February 1999. 1.

Sarvaš, Stefan. One Past, Two Futures? The NATO Enlargement Debate in the Czech Republic and Slovakia. Harmonie Paper 4. Groningen: Center for European Security Studies, 1999.

Savisaar, Edgar. "Skepsis Euroopa Liidu suhtes levib (Skepticism Concerning the European Union Is Spreading)." Postimees. 16 January 1999. 7.

Schlor, Wolfgang. "German Security Policy." Adelphi Papers, no. 277. New York: International Institute for Strategic Studies, June 1993.

Schmidt, Peter. "German Security Policy in the Framework of the EU, WEU, and NATO." Aussenpolitik 47, no. 3 (1996): 211–222.

Schollgen, Bregor. "Putting Germany's Post-Unification Foreign Policy to the Test." NATO Review 41, no. 2 (April 1993): 15–22.

Šedivý, Jiří. "Pull-Out of Soviet Troops from Czechoslovakia." Perspectives, no. 2 (Winter 1993/94): 21–39.

———. "From Dreaming to Realism—Czechoslovak Security Policy Since 1989." Perspectives, no. 4 (Winter 1994/95): 62–63.

———. "Czech Republic: Nuclear Controversy." Perspectives, no. 9 (Summer 1997/98): 77–88.

———. "Czech Republic." Security in Central and Eastern Europe: Problems—Perceptions—Policies. Vienna: Austrian Institute for International Affairs, 1999.

"Service of Soldiers Out of the State's Borders." Rzeczpospolita. 13 November 1998.

"Sejm: Hundred Words." Trybuna. 18 February 1999.

Sharp, Jane M. O. British Views on NATO Enlargement. 7 October 1997. Available online at http://www.nato.int/acad/conf/enlarg97/sharp.htm.

"Shorter, but Hard to Postpone." Gazeta Wyborcza. 20 November 1998.

Sikorski, R. "Courage in Draw of Conclusions." Rzeczpospolita. 20 November 1995.

Simon, Jeffrey. "Central European Civil-Military Relations and NATO Expansion." McNair Paper 39. Washington, D.C.: National Defense University, 1997.

Siwiec, M. Interview. "It Will Not Be So Easy." Trybuna. 23 June 1997.

Smyser, W. R. "USSR-Germany: A Link Restored." Foreign Policy, no. 84 (Fall 1991): 125–141.

———. "Germany's New Vision." Foreign Policy, no. 97 (Winter 1994-1995): 140–157.

Solano, S.G. Javier. "NATO-Russia Relations: A Key Feature of European Security." NATO Review. May 1997.

Somogyi, Ferenc. "NATO Accession and the Hungarian Public Opinion." Hungary: A Member of NATO. Ed. Rudolf Joó. Budapest: 1999. 77.

"SPD Plant Antrag zur NATO Erweitung." Frankfurter Allgemeine Zeitung. 7 June 1997.

"SPD Stimmt mit Reigerung überein in allen Wesentlichen Fragen der Aussen–und Sicherheitspolitik." Süddeutsche Zeitung. 19 June 1997.

Stan, Valentin. "The Government of Failure/Guvernul esecului." Sfera politicii 4 (1998): 6.

"Strategy for Russia (Theses for the Report of the Council on Foreign and Defense Policy)." Nezavisimaja Gazeta. 19 August 1992.

Stent, Angela. "The One Germany." *Foreign Policy,* no. 81 (Winter 1990–1991): 53–70.
"Summary of Poles' Opinions About Poland's Security." CBOS Focus Group Interview. December 1992. 4–14.
Szczepański, J. "Will Hornet Land?" *Rzeczpospolita.* 26 January 1999.
Szemerkényi, Reka. "Central European Civil-Military Reforms at Risk." *Adelphi Paper,* no. 306. London: International Institute for Strategic Studies, 1996.
Szeremietew, R. "Poland's Defense: Questions and Doubts." *Rzeczpospolita.* 22 January 1998.
Szlajfer, H. Interview. "Common Concert on NATO." *Gazeta Wyborcza.* 2 April 1997.
Szmajdziński, J. *"Seym's* About Defense." *Armia,* no. 3. 1998.
Talbott, Strobe. "Why NATO Should Grow." *The New York Review of Books.* 10 August 1995.
———. "Russia Has Nothing to Fear." *New York Times.* 18 February 1997, sec A: 25.
"Tartó bizonytalanságérzet (Permanent Uncertainty)." Editorial. *Heti Világgazdaság (World Economic Weekly).* 1 May 1999. 9.
Tertychnyj, V. "Rozshyrennja NATO: vijskovi aspekty." *Polityka I Chas,* no. 8 (1996): 20–21.
"There Will Be Money for Army." *Gzos.* 27 October 1997.
"Toward One Safe Europe." *Rzeczpospolita.* 14 November 1994.
Tracevskis, Rokas M. "Baltics Back NATO, Anxious About Russia." *The Baltic Times.* 1 April 1999.
Tréan, Clare. "Paris souhaite que la République tchéque intégre le plus rapidement possible l'OTAN et l'UE." *Le Monde.* 4 April 1997. 4.
"Union . . . amplificateur de puissance." *Le Monde.* December 1993.
United Kingdom. House of Commons. Defense Committee. *Britain's Army for the 90's.* CM1595. London: HMSO, July 1991.
———. *Defense Committee Third Report NATO Enlargement.* London: HMSO, 18 March 1998.
United Kingdom. House of Commons. *Hansard.* London: HMSO, 26 February 1997.
———. *Hansard.* London: HMSO, 9 July 1997.
———. *Hansard.* London: HMSO, 17 July 1997.
United Kingdom. House of Lords. *Hansard.* London: HMSO, 14 March 1997.
———. *Hansard.* London: HMSO, 31 July 1998.
United Kingdom. Ministry of Defense. *British Defense Policy 1990–1991.* Ministry of Defense public relations pamphlet. London: April 1990.
———. *Defending Our Future.* CM2270. London: HMSO, July 1993. Para 108.
———. *Statement on the Defense Estimates.* CM2550. London: HMSO, April 1994.
———. *Stable Forces in a Strong Britain.* CM2800. London: HMSO, May 1995.
———. *Statement on the Defense Estimates.* CM3223. London: HMSO, January 1996.
———. *The Strategic Defense Review.* CM3999. London: HMSO, July 1998.
United States. Department of Defense. Office of the Secretary of Defense. "Kievenaar—Report." *Executive Summary of Estonian Defense Assessment.* Washington, D.C.: 1998.
United States. Department of State. Office of the Spokesman. "Press Briefing with Italian Foreign Minister Lamberto Dini." Villa Madama, Rome, Italy. 16 February 1997.
United States. U.S. Congress. *Address by the President Before a Joint Session of Congress on the State of the Union.* Washington, D.C.: Presidential Documents 33, no. 6 (10 February 1997): 136–145.

———. *The Enlargement of NATO: Rationale, Benefits, Costs, and Implications.* Washington, D.C.: Section 1048 FY 1997 Defense Authorization Act, February 1997.

United States. U.S. Congress. Senate. *Message from the President Transmitting the Treaty on Conventional Armed Forces in Europe (CFE).* Washington, D.C.: GPO, 9 July 1991. 102–108.

———. *Resolution of Ratification to the Protocols to the North Atlantic Treaty of 1949 on the Accession of Poland, Hungary, and the Czech Republic.* Washington, D.C.: 30 April 1998.

United States. U.S. Information Service. *USIS Wireless File* EUR203. Washington, D.C.: 18 February 1997.

United States. White House. *A National Security Strategy of Engagement and Enlargement.* Washington, D.C.: July 1994. 29.

Urdze, Andrejs, ed. *Der baltische Weg: Das Ende des Sowjetkolonialismus.* Hamburg: Rowohlt, 1991.

"The U.S. Role in Europe." *Miller Center Journal* (May 1998): 115–130.

Vares, Peeter. "Dimensions and Orientations in the Foreign and Security Policies of the Baltic States." *New Actors on the International Arena: The Foreign Policies of the Baltic Countries, Research Report no. 50.* Ed. Pertti Joenniemi and Peeter Vares. Tampere: Tampere Peace Research Institute, 1993.

Végh, Ferenc. "The Hungarian Defense Forces: From Preparation to Full Interoperability." *Hungary: A Member of NATO.* Ed. Rudolf Joó. Budapest: 1999. 49.

Vernet, Daniel. "L'idée francaise d'un 'M. PESC' provoque la perplexité à Bonn." *Le Monde.* 21 March 1996. 2.

———. "Accord sur la réforme de l'OTAN." *Le Monde.* 12–13 May 1996.

———. "Une nouvelle Alliance pour une nouvelle Europe." *Le Monde.* 26 May 1997. 1.

———. "France-OTAN: Une bonne idée en panne." *Le Monde.* 30 June 1997.

Vesa, Unto. "Back to Deutsch: Integration, Peaceful Change, and Security Communities." *Changes in the Northern Hemisphere: Research Report no. 52.* Ed. Jyrki Käkönen. Tampere: Tampere Peace Research Institute, 1993. 159–164.

"Vneshniaja politika Rossii doizhna byf prezidentskoi. Prichiny i sledstvija porazhenia diplomatii Andreia Kozyreva." *Nezavisimaja Gazeta.* 17 May 1995.

Vogel, Heirich. "Opening NATO: A Cooperative Solution for an Ill-Defined Problem." *Aussenpolitik* 48, no. 1 (1997): 22–31.

"Voigt: Eine Unideologische Aussenpolitik." *Frankfurter Allgemeine Zeitung.* 14 January 1999.

"Voigt für Scnelle NATO-OST-Erweiterung." *Frankfurter Allgemeine Zeitung.* 10 May 1996.

Voigt, Karsten. "Eastward Enlargement of NATO." 1995.

———. Speech given at SPD Party Congress. "Rede auf dem Parteitag des UB Frankfurt." 19 April 1997.

———. Speech. "German Foreign Policy Beyond the East-West Conflict." 19 April 1997.

Walewska, D. "Preposition for Mielec." *Rzeczpospolita.* 17 November 1998.

Wêglarczyk, B. "Army Will Pay to Polish Enterprises." *Gazeta Wyborcza.* 29 October 1997.

"What Change in Polish Army After Accession to NATO?" *Wprost,* no. 41 (1998).

"Who Will Give Us Wings?" *Rzeczpospolita.* 2 February 1998.

Wigrowska, M. "Situation Without Precedent." *Rzeczpospolita.* 16 June 1997.

Wörner, Manfred. "NATO Transformed: The Significance of the Rome Summit." *NATO Review* 39, no. 6 (December 1991): 3–8.

Woyke, Richard. "NATO Faces New Challenges." *Aussenpolitik* 44, no. 2 (1993): 120–126.

Wroñski, P. "Strange Laze of the MND." *Gazeta Wyborcza.* 13 June 1997.

———. "Before Entrance of the Golf Club." *Gazeta Wyborcza.* 2 July 1997.

———. "When Poland Gives Us Order." *Gazeta Wyborcza,* 9 July 1997.

———. "Year of the Army." *Gazeta Wyborcza.* 15 November 1997.

———. "*Huzar* of Disagreement." *Gazeta Wyborcza.* 19 November 1997.

Zieleniec, Josef. Speech given at the House of Deputies of Parliament. 21 April 1993. Ministry of Foreign Affairs. *Documents 1993.* Prague: House of Deputies of Parliament, 1994.

Zielke, K. "Concept of Poland's and Central European Countries' Approach to Membership in NATO. Draft of Ministry of National Defense Bureau for Defense Policy from 27.07.1992" Reprint. *Central European Review,* no. 6 (1994): 30–36.

THE CONTRIBUTORS

Mariana Cernicova-Buca is a columnist in the Romanian regional press covering political events in the Central European region. She is a senior lecturer at Tibiscus University in Timisoara, where she teaches mass communication and European and Euro-Atlantic affairs. Her main fields of research are Romanian domestic and foreign policy (transition to democracy, political and administrative reform, civil control of the army, compensations for the abuses of communist regimes, the Romanian role in European and Euro-Atlantic structures, relations with neighboring countries, Romanian minorities in bordering countries, and the Romanian diaspora and lobby); Central European studies, and mass communication. She holds a Ph.D. in journalism from the University of Timisoara.

Paul Gallis is the section head for Europe and Eurasia at the Congressional Research Service, Library of Congress, Washington, D.C. Formerly he worked at the U.S. Department of State and was a speech writer for a U.S. senator. He was an assistant campaign manager for President Jimmy Carter from 1979 to 1980. He is widely published on European Security and is the author of numerous congressional research publications and reports, including the issue brief *NATO: Congress Addresses Expansion of the Alliance* and coordinator for a study for the U.S. Senate entitled *Operation Allied Force: Lessons Learned* (September 1999). He published most recently "Congrés d'Etats-Unis et les Mission de l'Otan," in *La revue internationale et strategique* (Winter 1998/99). He holds an M.A. from the University of Paris and a doctorate in European history from Brown University.

Sir Timothy Garden is a visiting professor at the Center for Defense Studies at King's College, London, where he is working on European defense issues. He spent over thirty years in the Royal Air Force as a military pilot and was the assistant chief of the air staff in 1991. His last appointment was as the 3-star officer running the Royal College of Defense Studies in London. He was the

director of the Royal Institute of International Affairs at Chatham House until
mid-1998. He has written extensively on strategic issues and his publications
include books on nuclear strategy and military technological issues. He has a
degree in physics from Oxford and a degree in international relations from
Cambridge.

Radek Khol joined the Institute of International Relations in Prague in 1996.
He has been a member of a long-term research project on security policy of
the Czech Republic. He has published articles on NATO enlargement, secu-
rity policies in Central Europe, and civil-military relations. In 1999 he was
PfP research fellow at NATO Defense College in Rome writing a study on old
strategic thinking in the new strategic environment. He graduated from the
Department of War Studies at King's College, London, in 1996 and from the
Department of International Relations at the Faculty of Social Sciences,
Charles University–Prague, in 1997.

Irena Kobrinskaya is a director at the Moscow Center of the East-West Institute. She worked at the U.S. and Canadian Institute at the Russian Academy
of Sciences, the Institute of Political Studies at the Polish Academy of Sciences, and the Moscow Carnegie Center. She is an expert on security and foreign policy as well as foreign policy decisionmaking. She is the author of several monographs, book chapters, and some 100 articles in Russian and
Western periodicals. She was born in Moscow and holds a Ph.D. in history
and international relations from Moscow State University.

Maria Kopylenko currently works as a news analyst for Deutsche Welle in Ger-
many. She received her Ph.D. in English literature from the University of
Kiev, and has studied politics at the Free University in Berlin. She was previ-
ously a research associate at the National Institute for Strategic Studies at the
Ministry of National Defense in Ukraine, and a political commentator for the
BBC in London.

Gale A. Mattox is a professor of political science at the U.S. Naval Academy
and is the president of Women in International Security (WIIS), an international, nonpartisan network with a membership of over 1,300 women working on international security issues located at the Center for International
Security Studies, University of Maryland. She served on the policy planning
staff (1994–1995) and in the Office for Strategic and Theater Nuclear Policy
(1985–1986), U.S. Department of State, and has held NATO, Bosch, and
Council on Foreign Relations fellowships. She has published on European
defense policies (1987), German-American affairs (1989), Germany at the

crossroads (1992), and Germany in transition (1999) as well as numerous articles and chapters. Mattox holds a Ph.D. from the University of Virginia.

Roberto Menotti is coordinator, Euro-American Studies, at an independent think tank, the CeSPI Research Center for International Political Studies, and executive assistant at the Council for the United States and Italy, a nonprofit organization for cultural exchanges based in Rome. He has been a lecturer at the International Relations Department of John Cabot University in Rome. His publications include an article on NATO enlargement and Clinton's policy toward Europe in *International Politics* and a book on the same topic in Italian in 1999. He is a regular contributor to Italian journals pertaining to international affairs and serves on the editorial boards of *Limes* and *The International Spectator*. He holds a degree from Libera Universita Internazionale degli Studi Sociali, Rome, and an M.A. in international securities studies from the University of Southern California.

Marcin Andrzej Piotrowski is currently a doctoral student at the University of Warsaw in the Institute of Political Science and International Relations, where he is completing research for a dissertation titled *The Armed Forces of the Russian Federation in a Time of Transformation*. He is a specialist in Russian affairs. Recent academic studies include most recently "Primakov's Mission Impossible" in *Sprawy Polityczne* (Warsaw: International Affairs, 1999) and "Russian Policy Toward Crisis in Kosovo," in *Polish Foundation of International Affairs* (1999).

Arthur R. Rachwald is a professor of political science at the U.S. Naval Academy in Annapolis, Maryland. He is also a professional lecturer at the Johns Hopkins University, School of Advanced International Studies, in Washington, D.C., as he was at the SAIS Bologna Center from 1996–1997. He is a specialist in Central European and Russian affairs and is the author of *Poland Between the Superpowers: Security vs. Economic Recovery* (1983) and *The Search for Poland* (1989), in addition to numerous scholarly articles and chapters. Born in Poland, he was educated at the University of Marie Curie-Sklodowska, School of Law, in Poland and holds a Ph.D. from the University of Southern California at Santa Barbara.

Bernd Schürmann is currently preparing a doctoral thesis on security by non-military means. He has been a research fellow at the Center on Transatlantic Foreign and Security Policy, where he is researching Central Eastern European elite attitudes toward integration in the European Union and NATO, since September 1996. His interests lie in the enlargement of the European

Union and NATO, the development of the Baltic states and the Baltic Sea region, and the transition process in Eastern Europe.

Csaba Törő has been an analyst in the Department of Strategic Planning, Hungarian Ministry of Foreign Affairs, since 2000. He was at the Zrinyi Miklos National Defense University and a lecturer of international politics and organizations at the Department of Diplomacy, College for Foreign Trade, in Budapest. He was also a visiting lecturer of European Community law and institutions at the Budapest campus of Western Maryland College in 1999–2000. He is a candidate for his Ph.D. in international relations at the Budapest University of Economics.

Daniel J. Whiteneck is the director of European Programs in the Center for Strategic Studies at the Center for Naval Analyses. He has taught political science at Towson University in Maryland and has been a visiting professor at the United States Air Force Academy and the University of Colorado at Boulder. He has published articles on NATO and the European Security and Defense Identity, alliances during wartime, coalition forming and cohesion, and the role of global leadership. His current research is on U.S. leadership of NATO. He holds a Ph.D. from the University of Washington.

INDEX

315

149; "defense in all directions" strategy, 112; ethnic communities, 15; "fortunate three," 209; French view, 66, 69; German support, 42, 49; Governmental Program of Modernization in the Armed Forces, 116–117, 122–123; "grey zone of security," 112; Industrial Defense Potential, 122; invitation to NACC, 259; and Italy, 100; membership in NATO, 11, 46, 111–125, 294; NATO enlargement, 125, 243–247, 248; parliamentary debates, 118–121; perceived political threats, 113–114; Polish-Lithuanian Commonwealth, 8; "Polish wonder," 118; Public Opinion Study Centre (CBOS) polls, 120–121; relations with Germany, 43–44; Round Table negotiations, 111; Russian threat, 181; Solidarity Party, 111–112; support for Ukraine, 197; technology gap, 115; UK position, 79, 82 84, 87

Polish American Congress, 25
Polish Peasant Party (PSL), 112
Politburo, 173
Porcari, Saverio, 101
Portillo, Michael, 77
Portugal, 5
Post–Cold War era, 2, 7, 10, 15, 38–40, 178, 191, 241; demands, 16
Post-Soviet period, 171, 181
Potsdam agreement (1945), 4
Powell, Colin, 30
Primakov, Yevgeny, 44, 176
Prodi, Romano, 91
Putin, Vladimir, 183

Qichen, Qian: on NATO expansion, 265

Rada, Verchovna, 187, 190, 194
RAND Corporation, 25, 116; Czech study, 152–153
Rapid reaction force (RRF), 43–44, 124, 206
Realpolitik, 93
Reconciliations: historic, 10, 202
"Red line" through Europe, 174
Republic of Moldova, 201, 203, 208, 210; Partnership for Peace membership, 261
Rice, Condoleezza, 27
Rifkind, Malcolm, 77
Rifondazione Comunista Party (RC), 91, 103
Rivolta, Dario, 102
Robertson, George, 81
Roman, Petre, 204
Romania, 3, 7, 28, 97, 101, 232, 243, 246–247; Appeal of the Parliament of Romania, 210; application to NATO and

EU, 201, 204, 208, 214; Basic Program, 209; Bulgarization, 203; College of National Defense, 206; Constantinescu, 202–203; costs of NATO and EU, 204–206, 210; defense budget, 205–206; Euro-Atlantic Center (Bucharest), 204; French support, 62, 66–67, 69, 213–214, 249, 265; General George Pomutz Association for Commemorating Heroes of Romanian Origin Abroad, 213; German support, of 49, 214, 249; Hungarian population, 202; President Illiescu, 203, 211; Inter-Ministerial Committee for Integration into NATO, 209; invitation to NACC, 259; King Michael I, 213; Madrid summit (1997), 202, 209, 212–214; military leadership, 207; National Consultative Council for Euro-Atlantic Integration (1994), 210, 213; NATO enlargement, 202; negotiations with Ukraine, 202; Open Sky Treaty, 202; Partnership for Peace, 204, 206, 208, 210; peacekeeping missions, 211; political parties, 210–211; proposed NATO membership, 21, 214; protests, 200; public support of NATO, 212; rapid reaction force, 206; quest for membership, 199–217; relations with Russia, 203; Securitate (police), 200; security in region, 203; Serbian ally, 202; Supreme Defense Council, 207; UK position, 79–80, 82, 85; U.S. ethnic groups, 213; U.S. support, 214; Warsaw Pact, 199–201; Washington summit (1999), 209, 211, 213–214, 249; Western relations, 208; *White Book on Romania and NATO,* 204, 206; Yugoslavian border, 201–202
Rome summit, 17, 259, 270
Rosner, Jerry: campaign for NATO enlargement, 23–24
Roth, William, 28
Rühe, Volker, 40–44, 47, 50
Russia, 1, 3, 5, 7–11, 19; alienation, 79; Baltic independence, 219; Bosnia, 263, 289; challenges to national security, 180; Civil Union, 176; decline as a superpower, 171; democracy, 15; election, 39; expansionism, 173; facism in, 179; German unification, 36–37; forces in Siberia, 189; France, 55, 57, 63–65, 70–71; in Latvia, 246; Italy, 96, 100, 102; Juzhmash missiles, 192; military budget, 180–181; nationalism, 179; NATO expansion, 169–184, 245, 248; NATO-Russia Founding Act, 11, 248, 253, 286–287, 293–294; "near abroad and far

ABOUT THE BOOK

Thoroughly examining the deliberations over NATO enlargement in twelve countries—five current members of the alliance; three invited to join in the first round of enlargement; two seeking membership; and Russia and Ukraine, both involved with NATO, but unlikely to join—the authors shed light on the political motives leading to each country's position. Their comparative analysis explores the interaction of domestic and international issues that is at the core of efforts to reshape the security map of Europe.

Gale A. Mattox and **Arthur R. Rachwald** are professors of political science at the U.S. Naval Academy. Both have published extensively on European security affairs.